SIR DANIEL GOOCH

Memoirs & Diary

SIR DANIEL GOOCH

Memoirs & Diary

TRANSCRIBED FROM THE ORIGINAL
MANUSCRIPT AND EDITED WITH
AN INTRODUCTION AND NOTES BY

ROGER BURDETT WILSON

David & Charles : Newton Abbot

ISBN o 7153 5609 7

Set in Monotype Baskerville
and printed in Great Britain
by Latimer Trend & Company Limited Plymouth
for David & Charles (Publishers) Limited
South Devon House   Newton Abbot   Devon

Contents

List of Illustrations

ACKNOWLEDGEMENTS

All the line illustrations are from material mounted by Gooch in the manuscript (Editor's collection).

Plates I–III were kindly supplied by Mr Stephen Martin of Stakeford (III photo Wm. Ward, Bedlington). Plate VI is reproduced by kind permission of Real Photographs Ltd, Broadstairs. Plate VII is reproduced by kind permission of Mr C. F. H. Oldham, and plate XI is from an official photograph reproduced by kind permission of British Railways, Western Region. Plate XIII is from a print kindly lent by Mr J. G. Burr, of Windsor.

The remaining plates are from material in the editor's collection.

For my godson Nicholas

Introduction

The vast literature of railways, mainly preoccupied with Parliamentary and inter-company struggles, with locomotive matters and with the minutiae of day-to-day operation, has to a large extent neglected the men who built, directed and managed the railways. Only a handful of the great engineers have received the attention they deserve, while the majority of the men who promoted our railways, whose perseverance secured the Acts of Parliament, and whose money paid the contractors, bought the rolling-stock and provided the working capital, are still shadowy figures whose very names are known only to the few.

Mention of the Great Western Railway inevitably brings to mind the name of Isambard Kingdom Brunel, the undoubted genius who planned and built a railway embodying enough unorthodox features to ensure the disapproval, opposition and even ridicule of his profession and many of the shareholders. Yet he had been dead almost a century before a biography worthy of the subject appeared. But of Brunel's associates we still know all too little. The memoirs and diary of Sir Daniel Gooch, who knew and worked with many of them, are now one of the very few sources from which we can obtain an authentic picture of their activities.

When, in 1837, Brunel selected Daniel Gooch, then barely twenty-one, to be the first locomotive superintendent of the Great Western, he made an inspired choice. Young though he was, Gooch proved a tower of strength during the company's early struggles, and by 1840 had designed a series of standard engines to be built by outside contractors. With the opening of the works at Swindon in 1843, the planning and management of which was largely Gooch's responsibility, the company was able to build its own locomotives, and Gooch's designs were soon giving the Great Western pre-eminence in terms of speed and reliability.

With the amalgamation of the West Midland Railway and the Great

Western in 1863 Gooch resigned, after twenty-seven years as the company's mechanical engineer, but his connection with Swindon was by no means severed. At the general election of 1865 he was asked to stand as a Conservative candidate for Cricklade division, in which the growing town of Swindon was situated, and was elected. He represented the constituency until his retirement from Parliament twenty years later.

Gooch had, for some time, been permitted by the Great Western board to undertake other work, and in 1860 he was appointed engineer of the *Great Eastern* steamship in succession to her designer Brunel, who had died in the previous year. Gooch took a keen interest in the 'Great Ship' and subsequently arranged for her to be converted for cable laying. In 1864 he joined the board of a new company, the Telegraph Construction & Maintenance Company, which chartered the *Great Eastern* to lay an Atlantic cable. The first attempt in 1865 was a failure, but Gooch, who was on board, was confident of success and sailed in her again in the following year, when a new cable was successfully laid and the earlier one recovered and completed. He returned to London to become the first engineer to receive a baronetcy. Gooch made a third voyage, to lay a French cable from Brest to St Pierre in 1869, by which time he had assumed the chairmanship of the Telegraph Construction & Maintenance Company which he held until his death in 1889.

On his return from the 1865 cable expedition Gooch, much to his surprise, was asked to become chairman of the Great Western Railway board. The company was in a serious financial position, but, with some reluctance, he accepted the challenge. The board's faith in him was fully justified; the company weathered the storm and he remained chairman until the end of his life.

It seems that it was the conferment of a baronetcy in 1866 that prompted Daniel Gooch to commence the memoirs which comprise the first part of the present volume, and which he subsequently continued in the form of a diary.

Gooch and Brunel were cast in very different moulds; their greatness stems from very different qualities. The fact that Gooch has always been rather overshadowed by his one-time chief is not only due to Brunel's flamboyant appearance, bold unorthodoxy and the sheer scale of his achievements. Gooch's own reticence and dislike of the limelight were as much responsible for limited acclaim in his lifetime and lack of interest in his career since his death. But without doubt Daniel Gooch the engineer and Daniel Gooch the business man each bears the unmistakable stamp of greatness. It is the rare combination of talent in the two fields, so unfortunately lacking in Brunel, which places him among the really great men of his day.

Daniel Gooch could hardly have been better fitted, by background and upbringing, for the profession he was to adopt. At the time of his birth in 1816 the steam locomotive was an accomplished fact, though still in its formative stage and still struggling for recognition. But if the time of his birth was significant, it was of infinitely greater moment that Daniel spent his early years in the very heart of the coal-fields of the north-east, where most of the development of the locomotive was then taking place. Within a few miles of Bedlington, where Daniel spent his boyhood, were the collieries of Killingworth and Wylam, whose names are writ large in the annals of the steam locomotive, while, living and working in this same small area were men who, by experiment and perseverance, were bringing the locomotive to perfection and laying the foundations of the Railway Age. William Hedley, George Stephenson and Timothy Hackworth, to name but three, are today honoured as pioneers of an era which is, now, already passing, but in Bedlington when Daniel Gooch was a boy these names were heard often in the family circle, for, like many who lived in the village, they were practical, working men, engaged in the staple industry of the district —coal mining.

A month after Daniel's ninth birthday, in 1825, the Stockton & Darlington Railway was opened. Though not the first public railway, it was easily the longest and most carefully planned. News of its opening must have been received with great joy throughout the north-east, and young Daniel Gooch may well have heard all about the line and its first engine, *Locomotion*, from George Stephenson himself. Stephenson was engineer to the line and, as Gooch tells us in the memoirs, was a frequent visitor to his Bedlington home. The reason for these visits is not far to seek; Stephenson was using on part of the Stockton & Darlington line the wrought-iron rail invented by John Birkinshaw, manager of Bedlington Ironworks where Daniel's father was employed. But this was not the only reason which made 'Old George' such a familiar figure in Bedlington, for in 1823 the firm of Robert Stephenson & Company was founded in Newcastle to manufacture locomotives, and the partners in that historic concern, with George Stephenson and his son Robert, were Edward Pease the Quaker and Michael Longridge, who was managing partner of the Bedlington works.

At exactly what age Daniel became interested in locomotives does not appear, but it is obvious enough that throughout his boyhood and early youth he was absorbing knowledge which was to stand him in good stead when he started his apprenticeship at the Tredegar Ironworks in South Wales in 1831. The Gooch family was large, but in the well-ordered, happy atmosphere of the Bedlington home, Daniel's talents were encouraged. His sensible (if strict) father, though not an engineer himself, was, as we read in the memoirs, 'very fond of a little carpentry and had a good idea of mechanics'. It is interesting to speculate on the possibility that Daniel Gooch, who was to be every bit as good a business man as he was an engineer, inherited these twin qualities from his father.

It is clear that this bright and likeable boy was marked out at an early age as a lad of more than usual promise, and the family's many relatives and friends in the engineering world ensured the further development of his gifts when the time was ripe. Through the interest of the Stephensons, the Longridges and the Hawkes, Daniel was placed in a succession of works where, in spite of far from robust health, he was able to gain a varied and extremely valuable insight into many branches of the engineering profession.

Perhaps the most revealing entries in the memoirs are the many instances of the help and encouragement Gooch received from the skilled workmen with whom he came in contact at Tredegar, Newton-le-Willows and elsewhere. This ability to get on with men in all walks of life which manifested itself in those early years was to develop into Gooch's outstanding qualities of leadership which were to prove so valuable on the cable-laying expeditions in the *Great Eastern* and in his chairmanship of the Great Western Railway.

A firm believer in the old adage 'a rolling stone gathers no moss', Gooch served the Great Western, with one brief break, for over half a century, and between Gooch and many of that company's directors and officers there developed a warm and abiding friendship. If, as an employer, Gooch demanded the loyalty of his company's servants, those who were privileged to share his friendship were likewise assured of loyalty of a high order.

Although Daniel Gooch spent most of his working life in London and Swindon, he was at heart a countryman, and he retained all his life a deep love and knowledge of the countryside and of nature, acquired as a boy at Bedlington. In later years he loved above all else the peace of his Thames-side home at Clewer—'pretty Clewer' as he called it. His greatest relaxation was in walking; he covered prodigious distances even in late middle-age, and could seldom resist an inviting hill-top or cliff if time could be spared to climb it. He had a more than superficial knowledge of trees and flowers, and his delight in them could hardly be better illustrated than by the charming pressed specimens mounted in the diary. The sea, in all its moods, seems to have held a fascination for him; he loved to watch a rough sea breaking on a rocky shore, or to gaze at the full moon from the rail of the 'Great Ship' in mid-Atlantic, with his faithful dog Norval at his side. He seems, too, to have been an excellent sailor, for he never reveals any discomfort (apart from lack of sleep) from the violent rolling of the *Great Eastern*.

Although he had to travel a great deal on railway and cable business, Gooch spent many of his holidays touring at home and abroad. He twice visited France and Switzerland, and managed to see something of America and Canada during the maiden voyage of the *Great Eastern* to New York in 1860. In 1863 he spent a long holiday in Italy when he indulged his interest in paintings and sculpture. This proved to be the last tour with his first wife Margaret. After her death in 1868 he sought solace in a trip to Ireland with his daughter Anna. His second wife seems to have been as enthusiastic a tourist (and walker) as her husband, and together they twice visited Ireland, toured the West Country in 1878, and sailed to Madeira in the cable ship *Scotia* in 1884. But Gooch was equally happy to spend a quiet week or two at Weymouth, Malvern or St Ives, seeing the surrounding country by carriage, and taking his regular three walks each day.

Gooch's deep religious convictions are exhibited throughout the memoirs and diary, and although he strongly disliked ritualism and 'high church', the often-repeated statement that he was a puritan is hardly borne out by the facts. He had an abiding faith and was a regular churchgoer, but he enjoyed his wine and his cigar and the creature comforts which his position brought with it.

It would, however, be naïve to suggest that Daniel Gooch did not possess some of the less laudable traits of the Victorian character. He was no less an autocrat than most other men of his time in similar positions, and he certainly did not suffer fools gladly.

Gooch fought hard for what he knew to be right, and defended his beloved Great Western Railway from many an onslaught from within and without, yet he understood the Christian virtue of magnanimity in victory. Corruption, double-dealing and place-seeking he abhorred; any reader who is tempted to call him a snob for his opinion of the West Midland Railway directors need not read much further to find vindication of his attitude as well as proof of his ability to sum up his fellow men.

In politics he was, of course, a thoroughgoing Conservative, but there is little to support the contention that Gooch entered Parliament because it was socially advantageous to do so. Certainly he had no political ambitions, and as the diary clearly shows, he disliked electioneering and all that went with it. There is little doubt, too, that public speaking did not come easily to him. Much play has been made, over the years, of the fact that Gooch never spoke in a debate throughout his twenty years in the Commons, but he attended the House as regularly as he could and played his part on committees and commissions appropriate to his knowledge and experience. In later years he found the late sittings of the House a great burden and would have gladly stood down at the 1880 election had the people of Swindon allowed him to do so.

When he died in 1889 *The Engineer* said of him '. . . so many years have elapsed since he practised as an engineer that the present generation has probably forgotten that he was really a great mechanician. He did his work quietly and well . . . Sir Daniel Gooch was a very remarkable man; far more remarkable than has been generally known. He made surprisingly few mistakes in his work.' No thorough assessment of his stature as an engineer has been made since then, and a great deal of research would be needed before his work could be properly appraised. This would have to include not only his Great Western locomotives, about which much is already known, but all the miscellaneous design work which he did for that company and for the many outside bodies and individuals to whom he acted as consulting engineer. Also to be taken into account is his contribution to the final fitting-out of the *Great Eastern* and her preparation for cable laying, which have hitherto been almost completely ignored.

The best of Gooch's broad-gauge engines, the eight-foot single 'Iron Duke' class, of which the first appeared in 1847, were without doubt magnificent machines, and the fact that they remained in use, with rebuilds, until 1892, illustrates the soundness of his designs and the splendid craftsmanship of Swindon men under his direction. But it also raises the question so often asked—why did the Great Western never exploit the potential, in power and speed, of Brunel's broad gauge, and why did the company's train services, stations and rolling stock deteriorate so much in the seventies and eighties?

No really satisfactory answer has ever been given, but the reasons were certainly in the field of economics and management rather than in engineering. There is no doubt at all that bigger and more powerful engines could have been built for the broad gauge, but the broad gauge was doomed, so that there was little enthusiasm either in the boardroom or at Swindon to do so. Yet, it seems, loyalty to Brunel's seven-foot way implanted a firm belief in Great Western minds that the narrow gauge could not, and indeed must not be allowed to outstrip it, so that on the narrow-gauge parts of the system there was stagnation too.

When Gooch became chairman in 1865 the company was certainly in a parlous state, and the board felt that he was the only man available who could save the day. In addition to his complete familiarity with locomotive and engineering matters, Gooch had acquired an immense fund of business experience, and had a firm grasp of the working of a great railway. He was thus in a position to dictate policy to an extent which must have been the envy of most other railway chairmen of the day. Gooch saw at once that a policy of strict economy and retrenchment was necessary, and there is no doubt that in those first few precarious years from 1865 he drove himself very hard in pulling the Great Western back from the verge of bankruptcy. In those first years, too, his work in connection with the Atlantic cable was occupying a great deal of his time and energy. It could be, therefore, that by the time the company's finances had been put in order, Gooch was to some extent a spent force, and that this fact, coupled with his firm hold over the board, was at least partly responsible for the lack of enterprise at Paddington in the later years of his regime. However, having said this, it is only fair to state most emphatically that but for Gooch's courage and dogged tenacity, aided by the splendid work of James Grierson as general manager, the Great Western would never have survived, and the renaissance which was to come under the chairmanship of Viscount Emlyn (later Earl Cawdor) in the middle nineties would never have occurred. The pity is that this revival came so late.

Whatever his shortcomings as chairman, Gooch could never be accused of apathy. The Great Western Railway was always uppermost in his mind; even in mid-Atlantic, amid the cares of cable laying, he would worry about the weekly traffic returns, and he missed the wedding of one of his sons because it was board day at Paddington. He had a very great affection for his old company, and in the eyes of directors, officers and staff, and indeed of the country at large, Daniel Gooch *was* the Great Western.

At the time of his death Gooch was best known to the general public for his Atlantic cable work and for the determination he showed during the seemingly endless troubles which beset the building of the Severn Tunnel. Here was a project which Gooch knew could greatly benefit the Great Western by shortening the coal route from South Wales, and in spite of setbacks which would have driven lesser men to abandon the work, his faith was rewarded with success only three years before he died. There is a strong hint in the diary that Gooch's part in the ultimate triumph was not only as chairman of the board which voted the money; he may well have had a good deal more say in the engineering direction than has hitherto been thought. The presence of his son Alfred as an assistant engineer on the site may have some significance in this connection.

Although he never lived in the town, it is at Swindon that he is best remembered, for this thriving industrial town owes its very existence to Gooch and Brunel. Gooch took a great personal interest in the welfare of the ever-increasing staff of the great works which he founded, subscribing liberally to its charities and keeping a fatherly eye on the Mechanics' Institution which was the educational and social centre of the town for generations. It hardly needs to be said that the government of the railway town was paternalistic, but the GWR was probably a better employer than many in the nineteenth century.

For more than eighty years after his death, the life and character of Daniel Gooch have remained largely unrevealed. Much that he did and said and thought will remain his secret for ever, but in the pages which follow, the reader will find his philosophy and character gradually unfolding, and when he reaches the end he may well feel, as the editor did when he turned the last of the 630 pages of the manuscript, that the title sometimes jokingly used among admirers of the Great Western Railway—Good Sir Daniel—is not undeserved.

The Manuscript of the Memoirs and Diary

Daniel Gooch was only fifty-one when, in October 1867, he began to write an account of the main events of his life down to that time, but there was already more to record than many men gather in a lifetime.

After the completion of the memoirs he began to keep a diary, the first entry in which is dated February 1868. This he continued, at rather irregular intervals, until about six months before his death. With the memoirs, the diary filled eight volumes. Of these, two, covering the period 1870–3 and 1886–9, have not survived so far as is known. The six volumes which are printed in full in the present edition are made up as follows:

I	Memoirs to 1846	Folios [i–iii], 1–94
II	Memoirs 1847–65	94*–189
III	Memoirs 1865–7	190–235
	Diary 1868–9	235–349
V	Diary 1874–7	[350–439]
VI	Diary 1878–80	[440–526]
VII	Diary 1881–5	[527–630]

* (Gooch only numbered the folios in the first three volumes, and folio 94 is repeated).

The manuscript is written on blue laid paper, unwatermarked, ruled with thirty-six or thirty-seven lines to a page, and measuring $8\frac{1}{2} \times 10\frac{3}{4}$ inches. The paper is laced with green silk thread into limp roan covers, volumes I–III scarlet, volumes V–VII black. Each volume has a manuscript label on the upper cover in Gooch's hand.

The memoirs and diary are written on the recto of each leaf, and on the verso of some leaves are mounted newspaper cuttings, reports of meetings, invitations, and, towards the end, New Year and Easter cards from his wife. In the first volume are two early Great Western Railway timetable bills dated 1839 and 1842, and a record card from the indicator tests with the engine *Great Britain* (*see plate VIII*). There are election posters, accounts of Masonic meetings, and a fine printed menu for the dinner at Weymouth on 16 June 1869 (*see plate XII*). Letters are few, but include one from Richard Jefferies dated 2 May 1878, enclosing a copy of an article on the works at Swindon he had written for *Fraser's Magazine*. Gooch also pasted into the third volume a series of printed forms, completed and signed by Capt Halpin, master of the *Great Eastern*, showing the ship's position, distance run and cable paid out each day during the French cable expedition of 1869 (*see fig* 14).

Many of these enclosures are referred to in the text by 'copy annexed' or 'on the other side'. It has not been practicable to reproduce all of these, but some of the more interesting ones are to be found as plates or line illustrations in the text.

The most surprising of all the enclosures in the six volumes are the pages of pressed flowers which Gooch mounted with great care and artistry. They each have their origin written underneath. There are ferns from the lanes around Neyland, seaweed from Portrush, a rose 'picked on the Great Eastern', and a charming posy gathered on the island of St Pierre when Gooch landed from the *Great Eastern* on 14 July 1869. There are also a few rough sketches in the text, some of which are reproduced in the appropriate place in the present edition.

Gooch makes it clear that he had kept a daily journal since he was a young man. He mentions, for instance, the entry he made in it when he first met his future wife in 1836, when he was nineteen, and after a holiday in Cornwall in 1843 he writes 'I find the scenery fully described in my daily journal'. Again on holiday, this time in France and Switzerland in 1853, he writes 'my daily journal will shew all the places visited'. This journal is now almost certainly lost; had it survived it must have been a treasure beyond price. As it is, we must be grateful for the distillation of it in the present manuscript, for it is clear that the journal provided the basis for the memoirs. Even so. Gooch also drew on his memory, and after thirty years it is hardly surprising that in a few relatively minor details, such as the dimensions of the early Great Western engines, his memory failed him.

After the commencement of the diary in 1868 it is probable that Gooch ceased to keep a daily journal. The uneven gaps between entries, the occasional incorrect date, and variations in pen, ink and handwriting, give the diary an air of spontaneity lacking in the early part of the MS, which has the appearance of a fair copy.

Volumes II and III, and V to VII, have pencil markings in the margins inserted by his widow to indicate passages which she did not wish to be printed in the edition which was published in 1892.* By no means all the remainder was, in fact, printed, and it seems likely that the personal friends, referred to at the end of the introduction to the book, selected the passages which they considered sufficiently interesting.

There is a major difference between the text of the present manuscript and the printed edition of 1892. In the latter the accounts of the 1865 and 1866 cable expeditions (pp 85–118 and 121–87) are taken from Gooch's daily journal, and not from the slightly less detailed account in the memoirs. The reason for this is most likely that Gooch's

* *Diaries of Sir Daniel Gooch, Baronet.* Kegan Paul, Trench, Trubner & Co Ltd, 1892.

connection with the Atlantic cable was, at the time of his death, regarded as his major claim to fame, and thus a more detailed account of these expeditions was appropriate. The fact that the printed account of the 1869 expedition was taken from the diary tends to confirm that by that time Gooch had ceased to keep a daily journal. In contrast to the space given to cable matters, railway affairs and Gooch's other interests were heavily abridged by the editors of the 1892 edition.

The manuscript of the memoirs and diary remained in the family until the six volumes appeared in a London saleroom in June 1969.* Their appearance came as something of a surprise to those interested in Gooch's life, for it had generally been assumed that the MS was no longer in existence. 'Sir Daniel Gooch's Diary' has been widely quoted by transport historians, but all, so far as can be ascertained, saw only the published version of 1892. Not even E. T. MacDermot, when writing the official history of the Great Western Railway, was able to peruse the original manuscript.

At the very beginning of his memoirs, Gooch makes it clear that he is writing for 'those who succeed me in the baronetcy' and for his other children. Later in life, it seems, he came to regard the work in a different light, for Sir Theodore Martin, in his introduction to the 1892 edition, specifically states that it was Gooch's wish that extracts should be published after his death, and as Martin knew Gooch well we are bound to accept this statement. Understandably, Lady Gooch, his widow, deleted some of the more personal passages which were certainly never intended for the public eye, but she and the editors removed so much else that the character of the work as a personal document was destroyed.

The fact remains that the only version of the memoirs and diary which has been available to the public and to historians is the edition of 1892. Of this, it has already been said that it was merely a selection, representing perhaps one third of the whole eight volumes of the manuscript. It only remains to comment briefly, and with as much restraint as duty permits, on the text which was then printed. This, unfortunately, shows Victorian editors at their worst; passages were omitted without any indication of the fact, the diarist's spelling was corrected, his occasional lapses of grammar brought up to drawing-room standard, and innumerable other alterations of various kinds were made.

Scarcely less excusable are some of the many errors in transcribing

* Sotheby & Co, 23 June 1969, lot 162.

Gooch's admittedly difficult hand. Right at the beginning of the book (page 4) comes the astonishing statement that the Bedlington ironworks was the property of 'the Langridges, and Mr Sorden of Linden'. It would have needed very little enquiry in Bedlington to discover that it was the Longridges (a large and respected family of which Daniel's mother was a member), and Mr Gordon of London, who owned the works. Similarly, on the next page, Gooch's school at Crow Hall became 'Condhall', an error constantly repeated in subsequent biographical works in spite of the ready availability of Ordnance Survey maps, on which the house is marked. At the other end of the book the SS *Scanderia* is repeatedly referred to as the *Scandinavia*. The two short lines on the death of Gooch's first wife in 1868 (page 189) are pure invention, and give the impression that the event hardly affected Gooch at all, whereas, as will be seen, he was completely prostrated by its suddenness. What appears to be the source of this passage is a note in the hand of his widow, written on Fulthorpe House paper, which is almost word for word as printed.

The handwriting in the early part of the memoirs is neat and not particularly difficult to read, but as the years go by the writing becomes increasingly careless and legibility declines. Words containing several characters of similar outline present formidable problems, especially as Gooch often inserts an extra minim in his haste. At times the writing is so difficult that considerable research has been necessary to decipher correctly proper names and technical phrases.

The spelling of the manuscript has been followed in the present edition; only where the sense may not be clear has a note been interposed or missing characters or words supplied in brackets. On occasions, particularly at the end of a line, Gooch finished a word with no more than a wavy line, and in such cases it has been assumed that the correct spelling was intended, but there are occasional lapses in spelling which are printed as written. His repeated use of 'bouy' for 'buoy', the two occasions when he omits the 's' from 'scenery', and the delightful 'tormence' for 'torments' are cases in point. Proper names, again, are printed as Gooch wrote them, but the correct spelling is used in the biographical index, with cross-references where necessary.

The MS abounds in capitals, and these have been reduced to conform to modern practice. Punctuation is almost non-existent, and each entry is written as a single, long paragraph. Punctuation has therefore been supplied and the longer entries have been broken up into suitable paragraphs. Some hyphens and apostrophes have been added, where omitted by Gooch, to improve readability.

In the course of his life, Gooch's varied interests and business activities brought him into contact with a very large number of people, many of whom he mentions in the memoirs and diary. About one third of these names may be found in the *Dictionary of National Biography*, which of course reflects Gooch's standing in his own day. Of the remainder, many are railway or telegraph engineers, officials and directors, and politicians, some of whom achieved prominence or even fame, while others have receded into obscurity. People who have been positively identified appear in the biographical index. Here the policy has been to give sufficient facts to show how their affairs brought them into contact with Gooch; it is obviously not practicable to deal with these persons at length, but reference is made to sources where appropriate.

It is natural that Gooch's relatives figure in his diary, and brief details of his brothers and sisters and his children are given, but Daniel being one of a family of ten, and he himself having six children, all of whom married, confronts the editor with formidable genealogical research, producing results of very limited interest, if all his distant relatives are to be traced. Therefore a handful of his relations, of whom he makes only passing mention, remain unidentified. Where the identity of any name is doubtful the available evidence is inserted in a note, rather than in the biographical index.

The notes at the end of each volume have been kept to the minimum necessary to render the text intelligible to the reader who is not a specialist in the subjects it covers. A great deal of additional information can be found in the sources cited in the notes and biographical index.

The fragments of volumes IV and VIII published in 1892 are here reprinted without alteration, except that the few footnotes are omitted and replaced by new notes.

Sources and Acknowledgements

In view of the diversity of subjects covered by the memoirs and diary it would be quite impracticable to list all the books and other sources which were consulted during the transcription of the manuscript and the preparation of the introduction, notes and biographies. The more important sources on specific matters are given in the notes or the biographical index.

There are, however, certain works which have been of more general use. On all matters connected with the Great Western Railway the basic source is E. T. MacDermot's *History of the Great Western Railway*, 2nd edn, revised by C. R. Clinker (2 vols 1964). This is referred to in the notes as MacDermot: *GWR*.

Many of the railway directors and officers mentioned by Gooch were identified in Bradshaw's *Railway Manual* and its predecessors (1848–1922), which also contains a mass of valuable data on railway matters generally.

The best short account of Gooch's life and work is by C. Hamilton Ellis in *Twenty Locomotive Men* (1958). Chapter V deals with Gooch, but the whole book is a useful starting point for research on railway mechanical engineers.

On political affairs, files of *The Times*, and the *British Almanac and Companion* (1827–88) were important sources. Gooch's election activities at Cricklade are well chronicled in the *North Wilts Herald*, of which microfilm copies are in Swindon Public Library.

Also frequently consulted were the *Dictionary of National Biography* (*DNB*), Burke's and Debrett's *Peerage, Baronetage & Knightage*, Haydn's *Dictionary of Dates* (ed Vincent, 1910), *Who Was Who*, George Ottley's invaluable *Bibliography of British Railway History* (1965) and the Ordnance Survey one-inch maps.

The author or editor of any book of this scope is bound to depend heavily on the help and advice of archivists, librarians and friends—including many new ones made in the course of the work.

I feel credit should first be given to Mrs H. E. Merritt, Sir Daniel Gooch's great-granddaughter, for bringing the manuscript out of obscurity and thus making it available for publication and ensuring its eventual preservation.

I have had to enlist the help of a large number of people in deciphering parts of the manuscript and in the preparation of the notes. I am especially grateful to Mr Brian Carter, whose enquiries in Newcastle-upon-Tyne led me to Mr Stephen Martin of Stakeford, to whom I owe a great debt. Mr Martin has spent many years recording the history of the Bedlington area, and he and his son, Mr Evan Martin of Bedlington, placed their great knowledge at my disposal and introduced me to

Gooch's boyhood haunts. In connection with the diarist's early life I also received every help from Mr R. M. Gard, Northumberland County Archivist, Mrs E. W. Mitchell JP, Mr W. H. Gibson and Mr A. Walker.

Mrs G. D. Wilkin, Sir Daniel Gooch's great-great-granddaughter, kindly lent me his family Bible containing valuable genealogical material.

Mr P. J. T. Reed kindly placed his unrivalled knowledge of GWR broad-gauge engines at my disposal.

In my researches at Swindon I was given every facility by the Borough Librarian, Mr T. S. McNeil FLA and the reference librarian, Mr K. E. Hardy FLA. The County Archivists of Berkshire, Caernarvonshire, Cornwall, Monmouthshire, Pembrokeshire, Somerset and Worcestershire, the City Librarians of Westminster, Dundee and Newcastle-upon-Tyne, and the librarian of Windsor reference library answered individual questions.

I received every help from Mr E. H. Fowkes, Archivist, British Transport Historical Records, Mr John Scholes, Curator of Historical Relics, British Railways Board, and Mr N. W. Sprinks, Public Relations Dept, British Railways (Western Region), from the staff of the reference department, Cheltenham Public Library, Mr Ian Rogerson, County Technical Librarian, Gloucestershire, and Miss P. Y. Lewis, librarian of Gloucestershire College of Art & Design.

I am also indebted to Col T. M. Simmons, department of transport, Science Museum; the librarian, University of Manchester Institute of Technology; the director of the National Portrait Gallery; the public relations manager, B. I. Callenders Cables Ltd; the Institut Français du Royaume-Uni; the Société des Amis de la Bibliothèque Nationale de France; Mr G. H. Somner of the World Ship Society; Mr R. A. Mann, manager, Luttrell Arms Hotel, Dunster; and the following individuals who have helped in various ways: Mr J. H. H. Bayley JP, Mr D. Bick, Mr M. Brooks, Mr J. G. Burr, the Rev T. Hine, Mr J. Hollingworth, Mr G. Littell, Mr D. B. Lyall, Mr B. R. Miller, Mr F. B. Robinson, Mr D. M. Stevens, Mr C. H. A. Townley and Mr J. Turnbull (the last occupant of Crow Hall, Cramlington).

I am also glad to acknowledge the help of my old tutor Mr E. R. C. Brinkworth in elucidating some of the more obstinate problems resulting from Gooch's troublesome handwriting. Mr Paul Morgan, as usual, has advised me on editorial matters, and Mr Michael Robbins has taken a great interest in the work and has given me the benefit of his knowledge of Gooch's life.

Finally, but by no means least, I wish to thank Mr M. J. Rix for his work on my behalf at the Bodleian Library, Oxford, and Mr T. Creswell who, during the past months, has read aloud the whole of the typescript for final checking with the manuscript, and again for proof correction.

Hutton House
Suffolk Place
Cheltenham
September, 1971   R.B.W.

VOLUME I

The Memoirs to 1846

London, Decr 1867

Her Majesty having by Royal Letters Patent conferred upon me the rank and dignity of a baronet, I feel it may not be uninteresting to those who succeed me in the baronetcy, and my other children, to know something of the life of him upon whom the title was first conferred.

Looking back as I now do for a period of 35 years, during which I have had to struggle with the world, I must first express my gratitude to God for the many and great blessings He has bestowed upon me. I feel and acknowledge all is due to His goodness, that many who have run the race of life with me, while falling greatly short in the result, have equally merited advancement. Some will say it is luck; I feel it is God's goodness and mercy, and I thank Him.

The principle which has guided me through life has been a steady perseverance in the path of duty to my employers, not being disheartened by a first failure but ever believing in the possibility of ultimate success, and a determination not to be led into changes by the inducement of immediate advancement. I feel proud of the thought that since I was a boy I have only been in one service, altho' I was on several occasions tempted by the offers of higher salary to make a change, but some words my father once used to me have ever been present with me: 'a rolling stone gathers no moss'. The experience of my life has fully supported the truth of this, and I would earnestly urge it upon my children and their children to adopt it as their motto.

Altho' I feel it is not possible for all men to succeed in life, yet I am sure few need fail to do well if they will win for themselves a character of strict honesty, and by this I do not mean that they will not steal, but that in their dealings with other men they will act with honour, not seeking to obtain an advantage by either supressing or magnifying the truth, but that a feeling may be created in the minds of them with

I

whom they are brought into contact, that what they say may be relied upon and will honourably be fulfilled. Thus you get the confidence and esteem of the outer world. With your immediate employers or associates, they should feel that, having embarked with them in their enterprises, you can be relied upon steadily to persevere in the pursuit of their interest, and so identify yourself with them that they can feel you are not ever seeking for a change, because you thus might earn a few pounds per annum extra. Be sure, as a general rule, your interests are in the end best promoted by such a course. It may be in some cases you will not be so rich, but you will be more esteemed. It ought to be every man's greatest happiness and pride to say 'I have been associated with the same men through life', and to my mind nothing speaks stronger against a man than for him, in describing his past life, to go through a long list of changes in his business associates, in the end trusted by none and esteemed by few.

I earnestly pray that my children and their children may avoid this, and pursue that straight and certain path I have before described.

Dan Gooch

Octr 1867

About the year 1827 my father, assisted by Mr Hodgson the historian of Northumberland, took great pains and expended much labour in tracing the pedigree of my family in the female line down to that period. I believe the cause of this was the restoration of the estates to some of the Border families that had been forfeited for rebellion and other political causes. I know that one case in which my father took much interest, and I believe spent some money, was an old man living in Bedlington as a labourer, who was thought to be the rightful owner of large estates of the Ford family. He, however, did not succeed, but the searching into pedigrees in this case induced my father to look into the matter for our own family, and he was greatly assisted by Mr Hodgson. Several of his letters are contained amongst the rough drafts of my father, now in my possession. This pedigree, together with such records of the family as my father collected, are now entered in my large family Bible, and to which I refer for information as to the past.

It shews that in the female line the family is of no mean descent, but may even claim the blood of Alfred the Great. The portraits, as far back as Mr Justice, are now in the family, the property of my eldest brother. The pedigree in the male line has not been investigated, but I hope

2

when I have a little leisure to be able to do this. As far as it has gone it is a Suffolk family. My father and mother were first cousins, in that both had the blood of the female line.[1] My grandfather Longridge was owner of some large iron works in Scotland called the Devon Iron Works, near Alloa, but I have no knowledge how he ceased to be connected with them or when he had a house in Newcastle. My uncle Longridge in his will describes himself [as] of Devon Iron Works.

I was born at Bedlington in Northumberland (or rather in the county of Durham, as this parish [is], on account of the remains of St Cuthbert having rested there when being removed from Holy Island to Durham), on the 24th day of August 1816.[2] I have often heard my mother say my birth occurred about 3 oclock in the morning during an awful thunderstorm. My father had then lived in Bedlington about a year. He was engaged[3] in the Bedlington Iron Works, at the time the property of my second cousins the Longridges and Mr Gordon of London.[4]

The village of Bedlington was a tolerably clean and large country village with half a dozen good houses in it. The house we then lived in stood at *a* in the annexed plan of the village. We removed from this

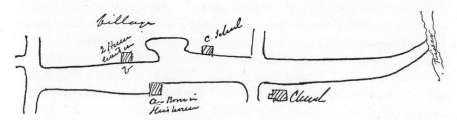

FIG 1   Gooch's sketch plan of Bedlington, showing 'a—born in this house', 'b—2nd house lived in', 'c—school' and the parish church. The river Blyth is at right

house to a house marked *b*[5] when I was probably about 3 years old, as I can remember my trying to carry part of my cot over the street. I certainly was not more than 3 years old at this time, as I was only 4 years of age when I went to school. How well I remember the first day I was led there by the servant, and also the appearance of the 2 ladies who kept it. Its situation is marked *c* on the plan.[6] The ladies were a Miss Robson and her sister Miss Betsey. They must have been kind to me as I was very fond of them, and long after looked back upon them as old friends. My mother has often told me I was sent so early to school as I was rather inclined to keep the house in hot water from one piece of mischief or other.

I do not know exactly how long I was at that school, but probably a few years, as the next I went to was at Mr Thompson's, the clergyman of Horton parish who lived at a place called Crow Hall,[7] not far from Cramlington and about 4 miles from Bedlington. It was a large school & the boys were chiefly the sons of farmers living round about, and most of us rode there either on donkeys or ponies. Probably some 30 of these animals were congregated in the old buildings used as stables at the school. We all had a great regard for Mr Thompson and also for Mrs Thompson; both were very kind to us. We, of course, took our dinners with us and dined in the school room, where Mrs Thompson looked after us and did all she could for our comfort. We used to have each a large basin of new milk, and I well remember the thick coating of cream upon it, into which we used to dip our bread. I even now look back upon the period I was at that school as a very happy period in my life.

Mr Thompson was very indulgent, and often when the Northumberland Pack of foxhounds, then belonging to Sir Matthew White Ridley, came past the place he did not punish us if we mounted our steeds and went after them. It was a great amusement for the gentlemen hunting to see some 30 donkeys & ponies and us boys. There were also times when Mr Thompson had either a wedding or a funeral to attend to at his church, which was a couple of miles from the school, and in his absence his eldest son used to take charge of the school; but not being much older than the eldest of the boys he had not very much command of us, and we used to have all kinds of fun in the school, shutting in the shutters to prevent people outside seeing what we were about. We thought little & cared little for the loss of time in our studies.

My chief play mate was George Marshall, who lived at Bedlington. He was the son of a widow, farming their own farm,[8] and he had a sweet girl as his sister, who died, as I will mention further on. He and I were inseparable companions; our evenings were always spent together, and our Saturdays, on which day there was no school, altho' I do not think there was a great similarity in our dispositions; he was quieter, had less mischief in him, and I believe most of the scrapes he got into was through my leading. His mother was very kind to me, and treated me as she did her own son. For some time we used to ride together on the same pony to school. My Saturdays were always spent either on the farm or at the collieries or iron works. I used to go often to a pit called The Glebe,[9] and nothing pleased me so much as going underground and driving the trams. In looking back at all the risks I ran at this pit it is a wonder to me I never met with an accident,[10] but it was not in my nature at that time to have any fear, and I could never rest an hour at home.

My father was rather strict with us on a Sunday. We went to church morning and afternoon, and at the afternoon service I, with the rest of the young people, had to say our Catechism before the congregation. We all stood in a circle round the reading desk, a large open space in the church was well fitted for it, and the questions were put by Mr Coates, the minister. He was a *true pattern* of a clergyman, a gentleman in every sense of the word, beloved by all. The church and church yard at that time (it has since been much altered, I think for the worse) was kept in the most beautiful order. It was the great pride of Mr Coates to see the church yard kept neat and filled with flowers and pretty shrubs, and so much was he liked that even us mischievous boys respected them for his sake altho' we used often to play there as it was always open, yet we never did any harm. A grandson of Mr Coates was also a play fellow of mine and I used often to be at the parsonage.

Old Mrs Coates was mad, and a strange old lady. At times she was very fond of us boys and would give us all kinds of good things, and at others, if she could get hold of us, she would beat us with her stick. We used often on such occasions to tease her, and of course keep out of her reach. I remember on one occasion when doing this I ran away, she following me, and in getting through the bars of an iron gate I got my leg fast, and she came up and gave it me with her stick. Poor old lady, it was a melancholy thing; some of her sons also became deranged. What has become of Henry, the grandson, I do not know; I did hear of him practicing as a surgeon in London. I should like to see him for the sake of old times. He was a dreadful coward and I fear I often made him unhappy as he used to be afraid of joining in our mischief, yet we forced him into it.

The old women of the village had a considerable dread of me, yet I believe they liked me all the better for the pranks I used to play upon them. Our great amusement was to fill a cow's horn with old tar rope and then to put a hot cinder in it, and insert the small end of the horn into the keyhole or any other opening we could get through the cottage door, and by blowing at the large end driving the smoke into the cottage. This we called *funking* the old women, and was generally a winter

5

evening's amusement. There were no policemen in those days to protect the subjects of His Majesty.

There were, however, two very serious scrapes we got into, and were threatened with the magistrates. Geo Marshall, Harry Coates and myself found some young girls in one of Marshall's fields; we told them to go out, instead of doing which they laughed at us. I had at the time a small frog in my hand, and as one of them opened her mouth in laughing rather wide, I slipped the frog into it. She said it went down her throat and they all went off screaming to the village. There was soon a hue & cry after us and we had to keep out of the way until night. There was a general enquiry into it next day and we were threatened with a visit to Morpeth jail, but somehow got out of the scrape. I am not sure to this day whether she did or did not actually swallow the frog. I certainly did not see it afterwards and believed at the time it had gone down her throat, a thing not impossible as it was very small.

Another serious scrape was our nearly hanging a boy. Four of us were playing in the rick yard at the back of Marshall's house. As the hay ricks had just been put up a ladder was standing up against one of them, and we proposed a game at hanging. I remember I was to be hanged last; of course one boy had to be first. We got a small rope and fastened it round his neck, getting the other end over one of the rounds of the ladder, and so pulled him up off the ground. This end we made fast, and thought it good fun to see him kick his legs about. Fortunately we heard the bailiff coming and all ran away. Still more fortunately he happened to go round that side of the rick and saw the boy hanging, and was just in time to get him down & save his life. He was black in the face and insensible. I have often thought since what a painful thing through life it would have been had we killed him; the poor boy carried the mark of the rope round his neck for some time afterwards, but in a few days we were playing together again, little feeling the escape we had all had. We got into considerable hot water about this.

Another amusement we used to have was for our school to challenge some other one to fight, for which we used to prepare ourselves with swords made of wood, and in these fights we got many very hard nocks. The last one I was at I was the captain, and the ground selected was a road leading from the bottom of the village to the iron works, a high hedge on one side and a steep bank down to the river on the other side. The plan of battle was to force each other's ranks, drawn up as we were across the road facing each other. This was a very hard battle, and a drawn one. I am not sure we did not get the worst of it; it was to be resumed at another time, but this was prevented by the school master. Many swords were broken, and sundry combatants sent down the bank into the bushes. These amusements, if rough, I think did us no harm; they taught us a certain amount of self reliance, and we never suffered any serious personal injury.

Bedlington at the time I was there was often the scene of sharp fights between the Excisemen and the smuglers who used to carry whiskey across the Scotch borders. These men used to ride generally a very good horse with kegs of whiskey hung like saddle bags on the saddle, and as the population of the village in all cases took the part of the smuglers, the Excise often got the worst of it. I remember one night a very hard fight with two smuglers; the Excise had got them off the horses and secured the kegs of whiskey which they placed against the side of a house while they were securing the men, and we, finding these kegs, stove the ends in and let the whiskey run to waste, much to the disgust of the Excisemen when they came to take them away. I used to enjoy these rows.

There was also great excitement in the village at the time of the Burke and Hare murders in Edinburgh. What were called resurrection men used to rob the graves of the bodies for the doctors, and all that winter the church yard was watched for some time after anyone had been buried. Hare, who had turned King's evidence, and was let off, was supposed to be at Bedlington one night; at any rate, a man believed to be him was there, and the whole place turned out to lynch him. It was a wonder he was not killed; had he not possessed good legs he certainly would have been, as his fleetness enabled him to keep ahead of those in chase and they did not get hold of him, but pelted him with stones until he got away in the dark. He certainly was a bad-looking fellow; I had seen him in the afternoon begging. My father, as churchwarden, and a constable used to go round to all the lodging houses for tramps to see who was in them at night, and I used often to accompany them. It was a winter of great dread which was made worse by many practical jokes, by a piece of sticking plaister being put over people's mouths in the dark, the belief being that a number of people were killed by the resurrection men in that way, they having a plaister which the person operated on could not get off. I had a dagger made out of an old bayonet that I used to carry about with me when out after dark, altho' I dare say I would have used my legs freely had I fancied any real danger.

7

When I was about 9 or 10 years old I broke my collar bone. I was spending the afternoon with Harry Coates and we had his donkey out, which I was riding. The girths of the saddle had not been pulled tight, and I was whipping it behind as it galloped, when the saddle slipped round and my feet got fast in the stirrup and dragged me amongst his legs, causing the accident. I was fortunate in only having this one as a boy.

When 11 or 12 years old my father indulged my taste for mechanics by buying me a lathe and box of tools, the former I still have, or rather what is left of it, and I took lessons in turning. This was a source of great amusement and usefulness to me, as it caused me to think, and also to read useful books on mechanics. I acquired a considerable amount of skill in fancy turning and got a good deal of employment from the ladies for screw handles, chess men &c. I collected all the large bones I could get, to make things in bone. My poor father took a great deal of interest in what I did. He was a man very fond of a little carpentry himself and had a good idea of mechanics, although he had received no mechanical training. I quite understood the details of the steam engine and, for a boy who had to depend upon himself, got from books and such experiments as I could make, a fair knowledge of natural philosophy. Arnold[11] was a very favourite book of mine; a plan I found very useful was to write down from memory what I had been reading. In science, to enable you to do this requires you to understand fully what you have read, as you have to put it in your own language.

I have ever looked back upon my years spent at Bedlington as very happy ones; I know they have been very useful to me in after life, giving me a feeling of self reliance which I have needed, having my way to fight in the world. My dear parents gave me all the education they could and such as was to be obtained in private schools, and while leaving me much liberty they set me a right example. I may say Sunday was the only day when my time was not at my own disposal out of school hours, and I often used to be out of the house on a Saturday morning before anyone was up. I remember eating my breakfast before going to bed to save time next morning.

Before I left Bedlington (I do not know in what year it was) I went to Morpeth to see a steam engine working on the common road. It was built by Messrs Hawthorn of Newcastle, and drew a threshing machine after it. I believe it was for the Duke of Northumberland; it was on its way from Newcastle to Anwick [Alnwick]. I found it at a stand, from

I   (*Above left*) Daniel Gooch's birthplace in Bedlington (the house behind the single-storey cottages)

II (*Above right*) Daniel Gooch's first school in the Market Place, Bedlington (with dormer windows)

III   (*Below*) The second house occupied by the Gooch family in Bedlington, where Daniel spent his boyhood, now the King's Arms Hotel. Note the plaque commemorating Daniel Gooch's association with the house

IV (*Right*) Daniel Gooch
with the model of his
Fire Fly engine. Photograph
said to have been taken in 1845,
as it appeared in the 1892
edition of the diary
V (*Below*) Bedlington
Ironworks at the time of
Daniel Gooch's boyhood, from
John Birkinshaw's *Remarks on
. . . Cast Metal and Malleable
Iron Rail-ways*, 1827

some defect, on a hill a little before reaching Morpeth, but waited to see it repaired, and it went on into the town, making the turnings of the streets capitally. It made a strong impression on me. I knew all about the iron horses, as they were then called, on the waggon ways; George Stephenson was frequently at my father's house and used to take a great deal of notice of me by taking me on his knee and talking to me about pits &c. At that time he was much engaged in advising on colliery matters & had just commenced his glorious career. My eldest brother Tom went to his works at Newcastle as a pupil.

Mr Locke was also there, and used frequently to come to Bedlington to spend his Sunday with my brother. I well remember the discussions about railways, then called waggon ways, and the first introduction of the long wrought iron rail.[12] Mr Birkinshaw, the manager of the Bedlington works, took out a patent for making these rails, fish-bellied as they were called, or this shape

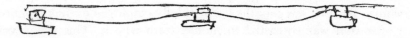

the chairs or supports being placed at the weak part of the rail and the bellied part giving strength between. It was at that time a great advance in the art of rolling to give this varying depth of bar.

Amongst my father's papers I found the annexed slip, shewing that he foresaw the great future in railways from the introduction of these wrought iron rails. He lived to see some considerable progress made.

[*Slip in John Gooch's hand*]
The only manufactory in this parish is that carried on under the firm of the B[edlington] I[ron] Co, in which Mess[rs] Gord[on] of L[ondo]n are the principal proprietors, the lead[in]g feature in which is the manufacture of mal[leab]le railway bars invented by Mr Birkinshaw, for which he obtained a patent, an improvement as connected with the present prospects of railways becoming of general use, from which the most beneficial results may be expected both from their superior durability to metal as well as from the increased facility given to locomotives from the lengths (from 15 to 18 feet) in which they can be laid down without a joint.

Since writing the above, I found on making an inspection of the Great Western Railway at Stratford-upon-Avon, these rails laid on an old line[13] purchased by the Gt Western Co between Stratford-on-Avon

C

and Mor[e]ton[-in-Marsh], and learned from Mr Greaves, whose father was interested in laying the road, that the present rails were those originally obtained from Bedlington in the year 1830. The line is worked by horses and the rails are still in good order now (1867). I have had a sample sent to me to keep as a relic of the early history of railways. This is now at Clewer, and it ought to be preserved.[14]

In February 1831 my father left Bedlington to go to Tredegar iron works in Monmouthshire, and took his family with him. I remember well what a pleasant journey it was. We had a kind of omnibus built, with curtains round it, in which we all travelled, posting. I do not know how many days it took us to make the journey, but I well remember it, and the beautiful view as we crossed the Malvern hills; it was a bright moon light evening.

When we were settled at Tredegar I began my professional career by working in the works. Mr Saml Homfray was the managing partner. I went first into the moulding dept, commencing work at 6 oclock in the morning. The first few months I was chiefly employed in making cores, but after that was entrusted to mould tram wheels. This was a very heavy job for me; the wheel pattern weighed 50 or 60 lbs, and I had nine boxes to mould twice a day, the first lot before 9 oclock in the morning, when the furnace was run off and they were cast. During this time I went to my breakfast for a couple of hours, when I returned and opened the boxes, tamped my sand and moulded the 2nd set. This was generally finished between 4 & 5 oclock. I had an hour for dinner. As this work was done in the atmosphere of the furnace house and the work was very hard I began to feel the effects of it in my health, and was sent a voyage to sea for a few weeks.

I went to Bristol and got a passage in a ship going to Liverpool & back. This was the first time I was in Liverpool. My brother John was at the time in Warrington, and I went to him to spend the few days the ship was unloading and loading to return. On my return to Tredegar I went into the pattern makers' shop and did not do any more moulding. The foreman of the moulders, Ben Williams, was very kind to me and gave me all the information he could.

I also obtained from those working the furnaces a good deal of information as to the mode of working them, and learned to know from the cinder and other indications the quality of the iron being produced. Here also my system of writing down any facts I collected was of great use, as it not only stimulated me to collect such facts but impressed them more strongly on my mind. Several of my books of notes are still in my possession.

The foreman in the pattern shop was a Mr Ellis. His son was the engineer of the works, that is, he had charge of all the mechanical department. Old Ellis, as we used to call him, was somewhat of a character, but he was always a kind friend to me and gave me any information he could. He had a book with a stock of facts, valuable at the time as the result of a life's experience, and this was always at my service. He gave me a pearl handle knife which I still have. One of the men in the shop was also most kind to me (his name was Jonathan Miles) taking great pains to instruct me in the proper use of my tools and assisting me in every way he could. I am glad to feel that I have, since that time, had it in my power to return some of his kindness by giving him employment at Swindon, where he has been for a great many years respected by all his fellow workmen. He is now, in 1867, a very old man and not able to do much, but he still is at the bench and is very sensitive about his ability to do as much as ever he used to do. Poor old Jonathan, I shall feel as tho' I had lost a friend when it pleases God to take him. We worked very much together at Tredegar, and often upon strange kind[s] of work.

One of the perquisites of the foreman of pattern makers was that he was *undertaker* for the works. He kept a shop in which he sold trimmings for coffins, also carpenters' tools, and these coffins were made in our shop by overtime. J. Miles was the chief man interested with them, and as we got paid extra for the work, I was glad to be allowed to assist, and many nights have Miles and I worked away together at our coffin making. Many of them had to be very elaborately decorated, and it took some time to complete it, sometimes as much as we could do in two nights. We then had to take them home and often have we, in the middle of the night, carried a coffin to the house of the dead. One winter's night, when so engaged, the ground was covered with snow, and to make a short cut to the place about a mile off we went across some old pit heaps, and when arriving at the foot of one of them we went plump into a small feeder with 5 or 6 feet of water in it. The surface of the water had been slightly frozen, and being all covered with snow we did not see it, and both of us, and the coffin, were in the water. We scrambled out and picked up our coffin and tried another road.

The cholera, on its first visit to this country, was very bad at Tredegar.

The first case was a man in our shop. He and I had been making a coffin, and I remember the side boards had been cut too short and were laid aside. 2 nights afterwards I used these very boards for his own coffin. Poor fellow, he little thought he was preparing part of his own coffin.

One of the advantages of being concerned in coffin making was that as undertaker one of us had to attend at the house the morning of the funeral to screw down the lid, and was not expected to go to work again that day. I used therefore to like this part of the work as it gave me all the afternoon to myself. I have often thought since of the face of a little child as I looked on it before putting on the lid; it looked so beautiful, more like a quiet sleep than death. It had none of that deadly white look of the dead. I have sometimes wondered whether the child was really dead or only in a trance. Poor little thing, it looked very beautiful, and still often comes before my mind.

One of the duties of our shop was to repair the valves of the blowing engines. They were made of wood, faced with leather, and one or other of the engines has to be done on a Saturday morning. I always went to this work as it took me amongst the engines, and we often had some excitement in performing the duty. This, on two occasions, was however rather too strong. There were 3 large blowing engines at Tredegar at that time, and they were all connected by the blowing pipes so that in case of accident to one engine the others could blow the furnaces. Each engine had a large regulator, or sort of iron baloon to equalise the blast from the varying stroke of the cylinders. To make these regulators tight it was the practice to put powdered lime into them. A young fellow, a little older than myself, of the name of Jenkins, and I were inside the blowing cylinder putting on a new valve when one of the furnacemen lifted the valve between our engine and the next one, when the blast came through the regulator upon us, bringing with it the lime powder, and we could not get out, for the pressure shut the valves where we were; but as one was off in another place the engine house was also soon filled with lime, and the engineer, knowing where we were and what had been done, ran as hard as he could to shut off the valve again, and returned to find us nearly dead from suffocation. A very little more and it would have been all over with us. We thought at the time the furnace man did it on purpose, as he knew we were there and had no business, in any case, to lift the valve. The old scamp—we played him some tricks for it afterwards—gave a dog his dinner, watered his beer &c. All the other men about the furnace condemned him and gave us every opportunity of clearing off scores with him.

Another occasion was, I believe, quite accidental, but careless, altho' the engineer was a great friend of mine and a good fellow. We were in the bottom of the cylinder and had just finished work. One of the men had gone out and we were just about to follow when we were much astonished to see the engine start. The piston at the time was about half stroke, so that we could stand nearly upright. Fortunately it made its first start upwards, or we would have been flattened like a cake between it and the bottom of the cylinder. Before it had time to make the up stroke and return we were able to creep down into the square valve box at the bottom (these holes being about 2 feet square and the same depth, just enough to crouch into), when down came the piston again within an inch or so of our heads. Fortunately the man who had left us was in the engine house and shouted to the engineer, who stopped the engine at once, before she could make another up stroke, or I fear the valves would have given us a hard squeeze. It was not at all uncommon for us to sit in these valve boxes when the engine was moved a little, but then we either had the valve off or made fast. I must say it was a curious sensation to be there and hear the roar of the air rushing in as the piston moved, or see the piston coming down upon us, shutting us up in this little hole until it moved up again.

With all this, I used to like these Saturday mornings in the blowing engines, and as that liking was not general in the shop it was readilly accorded to me. A boy was also a better size for the confined space than a man, if they could depend upon him to do the work properly. I therefore take it as a compliment to me that I was so much trusted.

I also had a very narrow escape when erecting a roof over the rolling mill. We were putting up a new one just over the large fly wheel, a very improper thing to be allowed to do when the mill was at work, as, if we happened to fall, nothing could save us amongst those great wheels. One morning while we were at breakfast the fly wheel broke and flew through the roof we were at work upon, carrying everything away before it; half an hour later and we would have gone with it.

I worked upon the iron roof of the market house, and as it was put up during the winter it was a dreadfully cold job. I have looked on it on the occasions I have been at Tredegar since, and recalled my feelings on those cold days.

I think on one occasion I saved the life of my brother William. He was a little fellow and had gone with me to the works. I missed him from the shop and went out to look for him, when I saw him between the rails of a road that passed the end of the shop. On going towards him I saw a locomotive coming,[15] within very few yards of which he was, taking no notice, and had just time to run and pull him out of the way. It made my heart jump and was a very narrow escape for him. Fortunately the engines on those roads did not travel very fast.

I was often employed by the ladies at Mr Homfray's house to make fancy things for them. My skill at the lathe was often brought into requisition. Mrs Homfray's mother, a Mrs Staples, was quite a character; it was said she managed everybody about her. One day she sent for me to assist in altering her carpets, and she and I had a long day of it in cutting and nailing down again. She also once gave me a curious kind of instrument to make: it was a back-scratcher. I had to carve a hand in bone, with the fingers at right angles to the hand, and fix it to a long, slender piece of whalebone. This I learned was employed to do a little bit of scratching where her own hand could not reach. She was a very fat woman & I daresay could not reach a great deal of her body.

Miss Fanny Staples, her unmarried daughter, who also lived with Mr Homfray, used to give me many commissions to do, such as workbox repairs (I mean handles and other kinds of fancy things). As it all went with the day's work, and was not quite so hard as I often had in the shop, I used to like it, besides being proud to serve a lady. Poor Mrs Homfray was a very nice kind woman and much liked by everybody. I cannot say there was the same feeling for the old lady, but she took a great deal of interest in me, and shortly before I left Tredegar, I thought, much more than I liked.

Mr Bevan & Mr Jones, the mineral agents, were also very kind to me. Altho' only a boy they always gladly told me anything I wished to know about the mines, and allowed me to go with them sometimes.

[A] large works of this kind is by far the best school for a young engineer; he gets so general a knowledge of what he needs in after life. It is in fact the foundation for all else. Every engineer ought to know & understand the manufacture of iron and working of mines. It is a kind of knowledge that is constantly coming in useful as he gets older, and I look back upon the time spent at Tredegar as by far the most important years of my life, and will ever feel grateful to those, many in number, who were so kind to me in enabling me to obtain, and in giving me, information. It was also at Tredegar where the feeling of having earned money for myself was first felt by me, a feeling that cannot come twice in a man's life. Those first few sovereigns gave me more pleasure than millions could do now.

When I first went to work the important question of my wages took some time to settle, and it was nearly 4 months before finally arranged. I had 14 weeks pay due to me, and the amount per week being 9s/-, I was indeed a proud boy as I walked away from the pay table with upwards of £6 in my hand. I did not think there was so rich a person in the world. Oh, those first feelings of life, once past, never to return with equal force or satisfaction.

About early in 1833 my father's health began to fail him, altho' we had no idea of any danger. He went to London for advice & stopped at my uncle Robinson's at Worcester on his return, where my mother went to meet him. He was very weak but quite cheerful. The evening before he died he sat up to the usual hour, then went to bed and fell asleep. A few hours afterwards my mother woke and found him dead, (28th August 1833). It was a great and unexpected blow to us all. I went to Worcester hoping to be in time to attend his funeral, but was too late, the funeral having taken place the day I reached there. My father was buried at a pretty country church yard a little distance from Worcester called Claines, where his sons put up a monument[16] to his memory a little later. I thus, at a very early age, lost a good father, and my poor mother was left to care for 4 others younger than myself, and nobly she performed her task.

I had few companions at Tredegar. Two young surgeons, pupils of a Mr Jackson who was the surgeon to the works, were the only young men I associated with. I spent a great deal of time with them at the surgery and learned the art of drawing teeth and making plaisters. I used sometimes to accompany them in their visits on the sick, and we often had some shooting together on the mountains. One was a nephew of Mr Homfray, named Alfred Homfray, and the other a Mr Fenton. Both are since dead. Mr Jackson's sister was a very pretty and a very nice woman; she and Mr Jackson are also dead. There was also one other family with two young ladies whom I used to visit. They are gone; the youngest rests in peace in a pretty little church yard called Llanelwedd, close to Builth in South Wales, where a stone marks the spot. She died in [blank].

My mother remained in the house at Tredegar after the death of my father and I continued at the works. During the time I was there the

Merthyr riots took place; I forget the year.[17] The Tredegar men did not join the rioters. On the Friday a large body of men, collected from Nant y Glo & Ebbw Vale, passed through Tredegar on their way to join the Dowlais & Merthyr men, where they attacked the Castle inn, in which a number of one of the Highland regiments and the magistrates were. The soldiers were obliged to fire from the windows upon the mob and I think 21 were killed. They were beaten off for the time, but determined to collect additional strength by the Monday.

Early on the Monday morning a much larger number passed through Tredegar and got hold of all the men they could to force them to go with them. I was amongst the unwilling ones, and with the others was placed in front, the men behind having sticks with spikes in the end to poke us on. There were 8 or 10,000 altogether. When we got to Rhymney we saw a lot of soldiers drawn up along the ridge of Dowlais hill, instead of meeting the Merthyr men there as had been arranged. A considerable amount of bluster took place as they ascended the hill, we in the front not liking the look of things at all. When we reached the soldiers some of the magistrates came forward to advise the men to disperse and return home. This could not be listened to, and they would march on to Merthyr in spite of the soldiers. The magistrates then retired and the soldiers were ordered to present arms, no pleasant sound to us in front, as one word of command more and who could say how many of us would roll in the dust?

A panic certainly took possession of us in the front and was as quickly communicated to those behind, and a general scramble down the hill took place, so that in very few minutes the word 'Fire' would have done us no harm. We Tredegar people were right glad to get back, and we had some revenge on our oppressors as they, in parties of 2 & 3, passed back through Tredegar on their way home. We gave them a fair amount of chaff. The soldiers managed this matter very well, as they took possession of the hill first and so prevented the two bodies of men meeting. This put an end to the riots.

On the Friday the men disarmed a troop of yeomanry coming up from Cardiff, I think, & got one of the bayonets off the musket of one [of] the Highlanders when they made a rush upon them at the Castle Hotel. This bayonet, with a small flag tied to it, was carried on a pole by the party with whom I had the honour of marching. I have often asked myself since whether I was really frightened at the position I was in, but I think not. It is true the number of lives lost on the Friday made me feel the soldiers would fire if necessary, but I seemed to enter into the spirit of the march and the excitement of the shouting and noise, and I had no real occasion to get into the mess. Had I stayed at home I would not have done so as they only went into the workmen's houses.

Just before leaving Tredegar I did a very foolish thing. I was dared to go down a pit about 30 yards deep by the chain and come up in the same way. This I did. It was a balance pit, with a large round-link chain; I thought by taking a piece of iron to put through the links to rest on, I could manage it easily. I went down easily enough and had no difficulty for more than half the distance in coming up, but as I got near the top I felt my muscular power failing me, and nothing but the struggle between life & death enabled me to hold on. My arms & legs began to tremble so I could hardly hold to the chain. I am sure if I had had a couple more yards to do when I reached the top I must have given up and gone crash to the bottom. It was a lesson I never forgot, and therefore had its use. I saw a man a year ago on board the Great Eastern in a similar predicament. He was sent up a rope to free a line and before he could get back his muscles gave out, and but for Halpin going up after him & supporting him on his shoulders down again, the man must have fallen down into the paddle engine room, but he shouted at the top of his voice; I made no move, but felt death almost certain.

The time for leaving Tredegar now arrived and I left it with a heavy heart. I had been very happy there, and liked not to part with old friends. One of my best and dearest friends[18] gave me, the night before I left, a small Bible & Prayer Book which I have deeply valued and ever will do so as long as life lasts, telling me ever to seek in it comfort & support in all my trials through life. I have never forgotten those kind words, and I pray God they may not have been used in vain.

We travelled from Tredegar in the same carriage as was used to take us there from Bedlington, leaving Tredegar on the 28 July 1834. My mother went to live at Coventry in a house about a mile out of the town near Lord Hood's place; I forget the name of the village.[19] I stayed there until I left for the Vulcan Foundry.*

* This short paragraph was added as an afterthought on the verso of folio 27 of the MS, except for the first four words which are on the last line of the recto. Furthermore, the year was added after the rest of the paragraph was written.

The date 28 July 1834 for his removal from Tredegar would seem to be an error, as it clearly clashes with all others at this period. It is significant that the date was omitted altogether from the 1892 edition of the diary.

On Jany 28th 1834 I left home to go and work at the Vulcan Foundry near Warrington in Lancashire, under Mr Robert Stephenson. He and a Mr Tayleur of Liverpool had just built their works; indeed, they were not quite finished when I went there. They were intended chiefly for building locomotives. This was the first time I had left my home, and my dear mother gave me much good advice, much of which has been of use to me through life. I remember well her telling me always to keep my thoughts fixed upon obtaining for myself a good position in life, never to be satisfied to stand still, and altho' I was going to the Vulcan as a boy and a pupil, to strive to one day become the manager.[20] I have often, in after life, thought over my mother's words and seen the wisdom of them. The road to success in life is open to all who will with determination and honour follow it, never looking back, but keeping the eyes & soul ever fixed forward. Men are much more indebted to their mothers, I think, for their feelings and impressions that guide them through life, than they are to their fathers. There is more of sympathy between the boy and his mother than with the father, the advice is probably given more in love, and less as a duty, from her, and comes nearer home to the heart of the boy, while from the father it appeals more to the reason, and all who have lived 50 years feel and know how much greater a power the heart is with us than the reason. The heart is ever true to itself, the reason argues with itself, and is often divided against itself, and so cannot stand. I left my mother's roof with great regret; I was going out alone into an unknown world amongst strangers, and I can quite well remember I did not feel very happy.

I arrived at the Newton Junction[21] late in the evening and found Mr Chas Tayleur, the manager of the Vulcan works, in the waiting room. I had a letter from Mr Stephenson for him, and presented it to him with great awe, as the arbitrator of my future. He, however, spoke in a kind, friendly way to me, and this did much to reassure me. Lodgings had been taken for me at a farm house close to Newton Junction, called The Moss. It belonged to two old maiden ladies, the Miss Houghtons. The farm was their own, and the origin of their taking young men to live with them was, when the works of the Liverpool & Manchester Railway were going on, they complained to Mr G. Stephenson of the damage done by the nav[v]ies to their farm. Mr Stephenson advised them to let some of his lads (as he called them) live in the house, and they would be able to keep the men in better order at that spot. This was done; Alcard & my brother Tom went there, and Mr G.

Stephenson made it his head quarters when he was in the neighbour-hood.

The old ladies got so accustomed to the society of the young people living with them that they, when the line was finished, continued it. They were perfect ladies, and did the honours of the table, and a capital table they kept. They were great favourites of all who were fortunate enough to live with them. When I was there, there were two others, a Mr Binns and a Mr Halliday. We all slept in the same room; it was a very large one with two large beds and a small one. Mr G. Stephenson continued to live there very frequently while I was there, often from the Saturday to the Monday. He and the old ladies were very fond of a rubber of whist, and one of us lads had to make up the 4. I was never fond of cards and did not much like it. One Sunday night I was kept up until the clock had struck 12 to play a rubber. Old George would al-ways have one of the large beds to himself, so that two of us had to get into the other. I remember one night we bothered him a little by having a string tied to the clothes on his bed, and the other end in our bed, and when he got to sleep we kept pulling the clothes quietly off him. As he got cold he pulled them up again, only to have the dose repeated. We amused ourselves thus as long as we could stand keeping awake, and in the morning he described what a restless kind of night he had spent.

I saw a great deal of Mr Stephenson at this place. The old ladies had a nephew and 3 nieces living in the village of Newton. They were very nice girls & were very kind to us. We used often to spend the evenings at their house and have a good supper, and they frequently came to their aunt's at The Moss. Ellen, the youngest, died the year after I left; she was my favourite but all were as kind as sisters to me.

The works were situated about a mile from The Moss, down a wretched dirty lane with ruts a foot deep. I had to be in the works not later than 10m past 6 in the morning, and a dreadful walk it was in the dark when I first went there, & as we were only allowed half an hour for breakfast I was obliged to take my breakfast with me, consisting of a can of new milk and bread & butter. This I used to eat in the stationary engine room. Matthew Kirtley, who has for so many years been the locomotive engineer of the Midland Railway Co, was at the time the engineman. Being allowed an hour for dinner I was able to walk up to The Moss and get that meal more comfortably, but it did not give me a very long time.

I worked very hard at these works. A man of the name of Ireland (who is now old but is still at the Vulcan) and I used to take jobs on piece work together, and both worked hard. I was much indebted to Ireland; he was a well-informed and respectable man, and gladly gave me all the instruction and assistance he could. I was always glad to go out with the new engines, and in this way was a good deal on the Liverpool & Manchester Railway, and became acquainted with old Melling at the Liverpool end & Mr Fife at the Manchester end. They were the loco-motive supts and gave me facilities to ride about on the engines. I there got a good deal of useful experience in the working of a railway which I could not have got in the workshops alone. Mr Tayleur was kind to me in this respect, as it was only by his permission I could get out of the factory.

I knew some very nice families in Warrington where I went occa-sionally to spend the Saturday afternoons; the Boltons, a Quaker family, were very nice people, and I here first made the acquaintance of Mr W. Wagstaff.

Towards the middle of the summer my health began to give way, and after the doctor at Warrington had doctored me for some time I was obliged to give up work and go home to Coventry, early in Septr 1834. I remained there until the end of the year. My brother Tom was the engineer on that part of the London & Birmingham Railway, and had his principal offices in Coventry. I used to go there and draw most days, or went out on the works with his assistants. This rest and my mother's care returned me to health, and instead of returning to Newton I arranged to go to the Dundee Foundry at Dundee as a draftsman, the hard work in the shops being considered more than my strength would bear.

I left home early in January 1835 and on my way to Dundee paid a visit to G. Marshall at Bedlington, and spent a few days in Edinburgh, arriving at Dundee on the 17th February. The Dundee Foundry did a class of work I had not before had an opportunity of seeing, such as marine engines, flax & other general machinery. Mr Jas Stirling (now of Edinburgh) was the chief manager, but the actual manager of the works was a Mr Leslie Meldrum (since dead).[22] I cannot say I ever liked him very much, but I always found Mr Stirling very kind. I had the large sal[ar]y of one pound per week, and am glad to say I made this keep me, and then ceased to be any burden upon my mother, a matter that gave me very great pleasure, as she could ill afford to help me. Living at Dundee was very cheap; I had very comfortable lodgings with an old Scotch lady who only charged me 7s/– per week for my room. It contained one of those shut up beds, looking like a chest of draws when not used, and was a good sized room comfortably furnished.

The old ladey, (Mrs Stephens *inserted in pencil*) (I am sorry I forget her name) took great care of me; she thought I was very like an only son she had lost, and in all things acted towards me like a mother, & looked sharply after my expenses. These, owing to the cheapness of food, were only 5s or 6s per week, so that I had 7s or 8s for clothes and pocket money, and did very well upon it.

I obtained a great deal of new and useful information at the foundry and also had an opportunity of seeing something of that part of Scotland. The habits of the people were somewhat different from what I had been accustomed to, and I cannot say I liked them. Living in a flat is also not one of the most agreeable things; the people who lived in the flat above me were a continual nuisance to me. Their sleeping room &, I suppose, nursery, was over mine, and they must have had a very cross child as no sooner did I get to bed than it was found necessary above to rock a cradle. It is only those who have experienced this amusement just overhead who can judge of the soothing influence it has upon you. I stood it as long as I could but then became desperate, and at first tried what getting on a chair and nocking the ceiling with a poker would do, but was at last driven to the use of the key bugle, an instrument I at that time pretended to play upon. This was much more effectual than the poker, and at last brought matters to a crisis; not only my enemy above but the neighbourhood protested against my practicing on such an instrument in the middle of the night, and a general explanation ensued and I got rid of the rocking, but it took a couple of months to get this grave question settled. My good old landlady took my part; after this there was peace between the flats.

I was fortunate in having in Dundee an old friend from Bedlington, a Mr Nicholson, who had been brought up at the Bedlington iron works, and was then manager of the Dundee & Newtyle Railway.[23] He had married there and Mrs Nicholson being a Dundee lady was connected with some of the best families there. She was a kind, good woman, and I received from both Mr & Mrs Nicholson the greatest kindness. I dined with them most Sundays and often spent the evenings with them. Their house was almost a home to me. A Miss Christy, who was a very pretty and nice girl, used often to stay with them. There was also a family of the name of Montgomery, who lived in the flat below Nicholsons, who were very nice people. Miss Montgomery was a pleasant, jolly girl.

The Sturrocks also lived here. Archie, who afterwards served under me on the Gt Western and afterwards was many years loco supt on the Gt Northern Railway, was serving his time at the foundry, so that I had plenty of pleasant society. There was a very good Mechanics' Institution here, of which I was a member and attended the lectures regularly. The library was also a good one for such purposes.

For three or 4 years I had been a great believer in making use of the galvanic battery as a power, instead of steam. When at Tredegar I tryed a great many experiments, and there constructed a small engine to be worked by this power. It had a very short glass cylinder with wrought iron ends, and I got my power my [ie by] magnetising these cylinder covers alternately, and with a good heavy flywheel got a rotating motion, but I then found what has ever since been discussed (altho' many ingenious contrivances have been invented) that the loss of power as the distance increased was so great that, to obtain motion very little real power could be obtained, and this difficulty is still the chief obstacle to its useful application. I have since that period taken much interest in several schemes that have been tried, and now in 1867 believe that even if this could be overcome the cost and weight would both be greater than steam.

There was a gentleman at Dundee when I was there, whose name I forget, contrived a plan for lighting collieries by the use of the galvanic battery; he had a series of small glass bottles or tubes through which he passed the wires, leaving a short break in the middle, and thus producing a spark. By having a quantity of these he got a constant but faint light, and his idea was, as this light was enclosed in sealed glass tubes, no danger of setting fire to the gas in a colliery existed. It came to no good result.

I had a very narrow escape for my life while at Dundee. There was a large fire at Borrey's foundry[24] on Saturday night, the 31st October. I, like other fools, went to it, not that I could do any good, but to look on. After it was nearly subdued I intended to go home, about 12 oclock at night, and to do so had to pass through the yard at the back of the works. It was quite dark with the exception of the light given by the burnt building, and I was about to pass near a fire engine some men were working, to do which I walked over a small heap of cable, when I suddenly found myself drop a considerable distance into water, and felt it splashing up about me, but I could feel no bottom. My first thought was I had fallen over the quay wall into the Tay, but feeling about I found walls all round me and then knew I was not in the river.

It is curious in these moments of danger how many thoughts will pass through your mind. I well remember thinking at that moment of a trouble I had as a boy with the hotwell of the mill engine at Bedlington in consequence of the trap in the floor being up & the engine house very dark. I suppose the splashing of the water about my face in the well being like the splashing of the water at each stroke of the air pump in the hot well of the engine recalled the circumstances. I was, however, not permitted many seconds for reflection in the well at Dundee, when a bucket came down splash into the water close beside me, fortunately missing me. This was too good a friend to part with, so I got hold of this bucket and then began to call out to let those who had sent it down know that I was there. I well remember thinking how impatient they were to pull me up, as in the fall I had lost my hat and a very favourite stick and I did not wish to part with either of them, and when I had got my legs across the bucket I felt about for them. My hat I got hold of, but they would not wait for me to find my stick, but hauled me up. When I got at the top the careless fellows pulled me on my side on the ground, with my hat under me, and so spoiled it also. I was glad to get out of the crowd and get home. When I got to my room and began to take my coat off, which unfortunately was a new one, a smart green coat only a few days old, I found both sleeves nearly torn off, and then discovered that my arms were also both badly scraped at the elbows and were very painful. I had not felt this pain before.

I learned next day from Mr Nicholson who called to see me, that when I fell into the well the men at the top who were drawing water to supply the fire engine knew something had fallen down, but settled it was a lump of coal from the heap close to it, and having settled this in their minds threw down the bucket again. I also learned, much to my disgust, that Mr Meldrum of the Dundee Foundry saw me pulled on the bank at the top, but did not condescend to ask me if I was any [the] worse or take the slightest notice of me.

It was fortunate for me that in falling a distance of about 20 feet I went down so plump; had I hit my head against the wall I would without doubt have been drowned, as a man was who performed the same operation after me. His face struck the opposite side of the well and, I suppose, stunned him; those at the top saw him fall but failed to get him out of the water in time to save his life. I have no doubt my arms were damaged by holding them out as I went down. I felt, after it was all over, how much reason I had to be thankful to God for preserving me, & made a resolution I have adhered to, not to go to fires when I could do no good.

JANY 1, 1836. As it was not my intention when I went to Dundee to stay there more than the year, I finished with the Foundry Co on the 31 Decr and on the 6th of Jany 1836 left all my kind friends in Dundee with very great regret. I had arranged with Mr R. Stephenson to go to his works at Newcastle,[25] and after spending a little time at Edinburgh & Bedlington, reached Newcastle on the 26th Jany, beginning my work at the works the following day. I got lodgings in Blacket Street at a Mrs St George's. She had a little girl called Julia who had a beautiful voice, and the old lady took a pleasure in letting the child (she might be 12 or 13 years old) come to my room in an evening to sing to me. This child has since been famous on the stage in London as Julia St George. I never heard her in London, but as a child she sang very sweetly and promised to be good looking.

I did not stay long in these lodgings, but joined Harry Birkinshaw, a son of the Mr Birkinshaw of the Bedlington iron works, in some lodgings in Carlisle St, where I went on the 16th Feby. I had plenty of friends in Newcastle, and scarcely ever spent an evening at home, and generally went to the theatre one evening a week. My cousin, Mr George Hawks, was very kind to me, and my Sundays were often spent with them.

My wages at the works were not large. To begin with I had a pound a week; I was in the drawing office. This, after a couple of months, was increased to 30s/–, when I certainly felt myself very rich and took an extra night at the theatre. Some drawings I made for locomotive engines for Russia were, oddly enough, afterwards two engines on the Gt Western Railway.[26] The Russian railway was a six-feet gauge and I was much delighted in having so much room to arrange the engine. From some financial reason all the engines we made were not sent out, and two of them were made into 7 feet gauge for the Gt Western Railway, the North Star and the Morning Star. I was very much impressed in making these drawings with the importance of a wider gauge, & no doubt thus early became an advocate for the broad-gauge system, altho' at the time Mr Brunel had not propounded his views on the subject and I did not foresee how important a matter it was to be in my future life.

I occasionally at this time used to go over to Sunderland to spend the Sunday at Miss Hubbard's and John Wilkinson's,[27] and I there met my wife[28] for the first time at a party on the 25th of July 1836. Why I should have mentioned this in my journal[29] I cannot tell. I had met her sister Mary before, but made no note of it. Providence had, I supposed, arranged the future. I find the entry in my journal now, and also when I met her on different occasions afterwards, but have no recollection that I had any particular fancy for her. Indeed, as far as recollection serves me I thought I liked Mary best.

In September Sir Robert Hawks, who had taken great notice of me both while in Newcastle and when I lived at Bedlington (he used to be pleased with my skill in turning) asked me to go to their works at Gateshead; he proposed they should build a locomotive engine works and take me in as a partner in this department. This matter was so arranged and I left Mr Stephenson on the 8th of October, and went to the Gateshead works. They were then building a couple of locomotives for the Newcastle and Carlisle Railway. I was engaged in getting out plans for the new works and looking after the engines then in hand. A Mr Thompson[30] was to join this new concern. Towards the end of the month Thompson and I went south to buy machinery and visited Leeds & Manchester. At this latter place I first became acquainted with Mr Whitworth; we ordered some tools from him. We spent a few weeks in visiting the various shops and seeing my old friends in this part of Lancashire, when Thompson returned to Newcastle and I went to pay a visit to Tredegar, where I arrived on the 17th November, from whence I went on to Bristol to see Mr Brunel to try and get an order for some of the Gt Western broad-gauge engines which they had then determined upon building. I went to the Gt Western offices and saw the directors, as it happened to be a board day, but found that Mr Brunel was not in Bristol.[31]

I then went to Warwick to see my mother, she having removed from Coventry there. I was here taken very unwell and was detained until the 2nd week in January 1837, when I returned to Newcastle. There is a great contrast in the travelling between that time & this. I left Coventry for Manchester at half past 8 at night and ought to have arrived there between 7 & 8 next morning, but owing to the bad state of the roads

D   25

did not reach it until 3 in the afternoon, or in nearly 19 hours. It now takes a little over 2½ hours to perform the same journey.

On my arrival at Newcastle I went to Bedlington and found poor Elisabeth Marshall[32] severely ill from consumption. She died Jany 19th at 23 years of age, a couple of days after I was there, and I attended her funeral on the 24th. Poor girl, she had been my playmate in early life and was a sweet girl.

Towards the end of February a difference of opinion occurred between Joseph Hawks and the other members of the firm about the new engine works, and it ended in the scheme being given up. The machinery ordered, as far as it could be, was countermanded, and I left there on the 15th March. This was a great discouragement to me, as I had given up my connexion with Robert Stephenson to go into this, and could not seek to return to him as the new works would have been to a certain extent a rival establishment with his. I was therefore left without anything to do, and not a very bright prospect before me.

I had frequently seen my wife since I first knew her and she came to stay with her aunt at Gateshead on the 10th Apl. I saw her nearly every day either in Newcastle or at her aunt's, and on the 17th she went with me to the museum alone, and we left it engaged. A few days afterwards her father called upon me and the matter was settled. Thus the most important step in my life was taken, probably with little thought and no consideration as to the future, for I had only a poor prospect before me, and with nothing at the time to do, yet she has been a loving and good wife.

I was, however, very anxious and unhappy at my position; there were many things to make me so. I felt I had been too hasty, but was firmly resolved to do all I could to redeem my pledge and thus to provide a suitable home for her. She returned home and I received the first letter from her on the 5th May. I spent a good deal of my time at Sunderland after I was engaged, and well recollect one day, in bemoaning my fate to my wife as we were walking together over Sunderland bridge, she pointed to the motto cast on the bridge 'Nill Desperandum', and told me to make that my motto in life and all would come right. I felt the truth of it and determined to banish despair and start with renewed hopes.

My brother Tom was then the engineer of the Manchester and Leeds Railway and I at once wrote to ask him to give me something to do, and this he kindly did. I therefore left Newcastle and went to him at Rochdale on the 25th May and began my work on that part of the railway. I went to the opening of the Grand Junction Railway on the 4th of June.[33]

While at Rochdale a young fellow of the name of Holland & I took it into our heads to have a long ride, and we hired a couple of horses, thinking to go as far as Halifax and back, but when we reached there we made up our minds to go to Leeds and got two fresh horses and reached Leeds, where we called upon Mr Tanner, uncle of Margaret, and started back. I thought I never would have reached Rochdale; I had not been on horseback for years, and was so fatigued I could hardly sit, feeling also very sick. The distance we rode was 75 miles, and this on hack horses. I was surprised to feel how little it affected me next day.

We were a large party living together at the Roebuck inn at Rochdale, and had some good fun. It was a pleasant time and I obtained some useful experience in levelling and surveying &c in connexion with the laying out of a railway.

Towards the end of July I heard that Mr Brunel wanted some one to take the post of locomotive engineer on the Great Western Railway, and I at once wrote to him on July 20th,[34] preferring that department to railway making.[35] The offices were removed from Rochdale to Manchester at the end of the month and I went to live there. I heard from Mr Brunel on the 2nd August saying he was coming into the north and that he would call and see me. This gave me some brighter hopes, and he called at the office on the 9th August and arranged I should go to him at once. I was very glad of this appointment, as I felt it was a permanent thing in which, by attention and perseverance, I might hope to get on. I was also very glad to have to manage the broad gauge, which filled my mind as the great advance of the age, and in the soundness of which I was a firm believer.

I left Manchester and went to London, beginning my duties with the Great Western on the 18th August 1837.[36] None of the engines had then been delivered, altho' several were ordered, 6 from the Vulcan Foundry (my old shop), 4 from Mather, Dixon & Co of Liverpool, and 2 from Sharp, Roberts & Co, Manchester;[37] 2 from Hawthorn & Co, Newcastle, and 2 by the Haigh Foundry Co; also the two altered Russian engines before mentioned, from Robt Stephenson & Co, Newcastle.

My first work was to prepare plans for the engine houses at Paddington & Maidenhead, and I then went to inspect the engines building. I was not much pleased with the design of the engines ordered; they had very small boilers & cylinders, and very large wheels. Those made by the Vulcan Co had wheels 8 feet dia, and 3 of them only 12″ cylinders with 18″ stroke.[38] 2 of Mather, Dixon's had 10 feet wheels and 14 inch cylinders with very small boilers.[39] Those made by Hawthorns were on a patent plan of Tom Harrison's, having the engine and boiler on separate carriages & coupled with ball and socket steam pipes; these were immense affairs, the boilers were large and the cylinders were, I think, 16″ dia and about 2 feet stroke.[40] In one the cylinders were coupled direct to the driving wheels, which were 10 feet dia,[41] and the other had a spur & pinion (3 to 1) with 6 feet wheels, making the wheels equal to 18 feet diameter.[42] The same plan of gearing was used in the 2 engines built by the Haigh Foundry; their wheels were 6 feet dia and the gearing 2 to 1, but the cylinders were small.[43]

I felt very uneasy about the working of these machines, feeling sure they would have enough to do to drive themselves along the road. The idea Mr Brunel acted upon was to get a slow speed in the piston with a high velocity in the wheel, and this was right enough if the power of the cylinders & boiler had been at all in proportion.

The Gt Western line had been laid out with very flat gradients, generally 4 feet per mile, and a maximum of 8 feet, with the exception of the inclines at Box & Wootton Bassett, which were 1 in 100. The idea was to concentrate the gradients in these inclines and work them with stationary power. In the directors' report to the shareholders of the 25th August 1836 these matters were referred to as follows:

> It is expected by these ultimate arrangements, (meaning the good gradients) the locomotive engines on the Gt Western Railway will have nowhere to surmount a greater inclination than 5 or 6 feet per mile and probably even less, the only two inclined planes of 1 in 107 at Box and Wootton Bassett being worked by stationary power. These very favourable gradients, unequalled on any railway of great extent now in progress, will ensure such an economy in the cost of locomotive power as materially to reduce the estimated annual expenses. They will, moreover, greatly facilitate the attainment of a higher speed of travelling. Under these peculiar circumstances and with the view of obtaining the full advantage of the regularity and the reduction of power effected by this near approach to a level, and also to remedy several serious inconveniences experienced in existing railways, an increased width of rails

has been recommended by your engineer, and after mature consideration has been determined upon by the board.

Difficulties and objections were at first supposed by some persons to
exist in the construction of engines for this increased width of rails, but
the directors have pleasure in stating that several of the most experienced locomotive engine manufacturers in the north have undertaken
to construct them, and several are now contracted for, and adapted to
the peculiar levels and dimensions of this railway calculated for a
minimum velocity of *30 miles per hour*. These engines will be capable of
attaining a rate of 35 or 40 miles per hour with the same facility as 25 to
30 miles is gained by those now constructed for other lines.

It was thus the great Battle of the Gauges had its beginning, & these
were the hopes of the speed to be obtained. As I before said, I liked the
gauge, and the scope it gave for improving the engines, but the designs
of the engines, then contracted for were as bad as they could be. I, however, had made up my mind to do my best to aid Mr Brunel in carrying
out his views, and therefore said nothing, but certainly dreaded the
result. While inspecting these engines I also bought a number of tools
for the repairing shops.

I spent the 24th of August, the day I came of age, with my mother at
Warwick, and on my return from the north I went to live at West
Drayton, as being a central place between London and Maidenhead.
The company provided me with a horse & gig. We also built an engine
house here, supposing that trains would start from West Drayton, and
the first piece of the line was finished between the Drayton engine
house and the Dog Kennel bridge, through the cutting towards
Maidenhead.

Mr Brunel had an idea that a very perfect road could be made by

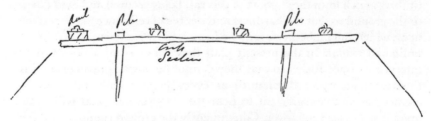

FIG 3   Brunel's broad-gauge baulk road. Gooch's sketch of section, showing the
longitudinal baulks carrying the two pairs of bridge rails, and the transoms which
maintained the correct gauge and were secured to the ground by piles

pinning it down with piles, and he made a system of wood framework to accomplish this. He used longitudinal timbers for screwing his bridge rail down upon; these were bolted to cross timbers secured to the piles thus:

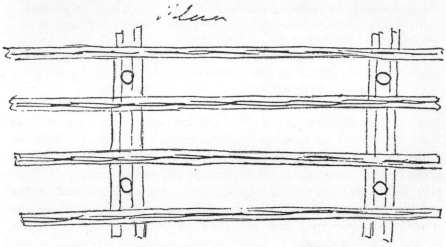

FIG 4   Gooch's plan of track, showing two pairs of rails on longitudinal baulks running from left to right, the transoms, and position of the piles

Mr Brunel thought by holding down the longitudinal timbers securely to the ground he could pack much harder under them, and so keep the road firmer. In Mr Brunel's report to the directors in February 1838 he says:

The peculiarity of the plan which has been adopted consists principally in two points. First, in the use of a light, flat rail secured to timbers and supported over its entire surface, instead of a deep, heavy rail supported only at intervals and depending upon its own rigidity. Secondly, in the timbers which form the support of this rail being secured and held down to the ground so that the hardness and degree of resistance of the surface upon which the timbers rest may be increased by ramming to an almost unlimited extent. In the present plan these timbers are held down at intervals of 15 or 16 feet so that they cannot be raised; gravel or sand is then rammed under them until at every point a solid resistance is created, more than sufficient to bear the greatest load that will come upon it as the load rolls over. Consequently the ground cannot yield, the timber which is held tight to the ground cannot yield, neither can it spring up as the weight leaves it; and if the rail be securely fixed every where in close contact with the timber, that also is immovable. Such is the theory of the plan, and the result of the exp[erimen]t has fully confirmed my expectations of its success.

But it was soon found that the settlement of the ground, more particularly on the banks, made the piles a series of props instead of holding-down pins, and in fact did much harm. They soon had to be cut off.

He also intended to carry the perfection of the road to the extent of grinding the surface of the rails, and a machine was made for this purpose, and we worked away with it for some time in the Dog Kennel cutting. The machine worked upon wheels carried by the rails, having two horizontal grindstones for grinding the surface of the rails. The winter was excessively cold and Mr Brunel kept very irregular hours, often coming down there before day light in the morning. Some nights, if it was moon light, we were on the line all night. A person of the name of Murphey had prophesied that one particular night would be the coldest night for many years. As luck, for him, would have it, it came true & made him for the time famous, and there was a grand rush for his almanack; but it was anything but good luck for us, as Mr Brunel kept us out all night and it certainly was awfully cold. We suffered dreadfully but nothing seemed to check the zeal of Mr Brunel in carrying on his experiments to perfect his road.

The first engine delivered to the railway was the Vulcan, built by the Vulcan Foundry Co. She was first in steam on the rails on 9th Jany 1838.[44] A second, from the same house, and two from Mather, Dixon and Co, followed in a week or so. These came by canal to West Drayton, and I had to get them from there to the engine house about a mile off.

One feature of Mr Brunel's character (and it was one that gave him a great deal of extra and unnecessary work) was, he fancied no one could do anything but himself, and I remember his giving me a scolding for unloading these engines and getting them onto the line without consulting him as to the mode of doing it. I certainly felt no difficulty in the task. There was a carriage sent by road from London which had to be got down the side of the cutting from the bridge, and he sent elaborate sketches and instructions how this was to be done. These took up a great deal of his time and of course were of no use in reality, as there was no kind of difficulty in the work, and circumstances were sure to alter his mode of doing it; but this was no doubt his mistake through life. As a rule he did not get experienced and qualified people about

31

him, and with them it was perhaps necessary, but the work was in consequence often badly done and always expensively.

Our experiments through the winter shewed that grinding the rails and the theoretical perfection of the road must be given up; altho' they were made in a nice gravel cutting the ground would not retain the perfection necessary to maintain the perfection in the surface of the rail.

The North Star engine was delivered by barge on the river at Maidenhead in Jany,[45] and as I was engaged elsewhere Mr Brunel went to see her unloaded from the barge and very nearly lost his life. There was a heavy chain used as a back guy for the shear legs, and a rope for the opposite one carried across the river. By some mistake this rope was let go and the weight of the chain brought the legs over with a crash, killing one man and just missed crushing Mr Brunel. But for the loss of the man's life I rather rejoiced, after the scolding I had had for doing the work at Drayton without him, that this accident should happen under his supervision, but of course said nothing.

The North Star was first in steam on the 15th Jany 1838. The first running of the engines was celebrated by a dinner at West Drayton on the 16 Jany. Some Irish gentlemen took more wine than was good for them and amused themselves by dancing an Irish war dance on our hats, which happened to be piled up in a corner of the room. I was rather disgusted with the termination of our dinner and resolved never to have anything to do with another. I was one of the stewards.

I went to my first London party on the 29th Jany; it was at Mrs Horsley's, Mrs Brunel's mother. I believe I did succeed in getting as far as the stair case, and left it disgusted with London parties, making a note in my mem[orandum] book never to go to another. I had to drive all the way from West Drayton to get there, and to walk from a public house where I put up and got a bed, in silk stockings and thin shoes. In those days we were not allowed to wear boots at a party. I spent my Christmas in the north, chiefly at Mr Tanner's, or rather my days were spent there with Margaret.

MARCH 1838. The time had now arrived when I thought myself sufficiently fixed in life to get married, and the day was fixed for the 20th March. I left London on the 16th and arrived at Sunderland on Sunday morning the 18th. On reaching Mr Tanner's I found Mrs Tanner had had a paraletic seisure that morning and was then hanging between life & death. This, of necessity, put the marriage off for the Monday and made the time of its taking place very uncertain. George Marshall, who was to be my bridegroom's man, came over to Sunderland on the Monday afternoon and staid over Tuesday, when he returned home. On the Wednesday afternoon Mrs Tanner was considered out of immediate danger, and it was then fixed that the marriage should take place on the Thursday morning. I went late at night to arrange the matter with the church authorities, and on Thursday morning March 22nd 1838 I was married at Bishop-Wearmouth church by Mr Grant. It took place, on account of Mrs Tanner's state of health, in a very quiet manner. A *post-chaise* (things that have gone out of use) was brought to the back door of Mr Tanner's house, and Margt and I, accompanied by a Mr Scurfield, an old friend of Mr Tanner's, went in it to church. The day was quietly spent at Mr Tanner's house.[46] I was anxious to get back to the railway, but did not leave Sunderland until Sunday night as it was uncertain whether my wife could accompany me in the then state of her mother, but a gradual improvement in her condition enabled Margt to leave with me on the Sunday. We went by a post-chaise to Durham, and took the coach early next morning for London, arriving there about 5 oclock on the Tuesday afternoon, or in 36 hours, a very different time from that now occupied by the same journey. We went on to West Drayton the same night, where I had taken part of a furnished house, and my mother was there to receive us. My married life had thus a somewhat sad beginning.

I took a good deal of interest at this time in the building of the Gt Western steam ship.[47] She was intended to sail between Bristol and America. She was a design of Mr Brunel's, and like many of his ideas, the world would not believe in her; indeed, Dr Lardner *proved* that she could not cross the Atlantic. However, on the 31st March 1838 steam was got up in her and a trial made. All went well with the ship but Mr Brunel had a serious accident by falling down one of the hatchways and seriously injuring himself.[48] It was a most unfortunate time for him, as every effort was being made to get the railway open. The Gt Western steam ship made her voyage to America and has since been a most successful ship. None, for her size, have done better. She was broken up about 1862–63,[49] altho' she had changed hands more than once.

I was much engaged up to the end of May in getting all ready for opening the portion of the Gt Western Railway from London to Maidenhead, and on the 31 May the directors made their first trip over the whole length of this portion, and it was opened to the public on the

4th June; and then my difficulties with the engines began. The North Star and the 6 built by the Vulcan Foundry Co were the only ones I could at all depend upon. Mather, Dixon's engines were so weak in the valve gearing they would not run more than a few miles without the gearing giving way, and those made by the Haigh Foundry Co with geared wheels, and on Harrison's plan by Hawthorn, as well as the 10 feet wheels by Mather & Dixon, were so weak they would hardly drag themselves, and could not work the trains. The two built by Sharp, Roberts & Co had cylindrical slide valves; these stuck fast or allowed the steam to pass them, and the result was I had to begin to, in a measure, rebuild one half of the stock I had to work with. For many weeks my nights were spent in a carriage in the engine house at Paddington, as repairs had to be done to the engines at night to get them to do their work next day.

The North Star, being the most powerful one and in other respects the best, was my chief reliance, but she was often getting into trouble from other causes. I began to think railway life was a very hard and anxious one. I was soon obliged to leave West Drayton and go to Paddington to live, having taken furnished lodgings in the Harrow Road. When I look back upon that time it is a marvel to me we escaped serious accidents. It was no uncommon thing to take an engine to look for a late train out on the line [on which] the train was expected, and many times have I seen the train coming and reversed the engine and run back out of its way as quickly as I could. What would be said to such a mode of proceeding now? And misfortunes never seemed to come along. I remember being sent for one Sunday night by a messenger, that the North Star had run off the line near Bull's Bridge.[50] I went down there and worked all night getting her on again; this I had completed about the time the first train next morning was due from London. I saw it coming, and wishing to send word to Maidenhead that the line was clear, gave a signal for it to stop. When it was doing so a tube burst and scalded the enginemen.

It was nearly middle day before I got the line into work, and was going up with a train to London when we got off again, and this kept me at work all the afternoon to get her on. I got into Paddington about 6 and was pretty well weary of railway life. As the last train from Maidenhead was due at 7 I stopped to see it arrive, and as I saw it pass into the station was congratulating myself nothing else could happen for that day, when a porter who was standing beside me ran to get on the carriage truck at the latter part of the train (on which the stage coaches were carried) and he fell under the wheels and I heard his legs crack. This made me almost ill, and very little would at that moment have tempted me to give up railways.

The failure of so many engines made the directors very anxious, and they called upon me, apart from Mr Brunel, to make them a report on each engine. I had hitherto done all I could to get them into working order and had reported to Mr Brunel alone, as my chief; but the directors having called upon me for a separate report, I felt I was placed in a great difficulty, as I could only tell what I believed to be the facts, and that such facts would be displeasing to Mr Brunel. I, however, had no choice, and had to make this report in which I condemned the construction of the engines. This alarmed the directors and obtained for me a rather angry letter from Mr Brunel. I will, however, do him the justice to say that he only shewed it in his letter, and was personally most kind and considerate to me, leaving me to deal with the stock as I thought best. His good sense told him what I said was correct & his kind heart did me justice.

I was shortly after, with his full consent and support, instructed to prepare designs for the future stock of which it had become necessary to order a large quantity. These drawings I took great pains with, giving every detail much thought and consideration, and the result was designs for 2 classes of engines, one[51] with a 7 feet driving wheel, 15″ cylinders & 18″ stroke, and another[52] with 6 feet wheels, 14″ cylinders and 18 stroke, both with ample boiler power, and I may with confidence, after these engines have been working for 28 years, say that no better engines for their weight have since been constructed either by myself or others. They have done, and continue to do, admirable duty. Advantage has been taken of new cylinders being required to give them an extra inch in dia and 4 inches more in stroke, and expansion gear has been added; in other respects the engines are the same.

When I had completed the drawings I had them lithographed and specifications printed, with iron templates for those parts it was essential should be interchangeable,[53] and these were supplied to the various engine builders with whom contracts were made. 142[54] engines were let, and all the makers did their work well; the best were built by Fenton, Murray & Jackson of Leeds, but the great durability of the engines has proved that all did their work well. I very frequently visited the various works where they were built.

35

1839

Great Western Railway.

LONDON to MAIDENHEAD and TWYFORD,

FIVE MILES FROM READING.

On & after the **19**th of August, *additional Trains will leave Paddington for Twyford, & Twyford for Paddington, at* **8** *o'clock in the Evening; and the Short Train will leave Paddington at Half-past* **8,** *Daily, excepting Sundays.*

Horses and Carriages being at the Paddington, Maidenhead, or Twyford Stations 10 minutes before the time specified for the departure of a Train, will be conveyed at the following Charges.

		CARRIAGES.		HORSES.	
		4-WHEEL.	2-WHEEL.	EACH.	PER PAIR, being the same Property.
BETWEEN	PADDINGTON and MAIDENHEAD	12s.	8s.	10s.	16s.
	PADDINGTON and TWYFORD	16s.	12s.	14s.	24s.
	MAIDENHEAD and TWYFORD	8s.	6s.	7s.	12s.

POST HORSES are kept in readiness at the above Stations; and upon sufficient notice being given at Paddington, or the Bull and Mouth Office, St. Martin's-le-Grand, would be sent to bring Carriages from any part of London to the Station at a moderate charge.

TRAINS, (Daily, excepting Sundays,)

DOWN TO | Hour.

	H.M.									
Twyford	8				Southall			Slough	Maidenhead	Twyford
Twyford	9							Slough	Maidenhead	Twyford
West Drayton	9.30	Ealing	Hanwell	Southall	West Drayton					
Twyford	10					West Drayton	Slough			Twyford
Twyford	12					West Drayton	Slough	Maidenhead	Twyford
West Drayton	1.30	Ealing	Hanwell	Southall	West Drayton					
Twyford	2					West Drayton	Slough	Maidenhead	Twyford
Twyford	4							Slough	Maidenhead	Twyford
West Drayton	4.30	Ealing	Hanwell	Southall	West Drayton					
Twyford	5		Hanwell					Slough	Maidenhead	Twyford
Twyford	6	Ealing			West Drayton	Slough			Twyford
Twyford	7			Southall				Slough	Maidenhead	Twyford
Twyford	8							Slough	Maidenhead	Twyford
Maidenhead	8.30	Ealing	Hanwell	Southall	West Drayton	Slough	Maidenhead		

(CALLING AT)

UP FROM | Hour.

	H.M.								
✳ Twyford	6	Maidenhead	Slough						Paddington
† Maidenhead	8.15	Maidenhead	Slough	West Drayton	Southall	Hanwell	Ealing	Paddington
Twyford	9	Maidenhead	Slough	West Drayton				Paddington
Twyford	10		Slough	West Drayton				Paddington
West Drayton	11			West Drayton	Southall	Hanwell	Ealing	Paddington
Twyford	12	Maidenhead	Slough	West Drayton				Paddington
Twyford	2		Slough		Southall			Paddington
West Drayton	3			West Drayton	Southall	Hanwell	Ealing	Paddington
Twyford	4	Maidenhead	Slough					Paddington
Twyford	5	Maidenhead	Slough			Hanwell		Paddington
Twyford	6		Slough	West Drayton				Paddington
West Drayton	7			West Drayton	Southall	Hanwell	Ealing	Paddington
Twyford	7	Maidenhead	Slough				Ealing	Paddington
Twyford	8	Maidenhead	Slough					Paddington

(CALLING AT)

✳ On Wednesday Mornings this Train will call at SOUTHALL, for the convenience of Persons attending the Market at that Place.
† On Monday Mornings this Train will start from TWYFORD, at a Quarter before 8, for the convenience of Persons attending the London Markets.

ON SUNDAYS,

DOWN TO | Hour.

	H.M.								
Twyford	8	Ealing					Slough	Maidenhead	Twyford
Maidenhead	8.30			Southall	West Drayton	Slough	Maidenhead	
Twyford	9						Slough	Maidenhead	Twyford
Maidenhead	9.30	Ealing	Hanwell	Southall	West Drayton	Slough	Maidenhead	
Twyford	5		Hanwell		West Drayton	Slough	Maidenhead	Twyford
Maidenhead	6	Ealing			West Drayton	Slough	Maidenhead	
Twyford	7						Slough	Maidenhead	Twyford
Maidenhead	8	Ealing	Hanwell	Southall	West Drayton	Slough	Maidenhead	

(CALLING AT)

UP FROM | Hour.

	H.M.								
Twyford	6	Maidenhead	Slough					Paddington
Maidenhead	8.15	Maidenhead	Slough	West Drayton	Southall	Hanwell	Ealing	Paddington
Twyford	9		Slough	West Drayton				Paddington
Twyford	5	Maidenhead	Slough			Hanwell		Paddington
Maidenhead	6.15	Maidenhead	Slough	West Drayton				Paddington
West Drayton	7			West Drayton	Southall	Hanwell	Ealing	Paddington
Twyford	7	Maidenhead	Slough					Paddington
Maidenhead	8.15	Maidenhead	Slough				Ealing	Paddington

(CALLING AT)

Passengers and Parcels between Twyford, Maidenhead, and Slough, and the short Stations, can proceed in either direction to West Drayton, or other Stations, and be taken on by the succeeding Train.

FARES.

PADDINGTON.	1st Class.	2nd Class Open Car.
To Ealing......	1 6	0 9
,, Hanwell	2 0	1 0
,, Southall ..	2 6	1 3
,, West Drayton	3 6	1 6
,, Slough.....	4 6	2 6
,, Maidenhead ..	5 6	3 6
,, Twyford	7 0	5 0

The Fares from *Slough* to *West Drayton* and from *Maidenhead* to *Slough*, are 2s. for the *First Class*, and 1s. for the *Second Class* Passengers.

Omnibuses and Coaches start from Princes-street, Bank one hour before the departure of each Train, calling at the Angel Inn, Islington; Bull Inn, Holborn; Moore's Green Man & Still, Griffin's Green Man & Still, Oxford-street; Golden Cross, Charing-cross; Chaplin's Universal Office, and Bull & Mouth, Regent-circus; and Gloucester Warehouse, Oxford-street, to the Paddington Station. Fare 6d. without Luggage.

TWYFORD.	1st Class.	2nd Class Open Car.
To Maidenhead.	2 6	1 6
,, Slough......	3 6	2 6
,, West Drayton	4 6	3 6
,, Southall }	6 0	4 0
,, Hanwell } ...		
,, Ealing	6 6	4 6
,, Paddington..	7 0	5 0

Conveyances for Reading, will leave the Twyford Station on the arrival of each Train, and to & from *Hurst & Wokingham*, to meet the **9** o'clock 12 o'clock, and 5 o'clock Trains up and down; also, Conveyances to and from *Henley*. LILLYWHITE'S Windsor Omnibuses meet every Train at *Slough*.

Parcels may be booked at the Railway Office, Princes-street, Bank; all the London Parcels Delivery Company's Receiving Houses; the above established Booking Offices; the Railway Stations; and the authorized Offices in the adjacent Places. Four Daily Deliveries will be made in Town, as well as in the Country, at the following Rate:—1s. for Parcels not exceeding 28-lbs. weight; 1s. 6d. for 56-lbs. weight; and so on 6d. for every additional Quarter of Cwt., including all Charge for Carriage, Porterage, and Delivery.

[W. Snell, Printer, 5s., Newcastle-place, Edgware-road.]

My chief draftsman at that time was also a clever fellow and he has made a good position for himself since as a contractor; his name is Thos Crampton (he died Apl 1888 *inserted at a later date*) and he has, in partnership with Peto & Betts, done a great deal of work. Unfortunately the position of their affairs at present, 1867, is unfortunate, and I fear they are all practically ruined.[55] A drawing now at Clewer of the 7 feet engine was made by him, and shews the design, but I also have a very perfect working model[56] of the engine at my house in London. This model is a very beautiful piece of work; many of the parts were made by Clements, who used to be in those days the best workman in London. The model is also valuable from the money it cost. I also value the drawing very much, and would wish both to be carefully preserved in the family by my eldest son.

No sooner was the Gt Western Railway opened than a strong party amongst the shareholders was organized in Lancashire and the north to condemn the broad gauge, and they appointed Mr Hawkshaw, then an engineer in Manchester, & Mr Nicholas Wood of Newcastle on Tyne to report upon it, for which purpose they required a great many experiments to be made, had instruments for testing the deflection of the road, &, as they did not give much of their promised attention to it, they appointed Dr Lardner to conduct the experiments for them, and the Doctor's calculations were little less [*i.e.* more] reliable in the matter of the power & speed of the locomotives than they had been with regard to the Gt Western S[team] S[hip] crossing the Atlantic. He said the North Star engine could only, at 45 miles per hour, draw a load of 15 tons. I tryed her the next day and took 50 tons.

Mr Hawkshaw had an instrument made for ascertaining the tractive power of the engines; it was simply a quadrant & weight, around which he passed a rope. I remember he came there to see the scale made for it, but getting his fingers in between the weight and the standard carrying it, he thought this was experiment enough for him and he never tried it with engines. A very elaborate report was made by both these gentlemen and presented to the shareholders of the Gt Western at a meeting held at the London Tavern on the 9th January 1839. Mr Hawkshaw in his report condemned the whole thing, while Mr Wood admitted many advantages in the broad gauge. These reports will be found with my papers giving full details. The resolutions submitted to the meeting were as follows:

By the directors: 'That this report be approved and adopted, and that this meeting being deeply sensible of the disastrous consequences inevitably arising from the continual discussion of the principles acted upon in carrying on the works, do request the directors to adhere to the principles laid down in their report as the most conducive to the welfare of the proprietors.'

Upon which the following amendment was proposed:

'That the reports of Messrs Wood & Hawkshaw contain sufficient evidence that the plans of construction pursued by Mr Brunel are injudicious, expensive, and ineffectual for their professed object, and therefore ought not to be proceeded with.'

As the shareholders were entering the meeting a very clever paper written by Mr George Clarke (who at the time was on the Gt Western acting as an engineer—he is now the manager of the Dowlais iron works) was put into their hands. This paper turned the dispute into ridicule, and there is no doubt had a good deal of effect on the result. There were 7,792 votes for the directors and 6,145 against them, so that as far as the Gt Western shareholders were concerned the matter was settled by a majority of 1,647 votes. This decision the shareholders never attempted to disturb.

I was very much interested in this fight and had devoted a great deal of time to counteract the conclusions of the n[arrow]-gauge party. A much better result was obtained from the North Star before the meeting than was obtained when Dr Lardner made his expts. I made some experiments on the blast pipe, by increasing its size and also taking great care that the steam was discharged up the middle of the chimney, and it was wonderful how much the larger size freed the cylinders and the care in discharging it still enabled us to get plenty of steam.

The effect and power of the blast pipe had not before been sufficiently considered in the locomotives. Mr Brunel had a notion that if the orifice was made in the form of a cross, thus it would be most effective, and he and I worked by ourselves most of Xmas day in the copper smiths' shop constructing a tip of this shape, but nothing succeeded so well as the plain round orifice. We kept our trials on these matters very quiet, intending to spring it as a mine against our opponents after they had committed themselves to their report, and it will be seen by reference to the report of the directors that they made good use of it.

Mr Brunel called upon me for a report upon the question of the gauge.

I wrote a very full one and was glad to get a kind letter from him, saying how much both he and the directors were pleased with it, and some portions of it were included in their report to the shareholders.

Before the end of 1838 I had taken rooms on Paddington Green,[57] and on 1st June 1839 my first child[58] was born there. The neighbourhood of Paddington at that time was very different from what it has since become. It was then almost impossible to get a house, and lodgings were very scarce, such as would suit me. My salary fixed by the company to begin with was only £550 per annum, and as I began life with the determination never to spend the whole of my income, be it what it might or the saving as small as it might, but [sic] if I only saved a pound I was sure I did not get into debt. I advise all young people to do this; it will add not only to their present peace of mind but to their future success in life. Nothing is so destructive to the mind as the feeling of being in debt. Illness or misfortune might force it upon you, but apart from these two causes it should be avoided as you would poison.[59]

Little occurred in railway matters during 1839 after the January meeting. We all much regretted the death of Mr Sims the chairman, who committed suicide by shooting himself, and Mr Charles Russell was appointed in his place who, as it will afterwards be seen, also destroyed himself.

Mr Brunel had rather an amusing victory over his enemies in the autumn of 1839. Maidenhead bridge consists chiefly of 2 flat brick arches of 120 feet span each. They were built in brickwork and the profession were pleased to say it would not stand, and the Railway Times, the authority of the day in railway matters, used to send a commission[er] down every week to report upon it. This he did by describing the cracks &c. (Braithwaite, I believe, was the man who went). They said, as it was resting on the centres, as soon as Mr Brunel took them away the bridge must follow. One Friday night there was a great storm of wind & rain, and the centres were blown down during the night. The Railway Times came out on the Saturday morning with statements and opinions rather stronger than usual, but before the paper was in the hands of the readers the arches were standing alone, and have stood well ever since. They had not been resting on the centering for some time before, but this the profession would not admit. The paper was certainly shut up in an unpleasant manner. The profession as a body condemned nearly all Mr Brunel did because he had the skill and courage to depart on a path of his own.

1840. During this year further portions of the Gt Western were opened, and agreements were made for leasing the Bristol and Exeter & the Swindon & Cheltenham Railways,[60] and it became necessary to furnish larger works for the repair &c of our stock. I was called upon to report on the best situation to build these works, and on full consideration I reported in favour of Swindon, it being the junction with the Cheltenham branch and also a convenient division of the Gt Western line for the engine working.[61] Mr Brunel and I went down to look at the ground, then only green fields, and he agreed with me as to its being the best place. The matter is referred to in the directors' report of Feby 1841.

By this time I was much more comfortable with regard to our engines. The new engines ordered to my drawings were being delivered; the Fire Fly, started in March 1840, was the first, and they all gave everyone general satisfaction. We could now calculate with some certainty not only upon the speed they could run, but upon their not breaking down upon the journey. We had no difficulty in running at 60 miles per hour with good loads. I may mention as a contrast of the locomotive expenses per mile up to that time as compared with what they have since become, that they were then about 18d per mile and are now between 7d & 8d. No doubt the cost of fuel was one of the chief sources of saving, and getting a greater mileage out of the engines.

My daughter Emily was born at Paddington Green on the 13 July 1840.

In November of this year, 1840, I took out a patent for steeling the surface of rails and tires, either by the mode of cementing the surface after the rail or tire was manufactured, or by welding a slab of steel on the surface in the pile. Careful experiments made at the Haigh Foundry Co's works at Wigan in Lancashire shewed that the latter mode was the best. Mr Stubs, the steel manufacturer, of Warrington, assisted us in these experiments, and altho' we never used it for rail making on account of the cost, we succeeded in making good sound tires, containing about 1/5th part of best shear steel. The large price paid at that time for steel made the tires costly in first cost and interfered with their general introduction, but I used them exclusively on our engines and tenders, and the results of their working shewed a very large economy in their use. Many of these ran a distance of between 200 & 300 thousand miles.

Laterly, from the great progress that has been made in the cheap

VI (*Above*) *Fire Fly*, the first engine designed by Gooch to be delivered to the Great
Western Railway in 1840
VII (*Below*) 'Castle' class locomotive *Sir Daniel Gooch*, one of a highly successful
class, designed by C. B. Collett and built at Swindon in 1938

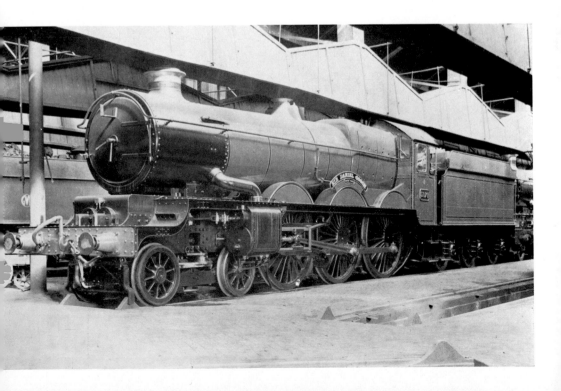

VIII   Record card of indicator tests made by Gooch with the locomotive *Great Britain* in 1850, with his initials and annotations manufacture of steel, solid steel tires and rails also have come into very general use, but I am still of opinion that for tires the plan I used of making the surface only of steel is much the best because they can be hardened, the iron in the tire being depended upon for toughness while the hard steel formed the wearing surface. A solid steel tire cannot be hardened as it would be brittle and dangerous. There is, therefore, in my opinion, as much difference in the life of the two kinds of tire as there would be between two anvils, one having the face hardened and the other left soft.

The extreme hardness of my steel tires made it impossible to turn them in the ordinary manner; I was therefore obliged to design machinery for grinding them. This was done by having on the slide rest a revolving grindstone a couple of feet in diameter running at about 1,000 revolutions per minute. This the labourers soon learned to use with as much care as a turner does his cutting tool. The wheels themselves were made to revolve in the opposite direction from the grindstone at the rate of about 200 rev per minute. Great truth was obtained in the wheels, and a very good job made of them at very little additional cost beyond turning the iron tires.

This patent did not pay me during the whole of its time more than between 5 & £6,000, and I found so much trouble connected with it, and the false position I felt it placed me in with our own company, that I never took out another, nor do I ever approve of engineers who have to advise large Cos being themselves interested in patents. I look upon the patent laws as a great curse to this country; it cannot be worked with perfect honesty. They are taken out for all kinds of absurd things, and by people with little or no practical knowledge of the work they undertake, and the really practical man in carrying out his work is met at all points by the claims of some patentee.

I have in my practice constantly found the disadvantage of the law, not that I object to reward a man for a real invention, but the real inventions are rare, while the patents are counted by thousands. The absence of a patent law would not retard invention; the human mind will scheme and study for the pleasure of the work, and the honour of being the originator of a real improvement would be sufficient stimulus. I have no doubt the day is not far distant when some important modification of the patent laws will be made. The existing law is a great improvement on the old one, when a man was not obliged to disclose his invention at the time of securing his patent. It was a common practice for a man to patent a general title and then wait his 6 months to see what ideas of other people he could pick up to put in his description.

1841. The whole of the Gt Western Railway between London and Bristol was opened on the 30th June 1841, and the question of working through the Box Tunnel[62] up a gradient of 1 in 100 was a source of much anxiety to Mr Brunel. We had found all difficulties at the Wootton Bassett incline disappear, but it was much shorter than Box and was also not in tunnel. I cannot say I felt any anxiety; I had seen how well our engines took their loads up Wootton Bassett without the help of a bank engine, and with the assistance of a bank engine at Box I felt we would have no difficulty.

Only one line of rails was compl[eted] through the tunnel the day we opened, and the trains had therefore to be worked on a single line. I undertook to accompany all the trains through the tunnel, and did so the 1st day and night, also the 2nd day, intending to be relieved when the mail came down on the 2nd night at about 11 oclock. That night we had a very narrow escape of a fearful accident. I was going up the tunnel with the last up train when I fancied I saw some green lights, placed as they were in front of our trains. A second's reflection convinced me it was the mail coming down. I lost no time in reversing the engine I was on and running back to Box station with my train as quickly as I could, when the mails came down close behind me. The policeman at the top of the tunnel had made some blunder and sent the mails on when they arrived there. Had the tunnel not been pretty clear of steam we must have met in full career and the smash would have been fearful, cutting short my career also.

But as tho' mishaps never came alone, when I was taking my train up again, from some cause or other the engine got off the rails in the tunnel, and I was detained there all night before I got all straight again. I need not say I was not sorry to get home and to bed at Paddington after 2 days and nights pretty hard work. Mr Brunel was at the time living in Bath, and he was very kind to me in sending me plenty of good food &c to keep my steam up. Box tunnel had a very pretty effect for the couple of days it was worked as a single line, from the number of candles used by the men working on the unfinished line. It was a perfect illumination extending through the whole tunnel nearly two miles long.

My wife's mother, Mrs Tanner, died on the 23rd of February 1841. I was unable to go down and attend the funeral.

I made at this time a number of experiments on the use of peat as a fuel. Lord Willoughby de Eresby took a great interest in the matter and we tried it in various ways, some coked and some merely compressed very hard. We were able to keep steam with it, but the consumption was very large, certainly 4 times that of ordinary coke made from coal. It would therefore require a very large difference in the value per ton to render such a fuel profitable.[63]

On Tuesday the 24 August 1841 I went to the House of Lords to hear the Queen read her speech,[64] and stayed there in the evening when I had an opportunity of hearing the Duke of Wellington speak. He moved an amendment to the address, and I was much struck with the methodical manner in which he referred to his papers; he had a packet of them in his hands and referred to them in turn, but always putting the paper away in its proper place in the packet when done with. Lord Melbourne was then Prime Minister, and answered him. The result was the Govt were beaten and went out of office. It was the only time I ever heard the great Duke speak.

My son Henry was born on the 30 Decb 1841.

1842. In January of this year the King of Prussia came over to England to attend the christening of the Prince of Wales. He travelled on our line to Windsor several times and when he left gave me a silver salver, which I of course keep, not that it is a very valuable one, but it is the gift of a king and they are not common.

The Queen of England had given up travelling between London and Windsor by road and had gone by us. A saloon carriage, very handsomely fitted up, was built for her use, and was used by her until a larger one was built.[65] When the old carriage was given up it was altered inside and I got the sofa which is now in my library at Paddington; it is oak. I also got the Queen's foot stool, also in carved oak. Great people have sat upon this sofa: the Queen of England, the Prince Consort, King of Prussia, King Louis Phillip and Queen of France, the late Emperor of Russia, the King & Queen of Saxony, (*in margin* the late King & Queen of the Belgians) and many big people besides. So I may call it a Royal Historical Sofa, and it should be preserved in the family.

While I held the ap[pointmen]t of locomotive engineer on the Gt Western I nearly in all cases took charge of the engine myself when the Queen travelled, and have been so fortunate as never to have a single delay with her, and she has travelled under my care a great many miles.

I was the first who had such a charge and it was some time before she had occasion to travel on any other line but the Great Western.

We started the machinery at the Swindon works on the 28 November 1842. A. Sturrock was our local manager, but the works were not put into regular operation until Monday the 2nd Jany 1843.[66]

1843. During this year further portions of the Gt Western Railway branches and the Bristol & Exeter were opened. The Great Britain steam ship, one of those large ideas of Mr Brunel's, was launched at Bristol. She was then considered a monster ship altho' now she is a very ordinary one, and everyone blamed Mr Brunel for building any thing so large. I took Prince Albert down by special train to the launch on the 19th July 1843. It was a lovely day & the sight a beautiful one. As the ship was built in a dry dock the launch only consisted in floating her out. On the down journey we had some long stops for the Prince to receive addresses, but having no delays on the return journey it was done in 2h 4m. Few runs have been made as quick as this ever since, over so long a distance.[67]

In September I went to spend a few weeks with Mr Tweedy at Truro in Cornwall, and travelled about there to see all the beautiful coast scenery of that county. I was very much pleased with its grandeur and the fine weather we had enabled us to see it to great advantage. Mr Tweedy & Jane were very kind in going about with us and shewing us all there was to be seen, and I have a very pleasant recollection of our visit. I find the scenery is fully described in my daily journal which is with my other papers of the kind.

1844. On the 1st of May in this year the railway was opened throughout to Exeter.[68] We had a special train with a large party from London to go down to the opening; a great dinner was given in the goods shed at Exeter station. I worked the train with the Actaeon engine,[69] one of our 7 feet class, with 6 carriages. We left London at 7.30 am and arrived at Exeter at 12.30, having had some detention over the new line. On the return journey we left Exeter at 5.20 pm and stopped at the Paddington platform at 10. Sir Thos Acland, who was with us, went at once to the House of Commons and by half past 10 got up and told the House he had been in Exeter at 5.20, the distance 195 miles. It was a very hard day's work for me, as apart from driving the engine a distance of 390 miles I had to be out early in the morning to see that all was right for our trip, and while at Exeter was busy with matters connected with the opening, so that my only chance of sitting down was for the hour we were at dinner. Next day my back ached so much I could hardly walk. Mr Brunel wrote me a very handsome letter thanking me for what I had done, and all were very pleased.

The question of the gauge of railways was beginning again to become an important question to us.[70] As the extension of lines took place it became a fight between the broad-gauge Cos and the narrow-gauge Cos as to who should get possession of the various adjoining districts, we contending that as the broad gauge was best we ought to be encouraged, and as will be seen, for the next few years my time & thoughts were nearly entirely devoted to this fight.

From what I saw on the occasion of this trip to Exeter, I felt we might safely put on a regular train that would perform the distance between London & Exeter in $4\frac{1}{2}$ hours, and advised the directors to do so as an express train at higher fares. This was shortly after done and was the beginning of that important system of express trains which has given so much comfort and accommodation to the public. I may therefore, I think, claim to be the father of express trains.

During the year 1844 I tried the expt of using corrugated copper fireboxes in our engines, thinking by that means I would greatly enlarge the heating surface. Experience shewed me what perhaps a little more reflection might have told me beforehand, that it did no good. The temperature of the gasses escaping from the chimney was not higher than it ought to be, and therefore as all the heat given out by the fire was already taken up I did not obtain any benefit, as I did not increase the bulk of the fire. It made a strong box but was a very costly one, and I only put it to two engines.

In May 1844 the late Emperor of Russia came over to stay with the Queen at Windsor. The King & Queen of Saxony were with her at the same time. I one day had charge of the engine when they came to London & back; in one carriage was the Queen of England & Prince Albert, King and Queen of Saxony, & the Emperor of Russia, with a large train of big wigs in attendance. This might fairly be called a royal train. The Emperor spent some time examining the electric telegraph which had been laid upon our line between London and Slough in the year 1839 by Mr Fothergill Cooke.[71] We had not used it very much; it was first laid in gas pipes, about one inch in diameter, the pipes being buried underground. Copper wires covered with silk were used as conductors, and then mixed with rosin. They did not do under ground and were then carried on the top of small stakes about a foot from the ground, & covered by a rail carried along the top. But these wires in the pipes were very difficult to get at and the present system of iron wires suspended from poles was adopted. The wonderful extension of this system is one of the marvels of the world, yet for several years this 18 miles was useless; no one seemed to believe in it and we did not use it for railway purposes. No doubt the plan of carrying it on poles was the means of getting over the chief difficulties that had been experienced.

One day it was serviceable in detecting a murderer. A man of the name of Tawell, a Quaker, murdered a woman at Slough and left by the train for London. The telegraph was used to describe him and when he arrived in London he was cared for by the police. This was much talked of at the time and helped to bring the telegraph into notice.

There was another great scheme connected with railways brought into operation this year, 1844, viz the atmospheric system of propulsion.[72] For some time an experimental piece of line had been laid by Samuda and his friends on what was commonly called Punch's line,[73] a short branch to Kensington from the Gt Western & London & North Western, but which line had then not been opened for the public. On this line about half a mile of atmospheric pipe had been laid and experimented upon. It was then laid on a short line between Kingston & Dalkey in Ireland. The gradient and curves were both very bad. Mr Brunel was at this time constructing the South Devon, and as the gradients and curves of that line were also very bad it was proposed to use the atmospheric system on it.

In September 1844 I went with Mr Brunel & several directors to Ireland to see the working of the system on the Dalkey line. From the calculations I then made of the power used to work the trains I found I could do the work much cheaper with locomotives. The result of our visit, however, was the determination to use the atmospheric pipes on the South Devon. I could not then understand how Mr Brunel could be so mislead as he was, and believe while he saw all the difficulties and expense of it on the Dalkey, he had so much faith in his being able to improve it that he shut his eyes to the consequences of failure, and there is no doubt the result of its trial on the South Devon between Exeter & Newton cost that company more money than would have well stocked their whole line with locomotives and worked them also. The cost on this 30 miles of line was about 350,000£. I may now say it was laid with all the care possible, and with all the improvements that could be suggested, and it miserably failed, and I was very soon called upon to provide locomotive engines to work the line.

I felt very sorry for Mr Brunel in this matter as it did him some harm, and figures shewed it never had a chance to compete with the locomotive in cost and handyness. Mr Robt Stephenson made a very careful report on the working on the Dalkey line after we were there, and arrived at the same conclusion I did. I may also mention a short piece was tried between London & Croydon which also was given up after a few months. This is certainly the greatest blunder that has been made in railways.

Louis Philip, King of the French, was at Windsor in October 1844 and travelled on our line.

On the 11th of December the Great Britain steam ship was ready for trial and I went down to Bristol to go out to sea with her.[74] When she entered the lock leading into the river she caught the stern works on each side and could not get through. Fortunately they were very quick in reversing her engines or she would have been a fixture and have probably been a wreck. She was, however, got free and back into the dock, and the lock walls were lowered and we got out the next tide, and the following day went into the Channel with her, when she performed admirably. She soon after began her voyages to America from Liverpool and after a few voyages was run aground in Dundrum Bay on the coast of Ireland, where she lay a whole winter exposed to the action of the sea, but stood it well and was then got off. She was a heavy loss to her shareholders, as she was then sold to Messrs Gibbs of Liverpool for a very small sum. They took her engines out and made sundry changes in her and she has since been employed profitably in the Australian trade.[75]

The engines as constructed originally drove the screw by a pitch chain from a large wheel worked by the engines to a smaller one on the screw shaft; I think the proportions were about 3 to 1. Altho' at the time of her first going to sea she was considered too large for any trade or port, she is now a very ordinary size ship; I think her tonnage is about 3,500.[76]

1845. In January of this year a very splendid service of plate was given to Mr Brunel by his friends at a large dinner; the cost was about 1,800£. He fully deserved it.

My son Charles was born on the 31 Jany. He was christened with

47

Jordan water. The late Duke of Cambridge paid me a visit at Swindon to see the works in March. Lord Barrington came with him. I found the old Duke full of questions and endless talk; he seemed very pleased with what he saw.

This year began our hardest gauge fight. The Gt Western went to Parliament for a line from Oxford through Worcester to Wolverhampton, then known as the Oxford, Worcester & Wolverhampton line. This was to be on the broad gauge, and it was strongly opposed by the London & Birmingham Co. I had to give evidence on the Bill and had prepared very elaborate tables shewing the speed and economy of the broad gauge. The committee of the House of Commons sat on it rather over 3 weeks and gave us the Bill on the 4th June. We met in a temporary committee room and the crowd and heat was excessive. Sitting in this heat all day and working most of the night in preparing evidence for the witnesses all most broke me down. I will never forget the passion poor old George Stephenson got into when the decision of the committee was announced. I thought he would have struck Brunel, and he also gave me his mind very freely for fighting the broad gauge against the narrow, in which, he said, I had been reared. I was not only fighting for my convictions, but also for my employers, who expressed themselves well satisfied with what I had done.

The London & North Western & Grand Junction[77] started express trains to Liverpool on the 1st of May, during this fight. I went by the first ones so as to be able to make use of any facts I could pick up in evidence. When the Bill was reported to the House the narrow gauge interests moved a resolution on the 20th June as follows:

> That a humble address be presented to Her Majesty to issue a Commission to enquire whether in all future Acts for the construction of railways, provision ought to be made for securing one uniform gauge, and whether it would be practicable and expedient to bring existing lines of railway in Great Britain and lines now in course of construction into uniform gauge, and if so, to report on the best mode of carrying these objects into effect in the present session of Parliament.

The motion was lost by a majority of 2 to 1 and our Bill passed; the Bill also got passed safely through the Lords without very much difficulty. It was afterwards moved by Mr Cobden in the House of Commons that the Commission should be appointed in pretty much the words of the previous resolution, which was carried unapposed.

The Commissioners appointed were: Sir F. Smith RE, Professor B.

Airy (Astronomer Royal), Professor P. Barlow, the latter father of the engineers of the Midland & South Eastern lines. Sir F. Smith had been for a time Inspector of Railways but knew nothing about them, and neither of the other Commissioners had any railway knowledge. They were certainly a most incompetent tribunal, yet when it is considered that the fight was to be between one railway Co on the broad gauge and the host of narrow-gauge companies, it would have been well to put some more practical men on the Commission. For one witness we could call, the narrow-gauge interests could call a dozen. Mr R. Stephenson, Mr Locke and Mr Bidder were the 3 engineers of highest standing who were opposed to us.

They met for the 1st time on the 6th August 1845. After the parliamentary fight was over Mr Brunel & Mr Saunders went abroad for a holiday and the question before the Commissioners was left to me alone, a responsibility I did not much like, but it was to be, so I undertook the task.

Mr R. Stephenson was the first witness called; he was followed by Mr Locke and a host of other officers and engineers of narrow-gauge lines. The general principles laid down by them against the broad gauge were, 1st, that the engines were too large & heavy and the large wheels used were not necessary, as the small wheels and engines of the n-gauge Cos were able to run at as high speeds as it was safe for the public to work the trains. 2nd, that the broad-gauge carriages were too large; the public did not like to sit 4 abreast. 3rd and that the cost of working was greater. A reference to the detail evidence in the Blue Book[78] will shew that these were the chief points attempted to be made by the n-gauge Cos. I may also say the question of the disadvantages of break of gauge was dwelt upon. I gave my evidence on the 17 & 21 of October, putting in a number of tables & calculations to disprove the above assertions, as shewn by the printed evidence, and to shew that the broad gauge could carry traffic at a higher speed and at a less cost than the narrow gauge.

Mr Brunel and Mr Saunders were examined on their return from the Continent at the end of November. As it was clear the Commissioners were unable to make up their minds upon these questions from the contradiction of the two opposing factions, we proposed to bring the matter to a practical test by direct experiment, and that we should each work trains of various weights over long lengths of railway to test the speed as well as cost. The n-gauge parties made great objections to this, altho' they had been getting new engines built of larger dimensions (but very faulty in construction) for the purpose of trying to work their express trains at our speeds. They constructed the boilers of great length without getting any more heating surface in the fire box, and allowed this excessive length to overhang the wheels at each end.

The White Horse of Kent built by Mr Stephenson and on which I had a number of experiments made, was so unsteady that it was necessary to be tied on to make expts on the smoke box temperature. She got the name of Stephenson's Rocking Horse, and the tube surface was carried to so great an extent that the heat in the smoke box was less than the temperature of the steam used, so that one end of the engine was actually acting as a condenser.

After much trouble, however, it was at last settled to make experiments, but not, as we proposed them, over a long length of railway as from London to Bristol & back, as against London to Birmingham and back, where there would be a variation in the gradients and the engines would be required, as in ordinary work, to take in cold water on the road, but it must be on a piece of short, level line, and the n-gauge parties selected the piece between York & Darlington, a practical level also, against about the same length of our line out of London, or 46 miles.

Experiments were to be made with trains of 50, 60, 70 and 80 tons, passenger, and 200 and 400 tons with goods. We made our experiments with our old engines, having no new ones built for the purpose. The Ixion was used for the passenger work and the Sampson for the goods.[79] Our experiments were gone through on the days and at the hours fixed, and we were unfortunate on two of the days in having a high wind on one and a small drizling rain on the other, making us slip. When it came to the turn of the 50 ton train the n-gauge party would not have it worked, saying after the result of the others it was useless.

We then went to York at the end of the year to run the n-gauge trains. Much to our astonishment, instead of beginning as was arranged, with the 80 ton train, they would only begin with the 50 ton, a weight they had cut out of our experiments. Not wishing to make any difficulties I agreed to its being worked. The engine employed was a new one just built by Mr Stephenson called the 'A' engine, with 6[ft] 6[in] wheels. She had the fire box overhanging the fire box [sic, ie the trailing axle]. I rode on the engine the first trip but she jumped about so much I would not go on her again and advised Mr Brunel not to ride on her. We got a very bad result in speed. We then, after much difficulty, got a start with an 80 ton train to Darlington. Before doing so, they put the engine over an artificial blast to get the water in the tender very hot, and a good strong wind was in our favour, but when we arrived at Darlington the n-gauge people made some excuse for not completing the expt. No doubt they did not like to face the wind which had helped them along on the down journey; so we returned to York by another engine, and the 80 tons was to be properly worked next day. This was a beautiful clear & bright day, with a very slight breeze, as good a day as possible for our experiment, but the n g would not run and after waiting for a couple of hours the expt was given up for that day, and the Commissioners went back to the hotel.

Mr Bidder then proposed to run a light train of about 30 tons to try the evaporation of the boiler. I made no objection to their doing as they liked, and accompanied the train. We attained a speed of 48 miles per hour at the 22nd mile, but shortly after passing this I found our carriage turn on its side into the ditch, in which position we fortunately soon came to a state of rest and I was not long in climbing out of the window. Bidder, Seymour Clarke and George Berkeley were in the same carriage with me. I & Clarke happened to be sitting on the side that was down, and altho' not a time to laugh, I could not help doing it afterwards at the recollection of the struggle of Bidder who was sitting at the other side, as he came tumbling down from seat to seat until he rested on me. When I got out I found engine and train all on its side and those on the engine more or less hurt. Mr Martley, who was there as my assistant, had his face a good deal scratched by being thrown into the hedge.

On walking along the line afterwards we found it sadly damaged for miles by the yawing about of the engine, and she at last broke her way through the rail. This put an end to our experiments for the day, and an enquiry was gone into the matter before the Commissioners the day following, when I certainly heard some as hard swearing that black was white as I ever heard in my life; the engineman asserted the engine was very steady, and his masters were weak enough to encourage him. Old Barlow[80] told me afterwards, as a good joke, that he was at the engine sheds of the Midland at Derby, with his son, when the engineman of the 'A' engine, not recognising him as one of the Commissioners, came to him to tell him about the accident, and ended by saying 'did not we humbug that fat old buffer', meaning the Professor himself.

This accident put an end to all further experiments, and we all returned to London on the 3rd Jany 1846 to make our reports, and the Commissioners were allowed to prepare their report upon such data as they had got. The conclusion they arrived at was that the narrow gauge should be the national gauge, but in referring to the experiments say 'that we consider them as confirming the statement and results given by Mr Gooch in his evidence, proving as they do that the broad-gauge engines possess greater capabilities for speed with equal loads and, generally speaking, of propelling greater loads with equal speed; and moreover that the working of such engines is economical where very high speeds are required or where the load to be conveyed requires the full power of the engines.'

It was a hard fight and there is no doubt, so far as the evil of brake [*ie* break] of gauge was concerned, we had a weak case altho' everything possible was done to strengthen it. A machine was constructed at Paddington by which loads could be easily transferred from one gauge to another by changing the body of [the] waggon, load & all, or by lifting the n-gauge waggons complete upon a broad-gauge platform. We also schemed a waggon with telescopic axles, adapted to run on either gauge, but I never had any faith in any of these plans as workable in practice. A break of gauge meant the unloading one set of waggons & putting the goods into another, as has since been done in practice with a platform between the two lines of waggons. The cost of this, apart from delay, is about 3d per ton on an average, and this may be taken as the maximum of the cost.[81]

The other points contended for by the n gauge during this fight they have since, in practice, given up. For they now make their engines quite as heavy as the broad gauge, their carriages are also as heavy and they put 4 people abreast, and they do run high speeds with express trains without any particular danger to the public.

While the Commission was sitting I went to France & Belgium in September for 10 days to see the plan adopted by the French for transferring the body of the dilligences upon railway trucks. This was my first visit to the Continent. My wife and her sister Mary went with me and I enjoyed the trip very much; it was a new world to me. I landed at Dieppe and went to Paris and from there to Bruxelles, and so home by Ostend.

A very carefully prepared answer[82] to the Commission's report was prepared by Mr Brunel, Mr Saunders and myself; we had some good fun over it. We met at Mr Saunders' house for a few hours each day until it was complete, and we, of course, proved that the Commission had come to quite a wrong conclusion, as will be seen in the printed papers or Blue Book, to which I refer those who take an interest in the question for all the details.

1846. On the 15th January the directors of the Great Western sent for me to the board room and Mr Russell, after very kindly speaking of what I had done in the gauge fight, presented me with a check for £500, and increased my salary by £300 a year. When I first joined the Gt Western it was fixed at £300 but when the line opened it was increased to 550 and in Jany 1841 to £700; the increase now made it £1,000. It was raised on the 1st Jany 1851 to 1,500£, at which it stood until I left the service. The following is a copy of the minute of the directors as to the 15 Jany 1846:

[*on a folded sheet of cream laid paper, probably in the hand of a clerk at Paddington*]

Extract from the minutes of the general committee. 15 Jany 1846.

"Mr Brunel having stated to the committee that Mr Gooch as superin-
"tendent of the locomotive department had exerted himself very much
"in furtherance of the interest of this company not only in his general
"duty, increasing as that is, but also in preparing evidence & state-
"ments on the gauge question & having recommended an increase of
"salary to be given——

It was resolved

"That the directors, in testimony of their approbation of Mr Gooch &
"in acknowledgement of his zeal in the service & of the highly credit-
"able state of efficiency of the locomotive department fix his salary at
"£1,000 p[er] annum from the 1st inst & present to him the sum of
"£500 as a reward for his former services—especially in relation to the
"enquiry before the Commissioners of the relative merits of the broad
"& narrow gauge."

The experiments and result of the gauge contest before the Commissioners induced us to build some larger engines, & I proposed one with 18 inch cylinders, 2 feet stroke and 8 feet wheels. This engine was ordered by the board and as it was important to get it to work before the next session of Parliament when a renewal of the fight would take place, I arranged for night and day work upon her and had her finished in 13 weeks from the day of getting the order, probably as quick a job as was ever done. She was first tried at the end of April 1846 and on the 13th June we made a sensational trip with her to Bristol with a load of 100 tons. Mr Russell & the directors & Brunel went down, a dinner was given to a large party at Bristol and a good deal of speech making took place. We attained a steady speed of 62 miles per hour with this load; the distance to Swindon was done in 1h 18m and to Bristol in 2h 12m including stoppages. Mr Russell called this a 'great fact' and it was a great fact. Had we had this engine ready in time for the gauge experiments how different would the results have been, altho' I don't suppose it would have altered the report. We called the engine the Gt Western.[83] She was built on 6 wheels, but finding the weight too much on the leading wheels I put another pair forward.

My 3rd son Alfred was born on the 2nd March of this year 1846.

NOTES

1 Daniel Gooch's father was John Gooch of Bedlington (1783–1833), son of another John Gooch of Beccles, Suffolk (1746–1818) and his wife Barbara, daughter of Michael Longridge of Newburn.

Michael Longridge's father was Thomas Longridge of Walbottle, from whom, through another son George Longridge of Sunderland, was descended Daniel's mother, Anna Longridge.

'Mr Justice' was Barbara Gooch's great-grandfather, whose wife was Barbara Fulthorpe. It was through this marriage that the name Fulthorpe, later used by Daniel for his Paddington house, came into the Gooch family.

2 Daniel was the sixth child and third son.

3 Variously described as book-keeper and cashier. Probably he would now be called the accountant. He was certainly a man of some standing and substance, though not wealthy.

4 Bedlington ironworks was purchased in 1809 by Biddulph, Gordon & Company of London. Michael Longridge, a nephew of a previous partner, Thomas Longridge (Daniel's maternal grandfather) was appointed manager in the same year and made managing partner soon afterwards. He later became manager of the Forth Street works of Robert Stephenson & Co at Newcastle as well.

Bedlington ironworks at the time of Gooch's boyhood was producing rolled iron bars and sheets, ships' anchors and chains, and iron nails. In 1837 a new works across the river was opened for the building of railway locomotives, of which over 150 were built before the works closed completely in 1867.

The history of this works, situated in the beautiful Blyth Dene, with its riverside quays, its workmen's institute and its clock tower, is a fascinating one which deserves to be better known. It is dealt with briefly in Chris Bergen's *History of Bedlington Ironworks 1736–1867*, printed locally after his death in 1940, and at length in an unpublished thesis by Mr Evan S. B. Martin of Bedlington. *See plate IV*

5 Now the King's Arms Hotel. Through the interest of a group of local people, a plaque now commemorates Daniel Gooch's connection with the building. Gooch's birthplace across the road has been demolished. *See plate I*

6 Now (1971) divided into two shops, Nos 15 & 16 Market Place. *See plate II*

7 Crow Hall was only demolished in 1970 to make way for an industrial estate.

8 The farm house, known as The Laird's House, a substantial stone building close to the Goochs' second house, is now Lloyds Bank.

9 Later called Willowbridge Pit, and now known as Barrington Pit. George Stephenson was at one time a partner in the Glebe Pit.

10 It may have occurred to Gooch (though he never says so) just how lucky he was in this respect. On no less than nine occasions he relates how he escaped death by the narrowest of margins. It is indeed tempting to suggest that he was predestined to be spared to live a long and productive life.

11 Possibly a mistake on Gooch's part; the book may have been Neil Arnott's *Elements of Physics, or Natural Philosophy* . . . (3rd edn 1828).

12 For discussion of this *see* Rolt, L. T. C. *George & Robert Stephenson* (1960), 72–4; Tomlinson, W. W. *The North Eastern Railway* (1914, new edn, David & Charles, 1967), 76–7; Young, R. *Timothy Hackworth and the Locomotive* (1923), 32–4.

Birkinshaw's malleable iron rail was first used on the wagon-way which carried coal from the Glebe pit to the ironworks at Bedlington.

13 This was the Stratford and Moreton Tramway. For a full account of this line see

Hadfield, C. and Norris, John, *Waterways to Stratford*, David & Charles, 2nd edn, 1968.

14 This is the first of several entries of this kind. It is very clear that Gooch was conscious of the historical significance of the events and innovations of his day, and likewise realised the importance of preserving not only the snuff boxes presented to him by royalty in later years, but even such seemingly mundane articles as this piece of rail.

15 In 1829 a locomotive engine *Britannia* from Robert Stephenson & Co of Newcastle, was running on the Sirhowy Tramroad which passed through Tredegar. Two further engines, *Speedwell* and *Hercules*, from the Neath Abbey Ironworks, came in 1831. In 1832 Tredegar works began building engines designed by Thomas Ellis, the engineer mentioned by Gooch.

See Jones, Oliver, 'The Sirhowy Tram Road and its Locomotives', in *Journal of Monmouthshire Local History Council*, No 20 (Autumn 1965).

16 There is now no trace of the grave or monument. Gooch gives the inscription as follows (*see* II, n 35).

Sacred to the beloved memory of John Gooch, late of Tredegar, Monmouthshire, and formerly of Bedlington in the County of Durham, who, after having in an exemplary manner discharged the relative duties of son, husband & father & brother, departed this life on the 28th Augst 1833 in the 51st year of his age.

On the 24th of November 1863 at Birmn, Anna Gooch his widow also 'fell asleep in Jesus' in her 81st year. Her remains are laid in this vault by the side of those of her husband by their children, to whom her memory will ever be precious.

'When Christ who is our life shall appear, then shall ye also appear with Him in glory.' Col 3, 4.

17 3 June 1831.

18 Possibly the young lady referred to on page 15.

19 Presumably to be near her eldest son Thomas, then working for Robert Stephenson on the London & Birmingham Rly. The village was Whitley.

20 It is interesting that, although Gooch never became manager of the Vulcan Foundry, he rose to a position which enabled him to place his brother William there as Managing Director in 1864. *See post*, page 95.

21 The Warrington & Newton Rly, opened in 1833, joined the Liverpool & Manchester at Newton Junction. The line later became part of the Grand Junction Rly from Birmingham, which was opened throughout on 4 July 1837.

22 This was the East Foundry, Dundee. James Stirling's nephew Patrick, who was apprenticed there two years after Gooch, was to become famous as the designer of the 'Stirling Singles' for the Great Northern Rly.

23 The East Foundry built some rather unorthodox engines with vertical cylinders for this line.

24 The fire was actually at a warehouse adjacent to Peter Borrie's Tay Foundry.

25 Robert Stephenson & Co, Forth Street Works.

See Warren, J. G. H. *A Century of Locomotive Building by Robert Stephenson & Co* (1923, reprinted 1970).

26 Gooch was almost certainly wrong in thinking that *North Star* and *Morning Star* were originally built for the Russian railways. It is now generally accepted that they were intended for the 5ft 6in gauge New Orleans Railway. What is more important is that they were the only engines ordered by Brunel for the opening of the GWR in 1838 which proved to be of any practical use at all.

The drawings which Gooch made at Newcastle formed the basis of the design of the first engines he built for the GWR after he became locomotive superintendent.

See Ahrons, E. L. *The British Steam Locomotive 1825–1925* (1927), 45. *Locomotives of the Great Western Railway* (Railway Correspondence & Travel Society), Part 2 (1952).

27 Probably John Wilkinson, junior, ironmaster, of Bishopwearmouth.

28 Margaret, daughter of Henry Tanner of Bishopwearmouth (*qv*).

29 It is clear from this and other references to his journal that Gooch kept a day-to-day note of important matters from a fairly early age.

30 The agreement for Gooch's partnership is preserved in the British Railways Board archives, together with a few other personal papers (HL 1/1/1). Mr Thompson was G. A. Thompson.

31 The Great Western Rly Co had obtained its Act to build a line from London to Bristol in 1835. At the time of Gooch's abortive visit to Bristol work had begun at both ends of the line, but the first section, from Paddington to Maidenhead, was not opened until 4 June 1838.

32 Elizabeth Marshall, sister of Gooch's schoolfellow, George Marshall of Bedlington.

33 This should be 4 July.

34 This famous letter is preserved in the GWR Museum, Swindon. *See Appendix.*

35 Even at this period civil and mechanical engineering were still one profession, though specialisation was on the increase.

36 As so often remarked, Gooch was a week short of his 21st birthday when he began his association with the company he was to serve, with one break of just over a year, until his death, at the age of 73, in 1889.

   Both before and after the delayed opening of the Great Western from Paddington to Maidenhead on 4 June 1838 the company had been beset by many problems, most of them the result of Brunel's novel and not always practical ideas both for the permanent way and the locomotives. Brunel's track, with a gauge of 7ft $\frac{1}{4}$in (as compared with 4ft 8$\frac{1}{2}$in of most other lines), consisted of light 'bridge' rail (*see fig 4*) on longitudinal timber baulks, the latter being rigidly secured by piles driven into the ground. When the embankments began to settle the piles caused unevenness in the track as well as a very hard ride, and they were soon dispensed with, but the longitudinal baulks remained until the end of the broad gauge in 1892, except for a few short stretches which were laid with sleepers.

   Brunel's specification supplied to manufacturers of the first batch of locomotives included the stipulation that the weight must not exceed 10$\frac{1}{2}$ tons and that the piston speed at 30mph must not be more than 280 feet per minute. The result was an assortment of largely experimental 'freak' engines, some with enormous driving wheels, which proved an endless source of trouble to the young Gooch. The two Stephenson engines (*see note 26*) alone could be relied upon.

   See MacDermot, *GWR*, I, chaps II and XV, and *Locomotives of the Great Western Railway* (Railway Correspondence & Travel Society), Part 2 (1952).

37 Gooch, obviously quoting from memory, is in error on some of the figures here. Mather, Dixon actually supplied six engines, and Sharp, Roberts supplied three.

38 This should be 16in stroke.

39 These were *Ajax* and *Mars*, whose 10ft wheels were of solid iron plate.

40 The stroke was 20in.

41 This was *Hurricane*.

42 *Thunderer*. The gear ratio was actually 27:10.

43 These were *Snake* and *Viper*. The wheels were 6ft 4in, and the gear ratio 3:2.

44 The diarist wrote here '16th Decr 1837', but deleted this and substituted '9th Jany 1838'. In fact, both *Vulcan* and *Aeolus* were delivered from Vulcan Foundry on 25 November 1837, together with *Premier* from Mather, Dixon. *Vulcan* was first run near Iver on 28 December 1837. For full details of delivery dates of the early engines see *Locomotives of the Great Western Railway* (Railway Correspondence & Travel Soc), Part 2 (1952).

45 According to MacDermot, *North Star* was unloaded on 28 November 1837.

46 There can hardly be any doubt that the young Daniel impressed Henry Tanner as much as a future husband for his daughter as he had impressed Brunel as an engineer for his railway. There are several letters at British Railways Board archives which show the mutual confidence which soon grew between Daniel and his father-in-law.

   Mr Tanner was evidently putting some money into railway shares and wrote on 1 January 1845 'I have every reason to be satisfied with your good management of the York & London shares'. But of railways in general Tanner was sceptical—'I have no great faith in railways tho' I certainly think more favorably of yours than I do of a

F

great many' he wrote on 5 December 1839. He continues, 'What are your engines about? I think I noticed one buried in an embankment & another with a broken wheel to the great terror of Her Majesty's liege subjects, this is not quite right for the Great Western.'
See BRB records ref HRP 1/6.

47 The paddle steamer *Great Western* (1,340 tons gross register) was the first of I. K. Brunel's three ships. The *Great Britain* (3,270 tons) was launched in 1843 and the gigantic *Great Eastern* (18,915 tons), with which Gooch was to be much involved, was launched in January 1858.
See Rolt, L. T. C. *Isambard Kingdom Brunel* (1957).

48 The diarist omits to say that a fire in the engine room of the *Great Western* was the real cause of Brunel's fall.
See Rolt, L. T. C. *Isambard Kingdom Brunel* (1957), 194–6.

49 This is incorrect. She was broken up in 1856–7.

50 Hayes.

51 The 'Fire Fly' class of 2–2–2 express passenger engines, of which 62 were built by various firms between March 1840 and December 1842. Six came from Longridge's works at Bedlington. *Ixion*, the last survivor, was withdrawn in 1879. Their mileage averaged half a million.
See *Locomotives of the Great Western Railway* (Railway Correspondence & Travel Soc), Part 2 (1952).

52 The 'Sun' class, 21 engines built between April 1840 and January 1842. They were similar to the 'Fire Fly' class, but with smaller wheels. They were later converted to tank engines and the last survivor was withdrawn in 1879.
See *Locomotives of the Great Western Railway* (Railway Correspondence & Travel Soc), Part 2 (1952).

53 Gooch's stipulation that the parts should be interchangeable shows great foresight for such a young man. Standardisation and interchangeability of parts was to become the keynote of GW practice, reaching its culmination in the work of G. J. Churchward in the early years of the present century.

54 It is not clear to what this figure of 142 refers. 62 of the 'Fire Fly' and 21 of the 'Sun' class were built.

55 The great contracting firm of Peto & Betts failed in the wake of the collapse of Overend & Gurney, the financiers, in May 1866.

56 This is the model in the photograph of Gooch taken in 1845 and reproduced in the 1892 edition of the diary, and elsewhere. According to the *Great Western Railway Magazine* (March 1936, 129–30) it represents *Leopard*, the second of the engines built by Sharp, Roberts & Co, which, ironically, suffered a boiler explosion at Bristol in 1857.
Clements may have been Joseph Clements, silversmith, jeweller and general electro-plater, of 214 Oxford Street (Pigot's *Directory*, 1838).
The model is now in the Science Museum, South Kensington. *See plate IV*

57 No 9 Paddington Green.

58 His daughter Anna (*qv*). Only just recovering from sleepless nights at Paddington engine shed, Gooch was soon to have his slumbers disturbed from an altogether different cause —little Anna cutting her teeth. His father-in-law wrote on 5 December 1839 'we hope Miss Anna may soon be relieved of her tooth ache & not trouble you so much at nights'. (BRB records HRP 1/6).

59 Even at this time, when he was only 23, Gooch had his first pupil. His elder brother, J. L. Gooch, writing to him on 25 December 1839, wrote, 'I think you should let Mr Russell [the chairman] know of your intention to take pupils, if it is not mentioned to him he may be annoyed, but you have probably done it already. I think you should have £400 [premium].' His father-in-law had written earlier in the month that he was 'glad to hear you have got a young pupil & trust he may lead to another. . . .' (BRB records HRP 1/6.)

60 The main line of the GWR was opened in sections, as follows:
Paddington–Maidenhead, 4 June 1838
Maidenhead–Twyford, 1 July 1839

Twyford–Reading, 30 March 1840
Reading–Steventon, 1 June 1840
Steventon–Faringdon Road, 20 July 1840
Bristol–Bath, 31 August 1840.
Faringdon Road–Hay Lane, 17 December 1840
Hay Lane–Chippenham, 31 May 1841
Chippenham–Bath, 30 June 1841

The Bristol & Exeter main line was opened in sections between 14 June 1841 and 1 May 1844, and the GW Cheltenham branch between 1841 and 1847.

See MacDermot, *GWR*, I, 452–3.

61 The significance of this passage is that the 7ft 'Fire Fly' class engines were to be used on the level road from Paddington to Swindon and the smaller, 6ft wheeled 'Sun' class on the Swindon–Bristol section with its Wootton Bassett and Box inclines, the change of engines being made at Swindon.

62 Box Tunnel is 3,212 yards long and on a uniform gradient of 1:100, falling towards Bristol.

63 An illustrated article on his compressing process appeared in *The Civil Engineer and Architect's Journal* for August 1839.

64 In fact, the Queen's Speech was read on this occasion by the Lord Chancellor.

65 For a description of the two early GWR royal carriages see *Great Western Railway Magazine*, January 1931, 33–5.

66 With these few modest words the diarist marks the beginnings of the Swindon factory where, for nearly 120 years an incomparable succession of locomotives, carriages and other vehicles was built to the designs of some of the greatest railway mechanical engineers.

No adequate history of the works has ever been published. The most complete account can be found in the series of articles by A. J. L. White in the *Great Western Railway Magazine* between 1911 and 1925.

67 The fastest regular run in 1970 (diesel traction) was 1hr 40min, including a stop at Bath, and in 1937–9 (steam traction) *The Bristolian* took 1hr 45min, non-stop.

68 The Bristol & Exeter Rly was leased to, and operated by, the Great Western from 1840 until 1849, after which the B & E regained independence until 1876, when it was amalgamated with the GWR.

See MacDermot, *GWR*, II, chap V.

69 The diarist left a space here, inserting the name of the engine later, evidently from memory. As recently as 1952 Gooch's report on this journey came to light at Swindon, in which the engine is given as *Orion*. The report is printed in detail in *British Railways Magazine*, Western Region, Vol 3 No 2 (February 1952), 30–1.

70 At this time the great majority of British railways were constructed to what is now known as standard gauge, ie 4ft 8½in. Brunel's decision to build the Great Western to a gauge of seven feet was criticised from the outset both on grounds of expense and for the inevitable difficulties of what became known as the 'break of gauge' at points where the two systems met. In 1846 a Royal Commission decided in favour of the narrow (4ft 8½in) gauge as the standard one for the whole country, and extensions to the broad gauge were henceforth confined to lines connected with the Great Western, mainly in the West Country and South Wales.

71 The telegraph system of W. F. Cooke and Prof C. Wheatstone was laid from Paddington to West Drayton in 1839. Although it attracted a great deal of attention from the public, it seems to have been of little use, and by 1842 had ceased to function. It was repaired and extended to Slough in 1843. The use of the telegraph to catch the murderer Tawell took place on 1 January 1845.

See MacDermot, *GWR*, I, 324–8. Hubbard, G. *Cooke & Wheatstone* (1965).

72 It seems extraordinary that an engineer of Brunel's calibre should have supported the thoroughly unpractical system of atmospheric traction. An iron pipe, in the top of which was a longitudinal slot covered by a flap valve of leather, was laid between the rails. Pumps stationed at intervals along the line created a partial vacuum in the pipe, and a piston running in the pipe and attached to the train opened the valve, admitting air, and was forced along by atmospheric pressure.

The system was tried on the South Devon Rly and found utterly unreliable. It had earlier been used on the London and Croydon line and on the Dublin and Kingstown branch to Dalkey. The principal proponents of the system were Samuel Clegg and Jacob and Joseph Samuda. *See* Hadfield, C. Atmospheric Railways (1967).

73 This was the West London Rly. Protracted endeavours to complete the line were often featured in the pages of *Punch*.

74 The floating of the *Great Britain* into the river was begun on the morning tide of the 10th, but she fouled the dock side and was not finally got clear until the night tide.

   See Rolt, L. T. C.. *Isambard Kingdom Brunel* (1957), 206–8. Rowland, K. T. *The Great Britain* (1971).

75 She looked like ending her days as a hulk in the Falkland Isles until, in 1970, she was towed home across the Atlantic to the port of Bristol, where she was launched in 1843, to be restored.

76 3,270 tons.

77 Gooch should have written 'London & Birmingham and Grand Junction', as the London & North Western, of which these two were the principal components, was not formed until the following year.

78 Report of the Gauge Commission, published in February 1846. For a full account of the gauge question as it affected the GWR *see* MacDermot, *GWR*, I, chap VI.

79 *Ixion* was one of Gooch's 'Fire Fly' class, and *Sampson* was one of five 0–6–0 goods engines built in 1842.

80 Professor Peter Barlow (*qv*).

81 The gauge fight provided plenty of ammunition for pamphleteers of the day; among the principal contributors being Sir Henry Cole and Samuel Sidney.

   See Ottley, G. *A Bibliography of British Railway History* (1965).

82 *Observations on the Report of the Gauge Commissioners*, published by James Bigg.

83 The *Great Western*, the first engine built entirely at Swindon Works, appeared in April 1846 and ran 370,687 miles before scrapping in 1870. She was built as a 2–2–2, with 8ft driving wheels, and later altered to 4–2–2, in which form she was the prototype for Gooch's celebrated 8ft single engines of the 'Iron Duke' class which, with rebuilds, were to see the broad gauge out in 1892.

   See Locomotives of the Great Western Railway (Railway Correspondence & Travel Soc), Part 2 (1952).

VOLUME II

The Memoirs 1847-65

1847. The passing of the direct line Oxford to Birmingham[1] again ra[ised]* the question of gauge, as the Gauge A[ct], on the recommendation of the Gauge Com[mission] required that all future lines sho[uld be] made on the narrow gauge (without P[arliament] sanction its being broad), and the House of Lords on the 25 June 1847 ordered an enquiry by the Railway Commissioners of the Board of Trade as to the accommodation of the lines between London & Bir[min]gham and whether it is expedient to lay the broad gauge to Bir[min]gham &c, such report to be made to the next session of Parliament.

The Railway Commissioners, in carrying out these instructions (these were not the *Gauge* Commissioners but the Board of Trade), sent out a series of printed questions to the London & North Western Company and the Gt Western; these questions referred chiefly to the resistance of railway trains and construction of locomotives. On the part of the London & North Western a joint answer was given by Mr R. Stephenson, Mr Locke, Mr McConnell & [Mr] Trevithick the two latter gentlemen being the locomotive supts of the L & N Western Co. Mr Brunel sent in his answer and I sent in mine separately on behalf of the Great Western.

To enable me to do this satisfactorily I felt a complete series of experiments was necessary, and having the authority of the board to spend what was necessary I designed and constructed an indicator to measure and accurately record the speed the train was running, and also on the same paper to record the tractive power used by the engine, measured by a spring; also on the same paper the force and direction of the wind. Annexed is a specimen of the record so obtained.[2] To check the traction I also, at the same time, took indicator cards from the

* A small piece of folio 94 of the MS has been torn off; missing words or parts of words are supplied in brackets.

cylinder of the engine so as accurately to measure the power exerted there. It also gave me the power expended in moving & working the engine. I made a great number of experiments over a level piece of line on the Bristol & Exeter line at various rates of speed and loads. They gave me results very different from those obtained by the n[arrow] gauge which, however, were done more by calculation than by actual experiment.

I read a paper at the Institution of Civil Engineers on these experiments in Apl 1848,[3] and a good deal of discussion took place on them for a couple of nights. It was, however, a simple party fight, Stephenson & Co against broad gauge, and was unworthy of the profession as party should there give place to science and truth. I still keep the original records of these experiments. They cost me a vast amount of labour both in calculations and in making the expts. It was rather a difficult task to sit on the buffer beam of the engine and take indicator cards at speeds of 60 miles per hour.

Mr Stephenson endeavoured to shew before the Board of Trade that it would be dangerous to have a mixed gauge (that is, 3 lines of rails) and produced some plans to shew the number of points and crossings. Many years experience has since proved him wrong. The report of the Commissioners was in favour of extending the broad gauge to Birmingham and making it a mixed-gauge line. This was the last of the real gauge fights; nothing has since transpired to raise the point again, and it may be said from all the evidence and reports that a difference in the gauge of the railways in this country, now they have so covered its surface and so large an interchange of traffic has to take place, is an evil and is now to be regretted, but that were the whole question now open to be decided, the broad gauge is safer, cheaper, more comfortable and attains a much higher speed than the narrow, and would be the best for the national gauge, but as the proportion of broad to narrow is so small there is no doubt the country must submit to a gradual displacement of the broad, and the day will come when it will cease. The fight has been of great benefit to the public; it has pricked on all parties to exertion, the competition of the gauges has introduced high speeds and great improvements in the engines, and was of great practical use to all those who were actively mixed up in the contest. They were forced to think & experiment; it was not allowed to them to rest quietly on speeds of 20 to 30 miles per hour. I know it was of great value to me by the practical information I obtained in investigations.

The South Devon line was opened in July this year 1847, between Newton & Totness, over long gradients of 1 in 42. I never saw Mr Brunel so anxious about any thing as he was about this opening. Relying upon the atmospheric principle[4] he had made these steep inclines, and he feared there might be difficulties in working them. These difficulties disappeared with the day of opening. All our trains went through very well, and at night it seemed a great relief to Mr Brunel to find it was so. He shook hands with me and thanked me in a very kind manner for my share in the day's work. He never forgot those who helped him in a difficulty.

I had a very narrow escape from being drowned this year. I was with my family staying at Exmouth in June, and arranged with J. Rea and Mr Smith[5] to go out fishing at 5 oclock one morning. We engaged the boat the day before and the man was to call us; this he did not do, but we all got up and found the boatman who said it was not safe to cross the bar. As it looked very nice from Exmouth we pretty well forced him to go, at any rate to go and see in the boat, so we started. The tide was running very quickly out and as we got near the breakers on the bar we began to think the boatman was right, and then proposed to return. We soon found this easier said than done, the tide was running so fast. It was clear, before we could get the boat round (even if, when round, we could pull her against the tide) we would be carried into the breakers. There was nothing left for us but to keep her head to the sea and trust to Providence. I was stearing the boat, and the boatman and a strong lad were rowing. The lad's oar broke and we had then only the one chance, but all we had to do was to give her sufficient stearage way through the water, the tide took us to sea quite quick enough. When we got amongst the breakers we had some heavy thumps and shipped some water. I saw one large sea nearly 6 feet high coming, and I felt sure it would swamp us, and then thought what a fool I had been to sacrifice my life in such a stupid way, for during those few seconds I felt certain of death. When the wave was within a few yards of us a merciful God made an opening for us by the sinking of the wave for a short distance, and we passed safely over it and were safe as it was the last. I will never forget the sense of relief I felt. Mr Smith & Rea were sitting in the bottom of the boat; the boatman said Mr Smith was on his knees praying. We had a flask of rum with us, and all seemed glad to get a glass of that. It was a lesson to me I have not forgotten, to believe the boatman was best judge in such matters, and we ought to have taken his advice.

During the latter part of 1846 and this year 1847 I had been building my present house[6] in Warwick Road, Paddington, and got it finished so that I could get into it at the end of September, which I did. My youngest boy Frank was born in the old house[7] on the 20th July 1847.

1848. On the 29th of May in 1848 I lost a friend for whom I had a great esteem. It was Stewart K. Rea, our medical man at Swindon. When we first started the works I induced him to settle at New Swindon as the surgeon to the works, and he was much liked by the men. He married a Miss Pavy in the neighbourhood, and she had not long been confined with her first child, for whom I stood god father. Rea had not been very well for some time, and a serious accident[8] we had to our express train on the 10 May at Shrivenham, by which 4 people were killed and several seriously hurt, caused him a great amount of anxiety and work, instead of taking care of himself, and he died on the 29th leaving his widow and child not very well provided for. I went for a holiday in June to visit the English Lakes and the Highlands of Scotland. My wife accompanied me and also Mr Stubs of Warrington & his niece. My daily journal of the trip will shew where we went. I saw a beautiful sun set one night from the top of Skiddaw; I went up by myself in the evening and it was a glorious sight as the sun set over the hills in the west. The moon rose beautifully over the Solway Firth in the east. I found it very cold when the sun went down but was well rewarded by the view. We had generally fine weather and enjoyed the trip very much; I needed some rest and change and it did me good.

The latter part of this year 1848 a steam carriage[9] built by Adams was tried on our line. It was a *very* small engine & carriage all on one frame, but was of little use. The Bristol & Exeter Co afterwards bought it to work the Weston branch. No more have been made.

1849. There was a good deal of frost & snow on the 16th & 17th of April in this year. I was very nearly lost in a bog in July. I went into Devonshire to attend an inquest on a fireman killed by the explosion of one of our engines at Plympton.[10] I went with an engine to meet Capt Simmons who was coming to attend the inquest on behalf of the Board of Trade. Having a couple of hours to spare at Kingsbridge Road[11] station I took a walk to the top of a high hill called Hill Moor. I came to some very wet places & seeing what I thought a sound piece of ground I made a jump upon it, but instead of its being sound it was a bog hole, and down I went. Feeling this, I let my body fall flat and so dragged myself out as there was no foot hold, and I might very easily have gone overhead & would have done so if I had not thrown myself down flat. I was pretty well saturated with bog and water. Fortunately it was a very bright hot day and I went on to the top of the mountain where there were some large rocks, and here took my clothes off and laid them in the sun on the hot stones, & I got into the shade while the drying process was going on. Fortunately the place was perfectly private and I got my clothes pretty well dried. How easily a man might disappear from the face of the earth in that way, leaving no trace behind.

In the August of this year we went to France and Belgium with Mr & Mrs Minet for nearly a month.

At the August meeting of the Gt Western shareholders a consultative committee was appointed to overhaul the directors. The railway excitement of '46 & '47 had been followed by a railway panic; new obligations reduced dividends and bred discontent among the shareholders. The committee so appointed were any thing but suitable men. They [k]new nothing of railways but had to make a report for the next meeting, and the chief point they made was to reduce the salaries of the officers of the company, mine amongst the number. The directors on the 7th Decb told me of this resolution of the committee, the proposal being to reduce me from £1,000 to 700. This I naturally objected to, but Mr Brunel advised me to take no notice of it as the directors would not carry it out without a vote of the shareholders was against them, and the early part of the year 1850 was occupied in a fight with the committee. The result was the committee were beaten by a large majority and my sal[ar]y was not reduced. I had quite made up my mind to refuse to accept a reduction; Seymour Clarke's sal[ar]y was reduced and this led to his leaving the service and doing very much better for himself on the Gt Northern Railway. But this attempt of the committee was after all a godsend to me as it opened my eyes to the little security there was in a railway situation, where directors who knew you might, by the votes of a lot of discontented shareholders, be displaced and others brought into power who knew not the officers or the services they had rendered the company.

Up to this time I had looked upon the Gt Western as an employment for life, & had refused a good offer from Mr Locke in 1842 to go to the Grand Junction, and also from Alderman Thompson to go to Italy, both at much higher sal[ar]y than I was getting, but I felt a rolling stone gathered no moss and was unwilling to leave a service where I was comfortable and well treated; but now I felt it was not safe to rely upon the permanency of such a state of things and I therefore determined to make myself in some degree independent of the railway, and for this purpose saw the chairman, Mr Russell, and obtained his consent to my doing any other work so long as I did not neglect the Gt Western. Acting on this principle I found no difficulty in making money by professional services in other ways, and it is thus what fortune I have realised has been obtained. I may therefore thank the consultative committee of 1849 for the views they took of railway management.

I was made a Free Mason[12] on the 14th of February 1850 by Mr Luxmore in St George's Lodge, Exeter. Many ridicule the Society of Free Masons, saying there is no secret and the only object is good dinners. Writing now, 18 years after I was made and during which time I took a very active part in it, passing the chair of several Lodges and getting high rank in the craft (being now Dep[u]t[y] Grand Master of Wilts) I look back on my connexion with Masonry as a very *useful* and a very pleasant part of my life. I have made many kind friends in the craft and have met with much kindness & have never regretted the day I was initiated into its mysteries. Nothing can be more pure and good than the teachings of Freemasonry; it needs only to be carried out in daily life to greatly improve the well being of society. I have myself initiated about 100. For the first few years it required hard work to learn all the ceremonies and attend the meeting of the Lodges. Now I leave this work to younger men but still enjoy my meetings with the craft.

My sister-in-law[13] Mary Laing died on the 30th March 1850. I was much grieved at her loss; she was a favourite of mine. She left 2 children.

Early in this year 1850 Lord Willoughby de Eresby, who had a great notion of ploughing by steam, asked me to design an engine for the purpose. This I did, and built it at Swindon, and I went down to his place at Grimsthorpe to try the ploughing. The arrang[emen]t of the plough was Lord Willoughby's own scheme. We succeeded very well, and I believe were the first to practically put steam ploughing into operation, as Ld Willoughby never gave it up afterwards and I built him two other engines. There is very little difference between the present mode of ploughing as patented by Fowler[14] & others, and that carried out by Ld Willoughby; nothing but in small details suggested by practice. There are drawings &c of the original engine &c in my possession.

The end of this year 1850 the South Devon Railway Co wished to have larger and more suitable engines to work their line. The directors of the Gt Western, who were working the line with small engines, declined to build new ones. I therefore proposed to the South Devon Co to find parties who would join me in finding capital to build the engines if a 10 years contract for working the line was made. This was agreed to by the South Devon, and I negotiated and completed the ag[reemen]t with Mr Brunel and was joined in carrying it out by Mr Chas Geach of Birmingham and Mr Evans of the Haigh Foundry Co, Wigan, and we had the engines built on the bogie principle. They have answered very well. I had before built some for the Gt Western of the same class & size. We began working the line in the autumn of 1851.[15]

1851. This year is chiefly remarkable for the 1st of those great exhibitions that have since become rather common. The one held in Hyde Park this year was a charming building and being the first of the kind the impression made upon the mind was stronger than with the following ones. The Gt Western Co sent a locomotive, the 'Lord of the Isles', one of our large class of passenger engines, and I am safe in saying she was a beautiful job and has ever since done her work on the line satisfactorily. This cannot be said of most of the engines exhibited. I got a medal[16] for her, but the highest class medal was given to Crampton for an engine certainly the most faulty in construction exhibited, and which has since never been repeated in this country. So much for the opinions of judges at such exhibitions; favour has generally too large a share in the award of prizes. The exhibition was on the whole a great success and made the year 1851 a remarkable one in London. I bought my first carriage this year, a brougham, and started our horse.

1852. Various portions of the Gt Western line were opened during this year, and the important piece between Banbury and Birmingham. This took place on the 30th September. We had made great preparations to give eclat to it, as it was the connecting link with our narrow-gauge system[17] and the completion of what had been so long a fight. Hitherto the numerous openings we have had have all gone off well, without any kind of hitch. A banquet was prepared at Leamington for a large number of visitors, a special train started with our Exhibition engine, the Lord of the Isles, from Paddington at about 8 oclock, to go to Birmingham & with the intention of returning from there to Leamington. The train and engine certainly looked beautiful and was filled with lots of ladies & gentlemen. I drove the engine and all went on well until we came near the Ayhno [*ie* Aynho] station. We knew an ordinary passenger train was ahead of us as far as Banbury, and when near Ayhno I saw a signal all right for us, having before shut off steam to slacken speed a little in case we got a danger signal, but seeing this signal all right I put on the steam again but had not gone many yards when I came in sight of another signal at the station, standing at danger. I then did all I could to stop, but it was then too late; I soon saw the train at the station. Fortunately there were some waggons behind the passenger carriages; these had just been uncoupled and the train engineman, seeing we were not going to stop, put his steam on and got a little way ahead with his passenger carriages. We soon went pretty sharp into the waggons, breaking some and sending some of them after the passenger train, which they struck, shaking the passengers a little but doing no one any serious harm. Our engine went jumping over the broken waggons and at last brought up in the ditch a little beyond the station. Mr Brunel was on the engine with me, but none of us sustained any injury, nor did any one in our train feel any shock. I afterwards found that the signal which had deceived me belonged to a ballast pit and was not worked from the station. It ought to have been taken down.

As we had no telegraph it was a long time before we could get another engine to take our party on; this was done at last. I had to stay and get our engine on the line. This I did, and got to Leamington when the feast was over, and as tho' misfortunes never came alone, a special train that was started from Birmingham got off the line in leaving that station, so that they did not get to Leamington in time. Altogether it was a day of misfortunes, and this was more annoying as we were particularly anxious to make a successful day, for our London & North Western friends were watching us. There is no doubt the opening was pushed on too quickly; we ought to have had another week. The police arrangements on the line had not been completed.

One of England's greatest men died this year, the Duke of Wellington. He was buried in St Paul's on the 18th Nov 1852. Lord Willoughby de Eresby kindly asked me to go to his house in Piccadilly to see the funeral pass; it was a grand and solemn sight. The Duke had not travelled upon the railway after the opening of the Liverpool & Manchester, when he saw Mr Huskisson killed, until he was called suddenly to Windsor on account of the riots at Newport in 1839. He travelled a few times after this. I was installed Master of the Lodge at Swindon [at] the end of 1852.

1853. We had a sad accident to our up express train on the morning of Feby 24, 1853. Some of the carriages got off the line near Ealing and one of our directors, Mr Gibbs of Bristol, was killed, & Dr Smith, another director was very much hurt. The other passengers were not much injured altho' many had a very narrow escape. The Govt Inspector could not find out the cause, altho' a bad rail made it plain enough to me.[18] It was not our policy to enlighten the public and it was put down as one of those cases which no fellow understands.

I left England for a holiday the last day of May in 1853 and travelled up the Rhine and into Switzerland. I also visited Chamonix, returning by way of France, reaching home on the 12th July. We were very much favoured with the weather, and my daily journal will shew all the places I visited. We got into the midst of an election row at a small place called Bulle in Switzerland. Cannon were brought out just opposite the hotel where we stopped to dine. I was half in hopes we would have a row in earnest but I think the soldiers coming out with the big guns was more than the people liked.

On September the 6th the Provincial Grand Lodge of Wilts was re-established, Lord Methuen as Grand Master, and I was appointed his deputy. The installation took place at Old Swindon. I was installed Master of the Swindon Lodge in December for the 2nd time and presented with a handsome gold Past Master's jewel by the members of the Lodge.

Decr 28, 1852 I first became a landed proprietor, having purchased the Nythe Farm in the parish of Wanborough in Wilts. It has been a good purchase; there are 232 acres. It cost me £13,400.

1854. I assisted to form a new Lodge at Calne on 17th Jany and was installed as Master. I also consecrated two Lodges, one at Trowbridge and the Methuen Lodge at New Swindon. We, at the same time as the Methuen Lodge was consecrated, laid the foundation stone of the Mechanics' Institution at New Swindon. There was a very large attendance of Masons, upwards of 500, and the day went off very well. We dined in the cricket ground under tents. Lord Methuen laid the stone and was also installed Master of the Methuen Lodge. The Mechanics' Institution has been a source of great benefit to our men there. I first let them have some spare rooms in the works, and a great change was gradually produced upon the general conduct of the men. As we required the rooms they occupied in the works a company was got up, in a great measure amongst the men, to build a hall & institution, also a market. This company has since paid a fair dividend of from 6 to 8 per cent, and the hall has been a great boon to the men. It is fit up with a stage where the men have performances &c.[19]

I had a sharp attack of illness in Apl of this year 1854, which kept me in the house for 3 weeks, the longest time I had hitherto been kept indoors. God has blessed me with very good health.

We had a hard railway fight in Parliament this year in obtaining the amalgamation act for the Shrewsbury lines between Wolverhampton & Chester. We succeeded, and had two great dinners on the strength of it, one at Greenwich and the other at the Gt Western Hotel.[20]

The members of the Middlesex Lodge gave me a dinner at Richmond, where we spent a very pleasant day. The party included ladies.

I built this year a common road locomotive for Lord Willoughby, intended to work on his farm at Grimsthorpe, and I went down there to see it tried. We had some good fun in learning to stear it; I found it very difficult to keep her on the narrow roads in the park and often, if we went fast, made a dash onto the grass. She weighed about 3 tons. I have made several designs for road engines, but I am satisfied they can only be used at a very slow speed, and may succeed in draging heavy weights, but are useless for anything else. I have often intended to build one to ride about on, but fancied it would not be satisfactory. Designs for some will be found amongst my drawings.

1855. I was installed as Master of the Britannia Lodge in London on the 11th May. It was an old Lodge revived. At the end of my year of office the Lodge presented me with a pretty gold jewel. I went to the continent on the 1st June. The Exhibition in Paris was open; it was only a poor affair after ours of 1851, but there was a good collection of pictures. When in Paris I saw 35,000 men reviewed by Napoleon, and 35 guns; it was a fine sight. I had never seen any thing like so many men together before. From Paris I went to Switzerland and crossed the Grimsel Pass into the valley of the Rhone. We were the first to do so this year and it was a very difficult operation. The snow had in no degree melted, and we had no path; the horses were constantly sinking to their belley and had to be lifted out. I, however, enjoyed that scramble very much. After crossing the Grimsel we crossed the Simplon into Italy and went on to Venice. I was very much pleased with the quiet and novelty of the old town. On our return from Italy we crossed the St Gothard, and so back home by way of Paris. We had fine weather and I enjoyed the journey very much. My journal of the trip will shew each day's route. We reached London on the 14th July. There is nothing so good for the health as the complete change obtained in going abroad.

Mr Russell retired from the chair of the Gt Western in the early part of this year, and Mr Walpole was elected in his place. Mr Russell was very much liked on the line by all, and he had always been very kind to me. We raised a fund to have his portrait painted for the board room, by Grant. It is a good picture and very like Mr Russell. We all much regretted his health would not admit of his retaining the chair.

The King of Sardinia was at Windsor Castle in December of this year 1855 and travelled several times on the line. The Emperor Napoleon the 3 of France and the Empress paid a visit to Windsor in the summer of 1855 and travelled over our line. He sent me afterwards a beautiful gold snuff box with the letter N and crown in diamonds on the lid.

1856. In the early part of this year I formed the Ruabon Coal Company. The circumstances were these: it had been found impossible to get a regular coal trade on our line, & I proposed to the company to have some collieries of their own, and went to Ruabon to look at those belonging to Mr Robertson and also some property of Sir Watkin W. Wynn's where a colliery might be sunk. Having obtained the best information I could, I advised the directors to buy up Robertson's works as they were in operation and could be made available for our purposes at once. This was finally agreed upon by the directors, and the price settled, but at this time a decision in regard to a similar plan in operation on the Eastern Counties Railway, [which] shewed it not to be within the powers of the company, stopped our plan. Mr Walpole then asked me if I could and would find private parties to form a company and enter into an agreement with the railway Co to send a large fixed quantity of coal over the Gt Western Railway. This I agreed to do, and took a large stake in it myself, or £20,000, about half the capital, and was to be chairman of the coal company.

Feeling that this might conflict with my position as an officer of the railway company I placed my resignation in the hands of Mr Walpole, but he and the directors did not think it right to accept it. I, however, left it in their hands to accept at any time should circumstances make it desirable. I felt there were interests in the coal trade amongst the shareholders of the railway who would no doubt object to what had been done, and such was the case, for 2 or 3 half-years afterwards it was the cause of a row at our meeting and some parties went to the Court of Chancery to put an end to the ag[reemen]t. In this they failed, and the Court expressed themselves strongly that what had been done was perfectly legal and right. I thus got a good deal of abuse by my trying to do good to the shareholders of the railway and risking a good deal of money in doing so. The colliery has, however, been a very good investment and has done good to both parties to the arrang[emen]t. Mr Walpole acted very well to me in this matter, as he never flinched from what he had told me, but did his best to carry out the arrangt and support those who had gone into it at his request.

On the 7th Feby I was installed as first Principal in the Moriah Chapter in London, and I consecrated a new Lodge at Devises, No 961, on the 18th of Apl 1856.

There was a grand review of the Fleet by the Queen at Portsmouth on the 23 Apl; there were 240 ships of various kinds reviewed. I was present on board a steamer belonging to the South Western Railway Co.[21] It was a very grand sight, but I had a narrow escape of losing my life. I was sitting on the top of the paddle box with two others, our legs hanging over the edge towards the sea, when a gun boat with a boat hanging over her side came alongside of us and so close that her boat mounted over the bulwarks and then went crashing over the top of the paddle box where we were sitting. We had just time to roll over onto the deck. It was a willful thing on the part of the officer of the gun boat. It appears the capt of our steamer would keep closer to the Queen's yacht than this gentleman liked, so he took this mode of driving us off. Had any one been killed, which he did his best to accomplish, he would have been guilty of murder and have found it rather a serious job for him. There was a great scramble to get back at night. The Lords & Commons did not get back until pretty well into next morning.

On the 15th of May 1856 I lost a very sincere friend in the death of poor Minet. I had a great affection and esteem for him; we had for many years seen a great deal of each other and I deeply regretted his loss. He left a wife and 7 children, and appointed me one of his executors to administer only a very spare fortune. He was buried at Kensal Green cemetery on the 21st.

There were great rejoicings & fireworks in London on the 29th May on the conclusion of peace after the Crimean war. Mr Walpole retired from the Gt Western board on his appointment to Home Secretary,[22] and Lord Barrington took the chair after the spring meeting. In the Augst meeting a committee of shareholders was appointed to enquire into the affairs of the company.

1857.* I was installed as Master of the Middlesex Lodge in London on the 16th Jany. I went over to Belgium in Apl, and also twice afterwards, to examine the coal works of that country, particularly their method of making compressed fuel. They have a very good machine for the purpose, a better one, I think, than that used at Swansea.

Minard Rea died at Swindon on the 18th June; he was a pupil of mine & for some time previous to his death had been the manager of the Swindon works. He died of consumption after a long illness and was buried in the church yard at Swindon where two of his brothers had before been laid, and since that time his mother. My brother William succeeded Rea as the manager at Swindon. He, at the time, was working the South Devon contract for me, but as the time was coming when I felt I might give up the hard work entailed by a railway appointment, the directors promised him my position when I retired if he would come to Swindon at the salary they could give. This was a very clear arrangt and on the faith of which he gave up a better sal[ar]y, looking to the future position, but he was afterwards grossly deceived.

The committee of shareholders appointed in August 1856 [1855] made their report early in 1857 [1856] and found great fault with the directors and their management. The result was a hot fight at the meeting in Feby 1857 [1856]; they wished to get Mr S. Baker and Mr Potter back into the directors and to effect other changes in the board, and a good deal of their attack was made on the agreement with the Ruabon Coal Company. The committee were beaten as usual by the directors at the Feby meeting.

Our old chairman, poor Mr Russell, destroyed himself this year [1856]. He suffered dreadfully from [a] heart complaint. Mr Ponsonby was elected chairman[23] in place of Lord Barrington who had only taken the office temporarily. In Great Western Railway affairs this has been a year of change and trouble.[24]

* The diarist is mistaken over some dates here. To make the text intelligible the correct years have been inserted in brackets.

I was laid up for a few weeks in September in consequence of an operation I was obliged to undergo. It freed me from the suffering I had previously for long endured.

1858. I went to the opera in Jany. The Queen went in state on the occasion of the marriage of the Princess Royal. The Opera House looked very splendid with all the rich dresses. In [*ie* on] February the 11th I went with a deputation of the presidents of the different Mechanics' Societies to present an address to Prince Albert. I forget what was the nature of the address. The movement was got up by the Society of Arts, and I daresay was for the glorification of some body or other. There was a total eclipse of the sun on the 15 March, and Swindon was the best place to see it. I went down; there were a large number of people there from all parts. Unfortunately the day was not quite clear and at time clouds passed over the sun, but a good deal of the eclipse was well seen. The atmosphere had a very gloomy appearance and feeling, but I did not see birds go to roost &c &c.

On the 19th of October 1858 my daughter Emily was married to Mr Ponsford. She was much too young and I should gladly have had it delayed a few years, but, perhaps unwisely, yielded to the wishes of the young people. Having only 2 girls it made a vacancy in the house.

On the 25th October my wife's father Mr Tanner died at Sunderland. His death was very sudden as he went to bed not making any complaint, but died from disease of the heart in a couple of hours. I went down to Sunderland to attend his funeral. He was very much respected by all the inhabitants of the town; all the shops were shut and thousands of people lined the streets between his home and the cemetery. He had been a kind and good father to his children and was in every way a most worthy man. I do not think I mentioned before that he married a second time in the year [*blank*] a Mrs Elstob, a widow; it was a very suitable marriage and she survived him until this year.

The Princess Royal was married to the Crown Prince of Prussia on the 25 Jany 1858. I took them after the marriage from Windsor to Basingstoke by train, and they sent me a gold snuff box, not a very grand one, but it was a royal gift.

1859. In the March of this year I bought Clewer Park,[25] or rather bought the lease of it from the widow of the late Hon[houra]b[l]e Ashley, and afterwards purchased the freehold from Doctor Proctor. I had been long looking out for a house in the neighbourhood of Windsor. I had spent my summers at Windsor for 5 or 6 years before, taking lodgings, and I was very fortunate to get a place so suitable for me in every respect as Clewer. When I went down to look at it a large bed of violets took my fancy very much, and I saw the timber &c was very fine and the faults I saw in the grounds easily remedied. I therefore had no difficulty in making up my mind to take it.[26]

The Cornwall Railway[27] opened on the 4th May, and was added to our contract for working the South Devon. I was of necessity a good deal down in Cornwall & Devonshire. I went to see the *Tor Rocks* near Newton on the *19th August*; it was a fine and enjoyable day.

On the 2nd August my daughter Anna married F. Newton. It was a sad loss to me losing both my girls at such an early age; they had hardly left school before they married, and I had little opportunity of having them with me at home. I hope it is for future happiness of both.

On the 15 Sept 1859 I lost my oldest and best friend in the death of Mr Brunel. He had been far from well for 2 or 3 years past, suffering much from pains in his head, and during that time had been much worried by the Great Eastern steam ship.[28] This was his last great work; not satisfied with the size of the Great Britain he conceived and designed this noble ship. Unfortunately he departed from the plan he adopted in building the Great Britain, not having a dock made to build her in, so that when finished she could be floated out, but had her built on land to be launched broad side on to the water. This was a mistake, as her launch proved. Her building was a long operation, money fell short and the work exceeded their calculations as to time, and it was not until the autumn of 1858 that she was ready for launching. The first attempt, owing to some misunderstanding by which some men at one of the capstans were killed, failed. That is, when the ship moved the accident caused her motion to be stopped, and then they could not get her to start again, and it now became a work of much labour and time to free her by degrees, with hydraulic presses, into the water, at a cost of about £70,000. Mr Brunel exposed himself to the wet and cold very much, and it no doubt had much to do with his last & fatal illness. When the ship was at last got into the water she was fitted up afloat and when ready to sail in the Sept of 1859 he was too ill to be with her.

Her first trip was a very unfortunate one; she was going round to Holyhead, but when passing down channel a water casing to one of the boilers which had been carelessly left without any opening for the steam to escape, burst and killed several of the men and did great damage to the ship. She went into Portland and landed the men who were killed and injured and afterwards went on to Holyhead. Here she was nearly lost in the heavy gale in which the Royal Charter was lost;[29] she dragged her anchor and was nearly on the rocks. She was afterwards taken to Southampton, where she was laid up for the winter. I went down to see her on the 12th November. Poor Brunel heard of the explosion a couple of days before he died.

By his death the greatest of England's engineers was lost; the man of the greatest originality of thought and power of execution, bold in his plans but right. The commercial world thought him extravagant, but altho' he was so, great things are not done by those who sit down and count the cost of every thought and act. He was a true and sincere friend, a man of the highest honour, and his loss was deeply deplored by all who have the pleasure to know him. He had a curious accident a few years before his death. Playing with a child he managed to swallow a half sovereign which went into his chest, and many attempts were made to get it out without success. He himself suggested the plan which succeeded: he had a frame made, swinging like a looking-glass on the centre, to which he was fastened and then suddenly turned with his head downwards. Two or 3 times they failed to get it out, but another attempt succeeded and it was a great joy to his medical men and all with him to see it fall on the floor. He did not die a rich man, as if he was extravagant with shareholders' money he never asked others to take up a scheme which he did not himself largely embark in, and he thus lost a great deal of money. I had some original shares in the Gt Ship before she was launched, or after (I am not sure which). The original capital & co[mpany] was displaced and a new company formed out of the wreck. I shall ever feel a deep sense of gratitude to Mr Brunel for all his kindness and support from the day I first saw him in 1837.

Lord She[l]burn[e] was elected chairman of the Gt Western Railway in the early part of 1859 in place of Mr Ponsonby. We all liked Mr Ponsonby very much and regretted his resignation.

1860. In January of this year I purchased the Hirwain [ie Hirwaun] colliery. Mr Saunders and a few others joined me in it. Also bought Bell Farm. The shareholders of the Great Eastern steam ship, being out of humour with their directors, at their meeting in February determined to turn them all out and elect a new board. I was requested to form one of the new board & was elected. After our election we determined to complete the ship fit for sea and send her a voyage to America as early as we could. I went down to Southampton and took the direction of all the engineering departments of the ship. Very many alterations were required both in the general fittings and machinery, the Board of Trade requirements being very large. We raised £100,000 by debentures and worked hard to get her ready to sail in June. The former captain of the ship who had been looking after her building (Capt Harrison) was drowned early in the year in Southampton dock, and we had to appoint a new man. We selected a Capt Hall. All was sufficiently complete for us to take our departure in June. I had settled to go with her and take my wife & Harry.

We joined the ship at Southampton on the Thursday, 14th June, intending to sail on the Saturday, but when all the people had been cleared out of the ship Hall told us the crew were not in a state to sail from drink. I was very vexed at this as it shewed a want of that which is necessary to success—discipline in the ship and more energy in the captain. We however sailed on the Sunday morning with about 20 passengers, so that we had plenty of room. Two of the other directors went with me, Mr Barber and Capt Carnegie. All went on most comfortably on our voyage, the weather was very fine and the ship as steady as an island, so much so that the game of skittles was played every day. One of the passengers, oddly enough, took some skittles on board with him and assumed the name of Skittles; a sister he had with him also went by the name of Miss Skittles. We had one sharp gale on the passage, lasting a great part of one night, making the ship roll a little. Our general run per day was about 330 knots. Our captain, thinking we would like to see the flying fish and other curiosities found in the Gulf Stream, took us a good way south out of our course, and altho' we all enjoyed the voyage very much and regretted the thought of getting to land, yet the credit of the ship needed that we ought to have made the run in 9 days, which she would have done if the right course had been steared, instead of the 10 days 19 hours we took.

We arrived off Sandy Hook very early on the morning of the 28 June and came to anchor to wait the tide. By 10 oclock craft of all kinds began to arrive from New York to look at us and our agents came off to us. The scene became very exciting and the day was a lovely one. When we began to run up to New York we were accompanied by hundreds of yachts, steamers &c, and it was certainly a grand and exciting scene.

77

As we passed up through that beautiful entrance to the Hudson the banks were lined with thousands of people, and the forts and American men of war saluted as we passed, so that it was one continued firing of guns and shouting of thousands of people all the way up to New York, and when we came close to that town the scene was wonderful. The wharfs, house tops, church towers and every spot where a human being could stand and get a sight of the ship was crowded. We reached the wharf where we were to lay about 5 or 6 oclock, and I was very glad when it was time for bed; I did not go ashore. It had been a really hard day's work; I will, however, never forget the beauty of the scene.

I now had to undertake a new kind of life, that was, to become a show man, as we expected to earn a very large sum of money by exhibiting the ship. We therefore had to advertise and organise our plans, and I cannot say, now it is all over, we were very clever at our work, nor were we well assisted by those appointed for that purpose in New York. Before leaving England we were told it would not do to charge less than a dollar for admission as the Yankies [k]new no less coin than the dollar. We soon found out this was a mistake, as the papers abused us for making so high a charge, and we after a few days had to reduce it to half a dollar. Certainly a great many people visited the ship; the highest number in one day was about 18,000, and I think we took about £20,000 altogether for exhibiting the ship.

We took up our quarters at the New York Hotel, a very comfortable house, and I must say my experience of the hotels in America places them considerably above any thing we do in England for the same or a greater cost. We were only charged 10s/- per day for food and room; the wines were bad—not fit to drink. At first we were kind of lions in New York; photographers wanted our photographs (in which I did not indulge them) and the first night we went to the theatre we, as modest people, went into the body of the house, but had not long taken our seats when a person came to invite us to go into a private box. This we did, and were greeted with God Save the Queen. All this kind of humbug lasted a very short time; we soon began to get out of favour as showmen, and before we actually left New York for good it was our first amusement every morning to read the abusive articles in the newspapers.

I was much disappointed with New York as a town; it is so mixed with good and bad houses that no good general effect was obtained excepting on the 5th Avenue. We had a great deal of annoyance from the want of ability in our Capt & officers to manage the internal matters of the ship. They seemed to care much more about shewing themselves off in their uniforms, about town, than attending to their duties. Hall certainly was a mighty *vain* man. The weather was dreadfully hot all the time we were in America. I went on the 9th July to Washington, spending a day at Philadelphia on the way. This latter place is a fine town, but Washington is certainly the most miserable place I ever was in to be called a town of importance. An old friend whom we knew in London was living in Washington, a Col Mann. He had been connected with the Government and shewed us great attention. We went with him to White House to be introduced to President Buchanan, who received us with great civility. The election for President was then going on, and Mann told me if Lincoln was elected the South would seccede; no doubt it had then been so settled, as Mann was afterwards one of the emmissaries to England from the South and was fully in the confidence of the party. I returned to New York on the 19th having spent 10 days in my visit south.

One curious thing happened while we were in New York, as shewing what the Yankies are. A man was to be hanged on Governor's Island, which is situated down the harbour. He was taken from New York in a steamer and the man in office invited a party of his friends to accompany him, providing them with ample refreshments on board, and by way of giving greater pleasure they steamed up the Hudson to the Gt Eastern to look at her, instead of taking the poor wretch they were about to hang direct to his doom.

On the 19 July we went for a trip to Niagara and the St Lawrence. We first went to Trenton Falls. The sail by steamer up the Hudson to Albany is very beautiful; it is done at a good speed by the large steamers they use. From Albany we went by rail to Utica, from whence we went next day to see the Trenton Falls. They are on a branch of the Mohawk; the falls are not large but are exceedingly beautiful. The narrow gorge in which they are situated is lined with trees and there is a comfortable hotel close at hand. The day was lovely and I enjoyed it very much. We returned to Utica in time to get the train to Niagara, travelling all night, and here we tried the American bed carriages. At the moderate speed at which they travel it is possible to lay flat very comfortably; the jar at high speeds prevents this. The berths were along each side of the carriage, the passage being between them. There are two tiers of berths and each one wide enough for two people; a curtain drawn across the front shuts you in very comfortably. As there were very few people travelling we were fortunate in getting the two berths to ourselves; my wife and I had one and Harry the other. But railway travelling in America is wretched; their republican notions of having only one class makes your company very mixed, and the carriages being all large open saloons with a door at each end and passage down the middle, prevents your having the slightest privacy even if you were a good large party of your own. The roads are dusty and the use of wood for fuel sends a quantity of charcoal into your carriage, mixed with the dust, so that when you have travelled all day you are as black as a sweep. People are also constantly passing through the carriages selling papers, books &c, and when the front end door is opened the rush of dust and dirt that comes in is very disagreeable.

Their plan of dealing with the luggage is a good one. An Express Co, as it is called, undertakes to take charge of it and deliver it to your hotel for a moderate cost. The fares are not low for the kind of accommodation you get, and your Yankee companions are the most free and easy people in the world. I was reading a book and a man behind me leaned over the back of my seat and read the pages with me, and complained I went on too fast as he was not ready to turn over at the same time I was; so I handed him the book and gave up my reading.

I was much disappointed with the general scenery of the country I travelled through, both in going to Washington & Niagara. There was no fine timber and most of the country was ugly in the extreme. We arrived at Niagara about 5 oclock on a lovely summer morning, and I need not say how grand the falls are, altho' the first impression is not equal to that left by a longer stay there. They grow upon you from day to day, each day seeming more grand. We were fortunate in having a full moon and the view of the falls by moonlight was wonderfully beautiful. I could have spent weeks here if time would have permitted me to do so. I stayed at a good hotel, the Clifton House, on the Canada side. The bridge across the river is a fine work, carrying both a railway and a common road; it is a suspension bridge. During our stay here we saw Blondin cross the river on a single rope and perform many wonderful feats on it. I cannot say the sensation was a pleasant one, and I was quite content with one day's exhibition.

We left Niagara on the 25th and crossed the Lake Ontario to Toronto, where we stayed with Mr Cumberland who was very attentive to us. Toronto is an imposing town with some fine public buildings.

From Toronto we went by a night train to take the steamer down the St Lawrence from Kingston. The sail down the St Lawrence is very beautiful, particularly the first part of it in passing the 1,000 Isles. These islands are small but covered with wood, & in the bright early morning were very, very beautiful. The whole distance to Montreal is very fine and passing down the rapids was a little exciting. Those near Montreal are any thing but safe; an Indian pilot was taken on board to pass them. It was about a 24 hours journey from Toronto to Montreal. The large bridge (tubular) built by Robt Stephenson[30] is a fine work 6,700 feet long and erected under great difficulties, as the ice coming down the river piles itself up to a great height. It was a costly affair and has not paid the railway companies. The town of Montreal is more than half French; the hotel not nearly so good as those in America.

From Montreal we returned to Albany by way of Lake Champlain and Lake George; these we passed in steamers. The scenery was truly beautiful, and interesting as being the great fighting ground between the English and French. We saw a number of Indians both here and in Montreal, many of them not bad looking but of a dark colour. The hotel where we stayed on Lake George is beautifully situated and the scenery by the bright moon was very fine. I was very much pleased with our trip and got back to New York on the 28 July.

On my return to N York we settled to carry out a pleasure trip with the big ship for two days; that is, we left New York on the Monday afternoon for Cape May, the mouth of the Delaware, spend the next day there and return the following night. We started with about 1,500 excursionists and a most extraordinary trip we had. The first night there was no end of fun, and as the moon was very bright and weather warm it did very well; but as the passengers had no beds to go to they laid about anywhere and in the morning woke up very cross, particularly the reporters to the press who thought they ought to have been supplied with comfortable cabins &c &c. An indignation meeting was held by them and they went ashore, not to return, the 2nd night. We did much better without them but the newspapers were full of abuse. Most of those who went the trip enjoyed it very much and passed resolutions accordingly, but on the whole this trip was not a success and did not pay us, and I was very glad when it was over. One thing I was glad to hear: on the first night a proposal was made having reference to Mr Brunel as the designer of the ship, and some hearty cheers given in his honour.

81

We had settled to take the ship to the Chesapeake for a week, and as soon as we returned to New York from Cape May we prepared to start, and sailed from New York on the 2nd August with about 100 passengers. We had none of the indignant press gentlemen, and had therefore a very pleasant voyage. We reached Old Point Comfort early the next morning and spent that day and night there; thousands of people crowded the little village to see the ship. I went over the large fort here and had also an opportunity of seeing a number of slaves who were brought by their masters to see the ship. The kindest and most friendly feeling seemed to exist amongst them, and I have never seen more happiness expressed in the face and manner of the working classes than appeared in these slaves. We left Point Comfort on the morning of the 5th Augt for Annapolis Roads in the Chesapeake, and had a beautiful sail all day. I was much amused at the disgust of the Yankee owners of one of the fast steamers. He had invited a large party to accompany him in the [*illegible*] steamer to meet us 30 or 40 miles down the bay, & his programme was he would steam round us and return ahead of us to Annapolis to be ready to receive us. When he met us he certainly turned round but did not succeed in keeping up with us, and when we cast anchor we could just see his smoke in the distance. Our ship certainly went along nobly at about 18 knots per hour, and the Yankees were mightly anoyed at the result of their trip. We had it dreadfully hot while we lay here, and thousands of people came from Baltimore and other places to visit the ship. The President visited us on the 9th; he lunched on board and had a large party of his cabinet with him. I had a long chat with him on American trade, as it was proposed to us to sail the ship between England & the South, with cotton. The President thought well of the scheme.

While here I went to Baltimore; it is a large and well built town. I returned by railway from Baltimore to New York on the 10 August, to get matters completed there to enable us to sail for England on the 16th from New York. I think I never was so entirely glad of any thing as I was when I felt, on that day, that our ship's head was turned towards England and I was quit of America. Of all the experiences I ever had in my life of dishonesty in business matters, none ever equalled the ordinary practice I met with as the ordinary practice in the dealings of the Yankees. Their word was of no value and their signature little better, without you were prepared to fight it in a court of law. There was no kind of imposition they did not practice upon us, and our agents, altho' a house of high standing in New York, did little to protect us. The jealousy between the North and South made it a matter of offence to them that we took the ship to the South. I left America with a feeling of rejoicing I never before experienced, and as I look back upon it after several years have passed my ideas are in no degree changed.

We had settled to call at Halifax, at the urgent request of the people there so that they might see the ship, and our run from New York was the quickest on record; a distance of 58 knots between two lighthouses was done in 3h 5m. We reached Halifax on the evening of the 18th Augt, and here we met with a little sharp practice, for altho' we thus went out of our way to please them they charged us 350£ for light dues and altho' we appealed to the Governor we failed to get it remitted. This was not much encouragement for us to stop in the place so we determined to start next morning and let the people see the ship in England if they liked. We worked all night putting our paddle floats out as far as we could as the ship would be very light before we reached England. The harbour of Halifax is a very fine one with very deep water up to the edge of the quay. Our ship went within very few yards of the quay wall.

We got up our anchor at 9 in the morning of Sunday the 19th and started direct for Milford Haven. We had a very pleasant run home, reaching Cape Clear on Sunday morning the 26th at 4am, and we dropped our anchor at Milford at 4pm. It was a very grand sight as we steamed up Milford Haven. The Channel Fleet, consisting of 11 or 12 ships was lying up the harbour in line, and as we passed them each ship manned her yards and gave us hearty cheers; a happy welcome to our home. A special train was waiting to take us to London but no one wanted to leave the ship that day, and our departure was postponed until the following morning, amid the cheers of the passengers. It is not often passengers wish to sleep another night on board ship after a voyage, but such is the comfort of the Gt Eastern that all felt regret that it was time to leave her.

The result of our voyage, altho' perfectly satisfactory as proving the speed and comfort of the ship, was not a profitable one. We carried very few passengers in either direction, and no goods, and the heavy expenses in America used up all the money we took for exhibiting her. Altho' this was our first voyage yet we were [not] stopped over much on account of any defect in the machinery. I was glad I had accompanied her, altho' I will not again undertake the duties of a show man, either of big ships or any thing else. We returned to Clewer on the 27th and was again comfortably settled in our home.

The Great Eastern was laid up at Milford for the winter and put on the gridiron there; a good deal was done to her—decks &c. My daily journal kept while away will give our proceedings more in detail than I have given them here.

I had two grand children from this year: Emily had a daughter in February and Anna one in August, so that I attained the dignity of a grandfather.

1861. My sister-in-law Elisabeth Ferguson died in Feby of this year at Cardiff; I went down to her funeral.

We had been hard at work on the Great Eastern all the winter at Milford, getting her ready for another trip to America. She sailed in May and made a good voyage, returning to Liverpool. She had about 7,000 tons of cargo on her return trip, chiefly corn, and the earnings of the voyage more than covered her expenses. We had some difficulty in getting her off the gridiron; it was an awful wet and rough night and by some blundering of the pilot her anchors were not let go in time, and she went into a man of war, doing her damage to the extent of 350£, which we had afterwards to pay. We sent her away again from Liverpool with a good lot of passengers in August. We were in capital spirits about her and I arranged after she sailed to go to Mr Baker's house near Worcester, who was at the time chairman of the Ship Co, to talk over our future, believing a bright one was in store for us. I went there and we had just finished dinner & were preparing to close in near a comfortable fire and have our chat, when the servant came in with a telegram saying the ship was off the Irish coast. This spoilt our wine and our hopes, and instead of discussing her future we had to speculate upon the cause of her return. Of course, this led us to no result and we went to bed hoping to hear news the following day.

I had not been very long asleep when a knock at my door awoke me and poor old Baker walked into my room with a fresh telegram in his hand. I will never forget the appearance of the old gentleman as he stood at the foot of my bed to read the telegram, wrapped up in a white flannel dressing gown and one of those old fashioned night caps on his head, a lamp in one hand and the telegram in the other. This telegram did not give us more information, so I went to sleep again, but in a short time another telegram arrived and a similar scene gone through. Next day we had full particulars: the ship had got into a heavy gale and her rudder shaft had broken, and she was left for a couple of days to the mercy of the wind & sea until a temporary arrang[emen]t could be made to steer her. She had a very bad time of it, but got safely into Queenstown. Both her paddles were carried away. We got her over to Milford again and put her on the gridiron for repairs; these repairs were very costly and cleared away much more than our profits. We, however, set about the work and during the winter got her all ready again for sea.

We started the new rail mill[31] at Swindon in May 1861. I had advised our directors to make their own rails, and at a cost of £25,000 put up a very good mill. I now began to think of retiring from the Gt Western. I had ample income independent of them and in my own mind settled to give up at the end of 25 years service, which would end in August 1862. I was further inclined to this by the prospect of an amalgamation taking place between the 3 companies, viz the Gt Western, the South Wales and the West Midland. I felt such an amalgamation would so alter our board that I would have new men to work with, strangers to me, and those likely to come from the West Midland not standing very high in character. I therefore quite resolved to leave them and wished to do so as I had no faith in the new directors carrying out the promise made to my brother William that he should succeed me. After events will shew I was right in my conclusions.[32]

I bought my steam yacht in August for Clewer.

1862. I was a good deal engaged this year in designing and building engines to work the Metropolitan underground railway, as our company had agreed to work it. Some years ago I tried some experiments as to the distance an engine would work without having any blast upon her fire, with a view of making such a line of railway where it would not do to have the gasses & steam from the chimney discharged into the tunnel. Mr Fowler had, with the assistance of Messrs Stephenson & Co of Newcastle, designed & built an engine for this purpose of the most extraordinary description and, as a trial soon found, quite useless. I simply made an ordinary engine but fitted it with tanks under the boiler into which I discharged the waste steam by reversing a valve at the bottom of the blast pipe, so that when the engine was in open cutting she worked like any other engine, but when in the tunnel the blast was stopped and a good ash pan damper destroyed the draft. This engine I found answered very well and has been the one used. Many suggestions were made; one was to fill the fire box with red hot bricks at the end of each trip, but such schemes never would have been practicable & Fowler's engine certainly was a complete failure.[33]

I stood god father to Dr Pavy's child on the 16th Jany 1862, and to my daughter Anna's on the 23 Jany.

The great exhibition at Kensington was held this year. Altho' the collection of things exhibited was very good, yet the building was far inferior to that held in 1851, and no doubt the first impression was wanting. The picture gallery was very good and 4 of my pictures were selected to go there. It was a nice lounge during the summer but will, I think, be the last that will be held.

Our big ship made 3 voyages to New York this year, each time increasing the number of her passengers. The last voyage, in August, she carried 1,530 out, but unfortunately, as she was entering Long Island Sound she toutched upon some rocks and did a great deal of damage to her outer skin, one hole being 80 feet long by 6 feet wide, with three other holes of less size. So little was this felt on board that none of the passengers had any knowledge of it until they got up in the morning at New York, and then only from a list she had got from the water between the skins on that side. This was a most unfortunate accident for us, and I fear to some extent a careless one. It was a fine moon light night when she struck and [she] was at the time slowing speed to take the pilot on board. The excuse made was that these rocks were not shewn on the chart. This accident detained the ship in New York for repairs until the early part of 1863. The work was very well arranged without putting her on a gridiron, but cost us about £70,000 and pretty well ruined us.

1863. The Metropolitan Railway was opened on the 10th Jany and I spent most of the day in the tunnel. On Sunday the 11th I had a serious attack of illness; it came on suddenly, as I fell down in the drawing room and was insensible for a few minutes. This confined me to the house for a few weeks. On the 13th of February the first gap was made in our family by the death of my favourite sister Anna. She had been a great sufferer for some time from cancer and was in London for advice. She was a good soul and well prepared to die. During the last ten days she was almost constantly asleep, and when she woke said 'has Jesus not taken me yet?'. God only knows whether her spirit might not have even then seen Heaven. Her loss was a great grief to us all. A family of 10 children had up to that time not had to mourn the death of one; all born had grown up into middle age. Poor Anna was buried in Kensall Green cemetery. Her husband married again but lived only a few months after his marriage.

Lord Shelburn having become Marquis of Landsdown resigned the Gt Western chair in the beginning of the year and Mr Walpole again took it for a time as a temporary arrangement. The medical men advised me to go abroad for a couple of months, and I left home with my wife and Harry on the 17th March. I went first to Paris where I stayed until the 23rd. Our friends Mr & Mrs Phill Pavy happened to be going to Paris at the same time and we went together. From Paris I went to Marseilles and on to Nice, which place we reached on the 27th. After staying here until the 31st we hired a capital carriage and 4 horses to take us to Pisa, on the way to Florence. This was a most lovely and enjoyable ride; I felt my health better and thoroughly appreciated it. We travelled about 25 to 30 miles per day & often had oxen or additional horses to help us up some steep hills. Being Easter we saw the Catholic churches &c in preparation. It is hard to believe so large a part of the people in this world can be misled by such unmeaning ceremonies—priest craft enforced by pomp and show.

We reached Pisa on the 8th Apl and went by rail from there to Florence, having arranged with our coachman to meet us at a station called Asinalunga on the line between Florence & Rome, and take us by the Terni road in the carriage. The railway was not then finished all the way, but we also wished to visit the interesting towns on the route. Florence is a very interesting place, richly filled with works of art; we stayed there until the 13th Apl and reached Rome on the 17th.

I had long wished to visit this famous city and was not disappointed. It is a place to spend months in, so filled is it with objects of deep interest. I look forward to paying it a longer visit at another time. We went on to Naples on the 21 Apl. This is a charmingly situated town but rather given to bad smells from defective drainage, and that being carried into the bay, when in certain winds it beats back upon the shore & would soon make any one ill. It drove me away before I intended. At other times the climate is delightful. I visited Vesuvius, going up to the top of the cone and eating egg roasted in the hot ashes. It was a dreadful job to get up the cone, but coming down was good fun. I would give much to see this mountain when in a state of eruption; it must indeed be a sublime sight.

I also visited and saw all that was to be seen of Herculaneum. There is not much; the excavations are very deep and only carried out to a small extent, but it shews the awful nature of the eruption that destroyed it. Sorrento, on the opposite side of the Bay from Naples is a charming place; I should like to have a good yacht here and spend some time. We went to see the blue grotto in the island of Capri; the effect of the light entering the cave through the water is most wonderful and extraordinary. The opening above the surface of the water is so small that only a small boat can get in, and then only in calm weather. I was very much pleased with the visit to this place. We crossed the bay in a boat from Capri to Naples, but the most deeply interesting day is to be spent amid the ruins of Pompeii, a town excavated from the ashes, with all the signs of actual former occupation. It is well such a town was buried 2,000 years ago and now brought to light. We thus see and learn the actual conditions under which men were at that time living. I could have dwelt for days amongst these ruins instead of a few hours accompanied by a guide. The tomb of Virgil shewn near Naples may or may not be the real one; no doubt he lived here and the tomb has been believed in for 17 centuries, so it would be sacrilege not to believe.

We left Naples on the 1st May and returned to Rome. When we arrived there there was a Sirroco blowing, what we in England would call a blight, but infinitely worse. I think it would be impossible to live many days in such an atmosphere; one felt as tho' there was nothing in the thick air to support life. Fortunately it only lasted a couple of days; it is said never to last more than three.

I saw a good deal of Mr Gibson & Mr Mozier, the sculptors, when I was in Rome, and bought some statuary from both. Gibson had just finished in clay a figure of a girl dancing. It was a beautiful work and I ordered one, but his death has prevented my getting it. I used to enjoy his studio, so many beautiful works were to be seen and he was a very pleasant man. It struck me as very singular how freely he gave up his time to visitors. The first time I went I knew nothing of him, nor had I any introduction, yet he received me most kindly and sat for fully an hour with us, telling us all kinds of amusing stories, and afterwards took much trouble to uncover some statues he had completed for us to see. Our sculptors in England make a mistake in this respect; they ought, as is done in Rome & Italy, to make their studios a kind of public exhibition where strangers would go and see their works, without feeling it was necessary to purchase or give an order, and so lead to a taste for sculpture in the many. Few men think of buying it as it is not placed before them. Had I felt, in visiting their studios, I must buy something, probabally I would not have gone and several things I purchased would have not been bought by me.

The Vatican contains a wonderful collection of works of art, a place to spend months in, and St Peter's is a glorious building. I did not see the Pope, but my wife and Harry did. I made an attempt one day to do so by going to a church where he was expected, but did not come. The church was something extraordinary for embelishment and there must have been several thousand candles lighted, altho' broad day light. I went to see some stairs said to be those up which our Saviour ascended into Pilate's house in Jerusalem. They are of marble but covered with wood to prevent their wearing out by the people who are constantly going up them on their knees. I did not try this plan but went up some ordinary ones to see the little chapel at the top. The Coliseum is a grand old ruin, but Rome is altogether a wonderful place, a place one could never weary of, and I left it with much regret on the 13th May.

We returned to Florence by water, by way of Civita Vechia and Leghorn, staying at Florence until the 18th, when we had a carriage and travelled for 2 days to Bologna by way of the Futa Pass. We stopped to see the curious escape of carburetted hydrogen gas from the surface of the earth at a place called Pietramala. It burns like a large Argand burner of about 12 feet in diameter, and the flame about 1 foot high. From Bologna we went by rail to Milan. I was much grieved in getting my letters there to find that my old friend Mrs Pavy had died at Elcombe on the 10th of May. I had for many years received from her great kindness. From Milan we went to Zurich, in Switzerland, by way of Como and the Splugen Pass. The scenery the whole way was very beautiful and grand. On leaving the valley the heat was very great, but when we got near the top of the Splugen it began to snow very hard and we travelled through 8 miles of snow, and dreadfully cold; with all our rugs &c and the carriage shut up we could not keep ourselves warm.

After spending a few days in Zurich, where I had a letter from Mr Saunders expressing a wish I should get back as early as I could, we started for home by way of Paris and reached London on the 1st of June. It was a great pleasure to get home again, for after all there is no place like it. I had enjoyed my trip very much, favoured with the most lovely weather, and Sardelli our courier took all trouble of my hands so that I had little to do but enjoy myself and acquire fresh health, which I did. My daily journal of the trip will give detail particulars of it.

On my return to London I found matters were getting into a difficulty with the Metropolitan Co, who read the agreement in a very different manner from what we did, and it ended in our giving them notice to cease working the line.

On the 30th June the Gt Eastern sailed again for New York with a very large number of passengers, and I went with her as far as Queenstown; but our funds had got so low that on her return from this trip we were obliged to lay her up, & the bondholders took possession of her, all the original capital having been lost. The two accidents cost us not less than 130,000£.

The amalgamation Act of the Gt Western with the West Midland and South Wales was passed this year,[34] and in Sept Mr Walpole resigned the chair and the amalgamated board appointed Mr Potter as chairman. This board consisted of 28 members, & there came in with the West Midland section a class of men we had not been accustomed to, viz Potter, Fenton, Parson, Watkin & Brown, men who were little guided by the usual principles that govern gentlemen of honour. They divided themselves into committees, and upon what was called the locomotive committee were put Parson, Brown & Watkin. Mr Talbot, who was chairman of the South Wales, was made chairman of this committee. When chairman of the South Wales he used to find fault with me to his shareholders because he thought I charged them too much for working his line. My first interview with them was well calculated to carry out what, there is no doubt, was their object, viz to disgust me with the concern in order that they might put in their own tools. I declined to remain in the room with them and got up and left, refusing again to go near them. A promise was made to me that a different course of conduct would be followed if I would again attend them. I therefore went, & at that meeting all went well enough. On the next occasion Parson & I got to pretty strong words and I left the room and never saw them again, nor did I ever attend the amalgamated board.

This of course could not last long, & I had before quite made up my mind to leave the company but had, and still did, refrain from doing so at the request of Mr Saunders and some of the other principal officers. As I before said, it would have played into the hands of those who had their own purpose to serve, and I was also anxious to help my brother William, if I could, before giving in my resignation, and I had some hopes that the old members of the Gt Western board would pull together against this West Midland gang. So I held my own.

My old friend Mr Saunders resigned in Septr, after, with some difficulty and much that was double dealing on the part of Potter, getting a pension of £1,250 a year granted him by the shareholders. Potter wanted him to resign and afterwards get his pension fixed, but Mr Saunders had to[o] good a knowledge of his man to do this. Had he done so he would have been sold, I have no doubt. But Mr Saunders gone was one of the difficulties removed from the path of Potter & Co.

Mr Gibson, the sculptor, came to spend a few days with me at Clewer. He was a most amusing man, but also had a high opinion of his own fame. When I was in Rome Mozier told me that Gibson was fond of giving them at their dinner club there an instance of the effect of his name. He was travelling once down the Gt Western Railway and fell asleep in the carriage, and so passed Reading station without getting out. He woke up at a small station where the train stopped afterwards, and there discovered his mistake and got out. He asked the porter on duty for his luggage, who told him it would be taken out at Reading. This Gibson could not understand and got into high words with the porter for not being able to let him have his luggage. When he asked the man if he knew who he was the man said no; when he told the porter he was John Gibson this so electrified the man that he immediately touched his hat and became exceedingly civil &, as Gibson thought, shewing the extent of his high reputation. When I explained to Mozier the real cause of the effect on the porter he was very delighted at the thought of the fun they would get out of poor old Gibson, as the fact was, the man thought the John Gibson was the gentleman of that name who was one of the chief officers of the company.

On the 24th of November 1863 I lost my dear mother, a heavy grief. What a good mother she had been to me, to us all. What an example of all that makes human nature true and noble, a true liberal-minded Christian, ever cheerful with a fine reliance on the mercy and goodness of her Maker. How often have I dwelt upon that calm, serene spirit. Oh my mother, how little, as we pass through life in your presence do we sufficiently value all that you are to us, the mother of 10 children, all of whom have benefited by her example and advice. She died with the knowledge that all had striven to rise to a creditable position in the world. We laid her on the 24th in the same vault at Claines church as my father. May I, my dear mother, be as well prepared for that change as you were. Some of her hair was sent to me, and the following very favourite verses.[35]

In March 1863, after a good deal of negotiation, I joined Mr Whitworth of Manchester in forming a company to carry on his works, my chief object being to place Harry there as a future provision for him, and I also thought the gun work would be an amusement for me when I retired from the Gt Western Railway. The company, [which] only consisted of 7, was to bring us within the Act. Lord Torrington, Sir J. E. Tennent, Mr Pender & Mr Aston, with Whitworth and myself were the directors, and in fact the company; & Mr Keeler, a nephew of Whitworth's, was the managing director.

1864. In the commencement of this year a great effort was being made to make another attempt to lay an Atlantic cable.[36] The Atlantic Co could not find the money and it was suggested to form a strong Co who would purchase Glass, Elliot's works and also the Gutta Percha works,[37] and by a good command of capital be able to undertake the contract with a large payment in shares & bonds. I was asked to join this combination and became a director; this I did, taking £20,000 in shares. Mr Pender of Manchester was elected chairman and we had no difficulty in completing all the arrangts. The Great Eastern ship was to form part of the work; we had not been able to do any thing with her and the company was wound up, the bond holders being in possession, and she was put up to auction in Liverpool. Mr Brassey, Mr Barber and myself being the largest bondholders (the bonds in the whole amounting to £100,000) we then determined to buy her if she went for 80,000 or less, and Mr Barber went down to Liverpool to attend the sale when, strange to state, a ship that had cost a million of money and was worth £100,000 for the materials in her, was sold to us for £25,000. We offered the bondholders the option of coming in to form a new company, allowing them to come in taking shares equal to the amount of their bonds as fully paid up. This about £75,000 did, and we paid the others their proportions of the 25,000 for which she sold. I then arranged with the Telegraph Construction Company (the Co we had formed for laying the Atlantic cable) to charter the ship to them, taking payment in cable shares to the extent of £50,000 for the work, they to make all the alterations and pay all expenses. I was elected chairman of the ship company, Mr T. Brassey jun & Mr Barber being the other directors.

Our Telegraph Construction Company was formed in Apl 1864 and we at once set to work in making preparations for the manufacture of the cable. I spent a great deal of time & took much interest in it.[38] We brought the ship from Liverpool to Shearness in July to fit her for the work. I came round in her and spent a few pleasant days at sea. Dr Pavy came round with me. The remainder of the year was very fully occupied in our preparations and I often visited the ship at Shear Ness; putting the large tanks[39] in her made a great havoc in her internal construction.

At the March meeting of the Great Western shareholders Parson was kicked out of the directors by the shareholders on account of some land transaction in connection with the Hammersmith line which did him little credit as an honourable man. I cannot say so marked a disapproval of his conduct was not his due. Having seen him out of the direction I felt the time had come when I could no longer hold my position either with credit or comfort to myself. I had seen nothing of the board or committees and had contented myself by writing written protests against many of their acts; one was a most injurious one to the interests of the company. Some years before we had bought a colliery[40] in South Wales for the purpose of supplying ourselves with coals so as to be independent of the coal owners who had, on two or three occasions, combined against us to keep up the price. This colliery had in a few years paid us a profit of about £90,000, taking the coals &c at the market price. Potter & Brown were interested in some collieries they had bought, and it came into their heads that however good a thing such a colliery was for the company, it was not good for their private interests, & that it ought to be sold. I, on hearing of this, wrote a strong report to Potter on the subject, calling his attention to the facts. Finding that he did not communicate this report to the board I sent a copy of it to several of the old Gt Western directors, but without succeeding in staying the improper act, and it was afterwards sold; a shameful transaction.

As I before said, having seen Parson kicked out, I made up my mind to resign at once, and called upon Potter. But before telling him what I intended I asked him what he proposed to do about my brother William[41] if I resigned, pointing out to him his qualifications for my successor and the conditions upon which he had come to Swindon. He then gave me his assurance that he would do his best to carry out that arrangt. I then told him I intended in a few days to send in my resignation (a very pleasant piece of information to him) and I did so, giving the required 6 months notice. But no sooner was this done than I found he had not the slightest intention to keep his word, and used every kind of tactics not only to set William aside but also Mr Armstrong, who had been my assistant on the Northern Division from the amalgamation of those lines. I spoke to him on the subject but found him false in every thing. I soon learned he had promised to appoint an engineer from Watkin's line, the Manchester & Sheffield,[42] and that he had asked this gentleman to attend the next board for the purpose of receiving the appointment. This was more than I could stand, and I at once wrote to each of the directors with whom I felt I had any influence telling them it was right they should either appoint my brother or Armstrong, both qualified men in their service. The result was they pulled together for once, and Potter was outvoted at the board and his friend from the north was sent back without his appointment, and they appointed Armstrong. I felt this was the best thing to do, as had my brother been appointed he would not have been comfortable with such men as the West Midland men always pulling against him. Armstrong being appointed, my responsibility was fixed to cease in June. My notice did not expire until the 5 October, and I attended at my office until the 7th September.

I then closed my connexion with the company as an officer after 27 years service. It was a source of great regret and vexation to me that I had been persuaded to remain the two last years; I wished I had carried out my intention of acting before the amalgamation Act came in force and I had never had anything to do with the new board. Up to that time, from my first joining the company in 1837, I had never had an angry word or a disagreeable feeling with any member of the board. I had always possessed their full and entire confidence, and my service under them had been a life of great contentment. I had ever striven hard for the companies interests and met with their entire support; nor, as I look back over those many years, can I recall one instance when a director forgot the companies interest for his own personal needs. They had ever been a high minded and honourable board, but what else could be expected from such men as Russell, Walpole, Ld Barrington, Mr Mills and the others equally to be esteemed? If they erred at any time in policy they never swerved from the course of honour. I am, and ever will be, deeply grateful for the many acts of kindness I have received at their hands, and will ever feel it a proud boast that with such men I, for 25 years, associated, and received their confidence and esteem. Had matters continued in their hands I doubt whether, as long as health & strength lasted me, I would have left the service; it would have been a task I might talk of, but one very difficult to fulfill.

After what had taken place it was not possible for my brother William to remain in the service of the company, so he sent in his resignation also. To assist him I formed a small company to buy the Vulcan Foundry works, near Warrington, he being appointed the managing director. I have since often thought of my mother's words when I went from home to those works in Jany 1834, when she told me not to be content until I was manager of the works. Altho' not a manager in the sense intended, I am so as being a director of the company, and the office of manager has fallen on a younger son. I was very sorry that my brother had been so badly used by Potter & Co; it was a great disappointment to him and to me, as I should have liked to hand over my work into his hands. I trust all is for the best.

After I gave up the Gt Western I attended every day at the offices of the Whitworth Company in Pall Mall, taking charge of the London department. It was an amusement to me, giving me an object in life without which I fear I could not get on with any happiness. It also left me at liberty to give a good deal of time to the cable work. We were trying hard to get Whitworth's guns adopted by the government, but this was a very uphill game and Whitworth somehow managed to offend all the people who he ought to have conciliated.

In the middle of this year I was asked to stand as Member for the Borough of Cricklade[43] at the next election, and after some hesitation I agreed to do so. Mr Merryweather, Sir John Wild and other landowners were anxious to get in a second Conservative, and I have no doubt thought my influence with the Swindon men would secure my election.

To oblige Mr Robt Tweedy of Truro I undertook a kind of contract for working the Colne Valley Railway. He had a large stake in it and while I took the working he took the risk. This was made for two years, 1865 & 1866; it gave me little trouble.[44]

On September the 22nd 1864 my old and good friend Mr Saunders died. He had enjoyed his pension only a year. He was one of the most able of our railway men and in his time had probably had a greater amount of influence than any other. He was a perfect gentleman and much liked by all the officers. We presented him with a very handsome testimonial in Jany. We had worked together for nearly my whole life and never had a disagreement. He was always a good friend to his brother officers and a man of high honour. I attended his funeral at Kensall Green cemetery; how many of those who have been my associates in life have passed from the world before me. I am glad to have a good marble bust of him by Durham.

1865. As Parliament was to be dissolved this year I had to begin my canvas. I went to Swindon on the 3rd March to meet a few of the leading workmen and appoint a committee. Odd enough, the man who was elected as chairman of the committee was a George Adams, who had been a Chartist in his time and still retained very liberal ideas. This was an odd chairman of a Conservative committee, and I felt a little anxious as to the wisdom of it, but I would be wrong if I did not state that Adams could not have taken a more earnest and zealous a part for me if he had been a Conservative all his life. I went again to Swindon to attend my first public meeting on the 22 March, and had to make my maiden political speech. The meeting passed off well, pledging them to give me their support, and the disagreeable job of making a canvas had to be undertaken. In a borough like Cricklade, spread over about 25 miles square, it was no light or short task; all April and half of May were consumed in this daily work. I took Adams and Geo Dicks with me and having, fortunately, very fine weather, we spent a jolly time, but the asking for votes is a detestable office, and more particularly from small tradesmen, a shoemaker most of all. It was necessary I should make this canvas early as the cable work was progressing fast and I intended to go out with the ship, and might not even be in England at the time of the election, as happened to be the case.

After I left the Gt Western the officers and servants of the company determined to present me with an address and to make a present to my wife. The 3rd of June 1865 was the day fixed for my receiving it at Swindon. Great preparations had been made and everything was done to shew their kindly feelings towards me. I hope those who succeed me will value that address more than any thing I can leave behind me, and also preserve the broach & earrings as heir looms in the family for ever. Man can receive no higher reward on earth than that of the good will and esteem of those with whom he has been associated through life, & my life had been passed in daily communication, both as master and brother officer, with those who gave expression to their feelings on this occasion, and I count this 3rd of June as the highest day in my life. The following printed account of the day's proceedings will best describe it.[45]

All things being ready for the cable expedition I joined the ship at Sheerness on the 10th July. We expected to sail on the 12th, but did not actually sail until the 15th. The work of the ship was all ready in time but the cable department were a little behind time. Capt James Anderson of the Cunard service had been appointed our captain, and future experience fully justified the choice; I found him a most able man.[46] While I was on board the ship the election at Cricklade took place. The nomination was on the 12 July; at this, Lord Elliot and myself were elected by shew of hands. The poll took place on the 13th when Goddard polled 978, Gooch 879, Elliot 772.

I have nothing to thank Goddard and some of his friends for in this election. He certainly acted a most selfish part, refusing to act in any way in my favour altho' I secured for him the votes of nearly all the men at New Swindon. Should I ever stand again I will certainly let him fight his own battles at New Swindon. Had he done, with his supporters, for me what I did for him I would have been at the head of the poll, or had I let our men plump for me the same would have been the result. I need not say I felt a little anxious as I waited on board the ship for the result of the election, and was kept a day longer in suspense than need have been the case by the telegram not reaching me, so that I did not know until the afternoon of the day following the election that I was elected, then having it from Mr Elliot[47] who came from London that day and also brought the papers with him. My brother William represented me at the election and they had a very rough time of it for, as usual, there was a great row at Cricklade, and I was glad to think I was saved the annoyance and excitement of it. This election cost me about £2,600—a great deal of money for very little. The men at Swindon voted very true for me.

We sailed from Sheerness on the 15th July, ship drawing 28ft 6in forward and 34ft 6in aft. Our departure was witnessed by a very large number of people and we were heartily cheered. The day was very fine and all looked bright and hopeful for our expedition. We did not make very rapid progress, the bottom of the ship being very foul and her trim not good as she was too much down by the stern. On the 18th we had very bad weather and overtook the Caroline steamer off The Lizard. She had sailed several days before us with the Irish shore end and we had hoped she would have reached Valentia and got it laid before we arrived there. The sea was too much for her and we took her in tow, but it was an awful sight to see how she laboured and the seas washed over her. I sat up until past 12 at night in the bridge house, watching her lights. That on her mast head, as we saw it over our stern, was performing most extraordinary gambols; now it sunk down out of sight and again shot up into the sky like a rocket, and rolled from side to side in a fearful manner. It was difficult to believe that in the hull of that ship a number of human beings were living. We all felt very anxious for her fate; not only for the lives of those on board, but also for the safety of our shore end. Early the next morning the towing cable parted, but fortunately the weather had a good deal moderated. I will never forget those hours we watched the Caroline

We reached Beerhaven in Bantry Bay in the evening of the 19th, having early in the morning reached Valencia and seen the Caroline safely into that harbour. We then also found the two men of war steamers appointed to accompany us, the Terrible and Sphinx, in readiness. As it might be several days before it would be possible for the shore end to be laid, our captain determined to return to Bantry Bay to wait. This is a beautiful harbour but there is no kind of port in it. The rush of the Irish on board when we dropped our anchor was an entertaining scene, bringing with them milk, eggs, poultry &c for sale, and our decks soon looked like a market—but it was not a cheap one; Paddy thought he would make a good harvest, if a short one. We were also visited while in this bay by most of the families living within a reasonable distance. Some young ladies living on the shore of Beerhaven were friends of Moriarty; there were 3 of them and we found them nice jolly girls; their name was O'Sullivan. We enjoyed our few idle days in this place very much, and were joined there by the two war steamers. The Terrible was commanded by a Capt Napier and the Sphinx by a Capt Hamilton, the latter a very nice fellow, the former did not seem to have his heart in the work and we did not fancy he would be of any use if we needed his services. His first officer, a Lieut Prince, fortunately did feel an interest in the work and he did what the Capt omitted. We received inteligence late at night on the 22nd that the shore end was laid, and we immediately started for Valencia where we arrived early in the morning of the 23rd. It was a glorious day and we had no difficulty in making the splice and got it completed by 4 oclock, when we started on our important & anxious task of laying the cable.

It was a beautiful sight as we started, the number of steamers collected and the fineness of the weather putting us all in hopeful spirits. I certainly had a full belief in the success of our work; no precautions seemed to have been lost sight of as far as human judgment could foresee. Sir Robt Peel, then Secretary for Ireland, the Knight of Kerry, Barber and many others came on board to see the splice made and gave us a hearty cheer when our paddles turned round and the ship's head commenced her westward course. W. Russell of The Times, H. O'Neil the painter and Robt Dudley, also a painter, went with us, Russell to write a report of our work for publication (which he did in a very able manner), Dudley went to make the sketches &c for the book, and O'Neil went in hopes he might get some scenes to paint. Altogether we had a very pleasant party on board, and our first evening was one full of hope as we watched the cable run out so smoothly and quietly into the deep, and I went to bed satisfied but was awoke at 3am on the following morning of the 24th by the paddles stopping. I was soon on deck and then found that a fault had shewn itself in the cable,[48] and the tests shewed it to be about 10 miles from the ship. This news was a sad damper on our spirits and hopes. The cable was at once cut and got round to the bows to begin the process of hauling in. Our machinery now proved defective in power and the process was a very slow one. Fortunately there was neither any sea or wind, but we only recovered about half a knot per hour. On the morning of the 25th as we were sitting at breakfast, it was reported to us that the fault had come on board. What a thrilling sensation of joy did this announcement produce in one's heart; we were all soon on deck. Just before breakfast Canning & I had agreed it would be better not to waste more time in getting in the fault, but to return to the splice and begin again. The object in continuing the hauling-in after that was to try some alterations we had made in the hauling-in machinery.

We soon set to work to make a new splice and had completed this by 2 oclock on the day, and the ship's head was again put to the west. In doing this I was standing on the paddle box with the Capt with the happy feeling of having got over our first mishap, when we saw Canning running towards us, calling out to stop the ship. This seemed to make one's heart to die within one; he told us all the signals had stopped. Steps were at once taken to discover the cause, but without effect, and we were just about to cut the cable and begin hauling in again when a signal was obtained from the shore, and we learned that it was a neglect of the instructions that had caused us this anxiety [and] that the cable was all right; but what a miserable 2 hours I had passed through. We started again at 4 and all went on well. We paid out the cable at about 6½ knots per hour with a strain of 13 to 15 cwt on the dynamometer, but on the 29th July, in the middle of the day, all signals with the shore stopped, shewing a more serious fault than the former one, & we were also in 2,000 fathoms water (in the former case only 500), and from the difficulty experienced in raising the cable from 500 it was an anxious question whether our machinery could lift it 2,000. All was perfectly calm, both sea & wind, and we made the attempt and succeeded in getting the fault in board about half past nine at night. We had paid out 707 miles when this 2nd fault occurred, and were 634 N[autical] miles from Valencia. We did not get all complete to start until 8 am on the 30th July. These faults occurring made us very anxious, and when we examined them we found them caused by a short piece of wire forced through the cable and in contact with the copper conductor, and this second one looked so like a wilfull damage that we suspected some one in the ship had done it. We took all strange men out of the tank and arranged for one of us to watch by turns in the tank, where the damage, if maliciously done, was effected.

All went well with us until the morning of the 2nd August, when Cyrus Field was on watch in the tank, and at 5 oclock another fault was reported and the ship stopped. We were then about 1,000 miles from Valencia and in Lat 51–25, Long 29–1. Steps were at once taken to haul in, the depth being about 2,000 fathoms. At 1.30 pm I was in my cabin when Canning came in to tell me the cable had broken and was lost. Oh what a sad blow this was; only the night before Canning & I had been calculating with some certainty on our reaching Heart's Content all right,[49] as another day would have taken us into comparatively shallow water whence we could pick up the cable if it did break. I will never forget this hour or the effect it had upon all engaged. Had we been one family and just lost a dear father or mother, our faces could not have worn a more down cast expression. No one spoke at dinner and all seemed to remain alone in their cabins. Poor O'Neil, I think, felt it more than any one, but indeed we all had heavy hearts; but it was necessary to take some steps about our lost friend, and we determined upon making an attempt to recover it.

The cause of this fracture, in my judgment, was putting a chain stopper on to it. The cable had caught on one of the projecting hawse holes in the bow of the ship, and to relieve it this stopper was put on and I have no doubt it cut the cable. Canning and the cable people blamed the bow of the ship but I am sure this was not so, as there was no part sharp enough to have such an effect. It was a mistake to use a chain stopper for such a purpose, and all the sailors and nautical part of our crew said no one but a land lubber would have done so. The cable people said a rope stopper would not hold it, but this was not so as we, in the next voyage, often used rope to hold the cable.

We had brought with us grapnels and lines to meet such a contingency, and lost no time in getting one down. Fortunately we had been able to get a capital observation of our position at 12 oclock, so that we knew exactly where to find the broken end. We let down the grapnel with 2,500 fathoms of line and allowed the ship to drift across the cable, and hooked it. We then hauled it up, but when it was about 700 fathoms from the end one of the shackles in the line broke, and our labour so far was lost. Fog and bad weather prevented us making another trial until the 7th, when we again lowered the grapnell. We hooked the cable and hauled at it all night with the ship's capstan, as our own machine had broken down, and at 7 in the morning of the 8th after raising the cable about 1,000 fathoms, another shackel of the line broke. This was very disheartening work and I felt certain our tackle was not strong enough to lift it to the surface. We had now also lost so much of our line that we had to make up a line out of what was left, assisted by some of the ship's cables. We were not inclined to give up the chance as long as we had any line left. We lowered the grapnel again on the 10th but it fouled the chain and did not hook the cable. It was again lowered on the 11th and we hooked the cable. It was raised about 700 fathoms when at 7 in the evening the line broke at the capstan and our last hope was gone. We had lost about 6 miles of line and could do no more, so orders were at once given to turn the ship's head for England, and by 9 oclock we had said good bye to the Terrible and were on our way home. We lost the Sphinx the 2nd day after starting; she stopped to make a sounding for us and never appeared in sight again. It was wonderful that in every case when we were in trouble the winds and sea became calm, and often, both before and after were very rough. We had now had no communication with England since the cable broke on the 2nd, and they were in ignorance of what had become of us.

We steamed direct for home, having a pleasant voyage and in good spirits, altho' we had failed, yet that very failure convinced me not only that we could lay a cable across the Atlantic but that with proper machinery and tackle we could recover the lost end. This feeling was universal in the ship, and all looked forward to its accomplishment the following year; we only considered our success postponed. Our confidence was greatly increased; we had also learned to place great confidence in the skill and judgment of Capt Anderson, who seemed to be able to handle the ship like a yacht. As Mr Russell and others have written a very full and detailed account of our expedition I refer to that for the public part of it, and to my own daily journal for my private views from day to day.

We made Crookhaven at 7 am on the 17 August and there landed Russell and sent our letters and telegrams to our friends, who were, we feared, getting very anxious about us; 16 days had passed without any inteligence of us. A common feeling existed that we had gone to the bottom and much anxiety was felt. We reached Brighton early in the morning of the 19th and as I was anxious to get home, as well as others, I arranged to be put ashore here. It was a foggy morning and we had difficulty in making the place and, much to the astonishment of the natives, they saw, when the fog rose about 8 oclock in the morning, the Gt Eastern lying about a mile off their pier. The landing was a most amusing scene; thousands of people crowded the shore, and if we had been people come down from the moon we could not have excited greater curiosity. I was truly glad to find my self back at pretty Clewer soon after 2 oclock in the afternoon. Emily was there to meet me, but my wife, who had been in Cornwall staying with her sister,[50] did not get home until later in the evening.

Thus concluded a very anxious and eventful voyage. I never spent so anxious a 6 weeks before. My son Alfred went with us, engaged in the engine staff.

NOTES

1 Birmingham & Oxford Junction Railway Act, 9 & 10 Vict cap 337, 3 August 1846.
2 The dynamometer car was almost certainly the first ever built, and is an indication of Gooch's very thorough and professional approach to his work.
  See MacDermot, *GWR*, I, 412. *Railway Magazine*, February 1940, 65–8.
3 'Observations of the resistences to railway trains at different velocities', read 18 April, 16 and 23 May and 6 June 1848.
4 It was intended that the atmospheric system (*see* p 46) should be used on the South Devon line, and in view of its alleged superiority to locomotives on steep gradients Brunel laid out the line with much steeper gradients than would otherwise have been acceptable. The atmospheric plant not being ready, the line was opened on 30 May 1846 using borrowed Great Western engines. Although some atmospheric trains did run later, the system proved to be a complete fiasco, and the company contracted with Gooch and his partners for the supply of locomotives (*see post*, p 67).
5 The identity of his fishing friends has not been established. J. Rea may be a relative of M. C. Rea or Rae, at that time locomotive superintendent of the Bristol & Exeter Rly and later works manager at Swindon (*qv*). An Elvira Rea of Exeter was godmother to Gooch's son Charles in 1845.
6 Fulthorpe House stood on the site of the gardens between Warwick Avenue, Harrow Road and Blomfield Road, near the Paddington Canal basin. Lucas's map of Paddington, 1855, shows Tunstall House, then occupied by the Croskey family (two of whose daughters married Henry and Frank Gooch) and Fulthorpe House, as a pair. Gooch acquired Tunstall House in 1868 and added it to his own house (*see* pp 145, 147).
7 8 Warwick Villas, Harrow Road. From correspondence with his father-in-law (BRB records HRP 1/6) it is clear that Gooch did contemplate building a house at Swindon. Writing on 2 March 1843 Mr Tanner says 'it seems a natural conclusion to come to . . . I think you should have quite a mansion for the sum you name'.
8 6 passengers were killed and 13 injured when an express ran into a horse-box and cattle truck.
  See MacDermot, *GWR*, I, 343.
9 This was the well-known *Fairfield* steam rail-car built by W. Bridges Adams. It was first used on the Tiverton branch and later on the Weston line.
  See Locomotives of the Great Western Railway (Railway Correspondence & Travel Society), Part 11 (1956).
10 The engine was *Goliah*, a six-coupled goods engine of 1842.
11 Later renamed Wrangaton.
12 For an account of Gooch's Masonic career see *The Freemason's Chronicle*, Vol VIII, No 191 (24 August 1878).
13 The diarist used the term 'sister-in-law' in a wider sense than is done today. Mary Laing was presumably the sister of the Rev William Laing, husband of Gooch's youngest sister Frances.
14 This was John Fowler (1826–64), pioneer of steam ploughing and builder of traction engines, and not John (later Sir John) Fowler, engineer of the Metropolitan Railway (*qv*.)
  Drawings of a ploughing engine, the *Australia*, are in the small book of locomotive drawings, *D. Gooch's Sketch Book*, now in the custody of the Curator of Historical Relics, British Railways Board.
  Lord Willoughby de Eresby exhibited a ploughing engine at the Great Exhibition in 1851 which may well have been the one constructed by Gooch. (*See* Official Catalogue, Vol III, Agricultural Machines, No 195.)

15 Under the contract, twelve 4–4–0 saddle tank engines (the 'bogie' engines) and four 0–6–0 saddle tank engines were built by outside firms, including some from Bedlington and some from Evans' Haigh Foundry. The contract was in the name of Evans and Geach only, though Gooch was clearly involved financially as well as being the designer of the engines.

William Gooch, Daniel's younger brother whom he had rescued from the path of a locomotive at Tredegar when he was a small boy, was placed in charge of the contract at the South Devon works at Newton (now Newton Abbot). A further 24 engines were built under a second contract in 1859.

See MacDermot, *GWR*, II, chap VI. *Locomotives of the Great Western Railway* (Railway Correspondence & Travel Society), Part 2 (1952).

16 A bronze medal, later given to Gooch by the board. *Lord of the Isles*, one of the 8-foot single class, was built in March 1851 and withdrawn in June 1884. She was preserved at Swindon until 1906 when, lamentably, she was broken up.

17 The Great Western was a purely broad-gauge line until the acquisition of the Shrewsbury & Chester and Shrewsbury & Birmingham lines in 1854. From that time its narrow-gauge mileage steadily increased and broad-gauge lines were gradually either made into mixed gauge or converted to 4ft 8½in, until, with the conversion of the lines in the West Country in 1892 the broad gauge was finally abolished.

18 Gooch's explanation differs from that in MacDermot's *History* (I, 343) where it is stated that the cause was believed to be a broken frame in the leading first-class carriage.

19 The Mechanics' Institution at Swindon, as Gooch says, was a very great benefit to the employees at the works, and it was, indeed, the centre of most social and educational activity in the new town for a long period. For a short account *see Studies in the History of Swindon* (Swindon, 1950), 117–20.

20 The long drawn out battle over the Shrewsbury & Chester and Shrewsbury & Birmingham lines is dealt with by MacDermot (I, chap VIII).

The Great Western Hotel, adjoining Paddington Station, was opened on 9 June 1854 and leased to a separate company until 1869, when it was taken over by the GWR.

See MacDermot, *GWR*, I, 162–3, 171; II, 269.

21 This may seem surprising in view of the long-standing hostility between the GWR and the LSWR, both of whom were eager to capture the West Country for the broad and narrow gauge respectively. But this is not the only instance of friendly relations between officers of rival companies, or between engineers with opposing views, as witness the close friendship between I. K. Brunel and Robert Stephenson.

22 The diarist is wrong here. Walpole only agreed to act as chairman during the parliamentary recess; he did not become Home Secretary again until 1858.

23 He became chairman in May 1857.

24 The GWR board at this time was faced with internal disagreements as well as a serious financial situation brought about by heavy expenditure in purchasing lines in the north and by poor traffic returns. The lowest dividend ever paid by the company was 1¼ per cent in 1858.

See MacDermot, *GWR*, I, chap IX.

25 Clewer Park, Windsor. *See plate XIII*

26 It is clear from the diary that Gooch had a great love of trees, and also of flowers, of which he frequently gathered specimens to press between the pages of his diary. This he did with more than usual artistry and skill, and they have survived for nearly a century in a remarkable state of preservation. *See plate XIV*

27 From Plymouth to Truro, later extended to Falmouth.

See MacDermot, *GWR*, II, chap VII. Woodfin, R. J. *The Centenary of the Cornwall Railway* (1960).

28 The *Great Eastern* was built by John Scott Russell for the Eastern Steam Navigation Co, formed in 1851. By the time the ship was launched on 31 January 1858 the company had run short of money, and at the end of the year a new company, the Great Ship Co, was formed, and work on the vessel continued. In January 1860 disagreements on the board over the continued employment of Russell led to the reorganisation referred to by

Gooch (p 76). Gooch became a director and also engineer to the company in succession to Brunel who had died just after the launching.

After the voyage to America in 1860 she twice suffered severe damage and the cost of repairs soon put the Great Ship Co into difficulties and, as described by the diarist (pp 92–3) she was sold by auction in 1864 to a new group of whom Gooch became chairman, with William Barber, the original chairman, and Thomas Brassey (*qqv*) as the other directors.

A notebook kept by Gooch in connection with his work on the ship appeared in Sotheby's saleroom on 23 June 1969 and is described in the catalogue of the sale (item 163). It is now in the National Maritime Museum.

The story of the *Great Eastern* is told, in a somewhat dramatised and journalistic manner, in James Dugan's *The Great Iron Ship* (1953). Her designer is given very different treatment in L. T. C. Rolt's fine biography *Isambard Kingdom Brunel* (1957), in which the building and launching of the ship are treated in detail.

29   26 October 1859. The *Royal Charter* was wrecked off Anglesey with the loss of more than 450 passengers and crew.

30   The Victoria Bridge over the St Lawrence at Montreal was the largest of Robert Stephenson's tubular bridges, of which the Conway and Britannia Bridges in North Wales were the first. The single tube of the Victoria Bridge was 6,588ft long. It was first used on 24 November 1859 and was officially opened by the Prince of Wales just after Gooch's visit.

See Rolt, L. T. C. *George & Robert Stephenson* (1960), 315–17.

31   The mill was for wrought iron bridge rail, then in general use on the GWR. Steel rail began to appear on the line in 1867 and the mill ceased to be used.

See MacDermot, *GWR*, II, 266.

32   See *ante*, p 73 and *post*, pp 90–1.

33   The GWR subscribed £175,000 to the North Metropolitan Rly Co for their line from Paddington to the City, hoping it would act as a feeder to their own line and give them a route to the heart of the City. The GWR supplied the rolling stock, including 22 2-4-0 tank engines, when the line opened from Bishop's Road to Farringdon Street on 10 January 1863. The GWR withdrew in the following August after disagreements.

The fireless engine designed by John Fowler, the Metropolitan engineer, and known as 'Fowler's Ghost', used hot bricks to maintain steam. Gooch's Metropolitan engines were the first condensing engines in the country.

See MacDermot, *GWR*, I, 229–31, 415–16. Baker, C, *The Metropolitan Railway* (1951). Robbins, M. *Points & Signals* (1967), 120–4.

34   The amalgamation of the West Midland with the GWR took effect on 1 August 1863. The Oxford, Worcester & Wolverhampton Rly, the principal constituent of the West Midland, had been one of the pawns in the gauge war as far back as the 1840s, and relations with the GW were never friendly and at times violently hostile. Under the amalgamation act six WM directors joined the GW board, and from the first they hardly endeared themselves to Gooch. Among the six were Edward Watkin (*qv*), one John Parson (*qv*) and Richard Potter (*qv*) who had resigned from the GW board in 1856. The WM chairman, William Fenton, became deputy chairman of the new GW board.

For a full account of the West Midland and the amalgamation *see* MacDermot, *GWR*, I, chap X.

35   The diarist has inadvertently repeated the date of death for the date of burial, which should read 1 December.

The verses are written on two folded sheets of mourning paper inserted in the diary together with a copy of the inscription on the vault at Claines (see I, n 16).

36   The first two attempts to lay a telegraph cable across the Atlantic, in 1857, were failures. In 1858 one was laid successfully from Ireland to Newfoundland, but after less than 300 messages had been sent the insulation broke down, partly owing to the use of too high a voltage.

The cables of 1857–8 were laid by the Atlantic Telegraph Company, founded in 1856, of which James Stuart-Wortley (*qv*) was chairman. The directors included Cyrus Field,

Curtis Lampson and John Pender (*qqv*). In 1864 the cable works of Glass, Elliot & Co and the Gutta Percha Co were merged into a new body, the Telegraph Construction & Maintenance Co, of which John Pender became chairman and Richard Glass (*qv*) joint managing director. On the board were Gooch and Elliot.

This new firm took the entire responsibility for laying the 1865 cable under contract to the Atlantic Telegraph Co. Gooch succeeded Pender as Chairman in 1867, and Sherard Osborn (*qv*) succeeded Glass as managing director in the same year.

After the failure of the 1865 cable the capital needed for a further expedition was raised by a third company, the Anglo-American Telegraph Co, founded in March 1866, with Gooch as chairman and some of the Telegraph Construction board as directors.

See Field, H. M. *History of the Atlantic Telegraph* (1866). Russell, W. H. *The Atlantic Telegraph* (nd, *c* 1866). For a detailed account *see* Bright, Charles. *Submarine Telegraphs, their history, construction and working* (1898).

37 The two firms manufacturing the cable. The new firm was known as the Telegraph Construction and Maintenance Company.

See *The Telcon Story*, 1850–1950 (The Telegraph Construction & Maintenance Co Ltd, 1950).

38 Thus began Gooch's association with the Atlantic cable. His role on the three expeditions of the *Great Eastern* has never been clearly defined or adequately assessed; it has often been assumed that he was on board merely as a director of the ship's owning company. The part he had played in the final preparation of the ship after her designer's death is often overlooked. The intimate knowledge of the *Great Eastern*'s construction and mechanical equipment he then gained must have been invaluable during the trials of the three cable expeditions. The fact that he was a director of both the cable companies meant that he had a personal interest in the success of the venture. His membership of all three boards made his intervention in the squabbles on board more effective, since he had both authority and impartiality.

Apart from his large financial interest in the cable schemes, and the challenge which the technical problems presented to him as an engineer, there is no doubt that Gooch acquired a great affection for 'the Gt Ship', in spite of her foibles and the hazards of cable-laying, and some, at least, of his faith in the vessel was prompted by his loyalty to the memory of her designer, I. K. Brunel.

39 These were round, open-topped tanks in the hold, for the stowage of the cable.

40 The Gyfeillon Colliery, Trehafod.

41 *See ante*, page 73.

42 The engineer in question was Charles Reboul Sacré (1831–89). He is mentioned by name in the minutes of the GW board meeting of 28 April 1864, when a letter was received from Sacré withdrawing his application for the post. His name had obviously been put forward by Watkin and Fenton, chairman and deputy chairman respectively of the Manchester, Sheffield & Lincolnshire Rly.

43 Swindon was then in the Cricklade Division.

44 There was little reason why it should; the line was only 6¾ miles long (from Chappel on the Great Eastern Rly to Halstead). It was later extended to Haverhill. Gooch's friend Robert Tweedy, possibly a brother of W. M. Tweedy (*qv*) was evidently a large shareholder though his name does not appear in *Bradshaw's Railway Manual* as a director. This little line remained independent right up to the grouping of 1923, when it became part of the LNER.

45 This was a 24-page pamphlet, reprinted from the *North Wilts Herald* of 10 June 1865. A copy is inserted in the diary.

46 Henry Fry, in *The History of North Atlantic Steam Navigation* (1896) says that the senior captains of the Cunard service, of which Anderson (*qv*) was one, were 'the very *crême de la crême* of the British mercantile service. Brave, bold, watchful, cautious, and stern, they were also, with perhaps one or two exceptions, accomplished gentlemen'.

47 This was not Lord Eliot, his fellow candidate in the election, but George Elliot of Glass, Elliot & Co (*qv*).

48 The cable was connected electrically with the Irish shore, and with instruments on board, with which a constant watch was kept for electrical flaws in the cable.
49 The western terminal of the cable, in Trinity Bay, on the north coast of Newfoundland.
50 Jane Tweedy, at Truro.

VOLUME III

The Memoirs 1865-7
The Diary 1868-9

1865. On my return to London I was surprised at a proposal made to me to take the chair of the Great Western Railway. I felt no hesitation in at once saying no, for I felt, apart from the labour and anxiety of the task, there were many men on the board with whom I had no inclination to work. The matter was much pressed upon me by Mr Walpole, who said if it was a question of pay with me the directors would advise the shareholders to pay me as much as £5,000 a year, but this was not what I hesitated about. I said if I take it I would only do so on the same terms as former chairmen had held the office; I would not, by receiving larger pay, become the servant of the company.[1] Several of the other old Gt Western directors urged me very strongly, but what induced me to yield was the strongly expressed wish of the officers and staff of the company. They had, under Potter, had a hard and very uncomfortable time of it. He knew no way of managing the concern but by constant changes, and the staff had lost all confidence in the security of their positions, and the whole line was in a state of disorganisation and discontent.

I therefore agreed that if the board as a body elected me I would accept the office. The difficulty of my being elected a director was great, as if any of the then directors resigned, the vacancy, by the Act of Parliament, could not be filled up. This was got over by Sir Watkin W. Wynn appointing me in his place, as he is a director by Act of Parliament so he can appoint me in his place. He therefore resigned and nominated me, and it was arranged that at the meeting of shareholders in February 1866[2] Mr John Williams of Chester would consent to the shareholders appointing me in his place. Thus the matter was arranged and I was elected as chairman on the 2nd November 1865 and took the chair at the board on the 16th Nov.

It is but just to those men who had done all in their power to get rid of me as an officer to say that after I took the chair they gave me their full support, and I had no reason to complain in any way of them. There is no doubt that when Potter proposed to resign the chair he had no idea such resignation would be so willingly accepted by the board. His object was to obtain more power, for, a couple of days before the election he went to Mr Walpole and several of the most influential directors, stating he was willing to retain the chair on certain conditions, the nature of such conditions being that he should have more power—in fact almost unlimited power—given to him. This, much to his disappointment, was rejected. Even at this time he did not go straight with me: at an interview I had with him before I had consented to take the chair, he told me it was his wish I should do so, yet up to the last hour he was plotting against me.

After my election the first thing I did was to look into the financial affairs of the company, when I was horified to find the amount of liabilities that had been incurred without any provision to meet them. Half a million of rolling stock had just been ordered, large new stations at Reading & Slough had been put in hand without any clear estimate or idea of their cost, temporary loans amounting to [£] 1,400,000 had been obtained, and other large obligations for new lines and works incurred. I now regretted the step I had taken, feeling a very anxious and difficult path lay before me, but having put my hand to the plough I had no alternative but to go on and do my best. I at once stopped all expenditure it was possible to do and began to look about for the means of meeting our engagements. Notices were accordingly given for a money Bill for the next session of Parliament.

I could not help feeling some gratification at the position I had taken, after the treatment I had received on leaving the company only a year before. It was certainly a victory over the West Midland lot, & I did not envy them their feelings in seeing me in the chair at their head. My duty, however, was plain: I had the interests of the company to serve, and not private feelings, and could not let the past in any way influence my conduct towards them. A united board was necessary and I did my best to make it so, and as is generally the case I found those who had before been most obnoxious to me were the most subservient.

With regard to our cable, I was much disappointed at the want of energy and determination of those interested in it. Shooting season came on and every one seemed to think shooting down poor birds a vastly more important thing than making efforts to raise new capital & make an attempt to complete the cable. I also urged the wisdom of laying a new cable throughout, and afterwards to retrieve and complete the old one. This, after a little, was the plan adopted, but valuable time was lost in making the financial arrangements, and the year closed without any certainty of the future. The Atlantic Company tried to issue shares with a preference, but as preference shares already existed this was found to be illegal, and they had no hope or chance of getting them out as a second preference, and had to abandon the scheme.

I had much reason to be dissatisfied, the latter part of this year, with the manner in which Harry was treated by Whitworth in Manchester. I therefore took him away and purchased for him an interest in some slate quarries at Bettws-y-Coed in North Wales, then chiefly belonging to Mr [? Cooper].[3] We formed a small joint stock company and Harry was appointed managing director. Harry also got married on the 25 Novr 1865 to Mary K. Croskey.[4] I was glad to see him settled & having known her from a child I felt she was in every respect a girl to make him happy. He was fortunate in getting a very comfortable house at Bettws and I pray it may be the beginning of a long and happy life. I am much blessed in the feeling that my boys are all good steady boys.

1866. The cable scheme occupied very much of my thoughts in the commencement of this year. All means of raising the capital by the Atlantic Company had failed and I saw no hopes of it doing any thing through their powers. Mr Cyrus Field came over from America to work at it and came to my house late one Sunday night in despair. I then proposed to him that we should start a new company, under an agreement with the Atlantic, to find the capital and lay the cables, paying them any profits we might get beyond a fixed amount. This scheme was at once acted upon and the Anglo-America Company was formed in March 1866, but the difficulty was still to raise the 600 thousand required. I proposed to our board at the Construction Co that each director should put his name down for £10,000 on a sheet of paper at once, to shew the public that we had confidence in our scheme. This made some long faces but I began the list with my name & 9 others added theirs, so that we had 100,000 round the table. This good start had the required effect and we succeeded in raising the capital, the Construction Co taking a good deal of it, and set to work in earnest to fit out the Great Eastern and complete the new cable.

Great consideration and attention was given to the machinery for hauling in the cable. Nothing could work better than our paying-out machine had done, but we required entirely new machinery for hauling in, with good and powerful engines to work them. We also put one of these machines to work in connexion with the paying-out gear, so that in case of a fault shewing itself the cable could be at once hauled back without cutting or disturbing it from the paying-out drums. Every other precaution we could think of from our former experience was taken. Special dresses were prepared for the men to be employed in the tanks so that they could not conceal any instrument by which damage might be done to the cable, altho' I do not believe the former faults were caused by wilfull damage. A full consideration of the matter last year convinced me of this, and that the damage was caused by broken wires in the cable itself sticking out and piercing it as it uncoiled from the tank.

I had at one time made up my mind not to go out with the expedition this year, feeling unwilling to leave my duties at the Gt Western, but as the time drew near I found such a jealous feeling springing up between Canning and Capt Anderson that I dreaded the consequences if no one was on board who could exercise some power and influence between them, and so I determined to go and I was afterwards very glad I did, for some one was greatly needed in the capacity of a director to settle their differences.

I took the chair at the [Great Western Railway] shareholders' meeting on the 2nd March for the first time, and was glad to receive from the proprietors a kind and hearty reception. It gave me confidence and I had no difficulty in stating upon what principles I would manage the concern, viz, to avoid all further obligations with new lines and extensions, to make, as far as possible, friendly relations with adjoining companies, and to cut down all capital expenditure to a minimum. Mr Potter had advised me to spend 3 millions in extending the works of the company; even if such a sum could have been obtained its expenditure would have been a wicked folly. A great mistake had been made by Potter in giving support to a line direct from the South Wales [line] near Lydney to Wootton Bassett.[5] He had even, to a certain extent, pledged the Gt Western to make it, and so cut off £80,000 a year from the traffic of their own line. I was not long in putting an end to this scheme as far as we were concerned, but Potter as a coal owner in South Wales had an object beyond the Co's interest in the matter: his coal company thought the line would be a benefit to them. Mr Fowler, as the consulting engineer of our company and the engineer of this new line, could have had little regard for our interest in projecting such a line, but it was the old story—suck the parent to death. There is no doubt had Potter's original intention been carried out the shareholders of the Gt Western would have probably never earned a dividend. He had also entered into any [*ie* an] agreement to build large carriage works at Oxford,[6] contrary to the advice of the officers, to cost about 90,000, which would have been entirely wasted as the place was unsuitable and the cost far exceeded any thing required. My belief is, had Potter remained in the chair a few years longer he would have brought ruin on the company and wiped out all the original capital and much of the preference. He was reckless in expenditure and a vain, soft headed fool, blown about by any wind.

Parliament met on the 6th Feby and I took the oaths and my seat that day. Parliament was opened by the Queen in person, but I did not go to see that. The Earl Russell was Prime Minister and Gladstone the Govt leader in the House of Commons. A Reform Bill was brought in, but it was in two Bills, one altering the franchise and the other dealing with the distribution of seats. The Conservative party, as also a considerable number of the Whig party, objected to this division but contended for the whole being dealt with in one complete and comprehensive Bill, and on this view I voted against the Government. Gladstone lost his temper sadly and bullied his party, and did himself and his cause much harm. In the early part of the session little else was done beyond the fight on this Reform Bill, and I am glad to say it was lost and the Government went out of office, being succeeded by Lord Derby as Prime Minister and Disraeli as leader in the House of Commons. This, however, did not take place until after I had left London to join the cable expedition. I dined with Disraeli in March & found him a much more genial fellow at dinner than he looks when sitting in the House.

By the middle of June all matters connected with our cable expedition had been nearly completed and I joined the ship at Sheerness on the 29th. I did so certainly with great hopes but perhaps not the same confidence as I did last year. I had then learned how many things might occur to destroy our hopes, but I felt perfect confidence that we could pick up the old cable now that we were prepared with proper machinery for such an enterprise. Yet this was one of the things in which the world at large had no belief, and I was often laughed at for what was called my madness. They had not seen what I saw last year.

My wife and Anna Newton went down to the ship with me and stayed on board all night. We moved out to the Nore on Saturday the 30th, where we parted with our friends, and on Sunday the 1st July commenced our voyage for Bantry Bay where we had arranged to complete our coaling and meet the other ships that were to accompany us. We had chartered two, the Albany and Medway, both fitted with hauling-in gear & lines, also bouys, the intention being that all 3 ships should assist in lifting the cable at the same time; one on each side of the big ship was to make a longer lift thus:

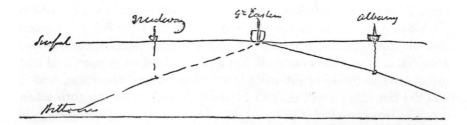

Such was the theory of our plan of lifting. After experience, as will be soon shewed, we could not in practice carry it out. Our old friend the Terrible was also to accompany us, commanded this time by Capt Commerel, a very different person from the last—his whole heart and soul was in the work from the first. We had a great many people on board going round to Bantry Bay. One great mistake made is allowing the ship to be so overrun with people, who do no good, and if they do no harm cost a great deal to [ie of] money to feed. Our run to Bantry Bay was a very rough one, and I got the first wetting on the deck of the ship I had had; I happened to be in the bows when a very heavy sea struck her and, mounting up her side, came on deck and soused me, but it was a very high, broken kind of sea.

The visitors got up a play to act; it was written by Woods of The Times and Parkinson of the Daily News. It caused some fun and helped to pass away the time. We reached our old moorings in Bantry Bay, or rather the part called Beerhaven, on Thursday morning July 5th. We found our coal ships waiting for us, and about 100 Irish labourers were set to work to do the coaling at the moderate rate of 5s/ per day. After a few days work they would not continue to work without they were paid the 5/– for every 6 hours. This is a specimen of Irish poverty; poverty is the fitting accompanyment of laziness. The result was we would not have them at all but coaled with our own crew, and they lost the wages. I went up the bay to a beautiful place called Glengariff. We had engaged a tug from Cork to attend upon the ships while in the haven, and oddly enough its name was Brunel; poor Brunel, what a deep interest he would have taken in this work had he lived.

When we arrived at Beerhaven none of the accompanying ships had arrived, nor had the ship with the Irish shore end come in, but she arrived on the 6th and Glass went away in her the same night for Valencia to take advantage of the first day to lay the shore end. We saw my old friends of last year, the Miss O'Sullivans, during our stay, and our old friend the Terrible joined us on the night of the 6th. The Albion [ie Albany] joined us on the 7th. On the night of the 8th we learned that the shore end had been laid the day before, so that our coaling and completion of machinery was all that now detained us. A good deal had to be done in finishing the machinery after leaving Sheerness, and it was the last thing finished. The Medway joined us on the 10th when our fleet was complete. On the 12th, all our work being complete, the Terrible, Albany and Medway started for Valencia on the 11th [sic] to find the shore end bouy ready for us next day. It was very foggy weather and these 3 ships had a most narrow escape from running upon the rocks called the Skillings; they only just saw them in time to stop.

We also left Beerhaven on the evening of the 12th and reached the shore end early next morning. It was unfortunately a rough day, both wind & sea, and wet, and it was with some difficulty the ships could be got into position to get the shore end on board of us. This was done about 12 oclock, and about 3 the splice & proper tests had been made, and our ship's head was once more turned to the west on the 13th and our cable running over the stern, and our real anxiety began. But we felt confidence in our arrangements for recovering the cable should any accident happen to break it, and we had determined to pay it out at a slower speed than was done last year. We arranged to get Greenwich time given to us every morning through the cable and we also had a daily telegram giving us the general news of the day.[7] It was wonderful to get, while in the Atlantic, the news of the morning from The Times, and as we got further west we used to have it at breakfast, the same as people living in the next street to the Times office. We were quite an imposing fleet of 4 large ships.

All went well with us each day until the night of the 17th, when I had just gone to bed about 10 oclock but had not fallen asleep when I fancied the ship had stopped, and I got up to look out of my port and saw the paddles were going, but the sea & wind was so rough and the night so dark I could not be sure, and at once put on my clothes and went on deck where I found our cable was in great danger, caused by the coils in the tank fouling and coming up in a regular knot and ravel. Fortunately every man had been at his post and attentive to his duty, as, as soon as the shout came up from the tank the ship was stopped, and before so much strain had been put upon the cable as to break it, for the ravel jammed in the machinery and so prevented more cable running out. The night was intensely dark with a heavy rain, also a high sea and wind. A rope stopper was fastened to the cable over the stern & Capt Anderson did what I should not have believed possible; he managed in such a night to keep the stern of that ship in such one position for the three hours it required to disentangle the cable. He could also only judge of the strain on the cable by watching the small phosforescent light in the water where the cable entered it. Great praise is due to Anderson for the masterly manner in which he thus saved our cable.

I never felt a more anxious 3 hours; I felt little hopes of our being able to save it. The night was so wild, dark and miserable, and the ravel in the cable so like a mess that could hardly be disentangled, and had we cut it the time to make a splice would have added much to the chance of losing it at the stern. We certainly never had so serious a difficulty to contend with the previous year, as we always had beautiful weather when in a difficulty, and as I have before said we then lost our cable not from bad weather but from doing a stupid thing likely to produce the result that followed. All, however, was got right and I sincerely rejoiced to see the cable quietly running out again, but this gave one's confidence a shake; here was a new danger we had not before experienced. We were paying out the new part of the cable which had been covered with white hemp instead of, as in last year's cable, with tarred hemp, and it was supposed that the want of stickyness permitted the coil below the one running out to spring up a little, or else the loose threads of hemp might knot with each other and so lift the lower coil. I believe the former was the case. We increased the number of men in the tanks so as to keep a closer watch on the coils. It was difficult to sleep sound again after this accident; before, all had gone so well I managed to sleep well, which I could not do the previous year, but now

I again felt I was listening to every change in the noise instead of getting sound sleep. The cable caught the lower coil 2 or 3 times afterwards but the men in the tank were always able to relieve it in time. I prefer the tar cable for paying out. We reduced the speed of the ship to 4½ knots.

On the 22 we passed the end of our old cable and the scene of last year's picking-up experiments. On the 25th we got into shallow water and felt no further fear of [not] being able to complete our work. What a relief this was; how slowly the hours had gone in anticipating this, but with the cable all had gone well, and we have had much reason to be satisfied with its electrical condition. We saw an iceberg off the Newfoundland coast on the 26th. Unfortunately it was about about 12 miles from us, but it gave us an idea of the size of these masses of ice, and lit up, as it was, by the evening sun, it had a very pretty effect. The Niger man of war joined us on the afternoon of the 26th, having come to pilot us up into Trinity Bay. It was very pleasant to feel we were so near the end of our task, but all our plans for being piloted into the bay were upset by a dense fog preventing us seeing any thing. We had therefore to stear the best way we could by compass, and when the fog cleared away early in the morning of the 27th July we were well up the bay. As we were going up the bay early in the morning a fault shewed itself in the tank from which the cable was being paid out. It was cut, and some in another tank used. The fog of the previous night lifted to give us a glorious day, glorious in every way—an unclouded sky and our light but deeply thankful hearts, thankful to Him who had given us success.

Preparations were made when we reached Heart's Content to connect the shore end to us, which we did about 9 oclock, and the Medway commenced to lay it after the splice was made. I received early in the morning a message from the Queen to the President of America; as this came before we had landed the shore end it did not go from land to land, which was a pity. We landed the cable at 4pm amid the wildest scenes of joy and excitement I ever witnessed. A great many people had collected at Heart's Content, and what with the wild shouting of every one, and the booming of the guns from all the ships, it was a scene, and produced feelings, never to be forgotten. The joy was almost painful; how impossible it is to give vent to such a feeling. A woman may shed tears of happiness, why should not a man yield to this also, as the only relief?

Having got the end of the cable into the office, during the time they were coupling it to the instruments, the clergyman of the little church at Heart's Content proposed we should go to church, and there offer up our thanks to God for our great success. None who could be spared hesitated to do this and the little church was well filled. Probably few churches have ever been filled with such deeply greatful hearts, for altho' we had had generally rough weather, yet with the one exception I have described, all had gone well, and when we remember the power of the angry Atlantic, to Him alone who stilled its waves was the glory due. The Evening Service was read and we had a short sermon from the text 'And there shall be no more sea'. Church over, I returned to the telegraph office and sent the first telegraph from shore to shore, as follows:

Gooch to Glass: Our shore end has just been laid and a most perfect cable under God's blessing has completed telegraphic communication between England and the continent of America. I cannot find words fully to express my deep sense of the untiring zeal and the earnest and chearful manner in which every one on board from the highest to the lowest have performed the anxious and arduous duties they in their several depts have had to perform. Their untiring energy and able and watchful care, night and day, for a period of 2 weeks required to complete this work, can only be fully understood and appreciated by one who, like myself, has seen it. All have faithfully done their duty and glory in their success, and heartily join with me in congratulations to our friends in England who have also laboured to carry out this great work.

I felt the first words our perfect child should speak should be thanks to God, and to those who had laboured in the work. I then telegraphed to Lord Stanley, the Foreign Secretary, as follows:

D. Gooch, Heart's Content, 6.30pm July 27, to Lord Stanly, Foreign Office, London: Mr Gooch has the pleasure to inform Lord Stanley that the Newfoundland shore end of the Atlantic cable was laid today, and the most perfect telegraphic communication established between England and the continent of America. God grant it may be a lasting source of great benefit to our country.

These were the first messages passed through the whole length of our cable; as I before said, during the voyage we had constant messages. Unfortunately the American Coy had not repaired their cable across the St Lawrence and we could not therefore telegraph direct to New York, the messages having to be conveyed by steamer across the Gulf of St Lawrence. I arranged with Capt Commerel of the Terrible to send one of the steamers at Heart's Content (The Niger) with the Queen's message, to Ashbee Bay,[8] and telegraph it from there to Washington. She started at 7pm; the message was as follows:

The Queen, Osborne, to the President of the United States, Washington: The Queen congratulates the President of the United States on the successful completion of an undertaking where she hopes may serve as an additional bond of union between the United States and England.

We did not get the answer to this until the 31st. It was at once telegraphed to Osborne, leaving Heart's Content at 4. It was delivered to the Queen at Osborne at 5 and the acknowledgt was received by us in 2h 35m. It was as follows:

The Executive Mansion, Washington, 11.30am July 30th. To Her Majesty the Queen of the United Kingdom of Great Britain and Ireland:
The President of the United States acknowledges with profound gratification the receipt of Her Majesties dispatch and cordially reciprocates the hopes that the cable that now unites the Eastern & Western hemispheres may serve to strengthen and perpetuate peace and amity between the governments of England and the Republic of the United States.

Andrew Johnson

Having done all that was necessary on shore the day we landed the cable, we returned to the ship, and it was a night of wild jollification; every one had his full swing, and singing and dancing and such fire works as we could get kept all awake until late at night. It was a glorious evening also in weather. Heart's Content is a quiet, sheltered bay, completely shut in from the outer bay by high land. It may be called pretty when the sun is shining, but the village is only a collection of fishermen's huts or wooden houses round the water's edge, the hills being covered with small stunted growth of firs. I was glad to get a message of congratulation on the 28 in answer to one I had sent to Clewer, and saying all was well at home. We were also glad to find our success fully appreciated in England; the leader in The Times said:

It is a great work, a glory to our age and nation, and the men who have achieved it deserve to be honoured amongst the benefactors of their country.

When this telegram was posted upon our news board which we put up in the ship so that all might read the news from day to day as we received it, I happened to be standing near and heard one sailor say to another 'I say Bill, we be benefactors to our race'. 'Yes', says Bill, 'we be', and they walked off with their backs straight & their heads well up, feeling at least some inches higher.

Everything was now done to prepare to go and make the attempt to recover our lost cable. We had coal ships at Heart's Content ready for us, and this had to be taken in. This occupied us until the 9th August. During this time our ship was a kind of open hotel; dozens of people came from various parts of Newfoundland and brought their bag[s] with them, quite looking upon us as a place where they might live at free quarters. Amongst them, however, were many very nice people from St John's, and also from Harbour Grace; a Doctor [? McKee] and his daughter were friends of the Captain's, and we saw a good deal of them. They sent the Capt a present of a young Newfoundland dog, 9 months old, born in Novr 1865. The Capt gave it to me and I was very pleased to have him. He is a beautiful pure blood Newfoundland, without a white hair upon him, and born of the same parents as the dog that was presented to the Prince of Wales. The breed is called the O'Sullivan breed. He & I soon became very fast friends and remain so. His name was given to him before I got him, it is Norval.

Mr Ridley of Harbour Grace gave us a grand ball at his home. He put up a large timber ball room and did the thing exceedingly well. I dined and slept at his house. The road to reach this place from Heart's Content was an awful one, the distance about 16 miles and time about 4 hours. He sent his carriage for us, or as many as it would hold. I fancied I never saw so many good-looking women in a room together before. A family at New Perlican, about 4 miles from Heart's Content, were also very kind to us, of the name of Howley. I am sorry to hear he is since dead; he considered himself a large farmer, having about 25 acres of land under cultivation. Land here may be bought at 1s/- per acre, yet it is not cultivated; the fishermen never seem even to cultivate a garden round their cottages, altho' they often have a great deal of time on their hands to spare.

While we were at Heart's Content the weather was very variable; when bright it was very hot, but the fogs and rain were cold. I scrambled about on the hills surrounding the harbour, but the thick scrub wood made it a very difficult task; but on the whole I very much enjoyed my stay there.

We lifted our anchor again on the afternoon of the 9th August. The Terrible and Albany had started on the 1st, the latter to grappel for the cable and try & get it bouyed ready for us; Moriarty went in her. We all sailed out of the harbour in full hopes of being back again in 10 or 12 days with the end of the lost cable. We had very rough weather in going from Heart's Content to the broken end, much the heaviest sea I had experienced in the ship. We reached it on Sunday the 12th. Here we found ourselves on the same ground we had left on the 11th of the same month the year before; it was singular enough our return to it should so nearly fit the day. We found the Terrible and Albany there. We then heard the Albany had hooked the cable and raised it about 150 fathoms when the chain near the grapnel broke; they had put down two mark bouys.

We began our work on the 13th, the weather having changed and given us a fine day, and our grapnel was lowered at one oclock. Canning had lost many valuable hours in thinking instead of acting, as was too often the case with him. In this case a nice breeze for our object had died away before the grapnel was down and we could do nothing but haul it up again; this was vexing. On the 14th the weather was very bad and we could do nothing. On the 15th the weather permitted us to put down the grapnel; this we did at 12 oclock. We began to drag at a little after 2 and about 8 hooked the cable. We then began to lift, which was done about 350 fathoms & then bouyed, which I thought a mistake. It would have been better to go on getting it up altho' it was dark, yet not so much so as to interfere with lifting. When the bouy was being attached at one oclock the splice of one of the eyes of the line gave way, and down went 1,600 fathoms of our line to add to that lost by the Albany, so that we were no further forward. We put down the grapnel again on the afternoon of the 16th and hooked the cable later. It was lifted about 100 fathoms and as it was very calm it was deemed best to discontinue the lifting until day light, as there was no danger of letting the ship hang by it. Lifting was begun early in the morning of the 17th and by breakfast time we had got it pretty near the surface. Arrangements were then made to have boats ready to get stoppers upon it as soon as it came up to the bows. We resumed the lifting and it came up out of the water, and we once more saw the cable deposited the year before. It was coming up at a great angle thus shewing there was great strain upon it. All were anxious yet joyous and could not restrain a loud cheer. This had hardly died away when snap went the cable and we were left to bitter—oh how bitter—a disappointment.

It was indeed hard, but there was nothing for it but to begin again. We had at any rate got a new end by this, left free from all the ropes &c of last year. After this failure we had rough weather until the morning of the 19th, when we again lowered the grapnel at 8 oclock, and we hooked it at 4pm and began to lift. By dark it had come up 1,200 fathoms. The Albany was also lifting it about a mile from us, and it was settled to bouy our lift and try to get hold of it again at another place so as to relieve the strain upon it. On the 20th & 21st & 22 the weather was too heavy for us to do any thing. On the 23rd we got a little better weather and let down the grapnel, but after drifting some time found we had passed over the line of cable without hooking it, so had to pull it up again.

August the 24 was my 50th birthday. I had a congratulatory message from Charlie, who was in the Medway, by the ship's signals. We put down a mark bouy this day, but did not attempt to grappel as the weather was very bad. On the 25th we put down the grapnel but a change of wind prevented the ship drifting in the right direction. We tryed her in steam with one paddle disconnected, but without success, and had to lift it again, but as the evening was favourable it was again lowered and draged until 2 in the morning, when the strain on the dynamometer indicated that we had hooked the cable, but in $\frac{1}{4}$ of an hour the strain was suddenly decreased and we hauled up the grapnel and found it much injured as tho' it had been dragging in gravel & rough ground, the only instance we had of this kind of bottom.

As the Medway had hooked the cable at this time, and lifted it about 600 fathoms not far from the bouy to which the cable was hanging, we then went to the south of her to let down our grapnel. A great deal of unnecessary delay took place in this by want of decision on the part of the cable people, and it was 3 oclock before it was down, but in the mean time the Medway had lost her hold of the cable, so we took her off; she pitched so much it was impossible for her safely to hold on by the cable. We also found the bight bouy so out of place that it must also have lost the cable. I began to feel very weary of this work, we seemed to make no progress, while the season during which we could hope for a chance fine day or two was rapidly passing away. I admit I began to lose heart, but resolved as long as we had coals and food to go on with, we would persevere. Our lines also began to get bad and we had lost a good deal in length. I went to bed on Sunday the 26 feeling any thing but jolly, and the same feeling seemed to pervade the ship.

During the night, or rather about 2 oclock in the morning, Capt Anderson knocked at my cabin door and said the Medway had just passed our bow, firing a gun and cheering, telling us that the Albany had got the cable and lifted the end on board & bouyed it. This was indeed good news. I got up soon after day light and went on deck, and at 7am Temple came on board with a piece of the cable he had cut off at the bight. Their grapnel had come up in very bad condition. We delayed taking the Gt Eastern to pick up the bouy for some time as there was a little wind, but by middle day we had got hold of it after many trials and much difficulty. We had lived in great hopes during the morning, but just as we were beginning to haul the cable in Moriarty came and told me that by an observation he had just taken of our position we were many miles away from the line of cable, and a short time served to prove this, as we hauled in and found it a short piece of about 2 miles long. I need not say this was a great disappointment to us all, but the sight of some of the old cable on deck put us in better spirits than we might otherwise have felt. So many disappointments had already taken place I think they began to lose their effect upon us.

We let down our grapnel again on the 28th, late in the evening, and after drifting all night it was hauled up in the morning of the 29th without having hooked the cable. I began now to despair of getting the cable in the plan we were trying; it had been so often hooked by the various ships and probably broken and pulled out of place that we might never get it. I therefore proposed that we should at once go along the cable about 90 miles, where we had an excellent observation when it was laid in the previous year, and also in only 1,650 fathoms of water, a great advantage over 2,000 fathoms. Many objections were urged by Canning and Anderson to this shift of ground. Anderson said it was admitting defeat, Canning soon yielded the point, and I was glad to see the ship's head turned east on the afternoon of the 29th, and we reached the new ground early [in] the morning of the 30th in Lat 51–52–30, Long 36–3–30. The weather on the 30th was very rough and we could do nothing, but on Friday August the 31, the day being very fine, we let down the grapnel. Owing to the bad state of our lines it took 2 hours to get it lowered, so that we did not begin to drag until half past 12, the depth being 1,900 fathoms; we were not as far east as I wished. The Medway also lowered her grapnel a couple of miles to the west so as to make a new end for us. We hooked the cable about 11pm when we hauled up about 800 fathoms, the weather being all we could desire, and we bouyed it, and on Saturday the 1st Sept crossed the cable again at 4 in the afternoon and began to lift. The Medway had also got the cable a couple of miles to the west, we being between her & the bouy we had put down, thus:

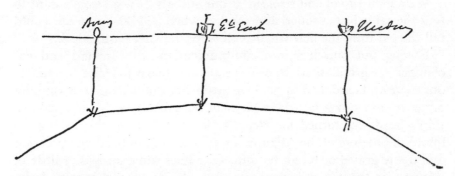

Having got the cable in the above position the Medway was ordered to heave away as fast as she could with the view of breaking the cable and so making an end for us. We also lifted gradually. The Medway broke the cable between 9 & 10pm and we had the satisfaction of seeing the cable come up to our ship's bow at 12.45. The night was fortunately very calm and all went well; we got the stoppers on and by 3am on Sunday morning the 2nd Sept we began to land the cable end on board.

This had been a night of intense anxiety; I felt it was our last hope. By 3am we had got the end into the instrument room where an anxious party was assembled. We had an end of the cable, but as yet did not know if it was any use. No time was lost in connecting it to the instruments, and then we had indeed an anxious $\frac{1}{4}$ of an hour until we had our signal acknowledged from Ireland. I think my heart ceased to beat during these few minutes. Fortunately for us the clerk in attendance in Ireland was not asleep but attending to his duties, and noticed our signal with very few minutes delay, and in something less than a quarter of an hour we were relieved and rejoiced to see the little light flash across our instrument.[9]

God only knows the sensation of such a moment. For 3 weeks we had, day and night, been striving (almost, for the last week, against hope) to recover this cable, but now all our anxieties & labours were fully rewarded. From the time we failed to recover it last year I had never doubted the possibility of our doing so. I had looked upon this as one of the things we could do, altho' often laughed at for such a mad idea as that we could go into the middle of the Atlantic and, from a depth of two miles, fish up a small piece of rope, and we did it. For the last week I, however, began to fear the weather; the season was getting late and the work was a hopeless one without good weather.

We all felt proud and rejoiced at our success. It was also pleasant to find the cable just as sound and good as when laid down; no one could tell the old from the new when both were together on the deck.

Having put ourselves into communication with Ireland and exchanged congratulations, steps were at once taken to splice the end to our cable on board, and by 7am we again saw the cable quietly running out over our stern & heard the pleasant hum of the machinery, and our ship's head was turned for Heart's Content. During this fishing we found the bottom of the Atlantic a soft oose, and only on one occasion found any gravel or rough bottom. Our lines came up with a little of this oose on them, and as they came in a dilligent search was made by us all for shells or any other curiosity. Once a piece of granite 5 or 6 inches long × 4 inches broad and about 1 inch thick came up. A small piece of stone was also brought up by the grapnel of the Medway, which Charlie got. I had a breast pin made out of it, also a ring for Charlie & myself. It is probable no piece of jewelry exists for which the stones have been fished from the Atlantic at the depth of two miles. They ought to be taken care of by my family as a relic of this expedition.

I was sorry Capt Commerel with the Terrible was not with us when we got the cable; he had been obliged to go to St John's for coals. No one could have taken a greater interest in our work and nothing was a trouble to him. He put lights on our bouys for us and made his boats useful whenever we wanted them.

Within very few hours of our starting towards Heart's Content the weather changed, and would have spoilt all our chances had it come on 8 or 10 hours sooner, but we now felt quite independent of the weather and steadily pursued our course, but feeling very anxious we should have no fault or mishap to retard us until we got into shallow water. I think I felt more anxious during the laying of this recovered cable than I did with the former one; having picked it up it would have been hard indeed had we failed to complete it. On the 6th of Sept we got into shallow water and felt all danger and risk at an end; on the 7th were off Trinity Bay, where we were joined by the Terrible, and on Saturday the 8th Sept we landed our shore end at Heart's Content and our work was complete.

Many of our old friends were there to receive us, and there was much rejoicing. We were also very glad to find the Queen in her speech on closing Parliament had referred to our success in the following words. Mr Walpole told me afterwards it was the first time any reference had ever been made in a speech from the throne to a private enterprise, so we feel so much more honoured:

Her Majesty has great satisfaction in congratulating the country, and the world at large, on the successful accomplishment of the great design of connecting Europe and America by means of an electric telegraph. It is hardly possible to anticipate the full extent of the benefits which may be conferred on the human race by this signal triumph of scientific enterprise, and Her Majesty has pleasure in expressing her deep sense of what is due to the private energy which, in spite of repeated failure and discouragement has at length, for the second time, succeeded in establishing direct communication between the two continents. Her Majesty trusts that no impediment may occur to interrupt the success of this great undertaking, calculated as it undoubtedly is, to cement yet closer the ties which bind Her Majesty's North American colonies to their mother country and to promote the unrestricted intercourse and friendly feeling which it is most desirable should subsist between Her Majesty's dominions and the great republic of the United States.

When our instruments were connected I sent the following message to Lord Stanley, the Foreign Secretary:

Sept 8th

Mr Gooch has the pleasure to inform Lord Stanley that the cable of 1865 was recovered from the bottom of the Atlantic on the 2nd of this month and has been safely landed today at Heart's Content, the recovered cable being in the most perfect condition. He also takes this opportunity of saying how much all here engaged in the undertaking were gratified, on receiving a newspaper today, to see the kind reference made to their efforts in Her Majesty's speech on the closing of Parliament.

We had a large party from St John's on board. They stayed all night on the ship and danced until 12. We had a very pressing invitation to go to St John's to a banquet they proposed to give us, but our ship was rather too costly an affair to keep idle for such a purpose, and we were all very anxious to get back to England. I therefore would not hear of any delay, but settled that we must leave Heart's Content on Sunday the 9th, and it was not without some difficulty we got all our visitors out of the ship by 10am on that day, and got our anchor up early in the afternoon, and we bid farewell to Heart's Content probably for ever and steamed once more for the Atlantic.

I gave the Bishop of Newfoundland, Dr Field, a passage home; he was a pleasant old gentleman. Mr Musgrave, the Governor of New-foundland, came to us when at Heart's Content this time, and stayed all night on board; he was from home when we were there before. Our passage home was a very rough one, the weather being bad and very high seas, making the old ship roll a good deal, but we reached Cape Clear early in the morning of the 17th and I landed at Liverpool early in the morning of the 19th.

A good deal of my pleasure for the last few weeks at sea was destroyed by the childish jealousy of Canning and others, a struggle as to who was to have the most credit for our success. When we returned the year before no one was anxious to struggle for the credit of the failure, but now there was nothing but bad feeling and I had constantly to interfere to keep things at all right. I am bound to say Anderson was free from this, & that the feeling was chiefly on the part of Canning and his staff, Moriarty siding with Canning; in fact the chief jealousy was against Anderson. Now in my opinion if any one had done more for the success of our work, or rather if the duties of any one had been more important than another, those duties were Anderson's. All did their best, and there was plenty of glory for all, and I pity the mind that could be selfish enough to be jealous of others sharing in it. If I had to lay a cable again I would, without hesitation, entrust it to Anderson. It ought to be done by one man; he ought to be the captain of the ship, and the cable and electric staffs, like the engineer's staff, ought to be under his control.

I was very pleased, accompanied by my constant companion Norval, to find myself at my pretty home at Clewer in the evening of the 19th Sept, grateful to God for His care of me and for His blessing on our work.

For more detail see my daily journal of the voyage.

The autumn meeting of the Great Western shareholders had been held in my absence, and they behaved very well about it, but I found money matters in England in a dreadfully depressed state. The failure of Overend, Gurney & Co, and the disclosures made of the affairs of the London, Chatham & Dover Railway, had put it almost out of the power of railways to get money to meet their debentures.[10] The rest of the year was spent in much anxiety on this account.

When we returned from the cable expedition a banquet was given to us at the Mansion House, London, also at Liverpool. I did not go to either of them. I was also invited to several other dinners given to celebrate the success, some of which I attended.

Mr Spencer H. Walpole, the Home Secretary, called at my office to see me on the 21st Sept, but as I was not there he wrote to ask me to go to his house and spend the afternoon with him on the Sunday following, the 23rd. This I did, and he then told me Lord Derby[11] had asked him to see me and offer me a baronetcy, and he wished to know something of the position &c of the others who had been engaged. He told me it was proposed to give a baronetcy to Lampson, one of the old Atlantic directors. I had no hesitation in telling him if there was one man who had placed difficulties in our way of success, this man was Lampson. I found that it had been offered by Lord Derby to Stewart Wortley, who was chairman of the Atlantic Co, and was at the time on a visit to Ld Derby, but he declined it and proposed Lampson in his stead, and the matter was too far gone to alter. I told Mr Walpole that Mr Glass was the proper person; he said they had been told Glass was only a speculator who had made a great deal of money by the cable and done little else for it. This, I told him, was not the case; that no one had done more than Glass, and I hoped he would not be passed over. The result was as follows:

Baronets: D. Gooch.   C. M. Lampson.

and in the London Gazette of the 13 Novr 1866 the following appeared,[12] and I was a baronet, a fate that had certainly never entered my head. Any acknowledgement of my services by the Government had certainly never formed any part of my hopes. I had gone into this matter of the cable from a desire to assist in completing so great a work, and would have been quite content with the feeling I had had success. When all equally did their best it seemed to me unfair that a few should be selected for any special reward. I earnestly pray that the dignity thus conferred upon me by the Queen will never be disgraced by myself or those who, in the course of nature, will succeed me. I feel pleased that the honour was not conferred in consequence either of wealth or because I had given a dinner to some great potentate, but that in the opinion of the Queen and her advisers I had done something for the good of my country and mankind, and that future baronets may with pride refer to the origin of the title.

1867. The early part of this year was a time of great anxiety to me in railway matters. It was impossible for us on the Great Western to meet our liabilities and we could not get money in any way. I deeply regretted ever having involved myself in so difficult a concern. As the time for our half-yearly meeting drew near I called a meeting of our largest shareholders and discussed the matter with them. I proposed to them to pay our dividends in stock instead of cash, and recommended a considerable reduction in the number of the board and that a committee of shareholders should be appointed by the Feby meeting to consult and advise with the directors. This was done and the meeting agreed to the payment of dividends in stock. The result was most beneficial to the company and not only relieved us from immediate difficulty but improved our credit and enabled us gradually to get rid of the large temporary loans. An Act of Parliament was obtained to reduce the board to 16, and it was arranged that all the directors should place their resignation in the hands of the committee and that they should select those who should be re-elected. This was a matter in which I could not take any part, but left it entirely to the committee. Amongst those selected to go were Mr Potter, Mr Fenton & Mr Brown, with others whose loss I regretted, yet those who remained were certainly the best of our directors. I could not feel regret at the loss of the others; they had acted badly towards me and I now saw all those who, in 1864, did their best to get rid of me by arrogance, now, themselves, out of the board.

The new board have worked with me as well as I could wish. We paid the dividends in the autumn also by stock, but one man went to the Court of Chancery to report what we had done as illegal, and I regret has so far succeeded as to prevent our doing the same thing in future, but we are going for a short Bill next session to enable us to do it, and I hope we will succeed;[13] it is needful for the interests of the company. A little time, if all work together, will enable us to get through all our difficulties; another year will shew what can be done—it is a very important one. I was elected chairman by the new board.

The session of Parliament of 1867 was a most important one. The question of reform was brought in by Lord Derby's government, and a franchise on a very extended scale was proposed & finally carried, giving a vote to every house holder who pays rates; it is a leap in the dark, as it is called. I supported it, feeling that any intermediate step would only be a temporary one, that it was better to go down to this at once than to have continued agitation on the subject, and I can only hope what has been done will be for the good of the country. Parliament met in November for 3 weeks to vote money for the Abassinia expedition, a costly and unsatisfactory expenditure but one forced upon us by the circumstances of the case.

I do not feel any great liking for Parliamentary life; the late hours do not suit me, and it is a great tie upon my time. What with Parliament and the railway I see no chance of even a few weeks rest and I often ask myself why, at my time of life, I should not have some leisure to travel abroad and feel now and then I can call a day my own. I must change my present intention if I try for a seat in the next Parliament.

I became a member of the Carlton Club in 1865 after my return from the Atlantic. On the 7th February 1867 a number of my engineering friends invited me to a banquet at the London Tavern. The Duke of Sutherland took the chair, and several other men of his class were good enough to attend, amongst them Lord Vane & the Earl of Caithness. The following is one of the tickets. My wife also persuaded me to

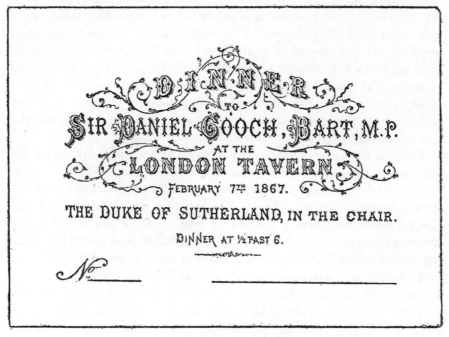

attend a Queen's Ball to which we were invited on the 25th June. It was a gay affair but not one I should care about often attending. I was glad to see it over; I annex the card of invitation. I had been appointed a Dep[u]t[y] Lieutenant of Berkshire early in the year, Feby 23, so was able to attend this and other full dress parties in uniform. It is a dreadful thing for a thin man to go in a Court dress. I was also appointed a magistrate for the County of Berks in the summer of 1867, and attended the Bench a few times at Windsor.

[*This point marks the end of the memoirs and the beginning of the diary*]

FEBRUARY 1868. The periodical called Engineering had a portrait of me in their number for Feby 21st, 1868, and a short account of my life.

SUNDAY, MAY 24, 1868. Within one short week how is my whole life changed. Only last Sunday my dear wife was sitting up, and altho' very ill, yet how little did I think she was so soon to leave me. Today I have strewed flowers on her coffin. Oh God how hard is this blow, the loss of one who has been my constant and loving companion for more than thirty years, one so pure, so unselfish, whose whole thoughts have been for my comfort and happiness, who never from one selfish feeling ever gave me a minute's pain, one so devoted and loving, falls to the lot of few men. We are assured by God Himself that those who love and obey Him on earth will receive a rich reward in Heaven. Oh how blessed must my dear wife be now she has gone to His blessed mansion, there to dwell in peace with Him for ever. Oh God make me worthy of one day joining her there; let our separation be short. Oh what a good wife she has been to me and a devoted mother to her children.

This loss has come upon us so suddenly, so unexpectedly, altho' for some months she has been complaining of not feeling well, yet I anticipated no danger until a week ago. The week before last she went out for a drive every day until Friday. On Saturday she was down stairs all the afternoon, on Sunday she got up and sat for a few hours in my dressing room where I joined her about one oclock and found her reading the Morning Service; she was reading the psalms of the day, but laid her book down to talk to me. As she felt fatigued I advised her to go to bed. From this time she sank very rapidly, suffering a good deal for a couple of days, but I thank God the pain left her and she only suffered from a feeling of extreme exhaustion. On Thursday afternoon the medical men told me she could not last more than 24 hours. Harry and Mary came up and were in time to see her while she was conscious, between 11 and 12 at night. Poor soul, when I told her they had come she wanted to get up and see if their room was comfortable. God was also

merciful to her in the arrival of a letter from Frank which was a fortnight behind its time and about which she had been very anxious. I
took it to her and will never forget the bright, glad expression that
lighted up her face when I told her he was well, and when I asked her if
she would like to hear the letter read she said yes, but immediately said
in the morning, and seemed to fall back into unconsciousness, and so
continued until the end came at half past 6 on Friday morning the 22nd
May. Harry, when he saw his mother, was sobbing very much, near her
on one side of the bed; I was close to her on the other with her hand in
mine. I think she fancied the sobs came from me, as she said Oh Dan,
love, don't. Her sister Jane and all her children, with the exception of
Frank, were with her to the last.

How my mind dwells upon the many happy years spent with her;
how much I owe to her for what has been good of my life; how much I
regret any pain I have given her. May her spirit now in Heaven watch
over me, may the thought of her goodness ever be present with me and
lead and guide me aright. My greatest treasure on earth is taken from
me; my fireside will be for ever lonely. Oh God give me strength to bear
the burden Thou has cast upon me.

CLEWER PARK, MAY 29TH, 1868. Yesterday my dear wife was laid in
her last resting place on earth. I came down here on Wednesday night
and Oh, how beautiful this place looked yesterday; how my heart filled
it all with her spirit. It ever asked itself how much she would have enjoyed it, and then came the sad, the bitter feeling that never more would
I share the beauty and happiness of the place with her. Amidst all the
joyous songs of the birds, the bright sun shine and the perfume of
flowers, she was carried to the cold and silent vault. Oh my beloved
wife, why did it not please God to take me first? But it is better to die
than to mourn; why should I wish her to bear my sorrow? No, God has
been merciful to her in casting this burden on me. All seems to speak
so audibly of her love; every spot is full of the past happiness with her,
yet what a void there seems. I cannot call to her, I cannot point out to
her the alterations I have made since she last saw the place.

There must have been some presentiment in my mind of this blow
that has come upon me, for it is only a few months ago since I asked Mr
Carter if I could have reserved a piece of ground in the church yard,
where I fancied I should like to make my last resting place, and Roake
the clerk was talking with me only a few weeks ago about it; and last

Saturday week as I walked to the station I walked to that corner of the church yard to look at the spot. She knew I had fixed upon that place. How little did I think what a fortnight would bring to pass, that within that fortnight I would again stand upon that spot and see my beloved wife's coffin lowered into the vault.

My friends have all been very kind. My wife's dear sister and all my dear children have done all that kind & loving hearts could do to give me comfort, to make me feel I am not entirely alone in the world. In this I have much to be thankful to God for; may He give me strength to lead a wise and good life, and may my end be like hers.

How busy has death been amongst my friends the last few months. 6 of us sat down on a committee at a table last autumn. One of the six is dead and 3 of them have lost their wives; another Great Western director died only 3 weeks ago. Mr Stewart,[14] the chairman of the Anglo-American Telegraph, with whom I was in almost daily communication, died suddenly a couple of months ago, and Sir F. Head,[15] who sat with me on the Royal Commission on Trades Unions, died suddenly at the same time, and a few weeks afterwards Mr Lane, the engineer on the Gt Western who I had known for 30 years also died suddenly. Death has indeed been scattering sorrow amongst my friends broad cast. How little do we know the end. My poor coachman also lost his wife suddenly a few days before my dear wife died.

SUNDAY, JUNE 14TH. How heavily time runs on; I so miss the loving companion of my life. Nature is all bright and beautiful but it seems to bring no sunshine to my heart. Oh that any earthly sacrifice could bring her back to me, to once more gladden my house. Looking on the past, all that may have given me pain seems to have passed away and only happy hours dwell upon my mind. How good and loving she ever was to me; how much more has all her care been for me than I felt it at the time. How much I underrated the blessing God had given me in her. Oh my beloved Peggy, how earnestly I would try and make up to you for any sorrow I may have caused you in the past if it were possible you could again come to me, again be my comfort and solace in sickness and health. Life seems so dreary without you; as I look into the future I see no joy, no comfort; alone I live. Friends have been very kind, but they are not a wife and, Oh, in sickness who can fill her place? None—no, not one living being. Had it been God's will to take me first I now feel how dark the hour would have been for her, and it is His mercy that she has been saved this woe. Time seems only to deepen my feeling of loss. In the ordinary affairs of life I seem ever to miss the feeling that they could be shared in by her.

My dear children are very kind, all I could wish, all I could hope, by the training and example set them by their loving mother. Oh God give me strength not to forget her, but to feel and believe that her angel spirit still watches over me and guides me in the path that will at Thy appointed day lead me to join her again for ever in that blessed world where she now is. The thought of this is my only comfort, and it does bring peace to the heart; it does soften the deep sorrow that rests on my soul.

GRESHAM HOTEL, DUBLIN. SEPT 8TH, 1868. Since I last wrote in this book I have felt far from well and [a] dreary feeling of loneliness has hung over me. I seem to have no one to call my own, with whom I can even share my thoughts, and feel that in sickness no loved one would be by my side to cheer and comfort me. My children and their children have been at Clewer with me and the summer has been a glorious one, hardly a day's rain. It at one time became very serious for the cattle, sheep &c; no grass and in many places no water. Fortunately we had a few days of very heavy rain a couple of weeks ago and this has made all Nature start again into life. It did not come a bit too soon.

Our half-yearly (G.W.R. *in margin*) meeting was held last Thursday and passed off very well, so I have taken advantage of this month to travel in Ireland, which I have not seen before excepting in merely passing through it by rail. I have brought Anna with me, and we look forward to a few pleasant weeks.

We left London this morning at 7.15am and arrived at the hotel here about 6.15pm. The passage was too rough for the ladies but to me it was a lovely one. There was a fine, fresh breeze and a bright sun; the sea was pretty high, making moving about rather difficult. Anna was very sick all the way.

During the last month I have been a good deal engaged in negotiations for the Construction Co, for making and laying a new Atlantic cable from Brest, on the French coast, to New York, calling at the island of St Pierre. I have also chartered the Great Eastern for the work and am glad to get another job for her as she has done nothing for a long time.

We have got capital rooms here, and as far as I can judge we will be very comfortable.

SEPT 9TH. We have been seeing the principal sights about Dublin; the College is, I think, the best of them in the shape of buildings. In the afternoon we had an Irish car and went to the Zoological Gardens in Phoenix Park; there are very few animals and the grounds are very badly kept. The situation is good & they might be made very pretty. We afterwards drove round the park; it is large and very pretty. The drive overlooking the River Liffey is very beautiful. Unfortunately it was a little thick over the Wicklow Mountains and we did not see them very well. There is a very large number of very fine large thorn trees, now covered with the red berry; they must be very beautiful when in flower. I went to one of the principal bog oak shops; the works they make are very beautiful. I bought some things and am having a clock made. One thing strikes me very much in Dublin; there are no public houses or gin palaces as you see them in English towns.

SEPT 10TH. This has been another beautiful day. We went in the morning to Kingstown and enjoyed a nice fresh sea breeze, sitting about on the end of the breakwater. The harbour is a fine sheltered piece of water of large extent and depth. The view of the Bay of Dublin from the end of this breakwater is very fine; it is often compared to the Bay of Naples, and I do not think it falls much short of it in beauty or in size and is very much the same shape and character. In the afternoon a military band was playing near the Yacht Club house. After enjoying this for a couple of hours we returned to our 7 oclock dinner having spent a very enjoyable day.

KILLARNEY, SEPT 11, 1868. We left Dublin at half past 8 this morning by the train for this place; it is a very uninteresting ride and there is plenty of time for reading. On passing Dundalk I noticed a ruin with a very high round tower, more like a factory chimney than a tower, it was so small. I see by Murray[16] it is about 150 feet high and is not larger in diameter than an ordinary chimney. Mallow is a very pretty place, the only one on the road. We were unfortunate in the day in arriving here, as soon after leaving Dublin it began to rain and continued until middle day, when it cleared up a little until we arrived here at a little before 4, since when it has been raining very hard. I am rather disappointed with this hotel (the Royal Victoria), the rooms are only small and not very well furnished. There is a table d'hôte at half past 6 and they cannot give you a private dinner between half past 5 and 8; in fact to dine at all you must dine at the table d'ote. The dinner was very well served and not of a very extensive character, but good. I have been amused tonight in the smoking room discussing Irish politics. I hope this rain will not continue as it makes the place look dreary; I dare say it is very pretty when you can see it, but today it is not very inviting, besides being very cold. The train from Dublin, as far as Mallow junction, is a very good one, travelling at a speed of about 45 miles per hour. After that it stops at all stations and is slow.

KILLARNEY, SEPT 12TH. This morning opened with a very doubtful prospect of a fine day, being cloudy and the mountains hid in cloud. It, however, did not rain, so we determined to see something and had an Irish car at 10 and started for Muckross Abbey. The drive is through the town of Killarney and along the Kenmare road until you come to the entrance gates to Mr Herbert's grounds, through which you drive to Muckross Abbey. This is a small ruin, the Abbey yard is still used [as] a burying ground for those who have a right to burial there. Little of the abbey is left in a perfect state beyond the cloisters, which are situated in the middle of the building forming a small square, and having a splendid specimen of the yew tree growing exactly in the middle, the stem being not less than 2ft 6in through and the branches spreading on each side far beyond the boundaries of the cloisters. From here we drove to the junction of the upper and lower lakes; it is a lovely drive. Mr Herbert's house is a large building. There are some oak trees planted here by the Queen and her children when on a visit to the lakes. We then drove to the Torc water fall; it is a pretty fall, but apart from this the views of the lakes from some points as you go to the top of the falls are very fine. Fortunately the weather had cleared up before middle day and we had a bright sun.

We took our lunch with us and eat it at the falls. The drive was a very lovely one and nothing could be finer than the views obtained both of the mountains and the lakes. The mosses were very fine, and the moss fern very plentiful and larger than any I have seen before. The hollies and arbutus are also in great abundance and quite as large as trees. As we passed through Killarney on our way here the market was going on, and we saw a good example of the Irish peasantry, a rough and ugly lot, both women and men. We got back to the hotel about half past 3 after a delightful drive.

KILLARNEY, SEPT 13TH. Today has been a very enjoyable day, altho'
the morning was a little doubtful; but we determined to go through the
Gap of Dunloe, and started at 10 oclock. We drove by car to the gap,
about 9 miles, and then walked across the pass to the head of the upper
lake. It is not so grand as I had expected, yet it is very fine on a small
scale. There is no reason why you should not cross in a carriage as the
road is a good one the whole way. You are pestered with women &
children begging and wishing to sell you a mixture of whiskey and
goat's milk, which it is quite as well to pay for but not drink. They also
work lace and sell it; I am no judge, but it is at any rate an honest employment and deserves to be encouraged. There are some fine echos in
the pass; a man plays on the bugle, the notes of which are very clearly
repeated. Cannon are also fired to astonish you, but the best was near
the top where an old Irishman plays on the fiddle and accompanies it
with a pretty good voice, & the echo repeats the music very clearly, and
the effect is very pretty.

I find the top of the pass was 800 feet above the lakes. The ascent is
very easy and no one able to walk a moderate distance ought to ride.
After gaining the summit you get a very beautiful view of the mountains
on the lake side and a pretty steep descent brings you to the head of the
upper lake. Today the mountains were very beautiful, the passing
clouds giving so much variety of light and shade. On reaching the lake
we had a boat waiting for us to take us back to the hotel by the lakes. It
is a lovely row, the upper lake is separated from the lower one by what
may be called between 2 & 3 miles of a river, it is so narrow. As you
approach the lower lake you pass down a short rapid with very little
water under your boat, and where the waters divide into the middle and
lower lakes it is called the meeting of the waters, but a more correct
name would be the dividing of the waters. We were at this place in our
drive yesterday. The row from here across the lower lake is very beautiful, all the shore and islands are so beautifully wooded. We arrived back
at the hotel at 4 after as enjoyable a trip as it is possible to make.

I have sat at dinner the last 3 days next a young lady, and a clever
girl she is, with very strong opinions on religion. Today I was told she
was a Methodist and was to preach this morning in Killarney. At
dinner today we had a very animated discussion on religious matters
and she told me she used to be wicked, but now she had seen the true
light and she was perfectly happy in feeling that she was at peace with

her God, and hoped I would soon be in the same state. In fact she seemed to think her future was certain; may not this be a greater state of danger than that of one who feels they much need God's mercy?

CRUISE'S HOTEL, LIMERICK, SEPT 14, 1868. We left Killarney this morning and came by rail to this place, arriving a little after 2. A ramble over the town has shewn us a nice clean and well built little place; the principal streets are wide, straight and good, and containing a great many good shops. The River Shannon is a noble river and I saw it to advantage today as it was high water. The river quays and town present a busy and active scene. The country, as we approached Limerick, is also richer and better cultivated than any I have noticed elsewhere. The cathedral is a very plain building both inside and out. There is a large stone placed upon a pedestal at the end of one of the bridges, said to be the stone upon which the treaty was signed in the time of James. Why something better than a stone could not be found for the purpose I don't understand. Killarncy looked very pretty as we left it today; the scenery there is certainly very lovely, and today the atmosphere was very bright. I will hope at some future day to again visit Killarney.

BERGIN'S HOTEL, OR PRINCE OF WALES, ATHLONE, SEPT 15. We left Limerick this morning at a $\frac{1}{4}$ before 11. Before starting I went down to the river to see it when the tide was out. It was even then a fine river, but not deep as there were a lot of loose rocks across it not covered with water. We first went to Nenagh, up the vally of the Shannon most of the way. At one place the river is within a couple of hundred yards of the railway. At Nenagh we got onto a different railway and had to wait $1\frac{1}{2}$ hours; this gave us time to explore the town. It is a tidy little place enough, with a large prison and court house. There is also a fine old round tower in good preservation. Leaving Nenagh we got to the main line of the Gt South[ern] & Western Railway again, passing a rather pretty place called Roscrea; the neighbourhood was very pretty. We got from the junction to Portarlington where we had to wait 2 hours for the down train to bring us on here. We got a car and drove about a mile into the town to try & get some dinner. It was not a very easy matter as our time was short and it took a long time to cook what they could give us, which was not much. However, it answered our purpose and the bitter beer was good.

Portarlington is a clean little town of one street, having some very good houses at the entrance of it. Very much of the country passed through today was well cultivated and had a rich appearance, but there was also a large quantity of bog. The hay was still out in the fields, some in small ricks and some being made; whether this was a 2nd crop or not I cannot tell. That in ricks may have been cut for some time; I saw in places they were beginning to carry them from the fields. We did not get here until 8 pm so that it was dark and I can form no notion of the place. I cannot say any thing for the hotel, it is a dirty hole.

MURRAY'S HOTEL, MULLINGAR, SEPT 16TH, 1868. I was very glad to get away from Athlone, the hotel is the most beastly place I ever was in. I could not get any sleep, my room happened to be over the kitchen and the fumes of burnt fat came up through the floor, and the noise of voices and jingling of plates lasted until very late. The bed was filthey and altogether it was a miserable place. I had made up my mind not to risk staying a night at Mullingar, fearing it might be no better, but as I was anxious to travel from here to Sligo by day light I asked the station master what kind of place the hotel was, and he gave a good account of it, so I made up my mind to risk it. It is a most comfortable place, clean and the rooms nice (at least those that I have) and I am quite content with it. We had a fire lighted as the evenings are now getting rather cold, so that we felt quite snug.

Before leaving Athlone we walked over the town to see all that was to be seen. The barracks are very large & are good buildings kept in good order. There is an old castle and some fortifications close to them. The Shannon is a fine river here; there is a weir and a lock for the navigation. The bridge over the river is a good & new structure. We left Athlone about 2pm and arrived here soon after 3. It did not take us long to see what there is to see here; it is a clean town with a good street running through it, altogether a much better place than Athlone, and I give every praise to the hotel. There are large barracks here.

VICTORIA HOTEL, SLIGO, SEPT 17TH. I was very comfortable at Mullingar last night and had doubts whether we would get as comfortable quarters here. This hotel is, however, a fair average; our rooms look clean, and that is the chief thing. It was market day in Mullingar today, and it was curious to see the number of geese, turkeys, ducks &c in the town. I cannot image where they would find people to purchase them; there were enough to supply London. We left at 11am and I was a little disappointed with the country from there here; I had expected to find it much more beautiful. We passed some lakes, and at Carrick crossed the Shannon, a fine view. Near here we passed Miss Ed[g]eworth's property;[17] it was a pretty village.

On our arrival here we took a long walk. The country round about the town is very beautiful, surrounded by high mountains. The bay is small and I expected to see a great deal more shipping; a dozen small vessels was the outside of the number. There was a good steamer ready to start for some place or other. As we left one of the stations, there was evidently a party about to emigrate, and a number of their friends were at the station to see them off. It was a curious sight, the howling was something frightful and it seemed quite possible for them to get up tears for the occasion. The train stayed longer at the station than they expected and it was impossible to howl all the time, so they left off for a little when they found the train was not ready, but as soon as the whistle sounded they began again.

There is very little to see in this place beyond the ruin of an old abbey, and this must have been on a small scale. Tomorrow I go up to the head of the Lake Gill to see my cousin Mrs Palmer. It is quite 32 or 33 years since I saw her; she was a pretty girl then—how will I find her tomorrow? A good deal changed, I expect. I fancied Ireland had more beautiful cenery than it has; there is a large quantity of the land occupied by bog, and today the country has been very flat. The railways keep pretty good time here.

SLIGO, SEPT 18TH. We had a very comfortable brougham this morning at half past 10 and went to spend the day with my cousin Mary Palmer. I was very pleased to find her looking so well and in every way so hearty. I could have fancied it was her mother I saw, the 32 years has brought her up to the standard of what her mother was when I saw her last. She was very pleased to see me and I confess I also was very glad to meet my cousin again. It brought back old and joyous times when all the world was before me and I dreaded it not, being in happy ignorance of its many cares and sorrows. Fortunately it is not permitted to us to see beyond the present. The day was fine and we enjoyed the drive up to the head of the Lake Gill; it is about 5 or 6 miles long and beautiful mountains rise up pretty steeply from its banks. The drive to get to my cousin's cottage, called Shriff, was about 10 miles. It stands well upon the hill side from the lake, but is a very small place. Some of the Peels of

Watlington were there; they have taken a house for shooting not far off.

My cousin took me to see some of the farms near at hand; poor people, they get 10 to 20 acres of land for which they pay a rent of from 26/ to 35/ per acre Irish, say 5 roods, but half of it is rock and it is impossible for them to make any living out of it. Indeed, I don't know how they can collect the rent even. I asked the men what would be the cure for their state of misery. Their great point was to have the land as such a rent as would enable them to get a living out of it; also they want to [sic] the landlords, they say, 'to live and let live'. This term was repeated to me a great many times, but there is no doubt if they got the land free the extent they hold is too small to enable them to live as men should live. We had an early dinner and tea, and left before 8 oclock for Sligo, after a pleasant day. We found our landlady had a nice comfortable fire ready for us, and as the nights are getting cold it was very cheerful.

ENNISKILLEN, IMPERIAL HOTEL, SEPT 19TH. We had to make a very early start this morning, or a $\frac{1}{4}$ before 7, in the carriage we had yesterday, for a place called Bundoran, said to be the fashionable watering place in this part of Ireland. With a cold east wind blowing this morning I cannot say I found the place at all tempting. We had to drive $22\frac{1}{2}$ miles from Sligo, along a very pretty road skirting the steep slopes of some beautiful mountains on the land side, and for some part of the way the sea on the other. At this watering place there is a wooden shed which does duty for a station, and where we got into the train for this place, passing Ballyshannon and up the north side of Lake Erne. This is a pretty, and a large, lake extending very nearly from Ballyshannon to this town. The town of Enniskillen is one long street, pretty clean and a fair width; it is surrounded by water. There is a monument in the shape of a Nelson's Column erected at one end of the town on some high ground, to the memory of the heroic deeds of Sir Lowry Cole, a Peninsula veteran. I went to the top of it, and the view is very fine—well repaid me for the scramble up it. I also saw my cousin Fanny Hawks (as was), now Mrs Brown; they live in Enniskillen, and after dinner we went to spend an hour with them. Mrs Dobree was staying with her; I believe she is my cousin Bessy Hawks, but do not feel quite sure. Anna Hawks, now Mrs Murphy, lives a few miles out of Enniskillen but I did not see her.

SUNDAY. We went to spend the day at Tempo, about 8 miles from here, with Sir J. Emerson Tennent. He has a very pretty place there and it is kept in very nice order; the house is also a very comfortable and good one on the cottage plan. We had a fine day and enjoyed it, getting home, or to the hotel, about half past 10 at night. Anna Murphy with two of her girls & a daughter of Mary's called to see me, but unfortunately I was out. The Imperial Hotel is a dirty place and does no credit to the town.

ANTRIM ARMS, PORTRUSH, SEPT 21. We left Enniskillen at a ¼ past 8 this morning by rail for Londonderry, where we were able to spend a couple of hours before coming on here. The country to Derry is very uninteresting with the exception of 2 or 3 small towns prettily situated as you get towards Derry. I was very much interested with Derry. We walked round the walls; they are kept up in good condition and make a nice walk. We also visited the cathedral; the interior has recently been restored and I think I have never seen a more comfortable and nice looking church. Some flags are kept there, [or] rather the staves of the flags taken from the French at the time of the siege of Derry. There is also a shell that was fired into the town containing messages, and not gun powder. From the top of the tower a very fine view is obtained of the town, the river and the surrounding country.

From Derry we came to Coleraine; this is, I think, the prettiest ride we have had in Ireland. It follows most of the way the water's edge, and the river Foyle down to the entrance of Lough Foyle is very beautiful. We had an hour to wait at the Coleraine station so we went into the town and [saw] all that could be seen there (not much) and we arrived here a little after 5. The hotel looks comfortable.

I have had today one of the most interesting excursions I ever made. The day, as to weather, has been all it could be. After breakfast we went for a ramble over the rocks which run out into the sea from this place, and afterwards along the beautiful sands. I wonder there are no bathing machines here as the ladies have to bathe, not on the beautiful sands, but upon some rocks close under the town, and it is rather a public place, particularly as there are no machines for them, but they must scramble over the rocks into the water.

At half past 12 we had a car and went to the Giant's Causeway. The ride there along the cliffs is most interesting and beautiful; you see the basalt coming up through and overlying the chalk. You also pass on the road Dunluce Castle; it is a large ruin but has never been a strong place, as it has more the appearance of the ruins of a large house than a castle, but its situation on a rock standing out into the sea is very fine (altho' I should say very cold), but the great interest of the day was the Giant's Causeway and the basaltic cliffs. They are not only wonderful in their formation but grand in the extreme, looking like mighty ranges of fine buildings supported by interminable columns. I did not expect so much variety in the form of the columns; I had thought they were perfectly regular and all hexagonal, but this is not so. There are all number of sides to them, altho' chiefly hexagonal. There are also some very fine caves into which we went. Boats are provided to take you round the cliffs and it is only by boat they can be seen to advantage. You then land upon the Causeway and examine the formation in detail, and a most interesting study it is. I got some very good photographs which shew it better than any description I can give.

On our return to Portrush we saw a very lovely sunset and did not get back until 6 oclock. There is a very good hotel at the Causeway and the guides are said to be civil; the man we had was so, and had a good deal to say about all the different spots. There are swarms of boys, girls & old people selling photographs, minerals, indeed doing any thing to gain a few pence; they are rather a bother.

CUSHENDALL, SEPT 23. I was very sorry to leave Portrush this morning as the place was very comfortable and the coast most enjoyable. I should have very much liked to stay a week or 10 days there. We had a roomy carriage and a pair of horses to take us to Belfast and started at about 10 oclock. We followed the same road we went yesterday as far as Bushmills, where we crossed inland at the back of Fairhead & to this place. We lunched as a place called Ballycastle; from there there is a very long pull to get over the mountain range of which Fairhead is the end. I measured it at 900 feet. The road is a very good one but not very interesting; some of the little valleys we passed were pretty, and as we got near this place the scenery became very good. We arrived here at 5pm and went for a walk upon the beach, not a good one. The hotel is clean but very 2nd rate; they were, however, anxious to make us as comfortable as the house would admit of. We had a lovely day for travelling.

IMPERIAL HOTEL, BELFAST, SEPT 24TH. We started from Cushendall at 9 this morning and followed the coast the whole of the way here; the drive the whole way is very beautiful. We had very fine weather and were able yesterday to see the island of Rathlin and also the Mull of Kintare [*ie* Kintyre] in Scotland very well, and today we could also see the Scotch coast very well. We had the horses fed at Glenarm, a pretty place—indeed all the villages we passed through were exceedingly well built and had many good houses in them. Carnlough is quite a nice watering place but there is a great want of bathing machines in all the places. Occasionally a little wooden box is put up, but the usual custom seems to be to do without, and today, after I left Glenarm (from which place I walked on while the horses were being fed) I came upon 5 ladies bathing in a little quiet nook, in a perfectly natural state.

The valleys we crossed were very beautiful; we also passed Garron Towers, a place belonging to the Londonderry family. The whole drive to Larne was very beautiful. The poor people seem to be generally employed on the coast gathering sea weed for turning into kelp; the smell is very strong and disagreeable. We arrived at Larne at one oclock, and as our train for this place did not start until a ¼ past 4 we had a long time to get through. We took a walk to the top of a hill and got a very fine view of Larne, also of the lakes, the rocks out at sea called The Sisters, as well as the Scotch coast; but there was nothing in the little town to see. We arrived here at half past 5.

The ride up Lough Belfast is very beautiful. As you get near Belfast the country is richly covered with houses and grounds. The view of the opposite side of the Lough is also very pretty. Belfast appears to be an exceedingly good town; very many fine buildings in it and the streets are good. There is a very good hotel and it is pleasant to get into such quarters again after the roughing we have had since we left Killarney. I begin to wish for a few quiet days; we have been working pretty hard and I shall be glad to feel when I get up in a morning I have no journey to make. I wish I could have stayed a little while quietly at Portrush; the sands, rocks &c are so enjoyable and I long for rest, but seem ever to be driving from place to place by one cause or another.

BETTWS Y COED, SEPT 27TH, 1868. I arrived here yesterday afternoon.[18] This place brings back sad memories; I have not been here before but in company with my dear wife, and all so strongly seems to speak of her. Oh my beloved Peggy how I miss you in every thing; how horid it is to be thus left alone. We have spent some happy days here, and what is the future to me? Dreary and lonely. I was never fitted for a solitary life; I need the home happiness of a wife, the one companion who shares with me all my existence and makes home home. I return to Clewer tomorrow, but how will I find it? It is indeed hard to think of.

We left Belfast on Friday morning by rail at 10.30am, after a walk about the town. It is certainly a thriving looking place; if all Ireland was like this it would be a prosperous and happy country, and it might be so to a much greater extent than it is if party and religious differences were not so rife and priest craft could be driven into the sea. The ride from Belfast to Dublin is through a rich and generally well cultivated country. It came on to blow and rain very hard; very fortunately we were quite independent of it, as it took us all day to get to Dublin, the train not being a very fast one. We, however, got to the Gresham Hotel soon after 5, we had dinner at 6 and I afterwards went to Booterstown to see Hannah.[19] She is getting quite fat; I spent an hour with her and returned to Dublin. Next morning we started by the train at 6.15am (an early start) and crossed to Holyhead. The passage was a rough one after the gale of the night previous, and [we] reached here soon after 3, where we found all well and glad to see us. I feel very glad to have a quiet day today as it has been rather hard work the last 3 weeks, moving about as much as we have. We have, however, seen a great deal of Ireland and on the whole I have very much enjoyed my trip; but as I said, I am not sorry to be quiet, and this trip, like many other happy days, will be of the past. Anna has been a very kind and cheerful companion and I think she has enjoyed her trip also. We have seen no place more beautiful than this.

CLEWER PARK, OCT 4TH. I reached here on Monday night and found all well. I am glad to get back; altho' I had no kind wife to receive me it was my own home and where she had made me happy. I have succeeded in getting some enlarged photographs of my wife; they are very good and I am very pleased to have them. Election matters will now, I fear, bother me. I have no wish or inclination to stand for Cricklade. I hear tonight we are to have opposition; if so, I certainly will not go through all the anxiety and worry of a fight; the price is not worth it. The next few days will decide my course.

OCT 11, 1868. I have last week been engaged in election matters. I attended a meeting at New Swindon on Tuesday night and met with a very good reception from the men. I have no inclination to go on with a contest; a Liberal candidate has offered himself and I have not perfect faith in the Conservative party as a whole. I have no intention to be used for the purpose of carrying Goddard's election. I have written a letter to each of the Conservative leaders in the borough and upon the answer to that will depend my future course. If I gave support to the Liberal side, or rather took no steps to get the Swindon men to help Goddard, they would vote for me very largely and so leave Goddard in the cold. I should prefer to get rid of Parliament altogether; it gives me no pleasure or position.

I was appointed Pro[vincial] Grand Master for Berks & Bucks yesterday, so that I must give up my office of D.P.G. Master of Wilts, which I regret.

Nov 15, 1868. Parliament was dissolved on the 11th, so today I am no longer a Member of Parliament, and this week will decide whether I ever will be one again, as if I do not get in for Cricklade I hardly think I will ever try any other place. A proposal was made to me on Thursday to go in for Gloucester, with an assurance of success, but I declined as I feel pretty safe at Cricklade. My committee have been working very hard; Armstrong & Dunn have taken a very active part, the latter is the chairman of my committee. All that men could do I feel they have done. By the returns made up to Thursday night by Goddard['s] agent and my agent going carefully through each name together, the promises are as follows: Gooch 2,722; Goddard 2,215; Cadogan 2,160; but 525 votes are not accounted for & they may go in a large degree against us, but if they do it cannot alter my position, should all my promises hold good. The polling on Wednesday will prove the result, and I may next Sunday be again a M.P. (whatever that honour may be worth).

I received my Patent last Sunday from the Grand Master, as Pro Grand Master of Berks & Bucks, and I shall, I think, hold the instalation in January some time, at Windsor.

I hope to get to town for the winter before the end of the month. I am adding the adjoining house to mine and the workmen have left the place in a sad mess. The two houses will make a very good house suitable for the future baronets who may have a family to fill it. How deeply I ever feel the loss of one who would have given it its sunshine to me; Oh my beloved wife, may your spirit still reach it and bless it.

CLEWER, Nov 24TH. My election is over and I have again been returned for Cricklade. I went to Swindon on Monday to attend the market dinner and on Tuesday went to Cricklade for the nomination. What a farce that ceremony is; it is perfectly useless for any effect it has upon the result of a contested election. We had to speak to an excited and not very quiet rabble in the street. After each of the candidates had been proposed and seconded, Capt Horsall of Wootton Bassett proposed me, and Armstrong of Swindon was my seconder. I made a very short speech and was listened to pretty fairly by the mob. The shew of hands was declared in favour of Cadogan and me. All passed off very peaceably and we returned to Swindon. The following day, Wednesday the 18th, the polling took place and produced a result very different from what I had calculated upon, the numbers being as follows: Cadogan 2,844 (Radical); Gooch 2,452; Goddard 2,009; so that I polled a great many less than I had received promises. Where the falling-off took place I have not yet learned. The Radicals proved much stronger than we expected.

I was truly glad when the day ended, and returned to Clewer by the 6pm train, leaving Foote to appear for me at the declaration of the poll on the Thursday; but it was a great pain and trial to come back to a lonely house, not a soul to give me a welcome or to offer me one word of congratulation. I felt how bitter it was and how valuless my victory. Poor Norval was glad to see me, and put his paws upon my shoulders to lick my face and give me all the welcome a poor dog could do. I lay down in bed that night thoroughly weary and sick of life, while I ought to have felt happy in my success; but what is success without a kind loving heart to share it with you and to sympathise with your feelings? I have often asked myself since whether the prize is worth the trouble, annoyance and cost in every way. I say not, and it is most certain I will never fight a contested election again, without my views change very much.

The present Parliament will have a hard session, yet I hope it may be many years before Gladstone carries the disendowment & disestablishment of the Irish church. I cannot help feeling the Radical party will not be so unanimous when they come to deal with the details of the measure. Gladstone has had a good lesson today in the loss of his election for South & West Lancashire; he was elected for Greenwich a week ago & he must be content with that. I have been present today at the opening of the new meat & poultry market in the City of London, on the site of the old Smithfield Market.[20] There was of course a great feed on the occasion, some 1,200 sat down to a cold collation. The ground we sat on has seen very different scenes; we had the satisfaction of feeling that what we assembled today to witness was a marked improvement upon former gatherings.[21] It will be a capital market, altho' I cannot say I admire the external architecture. The Gt Western Railway Co have capital premises under the market.

JANY 1ST, 1869. Another year has rolled away, a year of deep and lasting sorrow to me, the only real sorrow, by comparison, of my whole life. How little did I think when I entered upon 1868 how deep a grief was in store for me; the thought of losing my dear wife would have been the last thing to occur to me. How little can we look into the future; how merciful is this blindness. God alone knows what this year will bring to me. May He in His mercy comfort my stricken heart and give me courage and strength to submit with patient resignation to His will, and grant that when my call comes I may be prepared to join her in Heaven, never, never to part. Her spirit has been with me in my dreams twice within the last few weeks, once in great sadness; but there is comfort in the feeling left on the mind, even by a dream. I find it hard to realize the fact that I can never see her on earth again. My mind feels that she is only from home, and will come back; Oh, if this were really so, what a blessed meeting it would be. How I would strive to make up to her any sorrow I may have caused her in the past. She was ever one of the best and purest of wives & her absence has left a sad blank at my Christmas fireside. Her sister Jane Tweedy has kindly come to stay with me and is a great comfort; in so many things is she like her poor sister, kind and considerate in all things. I am very grateful to her for all she does to make me happy.

The alterations in the house at Paddington are nearly finished and will add very much to the comfort of it, but I can feel very little personal interest in the alterations. I ever think of the absence of the one who would have given sunshine to it. Now it seems as tho' I was acting only as an agent for those who are to succeed me. Before, when making improvements, I have always felt how much pleasure it would give my dear wife and looked forward to seeing her pleased with them.

FEBY 21, 1869. My poor sister Barbara died on the morning of the 18th at Birmingham; she had been long ill. So is a second void made in our family; it is probably seldom a family of 10 children are spared so long. William, the youngest of us, is about 40; Barbara was the oldest of the family and was upwards of 60. She has never been very strong; her end was peace.

147

Parliament was opened on the 16th. The Queen having a *head ache* could not be present, a poor excuse for neglect of duty, but it might be her dislike to her new ministers. She fixed to receive the Address at Buckingham Palace tomorrow, by the whole House; this has been put off in consequence of the illness of her son Leopold.

We have had a wonderfully mild month, not a flake of snow and scarcely a few hours frost, but very heavy rain and violent storms of wind. The park at Clewer has been flooded 3 times. Harry and his family have been staying with me since Xmas and left on Friday. I have also had my sister Mary Ann and her husband and 2 children staying with me for a fortnight. Today I am quite alone; it feels dreary work with a large house and not a soul to speak to. How heavy has been my loss; each month seems to make it more sad to me. I was never fitted to live alone; home has ever been a meeting place for me, but home is no home without a good and loving wife and will probably never be so again to me. I often try and picture to myself the possibility of another wife, but I now feel there is none living who can replace the one I have lost, and a lonely home is better than an unhappy one.

MARCH 1, 1869. I had a strange dream a few nights ago. Going to bed feeling very weary of life and almost longing for its end, I prayed to the spirit of my poor wife for comfort. I could not have been long asleep when, if it was a dream or a reality I know not, but she stood so plainly at my side, looking Oh how sad; yet she mentioned to me the name of a lady who is almost a stranger to me, one who I have certainly not met more than half a dozen times but who I have often heard my dear wife speak of in kind terms, and as one who stood very high in her good opinion. In such a matter she was generally right; I do not think I ever knew her take a fancy to any one who did not deserve it. They used to ride together occasionally. The vision was so clear to me that I awoke and almost put out my arms to grasp that which was gone. I wonder if there is any reality in dreams—are the lost ones permitted to thus visit us? I could almost believe it; my mind has been full of these thoughts since, yet it can be only a dream and like others will pass away and probably be forgotten.

MARCH 21, 1869. My poor sister Barbara was buried in the vault at Claines. I felt unequal to the task of attending the funeral.

Parliament is now engaged upon the question of the Irish Church. Gladstone brought in the Bill on the 1st March in a long and clear speech, and adjourned the 2nd reading until the 18th when Disraeli moved that it be read a 2nd time that day 6 months. He made a very good and powerful speech, and the division will take place on Tuesday night next. This is a beginning to serious and momentous changes in the relation between Church and State in this country; it will not stop at Ireland. There is a spirit of change abroad that will know no stopping place on this question, and the Church of England is doing its best by internal divisions to help its enemys. I may not live to see it, but many years cannot elapse until we find it also severed from the State. I feel this will be a sad day for England.

Our Trades Union Report was presented to the House last week. I wish it had been a stronger one against the unions. I fear it will not do much good in its present form.

The half-yearly meeting of Gt Western shareholders was held on the 12th and passed off very well. I, unfortunately, had a bad cold and very little voice, and feared I would break down, but I managed to get through it.

MARCH 22ND, 1869. Today is the 31st anniversary of my wedding day, the first time for the whole of that long period I have not been able to wish the sharer of my life many happy returns of the day. How little did I think just one year ago that the time during which we had yet to share life together was compressed into a few weeks. How much do I miss all her devoted love for me. If time has worn off the acuteness of the sorrow, it has but served to deepen the sense of my loss and to make more clear to my feelings the many great virtues she possessed. Oh Peggy, what of this world would I not sacrifice if I could have you again by my side, to look forward to ending my own life with you as my nurse and comforter. 31 years ago today we plighted our faith to each other; you promised to love and comfort me. How nobly have you kept that promise—aye, more than kept it, as this world goes. As I look back on all the years we have passed together, more deeply I feel your love and devotion. How much has any success in my own life been due to the happy home made for me by you, the care and prudence with which you managed all my household affairs. How much is my happiness now increased by your care and training of our children, who are all a comfort to me. Oh how dear is your memory in my heart.

GOOD FRIDAY, MARCH 26TH. On Tuesday night, or rather early on Wednesday morning, the division on the Irish Church was taken in the House of Commons. The return on the other side will shew the result. How far the Bill may be modified in committee it is difficult to say, but I fear the Church is gone and a step has been taken that will lead to further changes. God grant it may be for the good of my country, but I fear the contrary.

APL 4TH, 1869. Last Wednesday, the 31 March, the Masons of Wiltshire gave me a very splendid suit of Masonic regalia for the Pro Grand Master of Berks and Bucks, on my retirement from the office of Dep[u]ty P.G. Master of Wilts and my appointment to the head of the Province of Berks & Bucks. The meeting was held at Chippenham, for which purpose the Swindon Lodge (The Royal Sussex Lodge of Emulation) held their meeting in Chippenham to receive the Pro Grand Lodge. Lord Methuen presided at the Grand Lodge and there was a very full attendance of brethen from Wilts and other provinces. Lord Methuen presented the regalia to me in a very kind speech, and all the brethren shewed me great kindness and brotherly feeling. I had every reason to be much gratified with my reception. It is a happy feeling to receive, I will not say the applause of our fellow men, but rather the esteen and affection of those with whom we have been associated in any part of our life. The meare value of the gift to me was small compared with the warmth and sincerity of the kind wishes that accompanied it. I shall ever value this clothing and trust those who succeed me will consider it as something to be preserved in the family, of which they may ever feel proud.

After the Lodge was closed we dined at the Angel Hotel, a party of about 110, and all passed off very well. There is a curious bond of union between Masons, a something to be felt but cannot be described. I have never regretted joining the Brotherhood & have made very many good friends and have spent many happy hours in its ceremonies. I am glad some of my boys are Masons—they ought all to be so. How I miss my dear wife on an occasion of this kind. When I came home from Chippenham late at night I had not a soul to say a kind welcome to me, not one with whom I could share the pleasure the day had given me. My heart longed for the sympathy of her who had ever shared my joys and sorrows, doubling the former and greatly reducing the latter. Oh my dearest Peggy, I feel my life is now only a barren rock.

SUNDAY, MAY 17, 1869. Just 12 months ago today I first learned the danger of my poor wife and my eyes were opened to the sad prospect before me. I was at Clewer yesterday and all looked so beautiful, yet it lacked the feeling that she could share it with me. Bright tho' it was, I felt lonely and weary.

I went to Paris last Saturday with our dep[u]ty chairman Mr Wood & Grierson our general manager, to meet the chairmen of the Orleans & Western of France Railways with the view of seeing whether it was possible to arrange with them a service between Weymouth & Cherbourg. I do not think much will come of it.[22] I saw great change in Paris since my last visit in 1863. We dined with a French family of the name of Tiersonnier; it was the first time I had seen the family life of the French. They were very kind. I cannot say I like their plan of the gentlemen leaving the dinner table at the same time as the ladies. I went to the church of Notre Dame and was much pleased with it; it has been completely restored inside and is very beautiful, of a grand and quiet character. We returned on Wednesday to London. Paris looked very beautiful with the spring foliage & flowers on the trees; the Bois de Bologne is also very beautiful.

CLEWER PARK, MAY 22, '69. I came here last night to sleep and be alone today with my own thoughts and to dwell on the past. Clewer looks very beautiful, yet is there a sad want, the want of that one being who has for so many years shared with me the pleasure of looking on the flowers & fresh hues. It is very hard to be left alone in my old age when the care and love of a good wife is perhaps of most importance to us. I could picture today many happy hours spent at Clewer with my poor dear wife. I tried to recall every bright and happy look, and they were many. I looked in grief on the spot where all that is earthly of her lies, and asked God to permit me one day to be reunited with her spirit in Heaven. It is 12 months today since she was taken from me; to my mind the time looks much longer, and the future looks a dreary life of loneliness. What am I to do? My dear sister Jane Tweedy[23] has been a great comfort to me, so like my poor wife in many things, so kind and attentive to all that lessens my loss. If she could remain permanently with me it would be a great blessing, but that is not possible. May God in His mercy give me comfort.

LONDON, MAY 23, '69. On Friday I was installed as the Pro Grand Master of Berks and Bucks. The ceremony was performed by the Grand Secretary, Brother Hervey. There was a very large meeting of the brethren; the Lodge was held in the school room in the Batchelors Acre in Windsor, and the banquet in the Town Hall. Some 150 to 160 sat down to dinner; this was about as many as the hall could hold. Every thing passed off in a very satisfactory manner. After the meeting I went to Clewer and stayed there all night.

SUNDAY NIGHT, CLEWER, JUNE 13. I came down here on Friday with my belongings, and yesterday and today have been here alone with Alfred. I was glad to spend a couple of quiet days before leaving for the Great Eastern, and therefore had no one down. The place looks very beautiful to the eye, but it is a barren heath to the heart. I was never calculated to live alone; I need the quiet companionship of a wife. Oh that God had spared me her who was so true and so loving, yet judging of her feelings by my own it was a mercy to her to take her first. How hardly would she have borne my loss. Oh Peggy, how dear is your memory to me.

On Wednesday night I took the chair at the Railway Guards' Society at the Can[n]on Street Station hotel. It was a large and successful meeting, and they express themselves very much pleased with their success. Upwards of £600 was collected towards their funds and there must have been a couple of hundred at dinner.

GREAT EASTERN STEAM SHIP, PORTLAND. THURSDAY JUNE 18 [recte 17], 1869. Once more I am sitting in my cabin here, getting ready for another Atlantic cable expedition.[24] I well remember how often, in this cabin 3 years ago, I resolved I would not again go on such an expedition, and probably will often feel the same on this trip. But I love this old & noble ship and cannot pay her a visit without a strong longing to stay with her. I left town on Tuesday morning accompanied by the directors of the Great Western Railway, who have very kindly taken advantage of this occasion to give me a dinner, which was held at the Royal Hotel at Weymouth on Wednesday night. Some of the directors & officers of the Bristol & Exeter, the South Devon and the Cornwall Railway came. Nothing could be more gratifying than the kindness and warmth of the expressions used towards me in the speeches. About 50 sat down to dinner; Mr Wood, our deputy chairman, was in the chair. Probably to few men could a more agreeable compliment be made; the men who sat round that table were no strangers to me, but men with whom I had been associated for very many years. Some of those who have left our direction were present: Mr Williams of Chester, Mr Bodenham of Hereford and Mr D. Ogilvie of London. They travelled a long distance to shew me a kindness & I may rightly feel happy in the feeling that years of steady perseverance in the line of my duty have thus obtained the respect and esteem of so many old friends. I brought them on board the ship in the afternoon, with which they were very much pleased, and all went off very well. Mr Talbot kindly stated that altho' he had been opposed to my election as chairman, yet he was now very pleased he had been overruled. We kept up our party until nearly 12 oclock.

Yesterday the Mayor & Corporation of Weymouth gave us a breakfast in a tent, but first took us in a steamer to see round the harbour and Portland. Unfortunately the morning was very wet and we could not stay on deck, but by one oclock, when the breakfast time arrived, it cleared up and was a nice bright afternoon. All passed off very well and at 6 oclock I bid good bye to my friends and came on board the ship, glad to get the quiet we have here. We are all in excellent trim for our voyage; I never saw the old ship in so complete a state for a start. We have been a little disappointed about our coals; one of the 3 steamers that had to supply us with 2,000 tons put back from bad weather and only arrived in the middle of last night. We are taking as much out of her as we can, but do not intend to delay our voyage to take it all.

I had a telegram yesterday night saying the shore end was laid at Brest in the morning, so that I trust we will make the splice at Brest on Sunday and commence work across the Atlantic. Great credit is due to Halpin, who was first officer of the ship on her two former expeditions and now has the command. He has the great, and what I call unusual, power of doing things quietly yet well. The day is very wet but I hope it may clear up in the afternoon as we have given permission to the Weymouth people to come on board and see the ship. We have fixed to leave in the morning at 8. I had a kind letter last night from London. (*On opposite page* I ought to have been at the Queen's ball tonight, Thursday.)

JUNE 18, FRIDAY NIGHT. We had a large party of visitors on board this

BILL OF FARE.

Steam Ship
GREAT EASTERN.

19th Day of *June*

BREAKFAST.

Dishes of Beef Steaks
Do.   Mutton Chops
Do.   Pork Chops
Do.   Veal Cutlets
Do.   Smoked Salmon
Do.   Broiled Chicken
Do.   Fried Ham
Do.   Cold Meats
Do.   Stews
Eggs in Omelettes
Do.   Boiled
Hominy
Mush

DINNER.

	ROAST.	BOILED.
Soups... *Spring*		
Dishes Fish ...		
Do. Beef ... *Corn'd Round*		
Do. Mutton *Roast ...Legs*		
Do. Lamb...		
Do. Veal		
Do. Pork ... *Ox Tongue*		
Do. Pigs		
Do. Turkeys		
Do. Geese		
Do. Ducks *Roast*		
Do. Fowls		
Do. Curries *Chicken & Rice*		
Do. Stews		
Fricasé		
Made Dishes *Veal Cutlets*		
Calves' Heads		

VEGETABLES, ASSORTED.

PASTRY.

Apple Pies.
Ditto Puddings   *Cherry Tart*
Raspberry Tarts
Strawberry do.   *Gooseberry*
Cranberry do.
Plum do.   *Open*
Damson do.
Gooseberry do.   *French Pastry*
Roll Puddings
Plum do.   *Rice Pudding*
Rice do.
Pancakes   *Rhubarb*
Omelettes.

FIG 11   *Great Eastern* menu for 19 June 1869

afternoon, but it was dreadfully wet for them until between 3 & 4 oclock when it cleared up and has since been very fine. Sir Jas Anderson[25] and others came on board. I hope all will be here tonight or they will stand a chance of being left behind. I have been getting a cot rigged up today; to sleep in it will be more comfortable when the ship rolls than the fixed berth. I had a telegram today from Capt Osborn, saying the French directors & their friends hope we will not leave Brest before Monday as they have made their arrangts to visit the ship on that day. This is very stupid of them as I told Baron [D']Erlanger when I saw him at Sheerness that we would be ready to make the splice on Sunday if the weather permitted, and I am not very likely to delay our work for the pleasure of these gentlemen. They must therefore alter their plans if they wish to see us & we have suitable weather.

JUNE 19, SATURDAY NIGHT. We had a lovely morning for our start from Portland and were punctual to our time, the ship being fairly under weigh at half past 8. All was done in a quiet and ship shape manner and we have had a lovely day. The Scanderia started with us and is in company; our speed has been about 6½ knots, paddles making 6½ and screw 29 revolutions. It is a great treat to see the paddle engines doing their work again. The ship is drawing 27 feet forward and 34 feet aft, or a mean of 30½ feet. We passed the Start light a little before 5, and are now crossing over, hoping to be on the French coast in the morning early. The weather has changed this evening as it is now raining a little and very cloudy. I got no sleep last night but hope for a better result tonight.

BREST, SUNDAY NIGHT, JUNE 20TH. We made a good run across the Channel last night and were off Ushant this morning at 8 oclock, but our stupid French pilot said the land we made was not Ushant and we went off to sea again until he was lost in his own blunder, and after wondering where we were an observation shewed us we had passed to the west of Ushant, so we stood in again and about one oclock made the same point we had been at early in the morning. This was very vexing as it has lost us a tide. The ship made between 8 & 9 knots during the night.

We arrived in Brest Roads about 3 and found the Hawk and Chiltern waiting for us. The day has been very fine and the scene was a very pretty one as we came in, some 6 or 7 steamers having come out from

Brest to meet us, but we did not have any one on board as the sea was rather lively for a small boat. I cannot say I was sorry at this as we had no wish to see the ship covered with a multitude of people. I had to be pretty firm with Canning to induce him to get our splice attempted tonight; he was very anxious to wait for tomorrow, but the sea is very calm and the moon beautifully bright, and we know not what tomorrow may produce in weather; so there is no reason or sense in delay and the work is now going on and will, I hope, be finished by day light. Capt Osborn came on board from the Hawk for an hour. We had church service on board this morning. I like the homely character of these services, they are more impressive than in a church, to me at any rate. The crew were mustered in their Sunday clothing before church, and are a better looking lot of men than I thought they were from seeing them about on the deck. Our steam capstan brings in our anchor at the rate of about 6 feet per minute, very steady and well.

I had a good sound sleep last night, and a strange dream that my dear wife had come back to me. I was unable to make out how it was, but the impression of the dream was left very strongly upon my mind. Oh God, that it was true and that I could again hold her to my heart, and as in former voyages I could say 'good night my beloved one'.

The coast near here is very rockey and not a very safe port to enter, I should think, but it is very well lighted. There are large detatched rocks scattered about, shewing their heads above the water, all very well in clear weather when you can see them, but rather awkward in a fog or in the dark. The party from Paris came off in a steamer, but wisely did not attempt to come on board; it would not have been quite safe for landsmen, indeed even for sailors. It is not a very safe job when there is a little sea on, as the boat may so easily get under our side ladders and be swamped, or the people get their heads crushed. I will now go on deck and see how the work is getting on.

JUNE 21, MONDAY MORNING, 11 AM. I am very glad I did not yield yesterday to the persuasions and difficulties made by Canning & Halpin, and postpone making the splice until today. Nothing could have been better for us than the weather and every thing else last night, and our splice was made without difficulty; and at 2 this morning the ship's head was turned for the Atlantic and our voyage began, not to be interrupted again, I hope, until we reach its end. I went to bed about 12 after seeing that every thing necessary was being done to the splice, and

SOCIÉTÉ DU CABLE TRANSANTLANTIQUE FRANÇAIS (LIMITED)

———··∞··———

M ————————————

     Lé Conseil d'Administration a l'honneur de vous inviter à l'accompagner dans l'excursion qu'il fera à **Brest**, le 19 courant, afin d'assister au départ du **Great-Eastern** chargé de l'immersion du Câble.

     Le Conseil d'Administration vous sera reconnaissant, Monsieur, de vouloir bien renvoyer cette Carte avant le 15 de ce mois, s'il vous était impossible d'accepter l'Invitation.

M *Sir Daniel Gooch Membre du Parlement*

LES INVITATIONS SONT RIGOUREUSEMENT PERSONNELLES

PROGRAMME

DE

L'EXCURSION A BREST, A L'OCCASION DU DÉPART DU GREAT-EASTERN

POUR L'IMMERSION DU CABLE

———··∞··———

     Départ de **PARIS** par train spécial **(Gare Montparnasse)** lo samedi 19 Juin à 10 heures du soir.

     Déjeuner à **Saint-Brieuc** à 7 heures du matin.

     Arrivée à **Brest** le 20 Juin à 11 h. 20 m. du matin.

     Le 20 Juin à 7 heures 1/2 du soir: Banquet à la salle de Venise.

     Le 21 Juin, excursion pour visiter le **GREAT-EASTERN**, et assister à son départ. (Le lieu et l'heure d'embarquement seront indiqués.)

     Départ pour **PARIS** le 21 Juin par train spécial à 7 heures 50 minutes du soir.

     Arrivée à **PARIS** à 8 heures 30 minutes le lendemain matin.

———··∞··———

     NOTA. — A l'arrivée à **Brest** des Cartes seront remises à MM. les invités pour leur indiquer les Hôtels où leurs chambres seront retenues, et où ils pourront prendre leurs repas.

FIG 12   Invitation issued by the French cable company to visit the *Great Eastern* and witness her departure from Brest. Some modification of the programme must have been necessary as she did not arrive until 3pm on the 20th and set sail at 2am on the 21st

got up again when the gun fired about 2 this morning to signal our departure, and went on deck, where I remained until 4 and then turned into bed again. There was a glorious sunrise, but a red one, so we may have rain before the day is over, but it is, up to this time, a beautiful day & the sea like a sheet of glass. Our start has been an admirable one in every respect. The heavy portion of our cable is running out beautifully.

It is strange on both the occasions of my being in bed last night my dear wife was with me in my dreams. Since she was taken from me I have not dreamt of her more than 4 or 5 times, yet in the last two nights 3 times has she been with me. Is it indeed her spirit that has been permitted to visit my bedside and give me encouragement and hope? Oh my dear Peggy, if on earth I know how full your soul would be of anxiety and hope for me, and I will believe God has permitted your spirit to be with me for some wise purpose. I do not forget before my last voyage a dream you used to tell me of, assuring you of my success and which inspired you with so much confidence. You told me we would not fail; I will believe it is a God-sent dream to me now, and we will not fail.

MONDAY NIGHT, JUNE 21ST. This is the longest day and the end of the first day of our work; all has gone on as well as we could wish. There is some hitch with the people on shore as we cannot speak to them, altho' they speak to us. The electricians are a little puzzled with it and say it is owing to the arrangt of the cable in our tanks, and that when the heavy end is all out it will be all right. It cannot be any fault in the cable itself as that is perfect. At noon today we were in Lat 48–18, Long 5–40 and had done 41 miles from Brest, leaving about 2,300 miles to St Pierre. Cable payed out: [*blank*].

We have seen a great many ships today. Our depth at present is only about 60 fathoms. We are working only 3 boilers, 2 screw & one paddle; they are all connected so that the pressure of the steam is the same in each. With $14\frac{1}{2}$ lbs the pad[dles] made $4\frac{1}{2}$ rev[olutions] and the screw 17; this would give a speed including slip of 6·55 k[nots] in the pad & 7·3 in the screw. With steam at $16\frac{1}{2}$ lbs the pad gave 5·5 rev and the screw 21·5, = speed of pad 8·0 and screw 9·3—speed of ship 6 k. This shews a large amount of slip.

We had some rain this afternoon for an hour; it then cleared up but will, I think, rain again before morning, but the glass keeps high and steady. The sea is perfectly smooth and indeed the weather is all we could wish. I hope we will get some news from England tomorrow; we have had none today and I am anxious to hear what the Lords have done with the Irish Church Bill. Altho' this is the end of our first day it looks a long time to go on paying out the cable; say 5% is done. I think I shall be glad when it is done and I am once again in England. God bless all dear ones there.

TUESDAY NIGHT, JUN 22. All has gone on today as well as we could wish. The weather has been fine but dull, with the exception of 4 or 5 hours in the middle of the day, enabling good observations to be taken at noon. The shore end was all paid out about one oclock this morning, and we have since been paying out the main cable; it is running out beautifully from the large tank. Tonight, about one, we change to the forward tank. Good messages have been exchanged with the shore today and I was glad to learn the House of Lords had read the Irish Church Bill a second time. I hope they will materially alter its clauses; the majority was 33. No other message of any interest has come to us.

At noon today I had the following returns: Lat 48–30, Long 8–55. Distance run 130 miles. Total distance from Brest 171 miles. Cable payed out 177·7 do. Engine: pad 4·8 rev, screw 19·94. Coals consumed 117 tons.

We started a game at shuffle board today; when all is going on so well there is not much excitement and time hangs a little heavy, altho' I prefer this to the excitement. It is a week today since I left pretty Clewer; I wonder if all is well in England.

WEDNESDAY NIGHT, JUN 23. We have had a glorious day today. Nothing could have been finer than the weather, bright, warm sunshine, enabling capital observations to be made, and all has gone well with the cable. We changed from the main to the forward tank this morning at half past one and the cable is running out very well from this tank, as it is now carried the whole length of the ship. Our line of lamps tonight looks very well and gives us a good imitation of Oxford Street.[26] Since the change of tanks there has been a difficulty again in speaking with the shore, The electricians seem now to have made up their mind that the former difficulty arose from the coil we were paying out not being continuous with the remainder of the coil in the tank, and the signals being the result of induction, by which they were received on shore (so confusing them), and when they had got into the way of reading them

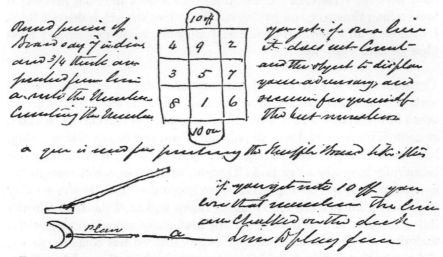

FIG 13 Notes and sketch by Gooch for the game of shuffle board played on
board the *Great Eastern*

our change of tanks has again altered it, and they learn slowly. We have
got some messages, though very slowly, but as they are improving I
hope by tomorrow all will be right and we will be able to get some
news. Our position &c today is as shewn on the annexed return.[27]

I have not felt very well last night and today. I could not sleep and
am weary; I hope to be all right tomorrow. I should like to call at
Paddington tonight and learn what our Gt Western receipts were last
week.

THURSDAY NIGHT, JUN 24. We had a fault in the cable this morning at
half past 3 oclock. The ship was stopped very quickly after the signal
was given from the testing room, the paying-out drums only making 60
revolutions; stoppers were put on and the cable cut forward and put
upon the hauling-in gear. $1\frac{1}{4}$ miles was then hauled back before the
fault was got on board at about a $\frac{1}{4}$ before 8. The splice was at once made
and the ship again under weigh at half past 9. The depth of the water
was about 2,200 fathoms and it gave a strain on the dynamometer of
about 4 tons, quite enough, as a good many wires were broken in the
cable pulled in. We held an inquest on it this afternoon and found the

fault was caused by a small puncture in the cover which must have been done before it was covered, as it was not new. There is no doubt the extra strain it had in paying out extended the injury sufficiently to bring it to light. It is a great satisfaction to find it is not caused by a broken wire in paying out, as we may hope it is not likely we will find such another fault. The hauling-in gear forward pulled the cable back very well, but with more strain on it than if the engine had been applied to the paying-out gear.

As tho' this fault and its anxieties was not sufficient for us, a false alarm was given at 20 to 11 of another fault. The light flew off the scale and did not come back. From the force with which the mirror had moved, causing it to stick, it is supposed some one on shore must have touched one of the wires by accident, giving dead earth. The ship was stopped but as the mistake was quickly discovered we went on again at once. Nothing could have been more favourable for dealing with such an accident as we had this morning than our weather; indeed, the sea has been like glass and the day hot and lovely. Annexed is the working up to noon today.

A swallow came on board yesterday and we saw some sea birds round the ship. We have had 2 or 3 ships pass us today. As our electricians do not seem able to speak with the shore we have not sent or received any messages today. They seem a little at sea as to the cause of this; it is not induction now.

11·30AM SATURDAY JUNE 26. After the fault on Thursday the cable went out very well and seemed going right. During yesterday, between 10am and about 7pm the cable was used for passing messages; they came much better, but still very slow. When Willoughby Smith, after dinner (or about 7pm) went to the test room he reversed the current and then saw a decrease in the resistance. He took steps to try and satisfy himself of the cause and the locality, but was quite unable to do so. About 9pm he told me that there appeared to be a small fault or some other cause on shore for the change in resistance, but he could not say where, or whether it might arise from some change in the wires on shore. We at once went to Canning and after fully discussing the matter determined to cut off the main and after tanks from the circuit and see if any better indication could be obtained on the shorter length. This was done, but the defect still shewed itself between the ship and shore. It was then settled to cut off the cable remaining in the forward tank (about 300 miles) so as still further to shorten our circuit. This was done without giving any further information. A consultation was then held with the engineers of the French Co at 2am, viz Capt Anderson, Mr Jenkins, Mr Varley and Mr Clarke.[28] I had Canning, Halpin & Willoughby Smith, and Mr Rawson was with me.

I asked the French engineers to give me their opinion frankly, as my desire was to do that which would be best for the success of the enterprise, rather than to consider the interest of the Telegraph Co alone. I regretted I did not get from them any decided opinion as to what was best to be done, but they rather pointed out the consequences to the shares of the French Co if the cable was compl[et]ed with the slightest fault in it. None of them could give me the slightest idea of where the fault might be; indeed, Mr Jenkins said it might be a ship had injured the cable in Brest.

There appeared to be only 3 courses open to us; one, to go on and try to complete the cable. All seemed to agree that the fault was so slight it might not for very many years interfere with the working of the cable (Varley said an indefinite time), and should the fault develop itself afterwards it might then be located and repaired. Another, to begin and pick up the cable in the hopes of recovering the fault; the 3rd, to cut, and go back to shallow water and lift the cable and test it there, and if then found good to the shore, to splice on to it and go on to lay as much cable as might be left in the ship, bouying the end until new cable could be made and sent out from England to complete it. This 3rd plan appeared to be too uncertain, the 2nd also was a very hopeless task, to begin pulling back cable without the slightest idea whether it was 20 or 300 miles we might have to recover, and the almost certainty, if it became a work of many days, we would break it in 2,400 fath water from weather. I therefore decided to go on. In this view I was supported by all our staff, and we at once began to make the splices and started the ship at 5am this morning.

As tho' we had not had anxiety enough for one night, a very bad fault shewed itself at 8; the ship was at once stopped and the cable pulled in. After getting in ¾ of a mile the fault was on board. An examination of this fault shews it to be a clean and sharp puncture of a very similar character to the former one, only this had not the appearance of age about it the other had. The yarn over the hole was discoloured, but it was impossible to say whether it was an old fault or not. The splice was made & the ship started at 11am. These faults are quite a new feature in cable laying; in 1865 our faults could be accounted for by broken wires, as the piece of wire was found in each, but here is simply a clean hole, and if done wilfully we know not how many we may have. It is very trying and enough to turn one's head grey. The weather continues all we could wish and the sea quite smooth. A large number of ships passed us yesterday; at one time 14 were in sight. We spoke 3 and reported them. It is just a week this morning since we left Weymouth.

Note: So little reason do I feel to be satisfied with the French engineers in this consultation that I am determined not again to trouble them. Their whole object, to my mind, was to protect themselves from having offered an opinion rather than to protect & secure the interests of their employers in assisting in any way they could in securing the completion of our work; would-be wise men, but are fools. One might suppose their selfish object was to procure further employment out of litigation. I will accept [ie except] Clarke from the above opinion, as he has in all cases acted with much more openness, and I think honesty, than the others.

This fault was very quickly treated; in 8 seconds after the gong sounded the engines were reversed, and in a distance of only 80 fathoms the ship was stopped. $\frac{3}{4}$ of a mile of cable was hauled back, the fault cut out and splice made, and ship under weigh again in $3\frac{1}{2}$ hours. Great credit is due to the men in the engine room for the prompt manner in which they acted on getting the signal in all the cases of fault or alarm.

JUNE 26, SATURDAY NIGHT. What an up and down life is this cable laying. For the last 20 hours I have believed we could not now lay a perfect cable on account of the small fault reported in it, and on which some 100,000£ depends to the Construction Co. At 4 this afternoon I was agreeably surprised by Willoughby Smith coming to my cabin and telling me the fault had disappeared suddenly, and up to the present time it remains allright. I trust therefore it has only been caused by some derangement of the wires on shore, but what anxiety has it cost me. I will, however, not be too sanguine until another day has passed. I may now be glad I decided as I did last night, not to pick up in search of this fault. We might have lost the cable and would certainly have lost our time and labour. At present the cable is perfect and as I am very tired and weary I hope I will get a long, comfortable sleep tonight. I stood on the paddle box tonight to watch a beautiful sun set, the first we have had in the Atlantic; the sight is very grand. The weather continues all we could desire. For particulars of log see other side.

SUNDAY NIGHT, JUNE 27. All has gone well with our cable since last night, altho' I was stupid enough to believe another fault had occurred in the night, and from 2 to 5am laid awake, picturing what was doing on deck, and then thought all was right & the ship went on again. I woke up at 2 and fancied the ship was stopped, and got up and looked out of the window and somehow came to the conclusion that the paddles were turning back, but was so weary and tired I thought I would not go on deck. Had I done so, or looked more carefully at the paddles, I would have saved myself 3 hours of considerable anxiety.

The day has been very hot but very beautiful, and the sea perfectly calm, all we could wish. I am glad to say the electrical condition of our cable is excellent and we were able to report it perfect today; God grant it may continue so. We will finish the forward tank tomorrow night; the ship is now more than 7 feet [down] by the stern. There is a very heavy dew, making the decks quite wet, but the sun set like a continuation of fine weather. I had a telegram from Osborn saying all was well in England. My head has felt very queer today, but I hope if I get a good night's rest all will be well tomorrow. The log at noon today is annexed. Jenkins wanted to telegraph today 'insulation of cable improving', which I refused to send, as it was not a true representation of the fact, and it was altered by giving the figures as to the resistance.

JUNE 28, MONDAY NIGHT. The weather today has been bright, hot and lovely, the sea like a lake; a couple of whales were alongside the ship, also a sun fish and a flying fish. It is unusual to see the latter fish so far north and must indicate fine weather. We certainly have so far been wonderfully favoured with the weather. Our cable has gone out very well today and we have just changed from the forward to the after tank, between 10 and half past; the change was done in a very quiet and admirable manner. Our ship is some 8 or 9 feet down by the stern, altho' we have got water in her bows; she will now come up quickly again as the after tank empties.

The supposed fault has shewn a loss of resistance this morning. They have been working the cable with 100 cells; this has now been reduced to 20. It is a very provoking thing, this defect, as we do not seem able to place it at all or, indeed, do our people feel certain it is a fault. It is so small and the same effect may be produced from other causes. How difficult it is to get a line 2,600 miles long without so much as the prick of a pin in it, and to get this safely stretched across the ocean. This matter shewing itself again has a little disheartened us, and we are not a very cheerful party today, so much are we ruled from hour to hour by the fluctuations in our cable's prospects. It looks a long time to look forward before we reach the end of our journey, and this night & day continued anxiety is very wearing, more than is good for me. This shall be the last time I will ever undertake so long an expedition; I cannot get any sound sleep. Log annexed.

TUESDAY JUNE 29TH. All has gone on well today in paying out the cable; log annexed. The weather has been very fine but much cooler and this morning there is a good deal of wind and broken sea from the south. Some of the sailors say it is going to blow, while others say not; time will shew. We are now a little over half way through the deep water, or to the southern point of the Banks of Newfoundland. If all goes well another week will take us there, when we have only 360 miles to lay in shallow water, and then home to England. How glad I shall be to see the ship's head turned in that direction & our work finished. The cable continues to improve in insulation, altho' the question of a fault or no fault is an open one yet between our electicians and the French ones. I hope I will be able to sleep tonight; I have had very little good sleep yet.

JUNE 30TH, WEDNESDAY MORNING, 11 AM. Those who said it was going to blow were certainly right last night. It is now blowing a very heavy gale from the S.E. and we had the additional misfortune to have a fault at 5 this morning; the light was seen to fly off the scale and immediately return, and in 5 minutes it again left it, not to return. The ship was at once stopped and hauling in begun, but the gale was too much for us and after getting a strain on the dynamometer of 5 tons the cable parted, fortunately between the paying-out machinery and the hauling-in gear forward. It was also very fortunate that the paying-out machinery and the stoppers held the end. It was at once bouyed & now rides by the bouy in the middle of the Atlantic. This is a great trouble to us; I cannot understand these constant faults as we find nothing like broken wires to account for them. It was also very singular that the light left the scale 5 m[inutes] before the fault was again seen, as tho' some sharp instrument had been pushed into the cable and at once withdrawn again. One does not like to suspect men of such wickedness, yet it is hard to believe these faults accidental, particularly as we had not a single one during the time the cable was being manufactured and stowed into the tanks.

The storm is now raging in a mad way, wind & rain and a very heavy sea. We are putting down a mark bouy; the Scanderia was told to do so also, but after trying we saw she gave up the task. It is awful to see these ships with the seas running clean over them; it makes one dread every minute seeing them go down. I cannot say I am sorry they are out of sight; I have stood in the bridge compass house for a couple of hours watching them. I at times felt that the bridge house itself would be blown away. Anderson thinks the gale is too heavy to last long, the glass fell 5/10ths of an inch; he says it is a very heavy gale—I have certainly not seen anything like it before, altho' I have seen larger waves. We must ever hope it will quickly subside and that we will be fortunate in recovering our end again; if not, I fear we must grapple for it, and then our work is very uncertain. It has fortunately happened in the shallowest water we have been in [in] the mid-Atlantic, being only between 1,800 and 1,900 fathoms. The fault was very nearly in when the cable broke, but if we had got it in the gale increased so much we could not have held on to it to splice.

We had fiddles[29] on the table for breakfast, but a French lamp stood on my cabin table all night until breakfast time, when I had it removed; I think some of our rolls made since would have upset it. Poor Norval is very unhappy; he will not leave my feet.[1] He would much prefer a run with his master in Clewer Park, poor dog. I feel for him as he cannot understand it. While the ship was backing her stern up against the wind, hauling in, 3 seas came in board, altho' not a great deal of water. It broke up the platform and part of the bullworks.

JUNE 30TH, WEDNESDAY NIGHT. Both wind and sea have gone down a good deal but the glass is still falling, and very different opinions are held as to the chances for tonight and tomorrow. We saw our bouys a little before dinner, one on the end of the cable and two mark bouys; they seemed all to be riding very well. We have been performing the very disagreeable duty all day of driving to windward for 10 or 12 miles and then turning round and running back again. Some of these turns in the cross seas gave us a very lively roll. There has not been much rain since morning. The old ship has behaved very well and has, as a rule, been very steady. As we can now do nothing but look after our bouys until we get fair weather I will have no anxiety on my mind tonight. I need not listen for a fault so I hope I will get a good sleep; I want a good long one very badly. I wonder if they know in England we have cut adrift from the cable, and if so, what they think of it; I daresay it will influence the shares. The end of our cable is in Lat 47–56, Long 30–05. Poor Norval is very unhappy with this weather; he got on the sofa beside me today and laid his head on my breast and squeezed his body in between me and the back of the sofa to keep him steady, and then thought himself all right.

THURSDAY JULY 1ST. The weather & sea today has not been such as to make it safe to attempt getting the cable on board, altho' it has gradually moderated, and if we could have been sure that it would have continued to improve I think we would have been tempted to try it, but the glass would not shew any signs of going up until evening. It has risen very slowly and we can only hope for suitable weather tomorrow, so we have had the pleasure of doing a little steaming and a little drifting about our bouys. They all seem riding very comfortably. I had a very good night's rest last night; I knew nothing could turn up to add to our difficulties, and my cot did very well as avoiding the rolling of the ship, but it is sad, weary work all day long with nothing to do. One tires of reading. I shall be very glad to see the wheels of the paying-out machinery running again, and that we are progressing towards the end of our voyage. On the other side is given the exact position of the end of the cable by *good* observation today. The Chiltern lost one of her life boats yesterday in the gale; no other damage has been done to either of the ships.

FRIDAY MORNING, JULY 2ND. I remember when a boy being much interested in reading a book called Lights & Shadows of a Scottish Life.[30] If I had the skill I think one might write an equally chequered description of the Lights and Shadows of Cable-Laying Life. We have just started on our voyage again with the cable all right over our stern. The morning was all we could wish for picking up the bouy and this work was begun between 4 and 5 this morning, and the end safely got on board by half past 7; and by 8 the fault was in, the splice made and the ship started at half past 10. We may indeed be very thankful we have got so well out of our difficulty, and we must only hope we have now had our share of them. I have just had a telegram from Osborn in answer to one I sent him a couple of hours ago. He says the French shares fell to 18 on the news of our trouble.

The Scanderia & Chiltern are picking up our mark bouys so that we will leave nothing behind beyond the one boat. I had a list of the people on board taken out yesterday; there are:

In Grand saloon	30
Electricians	21
Officers, engineers &c	42
Petty Officers	44
Seamen	84
Stewards & my servant	42
Firemen & trimmers	131
Leading cable hands	17
Ordinary do	32
Total	443

The cable was recovered over the stern this morning. All arrangts had been made to do so at the bow had the weather been at all unfavourable, but this being all we could wish it was done at the stern. The long lead of the cable along the deck, from the machinery forward & so on through the machinery aft, has this advantage, that there is most strain on the cable between these two points, and if it breaks as it did on Wednesday it is most likely to go there, and we have a better chance of securing the end before it gets overboard. I am therefore of opinion that this is the best arrangt, and we ought not to put the steam engine at the stern again. The leading sheaves would be better, I think, if they were a good deal larger, which can be easily done.

JULY 2, FRIDAY NIGHT. We examined the fault this afternoon. It, like the others, is a puncture, and the shape of this is exactly the shape of one of the scarfs of the iron wire round the cable, or thus [*small sketch*]. I have no doubt in my own mind it is caused in paying out, by one of these scarfs being broken and sticking into the coil below it in the tank. It is very provoking as there is no kind of security that we will not have a great many more of these. As a precaution we have put one of the officers of the ship into the tank with each watch, but I have given up all idea of its being the result of malice; this wire would hardly be put in so clean if done by a man's hand, it would be turned a little in the wound. We must therefore hope for fine weather so that if a fault does shew itself we have a better chance of cutting it out.

The weather has been very fine all day and there is every prospect of its continuance. The sun set was beautiful. There were a number of birds round the ship tonight, and some fish called skip jacks were seen; it is not usual to see them so far north. They are a small fish and jump out of the water. How glad I shall be when our head is turned towards England. The anxiety of the last few days is more than I can bear; it wears me down and makes me very weary, but we must do our best to complete our job. I should like to take the roofs off some houses in England and see my old friends, God bless them all.

SATURDAY NIGHT, JULY 3. Our cable has gone out all right today. We have put one of the officers of the ship and one of the French electrical staff to take watch in the tanks, altho' I do not think the faults were caused by willful act, yet it is wise to take every precaution in our power, and we are now coming to our deepest water, in fact the deepest water in which a cable has ever been laid, or 2,760 fathoms, or a little over 3 miles. I should be sorry to try the experiment of having to do any thing with the bottom in this part. A little after 5pm today the light left the scale again for a minute and made us all very anxious; it spoiled my dinner, for I could not eat. Just as we finished Willoughby Smith came down and told me he had been in communication with the shore & found one of the stupid clerks there had caused it by putting his hand on a naked wire. This carelessness is very vexing as it gives us great and un-necessary anxiety, but it is very satisfactory to learn the cause in this case as it no doubt explains the same things which have occurred before and been the cause of much discussion and anxiety; but I wish we had the careless fellow here and we would drum him round the ship. We have quite sufficient real cause for anxiety without being bothered with stupidity.

We had a good deal of news from shore today. I was glad to hear the Gt Western Bill[31] has passed the Lords. We also heard the Lords had been dealing with the Irish Church Bill in a way Gladstone does not like.

We must try some better plan of joining the ends of the iron wires; the present scarf system will not do. I have telegraphed today to Osborn to that effect, and Canning has also done so. We had very heavy rain this morning from about 7 until 11, when the wind got up and cleared it off, and the rest of the day has been very fine and sights were obtained at noon.

Several ships have been in sight today; we spoke one this evening and have reported her. If all goes on well another week will put us out of danger; just a fortnight today since we left Portland. It looks much longer & it seems a long time to look forward for a whole week. We have lost full 3 days by the faults. I wish I could sleep at nights; I scarcely got any sleep last night, and it is weary work lying in the dark, hour after hour, listening to every change in sound, expecting to hear a fault has gone over. If we have fine weather I do not fear a fault much, but the danger is they may happen in bad weather. The glass does not go up since it fell for the storm. Our sailors say the storm was equal to 10, 12 being the maximum number registered. It certainly blew great guns and I am not anxious to see another. Our consort ships today have been dipping their noses pretty deep into the seas while we have been as steady as an island. Our position &c is shewn on the annexed return.

How I should like to go and spend tomorrow at Clewer, and I am sure poor Norval would also, and get a good run in the park after the rabits instead of a promenade up and down our decks. Well, good night to all dear ones in England—they are asleep by this time.

SUNDAY, JULY 4TH. We had a good deal of news today from Brest. This is now my third Sunday on board; it looks a long time since I left home and still longer until I can hope to return to it. Yet why should I wish to return? The bright, loving face that has greeted me on former occasions is no longer there. I seem almost, at times, to feel the past is a dream and that my dear wife is waiting for me; oh God that it was so. As I sit and look at her portrait I can hardly think I am never in this world to look on that sweet face again; I may return to my home and not find one loving face to give me welcome.

All has gone on well today with our cable; the log is annexed. The weather has been very fine with a strong head wind & rather cold. To-night it is raining; I shall not care for rain if we do not get fogs and wind. We had a good deal of news from Brest today, and some ships have been in sight, but the time hangs heavy and it is difficult to get through the day. I should like to get a couple of hours sleep, but it will not come. We had church today as usual.

JULY 5TH, MONDAY NIGHT. All has gone well today with our cable, and its insulation is improving very rapidly as we get it into the water.[32] The day has been fine with a strong head wind and tonight the wind seems getting up; I hear the sea pretty rough outside my cabin. Some ships passed us very close this afternoon, but very few of the ships we fall in with have flags enabling them to speak to us. The annexed return will shew we have done a steady day's work. I had a very bad night again last night; I could not sleep and I think I felt much more weary this morning when I got up than I did when I went to bed. I fancy one's nervous system has been a little overstrained and nothing but perfect quiet and freedom from anxiety will put me right. The doctor has given me a bottle to take tonight, which he says will make me sleep without its giving me a headache or any other disagreeable tormence [torments].

Clark told me tonight that the faults we have cut out were a *million* times larger than the one they believe to be in the cable, and that he thinks for all practicable purposes, even if the fault exists, the cable will work as well and last as long as a prefect cable. Our insulation is now higher than the Atlantic cables are at present, and very much higher than when they were laid.

WEDNESDAY JULY 7TH. I was unable to write last night as the ship was rolling so heavily I could not burn a lamp in my cabin, and the candles hung up do not give sufficient light. The doctor's bottle has been of great use to me in giving me some sleep. I had a very good night the night before last and did not know until I woke at 5 yesterday morning what a gale had sprung up, and we have since had hard times of it. The gale was very heavy up to yesterday evening, blowing from the N.N.W., and has left such a heavy beam sea that we are rolling in a most uncomfortable manner. Getting our dinner was a task of no slight difficulty; in saving a tureen of soup I got a jug of milk over me. I felt the comfort of a cot last night, as while no one else got a wink of sleep I was very comfortable and with the help of the doctor's stuff got a good sleep, only disturbed at times by hearing things rolling about and heavy seas breaking with the noise of thunder under the paddle sponsons, making the ship tremble. Some of the rolls were measured at 28°, thus [*sketch*].

The gale was a very heavy one and the Scanderia fell astern almost out of sight early in the morning, but picked us up again in the middle of the day. Both ships were shipping awful seas; they at times disappeared in a mass of foam and rose up again on the crest of the next wave with the water pouring off their decks like waterfalls. I cannot say

I should like to be with them. The wind went down towards evening and there is very little of it this morning, but it has left a very heavy beam sea and we are rolling very heavily. It is with difficulty I can keep my seat to write and have an occasional slide to one side or the other of the cabin.

Poor Norval is very unhappy; he cannot find any resting place. Last night he got under my cot to be near me, and laid with his back hard against the side of the sofa; and there he lay all night. The noise and motion frightens him and he likes to be as near me as he can. Yesterday afternoon I was lying on the sofa and he got up and worked himself tight in between me and the back of the sofa, and then felt pretty happy.

Fortunately all has gone on well with our cable, altho' when the ship rolls and the cable is running out near the eye it flies about a great deal and requires close watching. The insulation of the cable is improving very much. We join on the main tank this afternoon and by about 10 tonight will finish the after tank. If all goes well for 48 hours now we will be in shallow water, and this will be a great relief to us all. It is very anxious work in this deep water; over 3 miles is an awful depth. There has been very little increased strain on the dynamometer in the deep water. We have had a good lot of shore news the last 2 days; the Lords appear to be making important changes in the Irish Church Bill. I think I may be back yet before that question is settled. I am glad the Great Western Bill has been read a 3rd time by the Lords, but regret to see so small an increase in our receipts yesterday.

Our position was as shewn on Halpin's return.

THURSDAY MORNING, JULY 8. The heavy sea continued all day yesterday and our rolling also; I was unable to write at night. We had a very bad time of it at dinner, for it seemed to select that particular time for making its worst efforts. It is rather fun to see the struggle every one has to make to keep their place at the table and also to look after their plate and glasses. A dreadful amount of breakage takes place.

The day yesterday was very fine, a nice bright sun and very pleasant temperature for sitting on deck. Our position at noon was as shewn in Halpin's return. We coupled the main tank in the afternoon and changed from the after to main tank at half past nine at night; it was very well done. The engines were stopped & reversed in 8 seconds and the ship was stopped dead in less than 100 fathoms, or her own length. The sea has gone down very much during the night but there is still a good deal of roll. We had heavy rain at 7 this morning, but the day is since fine, altho' cloudy, and I fear we will not get an observation at noon. By tonight we will get into 1,800 fathoms water & by day light in the morning about 800, and during tomorrow turn round the tail of the Banks of Newfoundland, so that I hope all will go on well for another 20 hours and we will be past any serious trouble.

Our cable is running out of the large tank very well. We have just had a meeting in my cabin (Sir Jas Anderson, Halpin, Canning and myself) to determine the point we are to make for on the tail of the Bank, and Anderson has marked on my chart the course we settled. There are strong symptoms of ice ahead of us; last night the temperature of the water fell from 67° to 52° in a couple of hours. I should like to see some good large bergs if they were not in our way and would not come across our path in the dark.

FRIDAY MORNING, JULY 9TH. The heavy swell has continued so that we still feel the rolling of the ship too much for a lamp to be quite safe on my table, so I did not write any last night. The day continues very fine and our cable has run out admirably. The log up to noon yesterday is shewn on the other side, and I am very thankful to say we are now getting into shallow water; by 2 oclock we will be in 7 or 800 fathoms. The Chiltern has gone ahead to take soundings in the tail of the Banks and to take up a position in 500 fathoms water, and we will then stear for her. We are now making for a point we call A, and will then alter our course due west until we get to the point B, when we turn up north on the west side of the big Bank. I am very thankful to God we have reached thus far in safety and all danger to the success of our work is over. It has been a long and anxious operation. The cable tests are extremely high— higher than the former Atlantic cables, and I hope when we get the end landed it will be found that the supposed fault is a myth. It must at any rate be very slight in its character.

We have been on the look out for ice since yesterday. The air became very cold in the afternoon, the thermometer in the sun shewing only 57°; this morning it is only 50, but there is no sun. We have had a little fog in the distance but only for a short time. The wind is blowing a good breeze from the north, and this is said to be the best possible wind for keeping away the fogs, a very important matter to us for the next few days. We have as yet had no fog; a rather singular occurrence to pass so long a time in the Atlantic and not have any. A large sun fish passed very close past the ship yesterday; I thought he would go under the paddle—he missed by only about 6 feet—but did not seem to be at all disturbed by its noise so close to him. The sun seems inclined to get out; I hope by 12 they may be able to get an observation and so fix our position exactly at the tail of the Bank. We ought to be at St Pierre on Tuesday early, and I hope we may be able to leave there for England on Wednesday, and I may then get to Clewer by Sunday fortnight. We have lost 3 days by the faults.

FRIDAY NIGHT, JULY 9. The sun got out quite bright by 12 oclock to-day, and we were able to get capital observations. We exactly made point A on the chart as arranged yesterday (our most southern point) and have since been running due west along the tail of the bank. At 12 tonight we will reach point B, and then alter our course north for St Pierre. The annexed log will shew we made a good distance up to 12 today, and we have now increased our speed a little as we are in shallow water, the cable running out at about 7 knots. Our consort ships took two soundings this afternoon, one 840 fathoms and the other 620. It is quite a pleasure to look at the cable running out of the large tank, and at night when the tank is lighted the effect inside is very pretty.

Halpin gave us some champagne today to celebrate our arrival in shoal water. It is a great relief to every[one] and they all shew it in their faces and conversation like people suddenly relieved from a great weight on their mind. We are most fortunate in the weather; we had every reason to expect to be in fogs, and instead we have had the most lovely afternoon one can imagine, and tonight the sun set was most glorious—beautiful far beyond the power of words to express or a painting to delineate. The sea was a sheet of glass and the sun set behind a heavy fog bank which seemed to enclose the view, making it a lake with a margin of trees and mountains. It is a scene never to be forgotten.

We cannot hope for such weather to continue. I fear fogs will come and I will have the pleasure of hearing the fog whistle just over my head. We have been unable to get news the last few days, owing to the rolling of the ship making the light fly about on the scale, but we have got some this afternoon. I have never known the rolling continue so long as it has this time. I think for 3 days we have had the fiddles on the tables; today we did without them. Beckwith has been at work getting his paddle floats ready to put on. Only half the number are on at present. This looks like getting towards the end of our work, & I shall be very glad

."GREAT EASTERN."   *19*

Date........ Noon....*July 9th*........ 18*69*....

Lat. obs. *42-57-0 N.* | Long. Chron. *49-13 W*

Lat. D. R.*42-53* N. | Long. D. R. *49-10*

Course and Dist. made good *S 62 W Dist 131*
distance Run 1885

Course and Dist. to next Position *AT West 65 mile*

Engine Run ....*Robert C Halpin*

4.88 - 22.41
Coals, *Total Cable paid out 2121.94*
115 Tons *Days Run 144.97*

FIG 14 Ship's log form, signed by Capt Halpin, with additional data by Gooch

when we make our start home. Jenkins telegraphed today that the cable may now be considered successfully laid. What about his fault?

SATURDAY NIGHT, JULY 10. I was awoke this morning by the sounding of the steam whistle, and when I went on deck I found a pretty thick fog and could have imagined myself at Paddington station, with the constant whistling of the 3 steamers and the bleating of the sheep. Towards 10 oclock the fog cleared away and since then the day has been beautifully fine. The sun set tonight with a strong indication of wind and rain before morning. Our cable has gone out very well and at a good speed, or 7 knots, and the ship has made a good run; but an error in the compass has placed us too much by about 12 miles to the S.W. and into deep water, or some 1,200 fathoms. The compass error was not discovered until observations were taken this afternoon, so there is no doubt our course since 12 has still been too much to the S.W. We are now hauling up stiff to the north so as to strike the shallow line again. The consort ships have been sounding and will go ahead and sound again tonight. As far as the cable is concerned it is an advantage to have it in deep water as it is safer than in the 100 fathom line on the Banks, but not so safe for us who are laying it.

We saw a very curious effect of mirage this morning; a large ship on the horizon was upside down, sailing on her mast heads and her hull up in the clouds. It is a singular effect; beyond her was a heavy fog bank. It was very easy to imagine land today in the distance on many occasions. We have had some news from England. The question of a certificate for the cable is now becoming important. As the time is getting near Anderson has telegraphed to ask the French board to meet at Brest so that he may get instructions from them, but he tells them the cable is commercially perfect, and if they have withheld from the public the doubts raised by their officers as to a fault and the great rise reported in the shares has taken place, they have placed themselves in a very awkward position. If they now raise any doubts it would be simple folly to do so as all are agreed (fault or no fault) for all speaking purposes the cable is perfect and will last as long as it would do if there was with certainty no fault. They would appear to me simply to go out of their way to damage their property. Our shore tests will give us more accurate information. We expect to meet the Wm Cory tomorrow afternoon and if all goes well to splice to the shore end middle day on Tuesday. Our ship is getting very light and the paddles get very little hold of the water.

SUNDAY NIGHT, JULY 11TH. I feel deeply greatful to God for His great mercy in permitting us to complete our work. As I look back on the voyage of, now, 3 weeks, how many difficulties have we had to encounter, how much of discouragement, yet we have struggled on full of confidence. I never doubted we would lay the cable; my only fear was we might lose it and have weeks delay in picking it up, and my only doubt was the question of time, not the ultimate success. We have lost 3 days on the road, but now we are in 50 fathoms and tomorrow will be free from the cable.

It came on very foggy last night and rained in torrents, so that it was difficult to stear a course. Frequent soundings were made and so we have fished out our way to what we call Point B, the place where the Wm Cory had to meet us. During the night I was called up to learn that a kink had taken place in the cable as it left the eye of the coil in the tank, but fortunately it untwisted itself as it went over the drum on the top of the tank. Had it got into the machinery it might have given us trouble.

When I went on deck this morning the fog was very thick and our whistle has been any thing but agreeable since daylight, and has almost driven one mad all the morning. We had no church this morning as the officers and hands were needed on deck. When we went on deck after lunch the fog was beginning to clear away and by two oclock it lifted up, and much to our joy and satisfaction there was the Wm Cory and the surveying ship, the Gulnare,[33] commanded by Capt Kerr, not a mile ahead of us and exactly in our course. I was doubly glad of this for Capt Halpin's sake, as fault had been found with his navigation both by Anderson & the others connected with the French Co, but here the fact proved him to be right to a yard—nay, I doubt if he would not have run the Wm Cory down, so exact did he hit the point where she was ordered to take up her position. The lifting of the fog at the moment it did was a kind act of Providence. It has been quite clear all the afternoon and we have followed our pilot ships, but now the fog has come on again and we can see nothing and our whistle is hard at work, likely, I fear, to interfere with one's night's rest.

The completion of such a work as this makes one feel very joyous and long to have one dear to you to share it with. How glad I should have been to send a telegram this afternoon to my dear wife had she been spared to me, feeling how truly her heart would have shared with me the happiness of success. As this is probably the last day those who have sat round our dinner table will all meet there, I proposed our Capt's health; he has done his work exceedingly well, nay, nothing could be better, and I asked Sir Jas Anderson to propose Canning's health. I should like to see that old feud between these two healed up, and I hope this voyage has done much to accomplish it.

Early in the morning we will be at the shore end, where we will hand the end of our cable over to the Scanderia to make the splice and we will go on to St Pierre. We have lost the Chiltern since 7 this morning. Our distance run to Point B, or up to 2 oclock today, was 154 miles, and we have paid out 2,446 miles of cable, the Lat being 45-15 & Long 55-15.

MONDAY JULY 12TH. The fog continued very thick all night, but we followed our pilot ships up to the bouy where the shore end finishes. As we could not see it we went on a couple of miles beyond the distance and then cut the cable from our ship and bouyed the end at 9 this morning, hoping to get it clear some time during the day to make the splice and get on to St Pierre. But in this we have been disappointed, the fog never having cleared up for one minute, and it has been a long and weary day, nothing to do but blow our steam whistle and occasionally fire a gun, but we have not once seen any of the other ships & have not heard of the Chiltern. She would most likely make for St Pierre when she lost us; we are quite helpless in this fog. Halpin tried to catch some fish this afternoon, but it was a failure; they were not to be caught.

When we cut the cable there had been laid, including the shore ends, 2,583 miles, and we have 209 miles left in the main tank and about 4 miles that we picked up during the faults. The slack has been 11·14 per cent on the whole distance. The course come by the ship is only 4 miles longer than the exact distance measured on the Great Circle. This is very creditable to Halpin and his officers.

I have been concocting a message to the Emperor of the French today to be sent as the first message from St Pierre through the whole cable. How I wish we were there to send it. Had it been clear today I might have started for home tomorrow afternoon. There is no knowing how long this fog may last; it is quite calm. What wind there is is from the S.W. or the worst quarter. Norval has been very much disgusted by the guns today; poor dog, he does not like them but tries to hide himself, and trembles for 10 minutes after they are fired. He will, I am sure, be glad to get home. I dreamt last night of my dear wife; not a very happy dream.

MIQUELON, TUESDAY NIGHT, JULY 13. When I had finished writing last night I went on deck a little before 10 oclock and was astonished at the change in the weather. I had come down only a couple of hours before, leaving it enveloped in a dense & very wet fog. When I went back all was clear and the moon and stars were shining bright. This gave us great hopes for today and we were not disappointed; I got up at day light and found the beginning of a lovely day. We at once made preparations to join up the cable, or rather to find the two bouys; this took us until 8 oclock and they were a couple of miles apart. The French engineers wanted to pick up one for a distance so as not [to] have so much bend in the cable. This I declined to do, so we spliced on to the shore end and from the Great Eastern paid out a couple of miles to the other bouy, so that on the main cable the first splice was made in the Scanderia and the Wm Cory was sent to pick up the other bouy ready to take the end from us when we reached it. On our coming up to him we found he had got the bouy but no cable. A pin in the shackle had worked out and so lost the end of the cable. This was a very vexatious thing as it was necessary to get the grapnels out in two of the ships and try to recover it. This was not done until 3 oclock when the Wm Cory got it. We then bouyed one end, leaving the small ships to complete the work as Halpin was anxious to get the Gt Eastern anchored before dark and we had 35 miles to go. We therefore started about 4 oclock and came on here. It is in some degree sheltered by the main land of New Foundland and the islands of Great & Little Miquelon, and St Pierre. There was a beautiful sun set as we came in, & our anchor was dropped between 8 & 9pm. (*in margin* Wednesday July 14th). The other ships finished their work about 11pm and then came on and anchored near us so that we formed a strong fleet this morning. The Gulnare piloted us in to the anchorage.

The weather this morning was very lovely & the sea like a mirror. We settled for the Gulnare to take us to the place on the island of St Pierre where the cable was landed and there leave the instruments and electricians to make the tests while we steamed on to the town of St Pierre on the opposite side of the island. We arrived there between 11 & 12; it is a miserable place but I think the Gt Eastern might have gone in if it had been any better than where we were for other purposes, but it was not nearer to our cable end by water, altho' only a couple of miles distant by walking across the island.

On our arrival at St Pierre we went first to pay our respects to the Governor. His house is not a very grand one, but had a little bit of garden and some green grass &c in it. I think some 8 or 10 of us called and were shewn into the drawing room. In a few minutes Col Cren the Gov[erno]r came in; he stood with his back to the fire place and we stood in a circle round him. I got Depecher to act as interpreter for me as the Govr could not speak English and I could not do much at French. He made us a long speech congratulating us upon our success and welcoming us to his islands. After a considerable amount of talk, champagne was introduced (and very good it was) and we each had one glass given to us. I then asked if he would wish to send a telegram to the Emperor. He had a clerk called and told him what to write; it was short, as on the other side.

[*On opposite page*]

Copy of telegram sent to French Emperor.

St Pierre, July 14, 1869
Sent 9.30pm Greenwich time.

To His Imperial Majesty the Emperor of the French:
Sire,

We have the honour to forward to your Imperial Majesty the first telegram passed through the French Transatlantic cable, announcing the satisfactory completion of the main section of that important work, and to congratulate your Imperial Majesty on the establishment of telegraphic communication between France and the island of St Pierre by a cable 2,583 knots long, laid in water in some parts 2,760 fathoms deep. The remaining short section from St Pierre to Duxbury (in shallow water) will be laid in the next 8 or 10 days, thus completing direct telegraphic connexion between France and the United States.

May this great work contribute to the welfare and happiness of your Imperial Majesty and of the two great countries which are brought into closer communication by its means.

Daniel Gooch
Chairman of the Telegraph Construction
& the Great Eastern Steam Ship Companies.
James Anderson
Director General of the French Trans-
atlantic Cable Company.

I then invited him to visit the ship, dine and sleep on board. He said he would be glad to do so but should like to return home at night. This Capt Kerr kindly undertook to effect with the Gulnare. I then asked if he would take his wife—we would be glad to see her and a few friends. This ended in a party of about 15, 7 or 8 of them being ladies.

Our confab over, we took our departure, arranging for the Gulnare to leave with him between 3 & 4 and go round to the cable end to pick me up, as I and the others intended to walk across and see what was doing with the tests. It took us nearly an hour to do this as there is no kind of road, so it was a scramble over stones and bogs, the island being a barren rock perhaps 100 to 150 feet high.

The town of St Pierre is a little, miserable place, chiefly built of wood, and was nearly all destroyed by fire a couple of years ago. There are

about 2,000 inhabitants; the church is a large building. I gathered a
few wild flowers as we crossed over, chiefly marsh plants.[34] I was in
hopes, from what Jenkins & Co told me in the morning, that 2 or 3
hours was all they would require to make their tests and I would find
on my arrival they were nearly done; but in this I was disappointed, and
they kept me hanging about there until half past 5. They then told me
they still considered there was a fault in the cable, of a very minute
character, and I left Willoughby Smith with them to continue the tests,
and as the Gulnare with the Governor had been waiting an hour I got
on board and returned to the ship.

We had dinner soon after 7; it took them a little by surprise my making an addition of 15 to our party, but all was managed very well and
the dinner went off very well. I was a little at a loss to talk as I had the
Governor's lady on my left, a French lady who thought she spoke
English (but did not) on my right, and the Governor opposite. I got
Despecher to sit next to him, so upon the whole all did very well. After
dinner the ladies, finding there was a piano in the saloon, would have a
dance; so some of the tables were cleared away and it was 11 oclock
before I got them away in the Gulnare, much to my satisfaction. It
reminded me of old days in Heart's Content to see the dancing, but the
ladies were not handsome, nor even good looking. One was an English-
woman and another American.

I telegraphed my message to the Emperor this evening (see other
side). The day has been a lovely one, a bright sun with a nice cool air.
There are still some patches of snow lying in the gullies very near the
water's edge.

[*On opposite page*]

Emperor's reply received at St Pierre July 15, 10am Greenwich time:
le 15 juillet, 1869, à 8-12 du matin,
Urgence recommendé
Monsieur Daniel Gooch, President du Comité du Cable Transatlantic
(? Miss[i]on)recommendé.
Je vous felicite de l'heureuse réussite de votre grande enterprise, et je
vous remercie de m'en avoir fait parti.

Napoleon

Translation:
I congratulate you on the happy success of your great enterprise and I
thank you for having informed me of it.

Napoleon

ATLANTIC, JULY 15TH, 1869. Thank God our ship's head is now turned for England and for home. The work and anxiety of this expedition has been much more severe than the former ones, partly from the length of time it has taken and also from the faults occurring in the cable. We have also had most unpractical and unreasonable people to deal with in Jenkins and Varley. Clark is not so bad and without the others I think he would do very well, but I trust my company will never again enter into any contract where Jenkins or Varley are to accompany the expedition.

I had arranged last night with Capt Kerr for the Gulnare to go to the cable station at 8 oclock to bring off Anderson and Willoughby Smith to the ship so that we might settle whether I was to give up the cable, and if so upon what terms; but Smith came alone, without any message from Anderson. I told Halpin to be ready to sail at 12 and we would stop at the cable station. Canning was also making his arrangts for laying the other shore end and getting away with the Boston work.[35] I think much that had to be done in this today might have been done yesterday, and the end laid in the early part of the day instead of the evening. A little before 12 I received from Anderson the following report from his engineers. I may mention that Smith told me as soon as I left the cable station last night. Anderson went over to St Pierre and Jenkins and Co followed him very soon, saying they would be back by daylight this morning, thus leaving him alone in his glory, but they did not get back until 8. The following is the report to Anderson:

Dear Sir James,

We have tested the Brest and St Pierre section of the cable of the Societé du Cable Transatlantique Français and we find that for all commercial purposes the line is in perfect working order. There is, how-ever, evidence of a very small fault existing in the line which we first observed when within —— miles of Brest, and which we can still detect by our tests. As far as we are able to judge at present we consider that with careful usage this fault is not likely to become worse, and we believe that with due care the line may be worked at its fullest speed for an in-definite time. We propose continuing our tests for the 30 days, leaving Mr Hackin at St Pierre with Sir Wm Thompson[36] at Brest to conduct them, and we do not advise the use of more than 100 cells battery power under any circumstances. In our fuller report to the board we shall not fail to allude to the efficient manner in which the enterprise has been carried out and the ample facilities which have been afforded to us for obtaining all the tests and data we have required.

We are, dear Sir James,
Your obt servants
Latimer Clark
Fleeming Jenkin

To Sir Jas Anderson.

Sir Jas Anderson,
    The foregoing letter of your engineers expresses exactly my own opinion.

C. F. Varley
Consulting Electrician.

This report was accompanied by the following letter from Sir Jas Anderson:

St Pierre Cable House
July 15, 1869

My Dear Sir Daniel Gooch,
    Enclosed please find copy of the report of our engineer and electrician.
    I much wish our enterprise, conducted with so much care and ability under so many adverse circumstances, could have been terminated by a certificate without any reserve whatever, but I will hope that the testing of the next 30 days will prove the cable to be in all respects as satisfactory as ever you could wish.

I am
My dear Sir Daniel
Yours truly
James Anderson

On reaching the cable house in the Gt Eastern I went ashore and handed Anderson the following letter:

Gt Eastern, St Pierre
July 15, 1869.

My dear Sir James,
    I am in receipt of your letter of today's date enclosing report of your engineer on the cable. While we do not admit the existence of a fault, however minute, I am prepared to hand over the cable to you upon the condition that it is so handed over without prejudice to any question

of a fault, which is to be left for settlement between the respective boards in London.

I am

Yours truly

Dan Gooch

Sir Jas Anderson.

To which I got the following reply, and then handed over the cable:

St Pierre Telegraph Station

July 15, 1869

My dear Sir Daniel Gooch,

I am in receipt of your note handing over the cable to us on certain conditions. I see nothing in the way of these conditions and all further details remaining for the consideration of the boards in London.

Yours truly,

Jas Anderson

I also saw Mr Jenkins and spoke to him as to the tests &c to be used during the 30 days. He read over to me the instructions he had given, which were to the following effect:

No land or subterranean lines to be connected to the cable at either end until the expiration of the 30 days. During the 30 days the tests as regards tension not to exceed those employed on the Atlantic cables (or 100 cells). No experiments of any kind to be made on the cable until the expiration of 30 days. During the 30 days the officers of the contractors to be constantly present in the instrument room and keep a joint record of all tests made.

Having taken these steps I handed over the cable to Sir J. Anderson and returned to the ship, telegraphing to Mr Glover[37] at Brest what I had done. Canning had now begun to lay the shore end for the Boston section, and was testing the cables in the other ships. He wished us to remain until this was done, so that we did not start until 7 oclock. The other ships started at the same time, the Wm Cory laying the cable. I was truly glad to find ourselves in motion towards home. The night is lovely and the old ship has been going 12 knots by the patent log. She is certainly going very quickly through the water. So we are done with this job so far as I am concerned. We have laid the following lengths of cable:

Brest shore end	8	nautical miles
Intermediate	106·96	
Main cable	2439·21	

St Pierre intermediate	20·0
Do shore end	10·0

2584·17

Distance 2,327 miles or a slack of 11·14 per cent. The greatest amount of slack paid out was during the heavy gale when it amounted to 20·79 per cent. I have been quite unable to make up my mind as to the cause of the faults. It is singular that none occurred after we put a better watch in the tank, yet the punctures were not such as would be made by a man without he had carefully studied the work of doing it, and prepared an instrument exactly the shape of one of the scarfs of the wire. He must then have been very careful, and this is not an easy thing to do, to push it into the cable without giving it the least twist. One thing is certain, we must in future take the same precautions we did in 1866. Every thing went as well as possible with this exception.

The wake of the ship as we came out tonight had exactly the appearance of a river, the rest of the sea looking like meadow land on each side, and as we made the turn to go east the winding appearance was very pretty. The moon is very bright and looks like fine weather. I forgot to mentioned I had an answer from the Emperor of France this morning to my telegram; I have copied it beside mine. Mine did not leave St Pierre before half past 10 last night, Greenwich time, and the Emperor's left Brest this morning at 9.50 Greenwich time, so that the Emperor must have answered it either very late last night or very early this morning. It was very civil of him to acknowledge it so quickly; I doubt whether the Queen would have been as quick.

Our party in the ship is now a small one, only 8 at dinner. I hope we may have a quick and pleasant voyage. Draft of water at starting: Fwd 22ft, Aft 24ft 6in.

FRIDAY JULY 16TH. This has been a lovely and very interesting day; the sea is like glass, with a nice light S.W. breeze, just sufficient to fill our sails, and the old ship looks splendid. It is realy a beautiful sight to stand on the top of the paddle box and see her when all her sails are set. She has been doing about 10 knots as an average, but the log shews more as our course has not been quite a straight one. Our distance has probably been much more than the chart measurement; her log is on the opposite page. Her paddles have been making 9 to 9½ rev & the

o

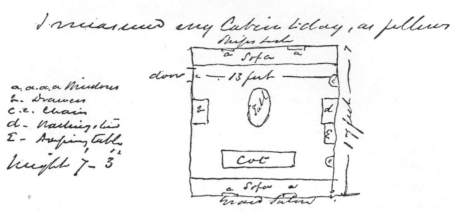

FIG 15   Gooch's sketch plan of his cabin on the *Great Eastern*

screw 33 to 34. We were very much interested during the forenoon in passing through a fleet of ice bergs; one was a very large one, Halpin estimated it at 8 to 900 feet long and very nearly as broad, and about 150 feet high. This, and another very large one, which looked like 3 churches clustered together, were something of the following shapes

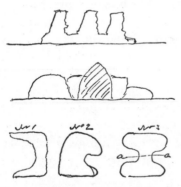

The crossed part was quite vertical and did not get the sun; it looked quite black. All the rest was white and shewing all the colours of the rainbow. The church one looked thus. We saw 8 bergs and some field ice. 3 that were in shore with a low fog bank behind them had a very curious appearance caused by the mirage; in fact it was doubled in height by the mirrored reflection, and they looked like this. No 3, as I watched it, separated in the middle at *a a* and there were two berghs, one in the water and the other in the cloud above it. The colours, and brightness of the ice in the bright sun were very beautiful. We went within 300 yards of one good sized one; all were pretty near. The air was very cold in their neighbourhood. I am very glad to have had this opportunity of seeing them, and under the most favourable circumstances—a very bright sun and clear atmosphere and smooth water. They must be very disagreeable things to run into with a steamer.

We also saw some immense flocks of sea birds, so thick that they cast a shadow on the water; they were very close to it, fishing. There was a beautiful sun set and every promise of a fine day tomorrow; the moon is now bright and clear. What a relief it is to be able to go to bed without the feeling that any moment I may be roused up to tell me something has gone wrong with the cable. I now feel I can lie down with some certainty that my rest will not be disturbed. In a few days and I will sleep quietly at pretty Clewer.

SATURDAY, JULY 17TH. I am a little disappointed in the distance we have run today. I had calculated upon 240 miles instead of 220. The wind has been from the south, not much of it, but we have kept our fore and aft sails set and appeared to be going quickly through the water, the paddle engines making about 9 rev and the screw 32. The weather was very fine all day and the sea smooth, but tonight it has come on a heavy rain and looks like more wind. The glass is falling. Yesterday the temperature of the water was only 47° while the air was 60°, shewing we are not far from the ice, but we have not seen any more, indeed we have seen nothing all day, and it is a slow and idle life; but a week of it, after the cable troubles, will do me no harm.

I find a purchase of fish was made at St Pierre; 132 cod, varying from 18 inches to 2 feet long, and a large basket of a small fish about 7 or 8 inches long was purchased for 13 shillings, large lobsters at 5d each. This is cheap, but I daresay the two men who sold them had caught them all in the night and it was not bad wages. I had my hair cut as a way of filling up time and making my head more comfortable. The coal dust is so bad it needs a good deal of washing, and for this purpose is better short.

SUNDAY, JULY 18TH. We have only made 220 miles again today. The night was wet and thick and it continued so up to 11 oclock today, when the sun came out, and we have had a lovely afternoon with a nice fresh breeze from the south west, making all our sails draw well. The Capt has lost a bet with Despecher that he will land us at Weymouth on Saturday. I doubt it, as to accomplish it we must do more speed than we are doing. It would be very pleasant to get home on Saturday night and have a quiet Sunday at Clewer before I begin the bother of my work in London. The sea is very smooth and this gives our paddles a good chance of doing their best. The speed of the engines is the same as yesterday. We had church service this morning as usual.

187

My dear wife was a great deal with me in my dreams last night, and were happy ones; I often pray that she may be with me. How hard it is, her bright face and loving heart will not greet me on my return to Clewer. It would have so gladdened her heart to see me back and congratulate me on my success. I feel in my soul that I am better fitted for quiet domestic happiness than this constant struggle with life, successful tho' I be, yet, now, I would like rest for the few years left me.

MONDAY JULY 19TH. The day has been all we could wish; a fine stiff breeze in our favour from the south, and we have made good progress. Tonight it has come on wet with squalls of rain and wind. One of the Cunard steamers passed us last night, but her speed was too much for us and she soon left us behind. Betting is going on as to our arrival at Weymouth; I think if this weather holds we will get there pretty early on Sunday morning, and I will most likely see Clewer on Sunday night, but Sunday is a wretched day for travel and it will be a long journey by a Sunday train—but its end will be home.

TUESDAY JULY 20TH. Our breeze has continued steady and favourable for us today and we have made our best run. The log this afternoon gives $10\frac{1}{2}$ knots. There has been a good deal of sea today, making us roll a little, but the sails do a great deal to steady her, as we have not rolled half as much today as we would have done in a similar sea cable-laying. Our speed is also in favour of her being steady. We have had no incident of any kind today.

It gives me ample time for reflection, this kind of life. I do not think I have slept 4 hours each of the last two nights, so that one has 20 hours a day to think. I wish I had a more pleasant prospect to think of on my return home; God only knows how desolate my heart feels.

If they have had good luck the Boston end of our cable ought to be pretty nearly laid by this time. I will hear of it when I get back to England.

WEDNESDAY JULY 21ST. It is said that between the 18th & 21 of this month there is a strong electrical current crosses the Atlantic in the track we are taking, which has the effect of reducing the barometer without producing a corresponding effect on the weather. It has been so in our case, as the barometer fell very much a couple of days ago and has remained low up to this time, and we have had fine weather with heavy showers of rain. During last night the wind got more astern and our fore and aft canvass was taken in about 2am but it was set again about 11 and has since continued. We have made a very good run.

We have had the excitement of meeting a ship and this evening, after dinner, we met the City of Cork steamer on her outward passage; but the days are very long and it is difficult to get through them. If I could sleep when I go to bed I should be glad to get there, but the last 3 nights I have slept very little, and it is weary work. There is plenty of time during the day to think of all one needs to think of, without tumbling about awake half the night. I will hope for a better result tonight.

THURSDAY JULY 22ND. We have had another beautiful day with fair but moderate wind and a smooth sea. Our run has not been quite so long, but we make good progress; a ship passed within a few hundred yards of our stern. It has been very enjoyable on deck and I have spent a great deal of time on our paddle boxes. Our sailors have been amusing themselves tonight by getting up a Rifle Corps. One of the men who acted as officer had a red uniform (where he got it I don't know) and his men were armed with brooms and hand spikes, and his band consisted of an accordion, a fife, and bones. It was an amusement to every body for an hour to see them do their drill and marching, and got through an hour after dinner very well. The moon is very bright tonight; how beautiful the sea is with the light of a full moon upon it. Saturday afternoon, if clear, we will see land and there is little doubt I will land early Sunday morning.

FRIDAY JULY 23RD. The weather has been all we could wish today, altho' not quite so much wind, but the air has been charming and very enjoyable on deck. We have been looking out for the coast of Ireland this evening, as we were off it, but a distance of about 35 miles and we did not see it. Tomorrow we will see the English coast once more; I need not say how glad we will all be, yet I don't know why we should— this week has been a most enjoyable one. We could not have had better weather if it had been left to our own making.

I went over the engines, boilers &c with Beckwith this afternoon. We have not seen as many ships today as I expected we would do, now we are getting so near the Channel; we only saw 3. I wish I could sleep at night; it is very wearing lying awake until 2 or 3 oclock in the morning.

I am going to take some of the doctor's stuff tonight to see if it will make me sleep.

SATURDAY NIGHT, JULY 24. This is my last night in the ship for this voyage at any rate, and I leave her with a good deal of regret mixed with pleasure in the thought of getting home, where I will arrive to-morrow evening. We made the Scilly Islands at 12 today, The Lizard at half past 5 and Eddystone a little after 9, so that we will be at Weymouth by 5. The day has been a very lovely one, perfectly calm, and our sails have therefore been of no use to us and our run has fallen off a little in consequence. There is no doubt the sails help this ship a good deal when there is a moderate breeze.

I was amused at Norval this afternoon. Beckwith wanted to clean up his colar for him; we got it off and Beckwith went away with it. We were on the bridge at the time. As soon as Norval saw him go down the steps he thought it was carrying the joke too far, and started off after him. He and Beckwith are very good friends, so he was content to follow him and keep his eye upon the colar, but when Beckwith went into the engine room and gave it to a man to do, Norval would not stand that but began to growl and would very probably have taken it from him if Beckwith had not coaxed him away. He was very glad when it was brought back.

CLEWER, AUGT 15, 1869. We reached Weymouth on Sunday morning the 25th July at 7 in the morning, and I at once prepared to land. This we did a little after 8, the crew giving us some hearty cheers as we left the ship. It was a lovely morning, and I left her side with feelings of regret. I felt I had little to tempt me home, not knowing whether I would find any but servants to receive me, instead of that dear loving face and heart that I felt would be rejoiced to welcome me on former occasions. How little can even success in life be enjoyed alone. How much worse must it be to bear in time of sickness or of sorrow.

After landing I went to the station to see about the times of trains, and then had a walk on the beach until the train started at 10.30. It is a dreadful day, a Sunday, to travel a long journey; this train did not reach Windsor until 6.30pm. I there found Anna, Fred & Charlie[38] on the platform. I was very glad to see them, and when I got to Clewer my grandchildren were at the door, each with a kiss and a bouquet of flowers for me. I did not feel so utterly alone, God bless them; it gave some comfort to my heart. I found Clewer looking very pretty and was very thankful to God for all the mercies of the voyage and that I had returned to my home with increased health.

I have, since my arrival, been quietly enjoying this place. The Seguins[39] have been with me for the last week. Anna and her family left a fortnight ago; Charlie has been here since the 2nd of the month. He leaves here for Russia tomorrow;[40] I pray God to bless his career in that country and soon enable him to return home in health and success. He is steady, and has both application and ability, and if all turns out as well as is anticipated he might, in a few years, to [sic] establish himself in a good position in life and soon be independent in a pecuniary sense.

When I look back upon the results of the last cable expedition I feel the experience we have gained must strengthen the opinion I had formed from former voyages; 1st, that for long, deep-sea work, your chance of success is very greatly enhanced by the use of such a ship as the Gt Eastern. It is very doubtful whether, with a smaller ship, we would have not on this occasion have lost the end of the cable, and I do not think there would be much chance of recovering it at 2 to 3 miles depth with a small ship. It may be said if a small ship was used and a difficulty occurred in bad weather, the cable could be bouyed (as we in fact had to do) but out of the 3 times we bouyed the cable we only had it done once as it should be—that, fortunately, in deep water. Once we lost is and another time it was very nearly lost; probably in rough water it would have been lost, so little hold had the stoppers upon it. It is also quite clear to me that the expedition as a whole should be under the command of the captain of the ship; he ought to be qualified by experience for the task. Halpin would be able to do all that could be done to lay a cable. All he would need would be a staff of cable hands, as he needs a staff of engineers for his engines, but they should be under his command and not have a divided command as we have always had. There is much discussion just now as to laying light, and therefore cheap, cables; I do not think they could be laid across the Atlantic. You need a cable of considerable strength, as difficulties are sure to occur, and a light cable would, in my opinion, be sure to break; and I doubt whether, in great depths, they could be picked up, as it would be impossible to tell when the grapnel had hold of them. If the experiment is tried I will certainly take no share in the work.

SEPTEMBER 11, 1869. Harry's son & heir was christened today at

Clewer church by Mr Carter; his name Daniel Fulthorpe. May God bless him and make his future life an honour to the position he is destined to fill.[41] No one was present but Harry, Mary and myself, and his little sister. Another day, in London, we must have a party in honour of the event.

OCTOBER 10TH, 1869. I was at Brighton a few days ago, & strange enough I met a lady walking on the promenade who has often been in my mind of late. I do not think I would have known her had she not been with her mother, whose face I seemed to recollect. I stopped, or I am not sure whether they did not stop and speak to me first. Why did my heart beat so? It brought back so suddenly a dream of a long time ago. Is it God's will that I am again to have a happy home and be cared for by a fond and loving wife? A vain hope, for my nature is not one likely to gain the love of a woman much younger than myself, and I feel sure my heart will never care for one who does not really love me or who, like my beloved Peggy, would devote her whole soul to me. I could not live with a woman indifferent or cold to me; rather a thousand times the lonely life I now lead. But why do I write thus on an incident so likely to happen? They were staying in Brighton, and I being there for a day, what so likely as that I should chance to meet them; but why should I so often have this girl in my thoughts? Oh Peggy, has God indeed permitted you to lead me to a happiness in the future? It is in God's hands; may He guide me for good.[42]

OCT 30, 1869. Weymouth, Great Eastern S[team] Ship. The old ship is here again, taking in coal for her voyage to India with the cable between Bombay and Suez. Capt Halpin is going in command of her. Osborn and me are down here for a couple of days to see all is getting ready. It is pleasant to be on board the old ship again and I hope she will have a good voyage.

The country has just lost, in the death of Lord Derby, one of her chief statesmen, at the age of 75. All shades of opinion agree in deep regret at his loss. I have to thank him for some kindness when, on his recommendation, I was made a baronet.

SATURDAY, CLEWER, Nov 6, 1869. The Great Eastern sailed today from Weymouth at 3.40 on her Indian voyage.[43] She has been detained since Thursday by a gale of wind. The Queen opened the new Blackfriars Bridge today, also Holborn Viaduct. She has had a fine day for it.

DECR 7. Frank is gazetted today as captain in the 4th Hussars. He is a very young captain; I hope his health may be spared to him to return to England. He is now with his regiment at Meerut in India. How pleased his dear mother would have been had she been spared to see him a captain. He was always her favourite boy and he was very devoted to her. Anna has since told me that when he left home his mother had an impression that she would never meet him again on earth, altho' she never mentioned such a thing to me.

DECR 26TH. Yesterday was Xmas Day and I had a large family party at my table. Anna & her husband & 6 children, and Emily's 6 children (she was not there), Harry and his wife and two children, so that I had 14 grand children; what a patriarch I felt. Jane Tweedy & Alfred made up the party. One dear face was missing. I have never dined from home on a Xmas Day since I was married, and but once before without her dear presence. Soon will this year be of the past; what will another year bring? Who can tell? It is well we know not the future, either for good or evil; sufficient for the day is the knowledge thereof. We can but trust in God and feel certain whether it is joy or sorrow that falls to our lot.

NOTES

1   This is borne out by a letter at BRB records (HL 1/1/1) from John Wright, locomotive superintendent of the South Devon Rly, congratulating Gooch on his appointment as chairman: '. . . I shall hope to see the G.W.R. as it was when you were there, for it has sadly fallen off lately, especially in our dept. It will be a happy day for many of your old servants, many of whom have had a rough time of it since you left.'

2   The meeting this year was on 2 March.

3   This name is difficult to decipher with any certainty, but it could be Cooper. A James C. Cooper was lessee of Penllyn Slate Quarry at Dolwyddelan, near Bettws-y-Coed.

4   The Croskeys lived next door to Gooch in Paddington. His youngest son Frank married Mary Croskey's sister Teresa in 1871.

5   This was the South Wales & Great Western Direct Rly. The engineer was John Fowler, already met with in connection with the Metropolitan Railway. The line would have run from Wootton Bassett to Chepstow, crossing the Severn by a bridge over two miles long. It was never built.

6   The proposed carriage works at Cripley Meadow, Oxford, was backed by the corporation but opposed by the university. Opposing views were aired in the press, including *The Times*, and *Punch* carried a cartoon in September 1865. The site was unsuitable, being liable to flooding, and, after the project had been abandoned, additional buildings were erected at Swindon for about a third of the cost.
    See MacDermot, *GWR*, II, 16–19.

7   They were, in effect, having a foretaste of the advantages of wireless telegraphy which came thirty years later.

8   Probably Aspy Bay, Cape Breton, Nova Scotia.

9   The mirror galvanometer, invented by Prof William Thomson (later Lord Kelvin). A highly sensitive instrument by which the engineers on board could immediately detect any change in the resistance of the cable. One of these instruments is in the Science Museum and is illustrated in the Museum's booklet *Lighting, 3: Other than in the Home* (1970).

10 The failure of the discount house of Overend, Gurney & Co had repercussions throughout the railway world. The London, Chatham & Dover Rly was in serious difficulty in 1866 and a receiver was appointed.
    See Marshall, C. F. Dendy. *A History of the Southern Railway* (1936), 456–7.

11 Lord Derby had been Prime Minister since July 1866.

12 Cutting from *London Gazette*, 10 November 1866: 'The Queen has been pleased to direct letters patent to be passed under the Great Seal, granting the dignity of a Baronet of the United Kingdom of Great Britain and Ireland unto Daniel Gooch, of Clewer Park, in the county of Berks, Esq, and the heirs male of his body lawfully begotten.'

13 The bill was passed, confirming the issues already made, but powers to continue this device were deleted from the bill as conditions had improved by the time it came before Parliament.
    See MacDermot, *GWR*, II, 22.

14 Charles Stewart, not to be confused with James Stuart-Wortley who was chairman of the Atlantic Telegraph Co.

15 The diarist made a slip here. It was Sir Francis Bond Head's brother, Sir Edmund Head, who was a member of the Royal Commission and who died on 28 January 1868.
    See *DNB*.

16 Those who could afford to make such tours at this time would get the best from their

stay by equipping themselves with a good guide book such as Murray's, Black's, Baddeley's or Baedeker's.

17 Edgeworthstown, home of the novelist Maria Edgeworth (1767–1849).

18 Gooch was evidently breaking his journey between Holyhead and London at his son Henry's house at Bettws-y-Coed. The London & North Western line from Llandudno Junction reached Bettws in the previous April.

19 Evidently another relative.

20 The new Smithfield was designed by the City architect, Horace Jones. The Great Western had a goods station in the basement of the building, reached over the Metropolitan line.

21 In this wryly humourous passage Gooch is referring to the burning of Protestant martyrs during the reign of Queen Mary.

22 Only in 1878 was the service commenced, but it only lasted until 1885, during which period one Great Western ship was completely wrecked. See *post*, page 318.
See MacDermot, *GWR*, II, 181.

23 Really sister-in-law. *See* TWEEDY, William.

24 This was to lay a cable from Brest to Newfoundland. The Telegraph Construction & Maintenance Co constructed and laid the cable for the Societé du Cable Transatlantique Français.
See Bright, C. *Submarine Telegraphs, their History, Construction and Working* (1898), 107.

25 Anderson (*qv*) was on board as director-general of the French cable company. The ship was commanded by Capt Halpin.

26 These were the lamps illuminating the paying-out machinery.

27 Printed daily log forms for this voyage, completed and signed by Capt Halpin, are mounted in the diary. *See fig. 14*, page 175.

28 The diarist has momentarily forgotten Anderson's knighthood! 'Mr Jenkins' is H. C. Fleeming Jenkin (*qv*) and 'Mr Clarke' is Latimer Clark (*qv*).

29 Fiddles were frames to prevent things falling from the table during rough weather.

30 By 'Christopher North' [Prof John Wilson] of *Blackwood's Magazine*.

31 The bill to legalise the issue of shares in lieu of dividends. *See* III, n 13.

32 In fact it was the conductivity of the cable which improved as immersion on the sea-bed caused the temperature to drop.

33 The *Gulnare* was a small Canadian survey vessel which was assisting the expedition.

34 They are preserved in the diary.

35 A branch cable was laid by the three smaller vessels, *William Cory, Scanderia* and *Chiltern*, to Duxbury, near Cape Cod, Mass.

36 Sir William Thomson (*qv*).

37 Probably Lt-Col Glover, RE, former director-general of telegraphs in India and later a director of the British-Indian Submarine Telegraph Co.

38 His daughter Anna and her husband Frederick Newton, and his son Charles.

39 *See post* VI, n 30.

40 Charles Gooch took a post with the New Russia Company. He returned to England in 1875 to join the Great Western Rly as mineral engineer.

41 Gooch's expectations were indeed fulfilled, and Daniel Fulthorpe Gooch succeeded his father as third baronet in 1919.

42 The diarist is here referring to the dream he had in the previous February (page 148). It is most unfortunate that the missing fourth volume of the manuscript covers the period during which Gooch met his second wife and was married. We shall probably never know if the chance meeting at Brighton was, in fact, the prelude to his second very happy marriage.

43 For a detailed account of this voyage *see* Parkinson, J. C., *The Ocean Telegraph to India* (1870).

VOLUME IV

The Diary 1870–3

It will probably never be known what Gooch wrote in the missing fourth volume of the manuscript, but from brief extracts in the 1892 edition and other sources it seems that his life went on much as before. He was as absorbed as ever in the affairs of the Great Western Railway, still hopeful of keeping the Great Eastern in commission, and still enjoying his Masonic meetings and his journeys to various parts of the country on railway or cable business. The Telegraph Construction & Maintenance Company was as prosperous as ever and he presided regularly over its meetings. Gooch still represented Cricklade in the Commons, though with even less relish than before.

Now a little more reconciled to the loss of his wife, he delighted in his garden at Clewer and looked forward to a warm welcome from the faithful Norval when he returned from his wanderings.

His youngest son, Frank, married Teresa Croskey, sister of Henry's wife, in 1871. His other children were all settled and in good positions. The one major event which we miss is his marriage to his second wife, Emily Burder, on 17 September 1870. There was not the slightest hint of this at the end of 1869, though the strange dream of March of that year, and the chance meeting at Brighton in the following October, may indeed have heralded this second and apparently very happy match.

By 1874, when volume V begins, he is again a happy man with a wife to give him the love and companionship he had missed since the tragic event of 1868. He was, of course, ageing, and was, as he mentions in the diary, putting on weight (he had gained nearly 1½ stone in the last few years), but even in 1876, at sixty, he was still able without apparent undue effort to ride a pony across the mountains to the Great Western colliery. His regular walks not only gave him much pleasure but kept him surprisingly fit for a man of his age.

On the G.W.R., 1872 saw the conversion of the South Wales main line from Swindon from broad to standard gauge, while the company's mileage was steadily increasing, as was its dividend. In February 1870 the various classes of shares were consolidated, and in July a dividend at the rate of 3% per annum was declared. By 1873 the company was able to pay a total of 6⅛%.

The following entries are all that appeared in the 1892 edition; they are reprinted here without alteration.

JANUARY 1ST, 1870. Another year has passed; what are the records to be left behind? As regards myself and children, I have much reason to be thankful, in so far as health and worldly considerations are concerned. The past pages will show my time has to some extent been engaged in a large enterprise, in laying the line of cable between France and America. This is the third cable I have stretched across the Atlantic, probably more than the traffic justifies, and it will take some time to fill them with work.

On the Great Western all has gone well, a quiet but sure improvement, and I look forward with confidence to the gradual growth of our dividends, and the general improvement of the financial condition of the Company. And now another year has begun, who will live to see its end?

THURSDAY, FEBRUARY 17TH. We had a most important meeting today of the shareholders of the Great Western Railway, for the purpose of consolidating the stocks or shares of the various sections forming the Company. It went off very well, and was unanimously approved. I have been for some weeks very anxious about it, and it is a great relief to my mind now it is settled. We intend to do the same with the preference stocks at the general meeting on the 11th of March.

The *Great Eastern* is now laying the British Indian telegraph. She reached Bombay on the 28th January, and started to lay the cable on the 1st February. I hope all will go well with her. It is the first cable she has laid without my being on board.

MARCH 11TH. At the general meeting of the Great Western shareholders today, they agreed to the scheme for consolidation of the preference stocks, and I trust we have now put the financial position of the line upon a sound and satisfactory basis. There is no doubt it is a most important thing for the future of the Company, and I am glad it has fallen to my lot to carry through so important a matter.

REGENT'S HOTEL, LEAMINGTON. SUNDAY, SEPTEMBER 18TH. I was

married yesterday at Christ Church, Lancaster Gate, London, to Miss Emily Burder.

NEWCASTLE, SUNDAY, OCTOBER 23RD. We had a carriage this morning, and started at 8.30 for Bedlington to spend the day with my old playfellow George Marshall. The morning was wet early, but it cleared up as we started, and we had a very fine day. How familiar the road seemed to me, particularly as we got towards Bedlington. I found my friend very well, and a hearty welcome. We went to church, where there is little change—a new tower has been built—and afterwards walked down the village and half-way to the ironworks. The village is very much changed for the worse, I think, since I was a boy; but perhaps this is not really so, as better houses have certainly been built, but many of my old landmarks are gone. The house in which I went to school as a child of four years old is exactly as it was, with the same pear-trees in front and the green rails. I was told one of the ladies is also still living in it, Miss Robson. I was very glad to pay another visit to the scenes of my boyhood. We returned to Newcastle at night.

MARCH 5TH, 1871. On Friday last we held our Great Western half-yearly meeting and paid $3\frac{3}{4}$ per cent. It is the highest dividend that has been paid for eighteen years, and will, I trust, be the lowest ever paid in the future. The meeting went off very well, with many very complimentary remarks with regard to myself. We agreed to issue a million of 5 per cent preferred stock, and to alter the gauge on the line from Swindon down through South Wales. It is a large expense, but I feel the time has come when it must be done. My Telegraph Construction meeting was last Tuesday; it went off very well, and we paid a large dividend.

JANUARY 1ST, 1872. The Great Western Railway has prospered to a great extent. Our receipts have been very good, and the shares are now at 118. A large rise since I first took the chair, when they were at less than 90. Telegraphs have also done well, and have largely increased in value. Upon the whole the last year has been one of great prosperity.

APRIL 7TH. The half-yearly meeting of the Great Western was held on the 29th February, and we were able to pay a good dividend of $5\frac{3}{8}$ per cent.[1] It is long since the Great Western divided such an amount as this, and I hope we may now go on slowly improving. The shareholders passed a resolution, giving me 5000 guineas, in very complimentary terms.[2]

At the next meeting of the Board, held at Paddington on the 21st of March, the following minutes were entered on the minute book:

March 21st, 1872. Referring to the resolution voting a testimonial to the Chairman, which was passed spontaneously by the shareholders at the half-yearly meeting on the 29th ult, it was proposed by Mr Miles and seconded by Mr Ponsonby, and resolved unanimously, that the following minute be communicated to the Chairman:
'That we, your brother directors, avail ourselves of the earliest opportunity to assure you how highly we estimate your services to the Company, both before and since your occupation of the chair, and we congratulate you on their recognition by this act of the shareholders. We feel assured that, although the words of the resolution require no action on the part of your colleagues, you will allow us to express our warm sympathy with those feelings of regard and confidence which are so deservedly entertained towards you by the shareholders of the Company, and which cannot fail to be most gratifying to you and your family.'

NOVEMBER 24TH, 1872. The *Daily Telegraph* of Christmas morning presented a very wonderful list of telegrams from all parts of the world sent on Christmas-Eve. It is a mighty thing that has been done in a few years, and it has worked a wonderful revolution.

JANUARY 1ST, 1873. We have again entered upon a new year, and in looking over the past, how much reason have we to be thankful to God for His many blessings. In all respects the year has been a prosperous one to me. I have been blessed with good health, and can look back with pleasure upon the expressions of regard and confidence given me by the Great Western shareholders and directors. The only real anxiety in my mind is the state of the working classes. I fear hard and difficult times must come before the present excitement as to wages and time is put upon such a level as will enable the trade of the country to bear it. Coals are nearly double the price they were eighteen months ago, and the men are earning so much in wages that they will only work three or four days a week, and then only do part work. So it is to a less extent with most of the trades. If continued, the only result will be to drive the trade from this country abroad, where wages are less. May God avert so sad an evil to this country, and the present year witness a change for the better in the relations of master and workman.[3] The year has opened with a glorious morning, an agreeable change after the constant rain and cloud.

MY OLD CABIN, 'GREAT EASTERN', THE NORE, MAY 13TH, 1873. Once more I am in my dear old cabin, where I have spent so many hours of anxiety, and many of joy and contentment. It seems as though I had hardly left the ship, everything is so familiar. I left London middle of day yesterday. We reached the ship soon after four. Osborne also came down by the same train. The day was a very lovely one, and the evening has also been very charming—full moon and beautifully clear. We were only a small party on board. Halpin is captain, and looks as jolly as ever.

After dining at seven we had a long stroll on the deck, and went early to bed. I read for half-an-hour, and then went to sleep, although my pillow is a very hard one. This morning all were astir early in the ship, getting up our anchor and casting off the moorings, and by 10am all was ready to make a start. The tide turned about eleven, and the last anchor having been lifted, we moved slowly and grandly away from our anchorage for the Nore. The day has been all we could wish, and everything has gone on well, and we came to anchor here about 1.30, to wait for one of the moorings, and hope to start in the morning about ten for Weymouth.

I feel little anxiety about laying this cable, the third between Valentia and Heart's Content; but a much more difficult and anxious task awaits the ship on her way home, viz, to repair the 1865 cable which broke a couple of months ago about seven hundred miles from Ireland in two thousand fathoms of water. What has caused it to break is a mystery to us. Is it from being stretched over a chasm and gradually weighted with shellfish or weeds, or has it become rotten and so broken from weakness? In the latter case, I fear we will not succeed in picking it up; but every effort will be made and I feel confident, if it can be done, Halpin will not fail.[4] The present cable is coated with compound, and will be less liable to decay; but, until we know the cause of the 1865 failing, we are quite in the dark as to the fate of these deep-sea cables.

'GREAT EASTERN', OFF THE ISLE OF WIGHT, MAY 15TH, 1873,

8AM. We picked up our anchor and left The Nore yesterday at 10am. Weather fine, although cloudy and rather cold. The old ship steamed along very steadily at about eight knots. We passed Dover at six in the evening, Dungeness Light at eight, and Hastings about 10.30. There were a great many fishing-boats about as well as ships, and we had to shift about a good deal to avoid them—one large steamer went close across our bows. This morning is fine but cloudy, and we expect to get comfortably in Portland by one or two o'clock. I am not sure I would like to go a voyage again.

FRIDAY, MAY 16TH. We dropped our anchor yesterday about three o'clock after a beautiful voyage down Channel. The day was lovely, and I enjoyed it very much. We did a little over eight knots in speed, and got into a quiet berth. The ironclad *Devastation* left Portland for Milford Haven soon after we came in. She is certainly a very ugly looking craft, and one I should not like to sail in. The after part of the hull is only about six feet out of the water, and with the light sea there was on yesterday the waves were constantly washing over her.

FULTHORPE, SUNDAY. I came home from the ship yesterday, leaving all on board in a very forward state. We never had an expedition in which all our arrangements were in so forward a state; in fact, all is quite complete, with the exception of coaling. This is to begin on Monday, and, as six thousand tons have to be taken in, it will not be completed before the end of the month.

WEYMOUTH, JUNE 7TH, 1873. I came down here yesterday; my wife and Charlie came with me; the latter is going the voyage with the *Great Eastern*. I did not go on board the ship yesterday. We took a long ramble and went on board the first thing this morning, and have spent the day on board, returning to the hotel for dinner. Captain Osborne and Barber dined with us. It has been a lovely day, the sea as calm as a mill-pond. Everything on board the ship is in admirable order, and we never started an expedition so complete, not a single thing left to do. Coaling all finished some days ago, and the ship got clean. We had a good lunch on board.

SUNDAY, JUNE 8TH. We went on board the ship this morning at 9am, and found her all ready with steam up for a start. The day has been lovely, without a ripple on the water. At a quarter past ten the anchor was lifted, and we moved away from the anchorage beautifully, accompanied by the *Hibernian*[5] and *Britannia*. The National liner had sailed with the Irish shore end on Thursday. We went with the ship until she turned round west, beyond the Shambles Lightship, about seven miles, and then got into the small steam tender, and watched for some time the fleet pass away to the west. It was a grand sight, and I trust under God's blessing the commencement of a prosperous voyage. The *Great Eastern* was deep, drawing 37 feet 4 inches aft and 31 feet forward, mean 34 feet 2 inches. She had 8,296 tons of coals, and with cables, tanks, and water, a total load of 16,405 tons. I felt it very hard to see her steam away leaving me behind, the first time she has done so in crossing the Atlantic for cable purposes, and I should much like to be with her in her attempt to repair the 1865 cable; but this cannot be, and I must remain content. We returned to Weymouth in time for lunch.

JULY 18TH. The 1873 Atlantic cable was safely landed, without a single hitch as far as the *Great Eastern* was concerned, on the 27th. The accompanying ships were driven from their course and left behind by a gale. It now only remains to pick up the 1865 cable, and the old ship will have done a good year's work. I confess I do not feel very sanguine as to this; all will depend upon the condition of the cable. We went to a large garden-party at Chiswick given by the Prince of Wales to the Shah of Persia. The day was fine, and the scene a very pretty one. The Queen and all the Royal Family were there.

AUGUST 28TH, 1873. The meeting of the Great Western shareholders was held today. We were able to pay 5¾ per cent dividend, a satisfactory result, being ¼ per cent beyond the corresponding half year, and as all the other large companies had only paid either no increase or a diminution, the meeting went off very well.

NOTES

1 The dividend was £2 13 9.
2 Gooch used a substantial part of the gift to purchase a service of plate, including a centre-piece with the engraved arms of the family and of the Great Western Railway. As an expression of his gratitude to the board and shareholders he commissioned a portrait of himself which was painted by Louis W. Desanges and which he gave to the company for the board room. It is now in the GWR Museum at Swindon. Of much greater significance was his gift of £1,000 to endow the new cottage hospital at Swindon, which was opened in 1872.
3 There had been a number of strikes and lockouts in 1872 and at the time Gooch was writing, a three months strike of miners in South Wales had just begun.
4 The 1865 cable was not recovered.
5 The *Hibernia*; she also accompanied the *Great Eastern* during the laying of the cable to India in 1870.

VOLUME V

The Diary 1874-7

JANY I, 1874. The new year has opened with a bright and glorious sunny day; may it be the emblem of the peace and happiness of England, and of myself and family. I have much cause for thankfulness to God for all the blessings of the past year.

MARCH 10TH, 1874. When I wrote the last few lines above I little thought that before many weeks were over a general election would have taken place throughout the country. On Saturday morning the 24th Jany an address from Gladstone to his Greenwich constituents announced the fact that he had advised the Queen to dissolve Parliament, and it was dissolved accordingly on the Tuesday following and the election had to take place at once. This was short notice, particularly to those who, like myself, had not made up their minds whether they would stand again. I went down to Swindon on the Monday and after seeing Foote, Armstrong and Dunn we agreed I would stand, and issued my address (copy annexed).[1] I also pretty well made up my mind that I would not stand with a 2nd Conservative, as I did not think we could carry two, and a circular (annexed) was written to all the leading Conservative gentlemen, and I returned to London. Young Goldney[2] of Chippenham had been asked to stand and was willing to do so; he called upon me on Wednesday but I advised him not. On the Thursday Goddard issued an address on the promise of his expenses being paid by Mr Poynder, who offered to do so. I had a pressing letter from Swindon to go down on Thursday and meet the members of the Conservative Association, as they thought they could convince me that two Conservatives could be carried. I went down and saw them in the evening and the matter was so much pressed upon me that I made no further objection to going on and doing all I could to carry both seats.

On Friday I went to Highworth and a meeting there, which was well attended and the church bells even ringing on the occasion (a thing I was assured had never been done before). This Highworth has always been a dreadfully radical place, but the present Lord Radnor is a Conservative and this has at any rate set free those who before might have voted to please the land lord, and I found a good Conservative feeling growing up. We returned to Swindon where I addressed a very large meeting in the Drill Hall, and it went off very well—not a word spoken against me, but much enthusiasm in my favour. On Saturday the 31st Jany I went to Cricklade to attend the nomination. The new plan under the Ballot Act is certainly a vast improvement upon the old system; it was done quietly in a room, without any trouble. I had a public meeting, pretty well attended, and went off very well. From here we went to Purton and Wootton Bassett; at the latter place I had a public meeting which went off all right, and I was very glad to get into the last train for London and look forward to a quiet Sunday. This election work is very hateful to me.

I went to Swindon again on Monday the 2nd Feby to attend the market dinner at the Old Town; also attended a meeting held by Sir Geo Jenkinson in the Corn Exchange, and in the evening I held a public meeting in the Corn Exchange at the Old Town at half past 7. Goddard had called a meeting for 7 in another part of the building and I found when I got there they had all joined in the Corn Exchange, so that our meetings would be held together. I did not like this, but could not help it. I, however, insisted upon appointing my own chairman (Mr Armstrong) and had the resolutions moved separately. The result was I got a very good hearing in a very crowded and somewhat noisy meeting, and my resolutions were carried; but they would not let Goddard speak and voted against him. It was a rough affair at last and I got away from it as soon as I could.

On Tuesday the 3rd I had to come to London for the day, but went back to Swindon in the afternoon. The Radicals had 4 members in the field; Cadogan & Tucker coupled, Morris and Arkell each on their own work. The only chance of getting Goddard in was to keep Morris on his legs, as he was sure to carry away from Cadogan a good many of the Radical voters. We did all we could, therefore, to encourage him to go to the poll; he tried to get each side to buy him. I am told he offered to retire if the Radicals would pay him £500. He sent to offer to continue to stand if I would pay him 250£, which I, of course, declined, and I suppose the other side did so also as he went to the poll, held on Wednesday the 4th Feby.

The day was a lovely one, bright and warm. I visited the polling places in New and Old Swindon and then had a carriage and drove to Highworth, Cricklade and Purton, and so got back to the station in time to get to London by the 4.5 pm train. The ballot certainly makes the election go on very quietly; there was not the slightest difficulty or noise and the weather was glorious. As we could not know the result until next day I returned to London very glad to feel it was all over, and pretty certain that my election was safe, as the next day proved with the following results, and we had the further satisfaction of carrying Goddard in also:

Gooch	2624
Goddard	2231
Cadogan	2092
Tucker	1578
Morris	497
Arkell	40

The result of the general election throughout the country has been a marvelous one in favour of the Conservatives. Gladstone had a party majority in the old House of at least 60 to 70 members, and now we have a majority of upwards of 50. The defeat of the Gladstone party is most complete, and arises very much, I believe, from the fear all the great interests in the country had of their meddling of govt in all their private arrangements; in fact no one felt safe that he would be allowed to manage his business in his own way and without the aid of a govt inspector. I hope the new govt will leave the private interests of the country alone, and this Parliament will likely have a long and quiet life.

On Tuesday the 3rd March I had the annual meeting of the Telegraph Construction Co. We declared at 25 per cent div[iden]d for the year, a pretty satisfactory result, and on Wednesday the 4th I had my Gt Western shareholders' meeting. We declared a 6¾ per cent divd which was satisfactory to both the shareholders and ourselves. The other large lines had paid a less dividend than in the corresponding period last year.

Yesterday, the 9th, I had the annual meeting of the Gt Ship Co, and we declared a divd for the half year at the rate of 10%, or 15% for the whole year. The meeting went off very well considering the disagreeable nature of some of the business. On Saturday last, the 7th, the Duke of

Edinburgh and his Russian bride landed at Gravesend and went by train to Windsor direct. The day was a lovely one, as well as Sunday, but yesterday and today have been cold and strong [*?* wind] with snow. They came with the Queen on Thursday by our line to make their entry into London, and great preparations are being made for their reception; I hope they will have fine weather.

MARCH 21, 1874. We came down to Malvern today to the Imperial Hotel to spend a couple of weeks. It has been a lovely spring day; we have our carriage and horses down.

APL 6TH, LONDON. We returned from Malvern today, having spent a very pleasant time there. The weather on the whole was very fine and both feel all the better for the change. It is a beautiful place and the air so fresh and bracing that one feels very little fatigue. Eastnor Park is a very beautiful drive and the wild flowers were splendid when we were there. The carriage & horses were a great advantage and we were very comfortable at the hotel, having the same rooms as last year.

APL 27, 1874. Frank with his wife and child came home today from India. He and they are all looking well, altho' he has been obliged to return on sick leave.

MAY 13TH. The Emperor of Russia arrived in England and went direct to Windsor, having landed at Dover instead of Gravesend as intended, in consequence of his ship getting aground at Flushing.

MAY 15. We brought the Emperor to London today; he is a fine looking man. I came up in the same carriage with Admiral Popoff and Count Schouveloff—two rather odd names, but both great ones at home.

On Monday the 18 I went to the Guild Hall where an address &c was presented to the Emperor. It was a pretty sight and in the evening I went to the Albert Hall where there was a concert for the Emperor. This was also a fine sight, as it was very full and the rich colouring of the dresses and uniforms had a fine effect. The Emperor left England on Thursday the 21st. On this day we went to Chepstow by 4.50 train to stay a few days with Alfred, and on the Friday I went to see the works at the Severn Tunnel[3] and on Saturday went over the Newport and Pontypool line and Lady L[l]anover lines in the Sirhowy Valley,[4] and on Sunday we went to Tintern Abbey, returning home on Monday the 25th.

WEDNESDAY MAY 27TH. I held the Pro Grand Lodge of Berks and Bucks today at Windsor. It was a very good meeting; about 120 dined in the Town Hall. The Lodge was held in the Carlton Club; all went off very well. Sir Watkin Williams Wynn went down with me.

JULY 1, 1874. We have just completed the laying of the cable to Brazil; it is a long distance and has been very successfully done with the exception of the piece between Lisbon & Madeira; this was laid last year and broken, the ends have been recovered in 2,500 fathoms of water and made good. Halpin laid the portion between Madeira and Brasil; it was carried in 3 ships so that two splices had to be made at sea. Halpin tells me he does not approve of the g[rea]t risk of this operation, but thinks even at an extra cost one large ship like the Gt Eastern is wiser.

MY OLD CABIN ON BOARD THE GREAT EASTERN, FRIDAY JULY 31ST, 1874, SHEERNESS. I left London today at 4.15pm to join the Great Eastern at Sheerness, reaching here a little after 6. I find the old ship looking very clean and nice, and it seems very natural for me to be sitting in this cabin where I have spent so many anxious and pleasant hours. The anxiety and excitement of starting on an Atlantic cable expedition is very different from what it was in 1865; all now is simply a matter of quiet business and there is no fuss or reporters. Capt Halpin is in charge of the expedition and has as first officer Capt Cato. I half wish I was going across the Atlantic with the ship, but am not quite sure this feeling will last until I get to Portland.

SATURDAY AUGT 1. We got our anchor up today at 1pm and at once steamed out of the harbour. The early part of the day was very dull and looked like rain, but the afternoon cleared up and it has been very calm and pleasant. Col. Le Estrange of the Artillery came with us as far as the Nore, from where he went back in the tug. Our speed is about 6 knots, drawing 32ft forward and 31 feet aft; we have just passed Dover (10pm) but at some distance from the shore. My bed is a very small one and pretty hard, but I managed to sleep well last night. Admiral Richards is with us and all is going well.

AUGT 2ND. There has been a good deal of fog during last night. I was awoke about one oclock by the fog whistle which continued to arouse us until between 5 & 6 this morning, putting all idea of sleep out of the question. I do not know any thing more disagreeable on board ship than hearing that whistle every 2 or 3 minutes. We were off Beachey Head at 6am and passed Brighton about 9. The day has been very dull and the weather so thick we could see nothing of the coast until we reached the Isle of Wyght. We passed St Catherine's Head about 5pm, the weather being clearer, and it afterwards got out bright with a fine clear moon, and we dropped our anchor in Portland at 12.45.

AUGT 3. I left the ship this morning and returned to Clewer by the 12.30 train, reaching here about 6. The Windsor Mechanics' Institution had a fete in Clewer Park today and did not behave themselves very well.

SUNDAY AUGT 9. The ship sailed from Portland today, direct for Trinity Bay, Newfoundland, as she is to lay the cable this time on her return. A successful and prosperous voyage to her is my sincere wish.

FRIDAY AUGT 28. The half-yearly meeting of the Gt Western share-holders was held today. We were not able to give them as good a dividend as we had hoped from the large falling-off in our mineral traffic, and increases in our expenditure, but the meeting went off very well and we paid 4%.

MARINE HOTEL, COWES, MONDAY AUGT 31. We left Clewer today by the 10.45am train for the Isle of Wight, travelling by Reading and Basingstoke to Southampton and crossing by steamer from there. We arrived at this hotel, the Marine, kept by a Mr Drover, at half past 3. It came on to rain soon after leaving Southampton and has been more or less wet all the afternoon, but we managed to get a walk.

SEPT 1ST, COWES. The day has been very wet, but fine at intervals, and we managed to get a good walk.

SEPT 2. This has been a very fine day and we got two very long walks. Bought a clock.

COWES, SEP 3. This has been a very wet day with a very heavy easterly gale in the evening. Mr Talbot[5] is here with his yacht the Lynx, and we went to lunch with him on board today. Miss Talbot is with him. But got very little walking.

FRIDAY 4TH. Very heavy showers of rain all day, so that we could only get a walk between them. This we managed to do.

SEP 5. This has been a very fine day and we walked to Whippingham church. It is a very pretty little church and the church yard is very neatly kept.

SEP 6, SUNDAY. It rained hard today until 5pm, when we started for a walk.

NEEDLES HOTEL, SEPT 7. We left our comfortable quarters at Cowes at 2pm today for this place, by a carriage. The drive is very pretty and the day has been fine until night. We liked Cowes; the rooms we had looked over the Roads, and there were a great many yachts there & a large passenger traffic by the steamers, so that from the cov[ere]d balcony in front of our window we could (even in the rain) sit outside and see a great deal of life going on. We were also very well fed and consider the hotel a very good one. On our way here we stopped to see Carisbrooke Castle, an interesting old ruin with very pretty cenery. This hotel is very comfortable, good clean rooms. The landlord, a Mr Beasley [&] his wife [are] both jolly fat; [she] is a happy looking woman and I have no doubt will make us very comfortable. Our rooms look over the cliffs and have a beautiful sea view as well as of the Needles and the English coast.

TUESDAY SEPT 8TH. I walked to the Needles this morning and along the headland to Colwell Bay, back over the hill. In the afternoon we walked along the downs to Freshwater Bay. This is a lovely walk; a splendid fresh air blowing. They rise about 600 feet sharply out of the sea. Freshwater Gate is a very pretty little bay with some curious chalk rocks, but is very much shut in; it cannot be so healthy as this place. There are only a couple of other houses near this hotel at Alum Bay; solitary, but wild and charming. The cliffs are very curious, being formed of different col[oure]d sands & clay in vertical beds; the beach is shingle and not good, but the hills is the real charm of the place.

There is a nice little pier as a landing place for the steamers which come 2 or 3 times a week, bringing large numbers of people to spend a few hours in the hills.

WEDNESDAY 9. A beautifully breezy morning. I went on to the hill in hopes of seeing the Gt Eastern pass, for she left Newfoundland on the 27th August and finished laying the cable on the 7th Sept, so was on her way to Sheerness and ought to pass here this morning. I, however, did not see her, but I enjoyed my walk on the hill. In the afternoon it came on heavy storms of wind and rain, but we got a short walk. (*In margin* Found she passed about 5am.) (*On opposite page* Ship left Portland Sunday 9th Augt at 10am, arrived in Heart's Content at 10am Augt 23rd. Started to lay cable Aug 27, finished on the 7th Sept.)

THURSDAY THE 10TH SEPR. A fine bright morning with high wind. We walked over the hill to Colwell Bay and back. It is a small place with only very few houses. In the afternoon we walked down to the beach but it came on to rain about 5 oclock and the night was very wet, with a heavy westerly gale blowing.

FRIDAY 11. Morning wet, but as it cleared a little after lunch we walked to Freshwater by the road, but just as we turned to come back it came on a heavy rain with a gale of wind, and we had a hard struggle to face it, getting very wet before we reached the hotel. I thought Bay[6] would break down; she had to keep close behind me so that I took the wind a little from her. The night was an awful one, the gale driving the small gravel against the windows of our room; I thought they would be all driven in. The hotel stands 270 feet above the shore.

SATURDAY 12. It was very showery all day today until 5pm, when [it] got out a lovely evening. I had a long walk on the beacon hill in the morning and was on the beach in the evening.

SUNDAY SEPT 13TH. This has been a beautiful day; I had a long walk on the hill in the morning and after lunch we had a carriage and drove to Yarmouth. It is a poor little place. From here we drove to Freshwater Gate and then sent the carriage home and sat about on the beach for an hour and walked home over the downs; a lovely walk and a beautiful sun set.

MONDAY 14, SAND ROCK HOTEL. We were sorry to leave Alum Bay today. They have made us very comfortable at the hotel, and as we were the only people staying in it most of the time we had no one to interfere with us. We started with a carriage at 2 oclock and passed through very pretty scenery, reaching here about 5; the day has been very fine. This looks a very nice, quiet place—quite a cottage, covered with ivy and other creepers & close to St Catherine's light house. I think we will like it; we had a walk before dinner. They charge high for carriages on the island.

TUESDAY 15. We walked to Black Gang Chine this morning and lunched at the hotel there. This chine is an overrated place; the beach is very pretty. I do not know what the hotel would be to stay at, it is a a good size and lots of people go there for the day. There is a large bazaar for the sale of all kinds of curiosities &c. After lunch we walked back over the hill to Niton, and so home; the fresh air was very delicious and we enjoyed our walk very much—it was a long tramp altogether. The hill is about 700 feet above the sea; the day was very lovely, hot when you did not get plenty of air.

WEDNESDAY 16TH SEPR. We walked along the coast this morning as far as St Lawrence and returned by the main road; a very nice walk but rather hot. In the afternoon we walked to Niton and had a look at the old church; it is in very good condition, wonderfully dark inside. The day has been very fine.

THURSDAY 17. Anniversary of my wedding day. In the morning we walked to the top of the hill & back by Niton, and after lunch had a carriage at 2 and drove to Ventnor and Bonchurch. This latter place is very quiet and pretty; we visited the old church, a remarkably small place.[7] We also saw on our way the little church at St Lawrence, said to be the smallest one in England; it is certainly not very large. The drive along the Undercliff is very pretty. We stayed a short time at Ventnor, but I did not like it well enough to care to go there; it is too much of a town and wants the quiet which to me is the great charm of the sea side. I do not like a crowd. On our return we called in at the sanatorium of the Consumption Hospital; there was a bazaar being held for the funds of the place, so it was very gay with ladies &c. We met Mr & Mrs Desange,[8] who are staying at Bonchurch. The day has been very fine.

FRIDAY 18 SEPT. We walked to Blackgang along the beach this morning, rather hard work as it is a very fine shingle and makes walking very difficult. After lunch we walked on the top of the hills towards St Lawrence; the air was very fine and the day has been hot.

SATURDAY 19. Walked on the beach. There was a grand sea running and we sat and enjoyed it. In the afternoon walked on the east hill. Day fine.

SUNDAY 20. Went this afternoon with a carriage to Shanklin, to see the place and secure rooms at the hotel if we liked it. It is a very pretty place and we liked the look of Hollier's Hotel and took rooms for Tuesday. The day was fine but it rained as we returned home and was a wet evening.

MONDAY 21. Did not feel very well this morning, so did not go out of the grounds until after lunch, when we had a walk on the east hills as far as St Lawrence. Day very fine.

HOLLIER'S HOTEL, SHANKLIN, TUESDAY 22 SEPT, 1874. There was a very rough sea on today, so we went in the morning to the beach to enjoy it, and at 2 left Sandrock Hotel for Shanklin. We were very sorry to leave this place; Mr Bush the landlord had made us very comfortable both in our rooms and our eating, and it is a charmingly quiet place. We were the only people staying in the house but parties came every day to lunch and walk about. If he had some good stables I should like to go here for a long visit and take my carriage, as from here it is within a day's drive to visit any part of the island. The air is also very nice, being open to all the winds that blow with the exception of the north. I will often look back with pleasure on our visit here. After dinner we went down to the beach at Shanklin; a lovely moon light night and the sea beautiful. It was certainly a charming evening; the day has been very fine. We called at the Desanges at Bonchurch on our way here: found him at home but not with his wife.

WEDNESDAY 23. We took a long walk about Shanklin this morning and after lunch walked along the cliffs to Sandown, a beautiful walk, and after seeing the place walked back by the sands; a good long walk. The Sandown Hotel looked the best. Day very fine.

SHANKLIN, SEPT 24, THURSDAY. It was wet part of this morning but got out beautifully fine in the middle of the day, and we walked on the cliffs to Bonchurch and back by the beach, a lovely walk. After dinner we went down to the Parade. The moon was lovely and we enjoyed our walk.

FRIDAY 25TH/74. We went by 10.30am train this morning to Ryde and lunched there, returning by train in the afternoon. The day was very hot. I did not fancy Ryde as a place to stay at, it is not quiet enough for my taste. The pier is a lively place and the scenery round is very pretty. In the evening we had a long walk in the light of a beautiful full moon. These moon light nights are very lovely here as the moon is over the sea and the effect is very fine.

SATURDAY 26. Walked this morning along the cliffs to Luccombe Chine and returned by the beach. The tide was unfortunately to[o] high and when we got near Shanklin we found we could not get round the point of the cliff. We sat some time waiting for the tide to go down, when an empty boat hailed us and offered to take us round. We were glad to avail ourselves of the chance and we must either have walked back and returned by the cliffs, or have waited an hour or two. The sun was very hot and the walk would have been a long one. After lunch we walked along the sands to Sandown and back. The day has been very hot but very enjoyable.

SUNDAY THE 27TH. We went to the old church this morning; it is a rough old place and the service was very nicely done. In the afternoon we walked to Sandown and back by the cliffs. The day has been hot, but very nice.

MONDAY 28. We walked on the beach this morning, and in the afternoon walked to Luccombe Chine by the cliffs and back by the sands; the day was very fine. If we come to this hotel again do not take No 25 sitting room.

MARINE HOTEL, COWES, TUESDAY 29. We had a walk on the beach

this morning and left Shanklin at 2.30 by carriage for Cowes. We have not been very much pleased with Hollier's Hotel; if I go to Shanklin again I will try the other one in the town. The hotel on the Parade is too much under the cliff & I do not think will be as comfortable and airy as those on the hill. This little town is very pretty, very undulating, and the houses are nearly all in little gardens, not in long rows as is usually the case. The drive to Cowes was very pretty. We were glad to find ourselves in our old rooms at this comfortable hotel. Day fine.

WEDNESDAY 30. Had two long walks today and the weather fine until night, when it came on very wet.

RADLEY'S HOTEL, SOUTHAMPTON, THURSDAY OCT 1/74. Had a walk this morning and left Cowes by the 3.30 steamer. Shortly before starting it came on a very heavy rain and has continued until dinner time. I got out for a walk in the town after dinner.

FRIDAY 2ND. It rained very hard with a gale of wind until 12 oclock this morning. I then had a stroll over the docks; everything looks very dead here and there seems to be very little doing. In the afternoon we had a long walk about the town as it got out very fine, & also after dinner.

CLEWER, SATURDAY 3. We left Southampton at 10.30 this morning and reached here at 3.30. Found Clewer looking very nice and pretty— and it is home. The hotel at Southampton is very badly done. We have had a very pleasant trip and are both much better for it. I like the quiet of the Isle of Wight and I begin to fancy there is more enjoyment in this quiet kind of travelling than in rushing about from place to place on the Continent. I should like to spend a few months at Sandrock Hotel and have my carriage and horses there; it would be a pleasant life. Well, we will see if it is ever my fate.

CLEWER, OCT 19TH, 1874. I have attended the funeral today of my oldest friend, poor Evans. When we returned home we heard he was very ill, and he died on the 15th. He was buried at [blank] church.

During June in this year we narrowed a large part of the broad gauge, all south of our main line between London and Bristol; it was done very well by the staff. Thus is the poor broad gauge gradually dieing out. It now only exists on our main line between London and Bristol, and the Windsor and Henly branches, and as we are mixing the whole of the bd gauge left by the end of this year we will have narrow gauge over the whole of our system.[9]

DECR 6TH, 1874. I heard last night of the death at 9am yesterday morning of Mr Young, our Gt Western solicitor. How busy death is about us; he had been with us in his usual health. He will be a great loss to us as he had a sound judgment and was an upright and honourable man, and a sound lawyer. Only a month ago Mr Leeman,[10] one of our directors, died very suddenly at Brighton. He was at our board on the Thursday before, apparently in very good health, & while out walking at Brighton with his brother complained of a pain in his chest, and died before they could get him to his house. Such is the uncertainty of life.

JANY 1, 1875. A new year has dawned upon us, and looking back on the past I have much reason to be thankful to God for all the many blessings I have enjoyed. Many old faces have been called away, and who can say which of us will be called during the present year? May we endeavour so to live as to be prepared through God's mercy to meet that call. My Christmas has been a sad one and we enter on the new year with a heavy heart. The day before Xmas Day our 10.15am train for the north was thrown off the line near Kirklington,[11] a few miles north of Oxford, by a tire in the first carriage breaking, and the result was a frightful smashing up of the carriages and the loss of 30 lives at the time, and, I fear, with those who have died since and are likely to die, the loss will not be much under 40, and at least 70 people injured, many very seriously. It is the most awful railway accident that has ever happened in England. As far as we can ascertain it is a pure accident; no one seems to have in any way neglected their duty. This is a comfort to us all. We have had a very hard frost now for more than a fortnight, and this caused the fracture of the tire, the metal of which was perfectly sound. Yesterday, the last day in the year, was a miserable day, so dark gas had to be used all day, cold and foggy.

FEBY 7, 1875. Parliament met on the 5th of this month, and so far we have had a very easy session. The 3 or 4 party divisions have shewn a majority on our side of nearly 100. I dined last night with Disraeli at the Treasury; there was a large party. On Thursday the 4th[12] we held our Gt Western meeting. The strikes in South Wales and the Forest of Dean[13] has reduced our revenue a good deal, and this, coupled with extra working charges, has prevented our paying more than 5% instead of the 6¾ we paid in the corresponding half year. Our meeting passed off very well. We have had very cold weather all this year, frost & snow, with a cold east wind.

MAY 5, 1875. Wednesday the 28th Apl was a great day amongst Masons, the Prince of Wales being installed as Grand Master in the Albert Hall that day in the presence of at least 7,000 Masons. The effect in the hall was very curious, as the building was filled from top to bottom and the blue Masonic collars gave a colour to the whole place. In saluting, the effect was very strange; it had also a curious feeling in the eyes. I fancy if it had continued many minutes we would all have been ill.

We spent Easter with Alfred, going to Bath on Saturday the 20 March and staying there until Thursday at the Pump Room Hotel, where we were not very comfortable as our rooms were bad, the hotel being full. We went to the cathedral on Sunday morning; it has been beautifully restored inside, and the service was very well performed and a good sermon. On Monday we went to Bristol and over the Clifton Extension line, saw Clifton and went in the afternoon to Chepstow. On Tuesday I went to the Severn Tunnel and on Wednesday to Milford, spent Thursday there in looking at the new docks &c, and returned to Chepstow in the evening. Spent the time with Billy until Monday when we returned to town.[14] The weather was very fine.

MAY 12TH, 1875. Went to Paris on the 8th to see the Bessemer steamer[15] tried across the Channel. There was a large party; Sir Massey Lopes & Mr Bassett and myself made a small party of our own. We had a special train and did not get to our quarters for dinner in Paris until nearly 9 oclock at night. The day was very fine and any steamer would have made a good passage. The saloon was fast so we had no opportunity of seeing it worked, and we ran down a lot of the west pier at Calais. The steamer is not fit for this service—too heavy and cumbersome. On Sunday we spent a very pleasant day in Paris, the weather being beautiful and all the shrubs and trees in perfection. We stayed at the Hotel Mirabeau, not a bad hotel but we were high up.

On Monday another special train brought us back to London. The Bessemer is no good for what she was designed.

We have had a great loss in the death of Admiral Sherard Osborne; he died very suddenly on the evening of the 13th while out at a dinner party. He is a great loss to the Telegraph Construction Co as he was a most able man, and a kind and certain friend.

MAY 14TH. I held my Pro Grand Lodge at Aylesbury today; we had a very good meeting and a fine day for the excursion.

MONDAY, MAY 24TH, 1875. We went to Leamington on Monday the 17th and stayed there until the Thursday at the Regent Hotel, having the same suite of rooms we had when we were first married. We enjoyed our couple of days. Charlie returned home from Russia on Saturday last, his connexion with the New Russia Co having terminated, and he is now joining the Gt Western Railway as mineral engineer.

TUESDAY, JUNE 29TH, 1875. On Sunday last, the 27th I had all my children with us in the evening. It is many years since this occurred before. Frank & Harry had their wives, and Anna her husband. Harry's 2 children and 3 of Anna's were also with us, so that we made a goodly party. Jane Tweedy left us today on her return home; she has been staying with us a few weeks. My wife and I went to a concert at Buckingham Palace last Wednesday; it was a pretty sight and very good music.

The Gt Western Railway Co have made an agreement to take over the Monmouthshire Railway Co this month.[16] It is a heavy undertaking and the terms are also the full value, but it has long been a thorn in our side in that district and I believe the result will be very beneficial to us both.

CLEWER, JULY 20, 1875. We came down to Clewer for the summer on the 2nd, but the weather has been very wet and the river in consequence very high, nearly over the banks into the park—a very unusual thing in the summer months. We went out in the steamer and had no difficulty at Bray Lock, the gates being open.

SHEERNESS. MY OLD CABIN IN THE GT EASTERN STEAM SHIP. FRIDAY NIGHT, JULY 23, 1875. I came from London today to the ship.

We sail tomorrow for Milford Haven, where we intend to lay her up, the charter with the Telegraph Construction Co ending this month. I have tonight Frank with me. It feels very natural to sit in this cabin again, where I have spent so many pleasant and so many anxious hours, and it may be a long time before I have a sail in the old ship again as I do not know how we are to employ her in the future; but we will not give up hope that some useful work may be found for her, as she is a noble ship and has done good service in the past.

SATURDAY 24TH. We got up our anchor today at 12, drawing 19ft 9in forward and 20ft 5in aft. As usual, the old ship could not move without some excitement, and we had several excursion steamers round us as we went away from Sheerness, with bands of music and the usual cheering, also great crowds of people on the shore to see us leave the harbour, which we accomplished all well but very slow from the dirty state of the bottom of the ship. The morning was stormy with showers of rain, but the afternoon was lovely. We passed the North Foreland at 6pm.

SUNDAY, JULY 25. We were off Brighton this morning at 9am, off Sandown at 3.30pm, St Catherine's Head at 5 and Portland Bill at 11pm. The day has been a lovely one, with a fine breeze; paddles doing about 6 rev & screw 24 rev. We had a fine view of the coast all the way.

MONDAY, 26TH. We passed the Start light house at 8am, Plymouth at 10, Lizard at 5.30, Land's End 7.30. It has been a bright and lovely day and I have enjoyed it very much. When we were off The Lizard there were 7 steamers near us and we had to thread our way with difficulty through hundreds of fishing boats who did not care to get out of our way. When off the Land's End we had a most glorious sun set, such as can only be seen at sea.

NEYLAND, TUESDAY, 27. We were of[f] the entrance to Milford at 9 this morning; there was a great deal of fog early and we had to wait to go in so that we would have the ebb tide to anchor. It was past 12 before we made a start for the harbour. We were joined here by some of the Gt Western directors who went into the Haven with us, and we dropped our anchor at 2pm opposite the town of Milford Haven. We landed and had a meeting with the directors of the new docks, and returned to Neyland in the evening. The day was very hot and lovely.[17]

NEYLAND, 28 JULY. We spent the day in looking over our station and steamers and in paying a visit to Capt Hamilton, the supt of the Pembroke dock yards, and seeing the new ships on the stocks. The day has been very hot & lovely.

CLEWER, 29TH JULY. We left by the early train from Neyland this morning and came as far as Newport to attend a meeting with the Monmouthshire directors, returning home in the evening.

AUGST 3, 1875. I was weighed today, and find myself 11 s[tone] 13 lb. My greatest weight before was 147 lb or 10 s 7 lb, so I have gained a good deal in the last few years. My wife says it is because I married her; it is not her fault if it is not so as she does all she can for my comfort.

TUESDAY, CLEWER, AUGT 31ST, 75. Our Great Western meeting of shareholders was held today. The long strike of the colliers in South Wales has reduced our dividend to $3\frac{3}{4}$ per cent per annum for the last half year. The meeting went off very well.

DOVER, WEDNESDAY, 1ST SEPT. We left London this afternoon at 2.30 for Dover, on our way to France. For journal of journey see special book.

CLEWER, OCT 9TH, 1875. Returned home today from our travels in France after a very pleasant time spent there, and both much better for our trip.

I found on my return the Bristol & Exeter had written to say they must offer their line to either us or the Midland, and had offered it to us. This is a great nuisance as we must pay too much for it.

OCT 12, 1875. At the Gt Western board today we agreed to take over the Bristol & Exeter as from the 1st Jany next, at 6% for 5 years and $6\frac{1}{2}$ in perpetuity. I am very sorry this has been necessary just now as we are not able to afford to pay the loss there will be on it for some time, but the London & the [sic] South Western and the Midland having taken over the Somerset & Dorset line[18] it would not have been wise for us to leave the B & E free.

LONDON, NOV 22, 1875. During my absence in France a great railway jubilee was held at Darlington to commemorate the 50th anniversary of the opening of the [Stockton &] Darlington Railway, the first of those great undertakings. It was very successful and largely attended by all the railway authorities. For particulars see the papers of the day. I was sorry not to be able to be present.

We have had dreadful floods all over the country the last month, doing a vast deal of damage and stopping the working of many railways. Our line at Oxford was stopped Monday & Tuesday in last week, and many parts of the line were under water. The first floods began on the 22 October when the water was over the park at Clewer and continued so for a week. They then subsided, but fresh rain began again about the 14th of this month, even higher than the previous ones, and are still out over the park and grounds about Windsor. The annexed account in the Eton paper will give a fuller account of the state of matters at Windsor, but the whole of England has been suffering in a like manner. The Bristol & Exeter line west of Bridgewater is flooded (see today's account in The Times, annexed). The last few days have been fine and we must hope that dry weather will prevail for the rest of the winter.

My poor old aunt Robinson died on the 16th Nov at York, at the good old age of 87. I saw her in 1870 when I was in York. She is the last of the past generation in our family. She left me a portrait of my grandfather Gooch.

DECR 20, 1875. One of our old Great Western guards was killed in an accident at Chippenham a few weeks ago. He was a man very much respected, and the following account of his funeral shews that a well spent life, in whatever scale of society, meets its reward in the esteem and respect of their fellow men.[19]

On Friday last, the 17th, the Gt Western Rly Co took a very important step in taking over the Bristol & Exeter and South Devon Railways. This matter has been forced upon us by the action of the Midland & London & South Western Railways in buying the Somerset & Dorset. Our shareholders were very unanimous in their approval. We give the B & E, as from the 1st Jany next, 6 per cent for 7 years and 6½ afterwards in perpetuity, and we give the South Devon, as from the 1st Feby next, 65 per cent of our divid for 7 years and 70% in perpetuity. I am sorry we have been forced into this at the present time as it must tell upon our dividend, at any rate for a few years.[20]

This makes our line the longest, I expect, in Europe. We have 2,018 miles & £72,367,650 of capital owned & leased by us.

Joint lines	85 miles
Lines worked at cost	24
Running powers exercised by us ..	119

2246

Canals   [*blank*]

JANY 1ST, 1876. Another year has passed, and I am grateful to God for all the blessings conferred upon me and mine. I have been blessed with good health and my dear wife and children have also all been well and happy. May God in His mercy grant that the new year we have entered upon today may also be rich in blessings and make us more and more worthy of His goodness.

We had a large party with us on Xmas Day; all my children but Emily, and we had about 13 grand children. It makes a large muster. The weather has been very mild and warm, tho' dull. Xmas Day was quite a spring day.

Charlie is to be married at Plymouth on the 4th of this month. I am sorry it will not be possible for me to go to the wedding as it is my Gt Western board week and important matters have to be settled.

MARCH 16TH, 1876. Our half-yearly meeting of G.W.R. shareholders went off very well, altho' we were only able to pay a ¼ per cent less dividend. The meeting was held on the 2nd March.

Charlie was married on the 4th Jany as arranged; I have since paid him a visit in his home at Cardiff, where he seems very comfortable. On the 10 Jany I went down into Cornwall and Devonshire to go over the lines there. Found them all in very fair order; we spent the whole week [there]. It was very cold and there was thick ice for skating at Penzance. I called upon Trevithick[21] there; he was very unwell. I also called upon Jane Tweedy at Truro.

On the 24 Jany we left London to go over the lines belonging to the Bristol & Exeter Co and had lovely weather, but I unfortunately had taken cold at the opening of the Westminster Aquarium on the Saturday before, and was far from well. The Bristol & Exeter directors gave me a splendid dinner at the hotel in College Green[22] (where we staid) on the Wednesday; it is a good house. We got home on the Friday night. Parliament opened on the 8th Feby.

My poor old dog Norval died during the night of Sunday the 5th. He had only been ill a week. When I went to Cardiff to Charlie on the Thursday the 24th Feby I left Norval very well, but when I returned home on Sunday night the poor old dog, instead of jumping up to welcome me as he has always done, had a difficulty in getting up the stairs, & only rubbed against my legs. He went up with me to my dressing room and got on the sofa, where he slept all night. On the Monday morning he was sick and looked so ill I sent for the veterinary surgeon who took him to his place, where he got weaker day by day as he could not keep any food in his stomach. I saw him a few times; poor old fellow, he tryed one morning to get up and go with me, but had no power in his hind legs. I saw him last on the Saturday morning; on the Monday morning he was found dead. Poor old dog, how I miss him; he has been for 9½ years my constant and faithful friend, he has been my only companion in many anxious hours. He was very, very true to me, altho' kind and good with others, yet he would not forsake me for any thing or any one. I feel as much grief as tho' I had lost a human friend. Bay & I went to Clewer on the Monday and buried him in the garden there, where I will put up something to mark the spot. He was a little over 10 years old as he was born in Nov 1875 [ie 1865], given to me when in the cable expedition of 1866, and died in March 1876.

APL 28, 1876. I have spent my Easter at Malvern this year. We went down on the 7th to the Imperial Hotel, taking carriage & horses with us. Our first day was lovely weather but it changed on the Sunday to rain and cold, and continued bad. On Thursday and Good Friday there was a heavy fall of snow, in many parts of the country deep enough to stop railway traffic. It did not leave the Malvern Hills until Easter Tuesday. We, on the whole and in spite of the weather, enjoyed our time at Malvern, leaving there on the 24th. On the Saturday before leaving we were able to get up to the top of the Beacon and were very fortunate—the views were lovely and with light & shade caused by light, passing clouds, the effect was very fine. It is a pity more water cannot be seen from this hill, only 4 little pieces of the Severn are visable. On the Friday we went to Worcester to see the cathedral; it is very beautiful. Dr Barry, one of the Canons, was kind enough to take us over it, and gave us a cup of tea afterwards.

MAY 19TH, 1876. We had a party fight in the House on the 11th on the question of the additional title of the Queen, viz Empress of India. The Opposition have tryed to make this simple and proper affair one of vast importance, saying it will destroy the feeling of Englishmen towards the Crown, and other such like nonsense. Much time and wind has been wasted upon the question, and we beat them on this division by 108.

The Prince of Wales arrived at home on the evening of the 11th from his Indian tour, looking very well. His visit to India has been most successful and great rejoicings have taken place on his happy return. I attended a Levée held by him on the 15th; there were an immense number present. He went to Windsor on the 17th and I saw him off by our train and had the pleasure of shaking hands with him.

I held my Provincial Grand Lodge at Reading on the 16th; we had a very large meeting, some 120 to dinner, and all went off very well. We are having a very cold month of May, a dry east wind; rain and warm weather being sadly wanted.

The Tel[e]g[rap]h Construction Co gave a large dinner at Willis's Rooms on the 10th to commemorate the completion of the cables to New Zealand. I was in the chair.

MAY 30, 1876. The ex-King & Queen of Hanover have been staying in London for a few weeks. The Queen, with her two daughters, went to Windsor yesterday by our 11am train and I went down to see them off. They had arrived early at the station; I was introduced to the Queen and had a long chat with her. She was a very motherly kind of woman, regretted she did not speak better English.

JULY 20. I have been put on a Select Committee of the House to report upon the question of compensation to be paid to servants in case of accident in the performance of their duty. The advocates claim that the master shall in all cases pay compensation when, from the neglect of a fellow servant, any one is injured. This would produce a wonderful revolution if made law, which it never will be. We have had some meetings and heard some evidence, but as there is no chance of completing the enquiry this session we have adjourned.

AUGT 15. Parliament was prorogued today. It has been a weary kind of session. The Opposition has been factious and talkative and much time has been lost, and consequently much time lost that might have been better employed. Some good work has been done.

AUGUST 26. We have had some dreadfully hot weather; on the 13 the temp in the sun at Clewer was 158° and in the shade 96°. Several days have been about the same. When I returned from Pad[dington] to Clewer today I found my poor dog Sailor had been killed by getting into the mill stream and carried under the wheel. He is a great loss to me as he was a splendid dog. He was brought by Beckwith in the Gt Ship from Newfoundland, and he gave him to me after I lost Norval, and I had become very fond of the poor fellow.

SEPT 2ND. I bought a ⅓rd share in Johnson & Co's graving docks for Frank, as from yesterday. I hope & believe if he looks well after it, it may be a good thing for him. Our Gt Western half-yearly meeting was held today. Our dividend not a very satisfactory one, the trade of the country continues in a most depressed state and consequently the railway traffic is very bad. All are suffering. Our dividend was the same as last year, or 3¾ per cent. The meeting went off very quietly.

CHEPSTOW, SEPT 5TH. We came down here by the 9.45 to stay a few days with Billy. The day was very fine and after our arrival we had a long walk, intending also to go and see the full moon through the east window of Tintern Abbey which is a great sight at this particular full moon, and large numbers of people go to see it. Unfortunately the night came on cloudy and wet and our excursion was stopped.

SEPT 6TH. I went to the Severn Tunnel this morning, and after lunch we drove to Tintern Abbey, Bay and I walking down the Windcliff; the view is very fine from the top of this cliff. The weather was fine for us until on our way back, when it rained pretty hard and so continued until we got home.

SEPT 7. We went over Chepstow Castle this morning (it is a fine old ruin) and had a good walk. Weather very fine. After lunch we went for a long drive but it came on very wet and we got a wetting before we got home.

SEPT 8. This has been a lovely day. We had a long walk in the morning and after lunch we drove to the Chase, some high land on the east side of the river. We also went to a point on the river called the double view;

from both these places the views are very beautiful, and the day was splendid.

SEPT 9. Had a walk in the morning and in the afternoon drove to Buckley [*ie* Beachley], the Old Passage. The day was very fine.

SUNDAY, SEP 10. Walked to the station and on to the Wye Valley junction in the morning. After lunch drove to Earlswood Common. This is high land and there is a splendid view of the Channel and country beyond from it. The wild flowers are also very plentiful and pretty; the day has been bright with some showers.

SEPT 11TH. We left Chepstow today and went to Cardiff to stay a few days with Charlie. Emily met us at the station. Day fine but cold.

SEP 12. Charlie and I went this morning to the comp[any']s Cilleli colliery[23] and returned to dinner. We went by the Taff [Vale line] and came back by the Eley Valley. Found all going on well at the pit.

SEPT 13. Charlie and I went today to the Avon Colliery. We went by Taff to Treherbert station, where we had ponies and had a rough ride across the mountain & back. The day was pretty fine with a few slight showers.

SOUTH WALES HOTEL, NEYLAND, SEP 14. We left Cardiff this morning for this place at 11am, and arrived here in time for a long walk before dinner. The day was very fine and our rooms here comfortable.

15TH SEP. Spent the morning with Capt Haswell at the station and on the steamers. After lunch the Capt gave us a sail up the Haven, after which we took a long walk before dinner. The day was very fine but rain came on at night.

SEPT 16. Spent the morning with the steamers. After lunch Beckwith brought us the Gt Eastern steam launch and we went down the Haven to visit the old ship. As we are putting a new deck to her she was in rather a mess, but it was pleasant to be on board of her again. I wonder what we will do with her. We went from Milford down the Haven to Dale Bay. On our return to Neyland there was a lovely sun set; day fine. Billy came to us last night. (*On opposite page* The lanes about Ney-land are very pretty and there are a very large variety of ferns. I found 5 different ones in the space of a few yards.)[24]

NEYLAND, SUNDAY, SEPT 17. We had a long walk this morning, and after lunch Beckwith brought us the steam launch and we went up the Haven to Picton Castle. Haswell went with us and dined with us in the evening; he has just been made an admiral. The day was fine and we enjoyed our sail, or rather steam, very much; Billy was with us. The scenery about this haven is very beautiful.

SEPT 18. We started at 7 oclock this morning in our Irish steamer the Waterford to go to Fishguard, as I wanted to see the fitness of the place for a harbour. The day was very bright, but a heavy sea, but I enjoyed our trip very much. We skirted close to the land in going. Bay was very ill all the time and did not enjoy her trip, but was very anxious to be put ashore anywhere, so as she got out of the ship. We got back to Milford at 4, having made the run from Fishguard in 3¼ hours. These steamers are splendid sea boats.[25]

SEPT 19TH, 1876. We spent today in sauntering about Neyland; the day was fine and hot. Billy went back to Chepstow.

SEP 20. We went by train this morning to Tenby, for the purpose of seeing the place and taking rooms should we like it. This we did, and got very comfortable rooms at the Gate House Hotel for Saturday. We had lunch and walked about the place for a few hours, returning to Neyland in the afternoon in time for dinner.

SEPT 21, THURSDAY. Spent the morning at the station, and after lunch we went by train to Pembroke station. Haswell went with us and we walked to the castle, a fine old ruin and of great extent. From here we had a pretty walk across some fields to the dock yard, where we called upon Capt Hamilton, the Supt, but did not find him at home and so returned to Neyland for dinner. The day was very fine and also very hot.

FRIDAY 22 SEP. At the station most of the morning. Took a long walk after lunch, and at the moment of our arrival back at the hotel it came on as heavy a shower of rain as I ever saw; a few minutes later and we would have got thoroughly wet.

SATURDAY 23 SEPT. A wet morning, so we determined to go to Tenby by way of Whitley [*ie* Whitland] Junction. It looked like getting wet to cross the ferry and get from it to the railway station, while by the other route, altho' much longer, we could be under cover all the way. We started by the 12 oclock train, by which time the rain had cleared up, and reached Tenby at half past 3, having had an hour's walk at Whitley. We had a walk on the sands before dinner, and found our rooms ready for us and very nice; they are very large. We enjoyed Neyland very much and were made very comfortable at the hotel.

SUNDAY SEPT 24. Went to the old church this morning; it is a large and fine old building and was very well filled, the service being also nicely done. We had a long walk to Saundersfoot and back after lunch; it was a stiff walk for Bay. The weather was fine altho' there had been a few showers during the day.

25TH SEPT. Walked on the south sands in the morning; afternoon had a nice walk to Waterwinch & back. The day was very fine.

SEP 26. The morning was wet but after lunch it cleared up, altho' not very fine, and we had a carriage and drove to Manorbeer Castle; it is a fine old ruin. Part of it has lately been fitted up as a residence by some gentleman. We returned to Tenby by the Ridgeway, some fine views. The lanes are very pretty about here with the ferns.

SEPT 27. We had a walk on the north sands this morning; weather fine, but it came on dull middle day. We, however, had a carriage and drove first to Gumfreston church, a pretty old place with some mineral springs close to it, but which do not seem to be much frequented. From here we drove to Carew Castle. This is a very interesting old ruin; part of it is not of very old date—in the time of Elisabeth, with mullion windows and fine large rooms. On our return we came by way of a pretty village called St Florence. The lanes are very narrow and fortunately there is not much traffic, as we could have come to a dead lock. The wet came on before we got home and the evening was very wet.

SEPT 28. This has been a very wet day. I got out for an hour in the morning with a mackintosh &c and at 4 it cleared up for a little and we had a walk on the south sands.

SEPT 29TH, 1876. This was a beautiful morning and we walked a couple of miles to find some caves called Hoyle's Mouth. After some difficulty we found the place and it was a disapp[ointmen]t; there is nothing to see worth the trouble. Old stories are told about the caves, but it is a small place. In the afternoon we walked along the south sands and climbed up upon the cliffs at Giltar Point. There is a beautiful sea view from here and along the top of the cliffs a delightful walk, grand fresh air and altogether, on such a lovely day as this, a very enjoyable place, and we, altho' tired, wished to have another day there.

SEP 30. A very heavy gale came on last night, a sad contrast to the lovely day, and most of my time during the night was spent in trying to wedge our bedroom windows; I never heard any thing rattle like them, and today the gale & rain has continued, making a very heavy sea. Bay has not got out at all. I protected myself as well as I could and got down to the Castle Hill in the afternoon for an hour. The sea was splendid and I watched it clearing away the sand from the beach for an hour or more. It made a kind of sand cliff, 3 or 4 feet high, and kept taking a little every wave. A roung sea is a grand sight, particularly on a rocky coast like this.

SUNDAY [OCTOBER] 1. The morning was very bright and fine and I went for a climb along the face of the north cliffs to get to Saundersfoot by that means, and also to [*blank* ? Monkstone] Point, but before I got there and nearly accomplishing the last part, the tide had come up to[o] high and in making an effort I slipped my foot of[f] a stone and went into the water, and a wave gave me a good wetting. I had to climb up the steep side of the cliff to get on high land again, and of course walked home in my wet clothes. Having changed & had lunch, we went for a walk as far as Gumfreston church and back; the afternoon was dull.

OCT 2ND. Wet all day until 4pm when we got a short walk on Castle Hill. In the evening went to hear the Alleganian bell ringers. The bell ringing was good, all rest bad.[26]

OCT 3. We had a walk on the north sands this morning. After lunch had a carriage and drove to Saundersfoot, from where we walked along the coast and up the pretty little valley to Issell church, a very pretty little place. We walked over the hill from here and so back to Saundersfoot. The ferns in all these narrow lanes are very abundant; in the spring they must, with the wild flowers, be beautiful. The day has been lovely and we enjoyed our ramble this afternoon very much.

OCT 4TH, TUESDAY [*ie* WEDNESDAY]. We left Tenby by train at 11am today to go to Chepstow and spend the night at Alfred's. The morning was wet but it got out fine in the middle of the day. We have liked Tenby very much; it is a quiet place with splendid sands and rock scenery, fairly open to the sea and very pretty walks and drives in the neighbourhood. There are also very good carriages to be had. We were very comfortable at the Gate House Hotel; cooking was good and we had capital rooms. Wine midling.

CLEWER, OCT 5. We left Chepstow at 1.30 today and arrived at home all right in time for dinner, where we were glad to find all right. Home is very comfortable after having been in hotels for a few weeks, as, however good the hotel there is no place like home. I thank God for mine and its many blessings.

NOV 16, 1876. We dined today with Prince & Princess Christian at Cumberland Lodge. Bulkeley was good enough to ask us to stay at his house for the night, and we went in his bus to Cumberland Lodge.[27] The dinner was punctually at 8, and we were a party of 16. The dinner was a very quiet one, and both the Prince & Princess were very affable and pleasant. We left at a ¼ to 11. The Prince's brother, Duke Frederick, was there and we had a long talk on iron making &c. He has some works of his own in Germany.

WEDNESDAY 22 Nov. I took Prince Christian and his brother by a special train to Swindon this morning, starting at half past 8. They spent a few hours in going over the works and seemed very much pleased; Bulkeley went with us. I left Swindon by a special at one to go to Warminster to attend the Pro Grand Lodge of Wilts. Prince Leopold was there, Lord Methuen & Sir Watkin Williams Wynn. After dinner

Sir Watkin & I went to Corsham Court with Lord Methuen. He has a splendid collection of pictures &c of the old masters. We stayed all night.

THURSDAY NOV 23, 1876. I was at Lord Methuen's until 12 oclock; had a long walk about his grounds. They are not very remarkable but there is some fine timber. I left Chippenham by train for Swindon, where I met my wife and Knatchbull Hugessen, who came down to attend the meeting at the Institution[28] in the evening, to give away the annual prizes. There was a large attendance and Hugessen made a good speech. Hellen Dunning went down with my wife and we returned home by special train. This Institution works very well and must be doing a great deal of good. We had a fine day.

LONDON, JANY 1ST, 1877. How quickly the New Year comes round. Time flys fast as we get older, but I have every reason to be thankful to God for the many blessings of the past year. To the country it has been a year of sad depression. All trade and commerce has been carried on either at a loss or with little or no profit, and the repudiation by Turkey & Egypt of the payment of interest on their debts has placed many thousands of people in great difficulty. The working classes have also been learning a lesson in the fact that trade unions cannot fix a standard of wages. There seems little present prospect of improvement; the world is unsettled by the chance of a war with Turkey. At present a European Conference is sitting at Constantinople, trying to arrive at a peaceful settlement, but all is uncertain, altho' a few weeks must decide it. If peace is fairly settled I hope commerce will improve. The value of money is nill.

We had a year of very bad weather; great heat for a few weeks in the summer, but a vast quantity of rain at other periods. The country has, for the last 3 weeks, been very seriously flooded. May God grant me and all those dear to me every blessing during the present year.

MARCH 12, 1877. The floods in the Thames lasted until the early part of Feby, 80 days. We had to keep every day and night baling water out of the stoke holes of the hot houses at Clewer. The flood was not higher than it was last year, but it has lasted such an unusual time. Much havoc has been done all over the country and we continue to have a great deal of wet, so that the farmers cannot get on their land.

The Queen opened Parliament in person on the 8th of Feby. Disraeli took his seat in the House of Lords on the same day. He will be greatly missed in the House of Commons. Sir Stafford Northcote is the new leader, but he is a poor substitute for Disraeli.

We held our Gt Western half-yearly meeting on the 6th March. It went off very quietly altho' we only paid 4¼ per cent as against 4¾, but the trade of the country is in a dreadful state, and our road has cost us a large extra cost.[29]

I enclose a copy of the Tatler as published in 1709. It has been again started and they have given this copy as a curiosity. A newspaper in those days was a very different thing from the present press, altho' they started with the price of a penny.

ATKINSON'S BELGRAVE HOTEL, TORQUAY. WEDNESDAY 28 MARCH. After our Gt Western board today we came down here. Bassett was with us, and we had a prosperous journey, getting here a little before 12, and was glad to get to bed.

TORQUAY, 29 MARCH. This has been a fine day; we had a walk in the morning and after lunch had a long one with Bassett. We have found Mr Lloyd and his daughter here, and we make up a nice little dinner party of 5 with Bassett. This is a very quiet and comfortable hotel, and the faishon is for you to dine in one of 3 or 4 dining rooms kept for the purpose, instead of your own room. Poor old Lloyd is very shaky, and we had a long chat over our cigars this morning. The effect of the moon light in the bay was lovely tonight.

GOOD FRIDAY, 30TH. We walked to Cockington this morning, a very pretty country lane walk, and after lunch drove to Watcombe. The day has been lovely. Bassett and I had a stroll after dinner.

SATURDAY 31. Bassett and I called on Froude this morning but found he was away for the day. Bay and I then went into Torquay and bought some marble work. After lunch we had a long walk to Daddy's Hole and round by other places, making us quite ready for dinner and a quiet sit indoors afterwards. The day has been very fine.

EASTER SUNDAY, 1ST APL. Went to Tor[re] church in the morning and walked after lunch to Mary Church & back; day very fine.

IX (*Above*) Interior of Swindon engine house, from J. C. Bourne's *History and Description of the Great Western Railway*, 1846

X (*Below*) The *Great Eastern* setting out from Valentia to lay the 1865 Atlantic cable, escorted by (*l to r*) the *Terrible, Sphinx, Hawk* and *Caroline*. Lithograph by Robert Dudley from W. H. Russell's book on the expedition

XI (*Left*) Daniel Gooch
in late middle-age

XII (*Right*) The exquisitely
printed menu
for the dinner given to
Gooch at Weymouth on 16
June 1869

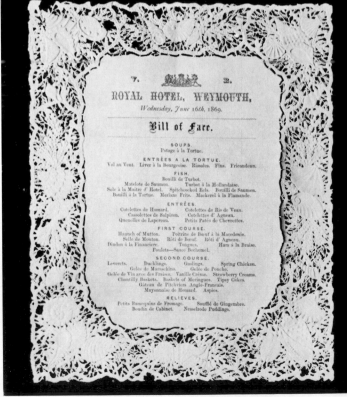

MONDAY 2ND APR. Walked to St Michael's Chapel in the morning. There is a very fine view from this hill. After lunch walked to Paignton & back, a long walk. Day very fine.

TUESDAY 3. Went to see the museum at Torquay this morning. It is a nice building with a small collection, but many very interesting things to be seen. After lunch we went to the Mary Church marble works and bought some pretty inlaid work &c. We have had some heavy rain today.

WEDNESDAY 4TH. A wet morning, but we had a carriage and drove to the Watcombe terra cotta works. Much interested in looking over them, and bought some specimens. After lunch the weather cleared up and Bassett and I walked to Petit Tor and Babbicombe, a very interesting walk. The rocks are very fine.

APL 5TH, THURSDAY. Had a walk this morning and went to lunch with Froude. Met a lot of people there. After lunch we went to see his works where he carrys on experiments for the Govt on form of ships &c. He is a very clever fellow. We returned to the hotel about 3 and with Bassett drove to Compton Castle, a good specimen of the old fortified house. It came on wet as we reached there, the rest of the day had been fine.

FRIDAY APL 6. We went to Newton [Abbot] today and had lunch with Wright. Returned to dinner.

SATURDAY 7 APL. Bassett and I went to Brixham this morning and on to Dartmouth. The latter place is very pretty; we took the steamer outside the entrance to the river. The day was fine, with some showers. Got back to the hotel about 3 oclock. Mrs Brunel called upon us. I was very glad to see her; it is a good many years since I last saw her. She was looking very well. We had a walk before dinner.

SUNDAY, 8 APL. There has been a good deal of rain today but we got a walk in the afternoon.

MONDAY, 9 APL. We left Torquay by 11.15 train this morning and returned home to Paddington. Had a fine day for the journey.

MAY 15TH, 1877. We had a very large division in the House of Commons this morning about 2 oclock, on Gladstone's resolution on the Eastern question which has been debated for a week. Govt had 354 votes and the Opposition 223, or a majority of 131. War has been declared by Russia against Turkey, a most unjustifiable war proclaimed in the name of Christianity and civilization by a nation as cruel and barbarous as savages in their dealings with the unfortunate people over whom they have obtained power. What will be the end of this beginning no one can tell, or where it may lead.

MAY 30TH, 1877. We went down to Chepstow on the 18th, Friday, to stay with Alfred a few days. On the 19 I went to the Severn Tunnel and went to the heading on the Monday. We went over the Wye Valley line to Monmouth and on Tuesday went to Cardiff to stay with Charlie. On the Thursday we went to the tunnel works of the Ogmore line and on to the Avon Colliery. The weather was fine all the week, but cold, and we returned home on the Friday. We walked to Llandaff Cathedral; it has been very nicely restored and is now a fine church.

JUNE 18TH, 1877. Our railway sustained a great loss on the 5th by the death of our rolling stock engineer Mr Armstrong.[30] His death was very sudden, he having been only a couple of weeks ill. He has been a very valuable servant to the company, being an able and upright man. I will also feel his loss very much. His department was a very large and important one, and my anxiety will not be diminished by having to place it in the hands of a fresh man. We have for some time had Mr Dean in our service as chief assistant to Armstrong, with the view of meeting such an event. I hope he will do well.

Mr Armstrong was buried at Swindon church on Saturday the 9th, in the presence of an immense number of sorrowing people. I and some of the directors went to the funeral, and all the officers of the company were there. No man could be more sincerely esteemed.

JUNE 25, 1877. I held the meeting of the Pro Grand Lodge today at Wycombe; we had a very full attendance both in the Lodge and at the banquet. The day was fine.

JUNE 29th. We went to Clewer today for the summer.

AUG 30TH. Today we had our half-yearly meeting of Gt Western share-holders. Our dividend was a ¼ per cent down, as we paid only at the rate of 3¾ per cent.[31] The times are very bad for railways and it is hard work to keep up dividends. The meeting went off very well.

SEPT I. The Medical Society[32] at Swindon had an excursion trip to Clewer today and had the use of my park. They had a very fine day and about 800 came.

QUEEN'S HOTEL, CHESTER. MONDAY, SEPT 3. We left Clewer this morning by the 9.45 am train for Chester, on our road to Ireland. The day was very fine and we had a stroll in the town before dinner.

SEPT 4. At Chester all day. Had two long walks; weather very fine.

ROYAL HOTEL, HOLYHEAD, SEPT 5. I had a long walk after breakfast. The morning was beautiful and we left Chester by the 11.45am train for Holyhead. Met Capt Dent, the marine supt of the London & North Western Co and spent the afternoon with him in looking over their ships and the extensive new works they are doing for dock accommodation.[33] We went by boat to see the wreck'd steamer lying in the harbour, and from there to the pier and ex[amine]d the light house. The L. & N.W. have spent and are spending a vast deal of money at this place for the Irish traffic. Capt Dent dined with us. The day has been lovely and the view of the Welsh mountains was very fine, Snowdon standing out as clear as possible. Dent told me it was a very rare thing to see the atmosphere so perfectly clear.

SHELBOURNE HOTEL, DUBLIN. SEPT 6. Had a long walk about the docks &c and left by the mail boat at 2pm and had a fine passage of 4¼ hours, and, at Kingstown, Bay was *not* ill. We reached the Shelbourne Hotel about 7 in good time for dinner. The day fine, with showers.

DUBLIN, FRIDAY SEPT 7. We spent the day in Dublin, walking about. The weather was fine with showers of rain in the morning, but cold.

SEP 8. I went to see Mr Ward, traffic manager of the Midland Gt Western of Ireland this morning, to get the benefit of his advice as to our route. He gave me useful assistance and wrote to the various hotels. In the afternoon we had a car and went to the Phoenix Park; there we saw a polo match being played. I had not seen it before; it appeared good fun but rough work. There was also a bycicle match going on. In the evening we went to Sanger's Circus. The day was fine but with a cold wind.

SUNDAY 9TH. We had a long walk before lunch and went in the afternoon to St Patrick's Cathedral. It is a fine building, but I cannot say I admired the way the service was done. The music was not good. Day has been cold but fine.

BLACK'S HOTEL, GALWAY. MONDAY 10TH. We left Dublin at 9am this morning by the Midland Great Western for Galway. Mr Ward kindly gave us a saloon carriage, and the chairman Sir [*blank* Ralph Cusack] and his daughter, who were going to stay near Athenry, went so far with us. We travelled pretty well and reached Galway between 2 & 3. Sir [*blank* Ralph Cusack] gave us a bottle of sherry and a bottle of champagne for our journey.

The early part of the day was fine, but it then came on very wet and continued so all the rest of the day. After getting our lunch I put on my mackintosh and, with an umbrella, started for a walk. I went to the bridge across the river, a little below the lake, and looking into the water I thought it had a very weedy bottom, but a closer inspection shewed me that what I thought were weeds were salmon, lying almost as thick as they could be stowed. Many hundreds were between the bridge and the weir out of the lake. They were waiting to go up into the lake. It certainly was a wonderful sight. This is a clean and pretty fair hotel.

RECESS HOTEL, SEPT 11. I have arranged with Mr Black, the proprietor of this hotel, to furnish us with a carriage and pair of horses to take us through Connemara, so we made a good start this morning. I first walked down to the bridge to see if the salmon were there and found they had not moved at all. The morning was very fine and the drive to Oughterard was very pretty, but I had gone over this ground a few years ago. When we were within a few yards of the hotel at Oughterard a very [*word missing*] thunder storm came on with violent wind and a down pour of rain. We fortunately just reached the hotel in time, or in the open carriage we were in we must have got drenched with the rain. It lasted a good hour, during which time we got our lunch and started again; the weather cleared up.

The drive from Oughterard here is very bleak, along the sides of lakes & the range of mountains called the 12 Pins partly in view. We reached Recess about 5pm and got into very good quarters. When I arrived a note was put into my hand from Mr Macready, who is the great man in this district as he holds all the fishing and shooting, and this hotel also belongs to him, altho' he lives in a big house on a hill close by. The note expressed his regret he could not be at the hotel to receive me as he had to attend a magistrates' meeting at a little distance, but he would call upon me in the evening, which he did. He is a rough kind of diamond, but was very kind and gave us a splendid dinner. The hotel is at the east end of Lake Glendalough. There is another hotel a little way down the lake and on the other side. The weather is cool and we were glad of even a peat fire. Rain came on late at night again. We got a walk along the lake before dinner and gathered a few flowers. As we came along people came out of the cottages and sold knited socks, 1s/– pr pair.

CASSON'S HOTEL, LETTERFRACK. WEDNESDAY SEPT 12TH. We left Recess this morning about 11am. The hotel was a very comfortable one, altho' the bed room accommodation was on a very small scale, yet it did very well for a night or two. There was a strong wind with some showers today, but the light and shade of the clouds and sun shine added very much to the beauty of the scenery as we drove down here by Lake Inach, a large and pretty lake with little wooded islands in it, and the 12 Pins mountains as a background. The road passed through Kylemore Pass, a beautiful pass in which Mr Michel Henry[34] has built a fine castle, but very much, I think, out of place. We met him on the road near his house and he was very anxious we should stop and spend a few days with him. I also met a Capt Ayres who was very civil, but I do not know who he is.

We reached Letterfrack at 2pm and had some lunch, after which we had a long walk. This is the cleanest little hotel I was ever in and the cooking is also good; it is very small. The view from here looking up the Kylemore Pass is very beautiful. The bay is also studded with islands. Altogether this is a very lovely place for a few days stay in fine weather.

THURSDAY SEPT 13, LETTERFRACK. The past night has been a very wet and stormy one, and today it has rained hard all day. I got out in the rain for a short walk but Bay could not go out at all. The Fushia grows here in a splendid manner, large thick hedges of it, 8 or 10 feet high and 3 or 4 feet thick, which was covered with flowers. It seems to be very much planted for hedges. I had my short walk under the shelter of a very fine hedge. I have not been able as yet to see more than 5 of the 12 Pins at the same time. We had intended to drive to Clifton and back today if the weather had permitted; it is only 7 miles from here. We have been burning peat all day; it makes a hot fire when the ashes are raked out and the draft is good.

HOTEL MCKEOWN, LEENANE. SEPT 14TH. We left our comfortable hotel this morning at 10. Our horses having had a day's rest were in [a] little better order. We drove round the coast road by way of the entrance to Killery Bay and past Lakes Muck and Fee to this place. The drive was very fine, the sea views with the islands in the bay very beautiful. We could see 6 of the 12 Pins at the same time and the views of the mountains were very fine. The day was dull but dry; we arrived here at one oclock. I cannot say much for the hotel; the bed room is pretty well, but the sitting room very bad. After lunch we walked along the upper part of the water or harbour as it is called, but I have not seen any ships. I had a message from Barber asking us to go to his house at Dhuloch tomorrow, and his son came to us in the evening. The night is very wet.

MR BARBER'S, DHULOUGH, SATURDAY SEPT 15. Barber sent a boat for us at 10 this morning to take us to his house at Dhulough. It was a lovely morning and we were not sorry to leave the hotel at Leenane; it was very bad, food and every thing. I sent John[35] with the carriage and some of the luggage on to Westport to wait for us there. The boat took us down the harbour to the quay or landing place at Dhulough. There are only a few cottages here, and Barber has some kitchen gardens and vineries. From here we drove about 3 miles up a valley to his house, passed a house called Delphi, and found Barber looking very well and glad to see us. We had a walk in the grounds before lunch and afterwards went on the lake in a boat and spent a very pleasant afternoon. The lake and surrounding mountains are very beautiful. The Fushia grows to a wonderful extent in Barber's grounds, and indeed every thing grows well. It has been a lovely day.

DHULOUGH, SUNDAY SEPT 16. The weather today has been lovely. We spent the morning in the grounds, a nice place for a quiet smoke, and after lunch drove to the quay on Killery Bay and then had a boat and rowed down to the entrance of the bay and landed on the sands where we spent an hour. The sands are very extensive and nice; we returned in time for dinner. The sail was very pretty, the light clouds floating about among the hills and the bright sunshine produced some very beautiful effects. We were glad of our dinner at half past 7. The effect of the moon on the mountains in the evening was very beautiful.

RAILWAY HOTEL, WESTPORT. SEPT 17TH, MY WEDDING DAY. We left Barber's at ¼ past 10 this morning on a car with 4 wheels and a good pair of horses hired from Westport. We passed through very pretty scenery for 8 or 10 miles and then came to open moorland until we got near Westport, where we had some beautiful views over the sea, and there is also a fine view of Patrick Mountain, from the top of which St Patrick banished snakes &c from Ireland. We reached our hotel a little before 2 and after lunch walked down to the head of the bay, a good mile away from the town. I was very disappointed in the place, it is very dirty and in a ruinous kind such [*sic*] condition. As we returned from the pier we walked through Lord Sligo's park which reaches all the way from the town to the bay, and the public are allowed to use that route. It is very pretty with some good trees. The house is a fine plain square building. After our walk we wrote our letters and turned out again for half an hour before dinner, which was a very bad one, and the hotel not a place to stop at longer than you like. The day has been a glorious one.

VICTORIA HOTEL, SLIGO, TUESDAY 18. We left Westport this morning by rail at 9.30 and travelled to Ballina where we arrived at a little before 12 and had some lunch, and started at one with a carriage and pair of horses for this place, a distance of 37 miles. The first part of the road was very interesting, over high ground from which we got some pretty views of the bay of Killary and afterwards we had very pretty views over Sligo Bay. The country is well cultivated and there is a good change for the better in the cottages and appearance of the people over what we saw in Connemara. The people are better dressed and the cottages look clean and comfortable. It is wretched slow travelling by post in Ireland. We only make good about 5 miles per hour; the same small horses came all the way with us, but starting at 12.25 it was 7.20 when we reached here. The day has been a lovely one, but after sun set it was cold and we were tired and cross at being so long on the journey. This hotel is comfortable; we have the same sitting room I had when here some years ago.

(*On opposite page* SLIGO, SEP 19TH. At Sligo all day and walked over the town and neighbourhood. Fine day.)

ANTRIM ARMS, PORTRUSH, SEP 20. We made an early start from Sligo this morning, breakfasting at ½ past 6 and starting in a carriage at 7. It took us 3 hours to reach Bundoran. The country is well cultivated and there is a good deal of wood. We also had some fine sea views. All the houses and cottages are comfortable and clean compared with what we have been accustomed to. We had an hour to wait at Bundoran and took a walk along the cliffs; it looks a nice sea side place. We left by train at 11 and went to Bundoran Junction; this is a very pretty ride, most of the way along the side of Lake Earne and past Belleek, where the pottery is made. We reached the junction at 12.30 and had to wait until 1.40 for the down train to Derry, so took a walk. We reached Derry at 3 and took a walk into the town. I was sorry we had not more time to see it properly, but our train for this place started at 5, so we had little time at our disposal. The ride from Derry to Coleraine along the banks of Lough Foyle is very pretty. We arrived here at 6 and have very comfortable rooms. The day has been fine, with a few showers in the afternoon. All the country we passed through looks rich and well cultivated.

LINDEN'S ANTRIM ARMS HOTEL, PORTRUSH. FRIDAY 21ST. This has been a fine day and we have enjoyed the fresh, beautiful air of this place. The small town stands on a point of rocks jutting out into the Atlantic, with beautiful sandy bays on each side, where you can take long walks on a fine, firm sand, and select according to the weather which bay you take. We are very comfortable at our hotel.

PORTRUSH, SEP 22, SATURDAY. This has been a most perfect day for the sea side, and I have seen no place where it can be so thoroughly enjoyed as here—beautiful cliff scenery and rocks, with splendid sands also. Before lunch we had a long stroll and sat on the rocks and after lunch we walked along the sands to Dunluce Castle, or as far as we could, and then climbed up the cliff. The caves in the chalk formation are very fine; this is a most interesting geological place. On the west of the town the exposed rocks are basaltic overlying a blue lias shale in flat, stratified beds, which have been subject to great heat and are almost like flint. There are veins of trap and masses of granite, and up through the whole rises a mass of hard chalk, very full of flints, and this is overlaid with a thin layer of basalt as tho' it had flowed in a thin stream over the surface and filled up the fissures. This is joined to the east by the basaltic rocks of the Giant's Causeway. The whole is a most interesting study and well worth a visit to see it alone. The evenings are cold and we are glad to have a fire. A large addition has just been made to this hotel, and we are located in the new part, and as the walls have not been papered it has rather a cold look. The rooms are a good size, and they are at any rate clean.

SEPT 23, SUNDAY. We went to church this morning and I was very pleased with the service. It was simple, and, as it ought to be, free from all operatic performances, and a large and attentive congregation. The sermon was also a good one, and I felt if all churches would follow the example of this, how little dissent there would be. There are two churches here, & a large Catholic chapel. The sea on the rocks was very fine this morning; before church I stood for an hour on the point, watching the waves break over the rocks. There is to me something very fascinating in watching the sea. There was a good deal of wind yesterday and this has left a heavy sea; we are pretty open to the Atlantic. There is a breakwater of rocks across the east bay here, on which the breaking of the sea is very fine. They are called the Skerries. A coastguard yacht came inside of them yesterday afternoon and made pretty rough weather of it until she was safely inside the Skerries, where she lay as quietly as if in a harbour. The wind was from the north.

There is a perfect remains of a forest on the shore of the west bay where the sea now is; has been dry land with a fine forest. The trees are lying quite thick, covered by 3 or 4 feet of peat, and this peat buried in the sand hills. The section is as follows [sketch]. The timber in the trees is still quite sound; how long have they been there? The action of the fire is beautifully shewn amongst the rocks round this bay. I have been glad of my great coat today.

MONDAY SEP 24. We had a carriage and drove to the Giant's Causeway today, and we could not have had a more lovely day for the purpose. This is a wonderfully interesting place; we went through all the usual ceremony; picked up a guide, a very civil fellow called Mac Glaughlin. His proper fee, which is settled by some authority, is from 2/6 to 5/– according to the extent of services rendered. They are attached to the hotels, of which there are two large ones, one belonging to the landlord of the Antrim Arms at Portrush. They provide boats and men to row them all at a fixed scale of prices. We therefore took our boat, the sea being nice and calm, and rowed into the large cavern where a boy is stationed to fire off a pistol for a consideration. We then rowed across to the landing place on the Causeway. I need not describe the wonders of the Causeway—they are so well known.

You are asked by the boatmen to buy boxes of what they call mineral specimens, but of no value. Collecting them is an employment during the winter and spare days, so one does not grudge them the couple of shillings. They also suggest the bonus of something for themselves when you leave the boat. A great nuisance at this place is the number of wretched old beggars, women and men, who pester you and destroy much of the enjoyment of the place. There is a very fine spring of fresh water in the Causeway of which you are of course asked to taste, and can have a little whiskey with it if you like. We had some lunch at a little public house on the top of the hill, instead of going to one of the large hotels. The old guide, when I asked him his fee, said 5/–, but gentlemen like me often gave him more if they were satisfied, so he got his half sovereign. He told us, of course, all the stories of the rocks &c. We got back to Portrush before dark, having very much enjoyed our day.

PORTRUSH, 25 SEPT. This has been a fine, tho' not a sunny, day, & I have been out most of it. We walked in the afternoon along the coast road to very near Port Stewart, near enough to see into it from the hill. It seems a prettily situated place, on the sea.

PORTRUSH, SEPT 26, WED. We had a beautiful walk this morning along the sands to the chalk cliffs. The weather was very bright and just sufficient sea on to give life to the scene. It is very curious to see the trap coming up through the chalk thus [sketch]. This has evidently been an overflow of the lava. After lunch we had another walk. The view from the hotel here is very fine, looking towards the north-east. The Skerries lie across the bay, forming a natural breakwater, and the cliffs along the coast are very fine. A number of large steamers & ships pass.

PORTRUSH, THURSDAY THE 27. This has been a lovely day and the warmest we have had. We had great excitement this morning in watching the launching and landing of the life boat which is taken out every two months for practice. They certainly were a long time in launching her and many lives might be lost in the time. There is a want of proper appliances and plan, the same in getting her back into the house which, however, of course does not matter so much. It was a morning amusement to us. After lunch we walked to the chalk cliffs. I have had a letter from Alfred telling me about his marriage, foolish boy; but as an honourable man he could not have done otherwise. May they be happy, and all will be well. I should have felt it much more had he acted dishonourably in the matter to avoid the necessity of marriage.[36]

FRIDAY 28TH. This has been a fine warm day, and we had a good long walk both before and after lunch, and watched a beautiful sunset from the east sandhills. The only excitement was the rifle practice of the coast guard; they fired very well.

SATURDAY 29TH SEPT. A fine day, but colder, wind from the east; so we had our walks on the west sands.

SUNDAY 30TH. We went to the same church today but the old gentleman did not preach and the curate's sermon was not so good, but I like the quiet service. Day has been fine, wind S.E.

IMPERIAL HOTEL, BELFAST, OCT 1. We left Portrush this morning at 11.30. Very sorry to leave a place where we had spent so pleasant a time and felt so well in health. It certainly is the nicest sea side place I have been at; it also suited Bay very well. The railway Co sent us a saloon carriage, so we travelled in some state from Portrush here. The country is very well cultivated and looks rich & good land. All the farms, cottages &c are also good and a great contrast to the west coast. How is this, if not that one side of the island is Protestant and the other Catholic? The day has been warm and sunny. Before dinner we had a long walk in Belfast; it is a fine and prosperous town. I do not much like this hotel, it is dirty and not comfortable, dinner bad. I had a long stroll after dinner.

SHELBOURNE HOTEL, DUBLIN. OCT 2ND. We left Belfast at 1.30 today for here, having had a long walk in the town before starting. Not sorry to leave the Imperial, it is bad and extortionate in its charges. Try another hotel next time we visit Belfast. We found our old rooms here ready for us and had a good dinner; this is a good hotel. Day very fine.

DUBLIN, OCT 3. We stayed in Dublin all day today. Went to see Mr Ward at the Midland Gt Western station and in the evening we went to the Gaiety Theatre to see the play of Our Boys. It was fairly acted but seemed to go a little slow. I had seen it some time ago in London.

QUEEN'S HOTEL, CHESTER. OCT 3. We left Dublin at 9.30 this morning by the London and North Western express boat; time on voyage 4½ hours. A lovely day and calm sea. These are fine boats, but I fancy they will roll in a cross sea a good deal. We came on direct here by the train. Bay stood the voyage very well; she had a private cabin and was very comfortable. After dinner we turned out for a walk and went into the skating rink and saw some wonderful boys on the trapese.

CLEWER, FRIDAY THE 5TH OCT. We left Chester by G.W.R. train at 9.10 and travelled home to Clewer. Day fine and found all well at home. We have enjoyed our trip very much and are both better for it. The weather has been all we could desire for, with the exception of the day at Letterfrack, we have never been kept indoors from the wet. Clewer looks very pretty and home is home; God grant it may always be as happy a haven as it ever has been for me.

LONDON, NOV 29TH, 1877. We went to Swindon yesterday to distribute the annual prizes to the young people at the Institution. Tom Brassey went with us and made a sensible speech to them. Sir A[le]x-[ander] Wood and Robinson also went down. The meeting passed off very well and we returned home by a special train. This Institution is working much good at Swindon and is steadily increasing in numbers. We missed our old friend Armstrong; how, year by year, vacancies occur in our Gt Western ranks; how few of those who began with me are left. One by one they drop off, and the time cannot be far distant when the whole of the old officers will have passed away.

LONDON, DECR 28th, 1877. We have now reached the close of another year, a year of great depression in all trade and commerce. We all feel as if we never knew it to be so bad, but certainly the return to prosperity never seemed so hopeless. It is not only in the coal and iron trades that the stagnation exists, but in every branch of manufacture, not only in England but all over the world. No country seems free from the blight, the savage and barbarous war carried on by Russia against the Turks no doubt has something to do with it, but this should hardly extend to America, where the suffering has been even worse than with us. The depression of trade makes railway receipts bad also, so in fact the ramification is carried far beyond those who are themselves in trade.

The political aspect of Europe is also at the present time of a very doubtful character. Russia is playing her old game of conquest under the guise of Christianity and is committing horrible crimes. Can England stand by as a neutral and see this go on? It is doubtful. The disgust and anger of the country is every day growing stronger. Parliament has been summoned for the 17th Jany and the result of it all will, I fear, be we will be led into war; better this than dishonour, which it would be if we allowed Russia to tear up, and cast the fragments in our face, the treaties made after the Crimean War.

The 3rd vol[ume] of the life of the Prince Consort has just been published,[37] and it deals with the period of the Crimean War, and it is strange what an exact counterpart the present action of Russia is of the last. Gladstone and a few of his friends have, I believe, led the Russians into this war by their wild and senseless outcry against the Turks, leading Russia to think England would not on any account go to war. The Parliament of last session did not do much work, but it has this merit—we did not do any harm. Some Irish Home Rulers took it into their hands to attempt a systematic obstruction of the business of the House, and as will be seen in the account I have enclosed, the House sat from 4 oclock one afternoon until past six on the following afternoon. I hope some steps will be taken next session to stop such a proceeding as this, bringing as it did the House into contempt.

I have not had any additions to my grandchildren this year, but had my usual large party on Xmas Day, and have much reason to be thankful to God for, good health and the many (oh, when I look round me, how many and great) blessings I have enjoyed. May I ever lean on and trust the hand from which they flow as my only guide and support. My dear loving wife is a great comfort to me, so good and unselfish, her only thought being my happiness, and that of my children. May God preserve her to me in health until the end.

The directors of the Great Western Railway presented me this year with a portrait of Mr Brunel, painted by C. A. Horsley R.A. from the original picture he painted during Mr Brunel's life. Horsley is brother-in-law to Mr Brunel. I value the picture very much both for the sake of Mr Brunel and the kindly feeling of our board.

NOTES

1   Gooch was nominated as a candidate by Joseph Armstrong (*qv*) and seconded by Horatio Dunn, storekeeper at Swindon works.

    There were six candidates: A. L. Goddard (*qv*) and Gooch (Conservative), F. W. Cadogan (*qv*) and Henry Tucker of Shrivenham (Liberal), William Morris, a colourful local reformer and agnostic ('working man's candidate') and John Arkell, of Stratton St Margaret (Independent Liberal).

2   Gabriel (later Sir Gabriel) Goldney, of Beechfield House, Chippenham, was MP for Chippenham for a long period. 'Young Goldney' may have been his son.

3   The Severn Tunnel, from Pilning to Rogiet, was first suggested by Charles Richardson, one of Brunel's assistants, as early as 1865, but an act for the tunnel and connecting lines was only obtained by the GWR in 1872. Richardson was the first engineer and exploratory work commenced in 1873. The work progressed slowly until in October 1879 a large spring was tapped and the workings flooded.

    In January 1880 work began afresh, with Sir John Hawkshaw (*qv*) as engineer and T. A. Walker as contractor. After several serious floodings the tunnel was finally completed and opened at the end of 1886. Alfred Gooch was an assistant engineer on the tunnel, living at Ashfield House, Chepstow.

    See Walker, T. A. *The Severn Tunnel* (1888). MacDermot, *GWR*, II, 186–91.

4   The Pontypool, Caerleon & Newport Rly was then nearing completion. It was opened on 21 December 1874.

    The 'Lady Llanover lines' refers to Hall's Tramroad, which the Great Western was negotiating to purchase in order to counter the London & North Western's purchase of the other line in the Sirhowy Valley. The GWR leased the tramroad and later converted it into a railway.

    See MacDermot, *GWR*, II, 64.

5   This, of course, is C. R. M. Talbot of Margam (*qv*), Gooch's old adversary when he was chairman of the South Wales Rly. Time had healed the breach.

6   'Bay' was Gooch's nickname for his second wife, Emily (*qv*). Throughout the succeeding pages of the diary this is deleted in pencil and 'my wife' substituted in her hand, presumably for the published extracts, though many of the passages were never, in fact, included in the 1892 edition.

7   Little did Gooch know that in that churchyard was buried the one-time arch-enemy of the Great Western Railway, Captain Mark Huish, general manager of the London & North Western Railway.

8   This was almost certainly Louis Desanges, the artist who painted the portrait of Gooch (*see* IV, n 2).

9   Even Gooch realised that the broad gauge would have to go sooner or later. The GWR lines were gradually converted to either mixed or narrow gauge until the seven-foot way was only retained from Paddington to Bristol because the Bristol & Exeter, South Devon and Cornwall lines were still broad. The conversion of these was to take place in a splendidly organised operation in May 1892.

    See MacDermot, *GWR*, *passim*.

10   This should be Edward Leeming, of Richmond.

11   The accident was near Kirtlington, later renamed Bletchington. The coach was an old Newport, Abergavenny & Hereford Rly four-wheeler with rivetted tyres. This method of fixing tyres had long been discontinued on the GWR as it was known to be dangerous, but evidently a few vehicles from absorbed companies remained. The company was severely censured by the Board of Trade enquiry.

    See MacDermot, *GWR*, II, 48–9.

12 4 March.

13 A South Wales miners' strike began on 2 January 1875 and did not end completely until May.

14 The Clifton Extension Rly, a joint GWR–MR line, was opened from Ashley Hill Junction to Clifton Down on 1 October 1874.

For Milford Docks *see* Rees, J. F. *The Story of Milford* (Cardiff, 1954), chap VI.

Gooch refers to his third son both as Alfred and Billy.

15 This vessel, designed by Henry (later Sir Henry) Bessemer and E. J. Reed, had among other features a swinging cabin controlled hydraulically, which was supposed to counteract the motion of the ship and prevent seasickness. On this maiden voyage the cabin was locked and never demonstrated. The whole scheme was ridiculed in the press.

16 The GWR was granted running powers over the Monmouthshire Rly in return for a guaranteed return for the Monmouthshire shareholders. The line was managed by a joint committee of three directors from each company. The Monmouthshire became part of the GW in 1880.

See MacDermot, *GWR*, II, chap IV.

17 The original terminus of the South Wales Rly (opened 1856) was Neyland Point on the north side of Milford Haven, whence steamers ran to Waterford and Cork. In 1859 the GW renamed the port 'New Milford', but when it was superceded by the new port of Fishguard in 1906 it reverted to its old name. The 'new docks' referred to by Gooch were at the town of Milford Haven ('Old Milford').

The South Wales Rly opened the South Wales Hotel near the station at Neyland, where the diarist often stayed during his visits to Milford Haven. It was taken over by the GWR with the SWR in 1863 and was closed when the opening of Fishguard Harbour deprived it of most of its trade. It is now (1970) a sad ruin.

See MacDermot, *GWR*, I, chap XI. Rees, J. F. *The Story of Milford* (Cardiff, 1954).

18 The impoverished Somerset & Dorset Rly was taken over jointly by the London & South Western and Midland Rlys after some double-dealing on the part of the LSWR while negotiations were in progress for the GWR to buy the line. The S & D Joint Rly was ever after a sore point in Great Western circles.

The Bristol & Exeter was, of course, an essential part of the route to the south-west, and no chances could be taken over that company.

See MacDermot, *GWR*, II, 51–4.

19 This was guard Henry Painter, thirty-six years on the GWR. More than seventy officials and staff attended the funeral.

20 The figures given by Gooch for the terms of the amalgamation are correct, but it is difficult to verify the statistics which follow without knowing the basis of his calculations. Bradshaw's *Railway Manual* gave the following figures as at 31st July 1876, ie, after the absorption of the Bristol & Exeter and South Devon: Capital authorised £55,502,685. Mileage (excluding lines under construction): lines owned 1,003¼; partly owned 19½; leased or rented 1,006½. Total 2,029¼ miles.

The Great Western had the greatest route mileage in the British Isles, but on the Continent both the Paris, Lyons & Mediterranean and the Paris & Orleans had over 2,500 miles at that time.

21 An F. Trevithick was locomotive superintendent of the Cornwall Minerals Rly, but it is not certain whether this was the former LNWR engineer from Crewe or his brother Frederick Henry.

See MacDermot, *GWR*, II, 287, n 2.

22 The Royal Hotel.

23 To replace the colliery sold in 1865 (*see ante*, p 93) the GWR purchased in 1874 the Cilely pit near Tonyrefail and the Avon Colliery near Abergwynfi. Charles Gooch, as mineral manager, was responsible for them.

See MacDermot, *GWR*, II, 45.

24 The diarist mounted a number of these ferns in the diary to make two very charming pages.

25 The Great Western did build a new port at Fishguard, which was opened in 1906.

See MacDermot, *GWR*, II, chap XI.

26 These were a company of Swiss bellringers, the Alleghanian Ringers, who were visiting Pembrokeshire at the time. They also sang as a quartet, and it was presumably this which displeased Gooch.

27 Cumberland Lodge was in Windsor Great Park. It being winter, Gooch was living at Paddington, and stayed with Capt Bulkeley in Windsor to avoid the journey back to town late at night. Clewer would be swathed in dust-sheets while the family was away.

28 Swindon Mechanics' Institution. The presentation of the prizes was one of the chairman's annual duties!
    See ante, II, n 19.

29 A large part of this was the quadrupling of the main line out of Paddington, including the Wharncliffe viaduct at Hanwell, completed as far as Southall on 1 October 1877.

30 More correctly Locomotive and Carriage Superintendent. As we have seen, Joseph Armstrong (*qv*) was a staunch supporter at Gooch's election campaigns as well as a railway colleague. He was sixty.

31 This should be $3\frac{1}{2}$ per cent.

32 For a full account of this important body in Swindon *see* Darwin, B. *A Century of Medical Service, the story of the Great Western Railway Medical Fund Society, 1847–1947* (Swindon, 1947).

33 Capt C. B. C. Dent, RN. The new harbour built by the LNWR was opened by the Prince of Wales on 17 June 1880 (*see post*, p 281).

35 Mitchell Henry (Murray's *Handbook for Travellers in Ireland* (1912), 279).

35 This is the only one of Gooch's servants he mentions by name. It would be usual for a man in his position to take a servant on his travels, to wait at table and attend to the luggage. When he took his own carriage there would be the coachman as well.

36 The meaning of this cryptic passage is obvious. The lady in question was Frances Elizabeth Jones of Oxford.
    It says much for Gooch that he took such a kindly view of the affair.

37 By Sir Theodore Martin (*qv*).

VOLUME VI

The Diary 1878-81

LONDON, JANY 1ST, 1878. May God grant His blessing to me and mine during this year and preserve us in health and happiness. Throughout the world the year presents a most gloomy appearance. The cruel and barbarous war in the East gives daily cause of anxiety and sorrow. Whether we will be preserved from being led into it is very doubtful. The sympathy for the Turks is nearly universal, but for the Turks alone this country will not fight. There is a universal distrust in the Russians; they are not to be trusted either in their word or bond, and are now fighting under the false colours of religion. How that sacred cause is misused by nations. In the question of trade in this country, such depression was certainly unknown and there is a widespread distress throughout the working classes, particularly in Wales and other coal and iron districts. There is not the slightest gleam of sunshine in the future. God alone knows how it will all end, but may He in His mercy protect and preserve our country.

FEBY 11TH, 1878. Alfred had a son born on the [*blank*] of which he seems very proud.

Political affairs have presented a very anxious appearance this year. Parliament was called together early, on the 17th Jany, and the Govt have asked for a vote of £6,000,000 over which there has been long and weary debate for the last 10 days, but it was carried on Friday last by a vote of 328 against 124. The Liberal party seems to be broken up into factions, Gladstone leading the Radicals and Lord Hartington the moderate men, while the Home Rulers form a 3rd party. I hope we may be spared a war.

MARCH 4. I had 3 shareholders' meetings last week; 1st the Gt Ship, 2nd the Telg Construction Co (we had a good dividend) and on the 25

Feby[1] the Gt Western Railway. We were able to pay the same divd as the corresponding half year, viz 4¼ per cent. This was fully as much as we expected considering the dreadful state of trade in all the coal and iron districts, and the meeting passed off very well. I have been a little out of condition this last week or two and have called in the doctor.

I was curious a few days ago to see how many public offices I hold at the present time; the following is a list:[2]

1. Member of Parliament for Cricklade.
2. Chairman of Gt Western Railway.
3.   do   Ross and Ledbury.
4.   do   Newant [ie Newent] and Gloucester.
5.   do   Balla & Festignog [ie Bala & Ffestiniog].
6.   do   Telegraph Construction [& Maintenance] Co.
7.   do   Gt Eastern Steam Ship.
7a.   do   Coleford Railway.
8.   do   North Wales Coke Co.
8a.   do   Swansea & Clydach Railway.
9. Alternate chairman of meetings of
        L[ondon] & N[orth] Western & Gt Western Joint
          Committee.
10.   do   Gt Western & Midland   do
11.   do   Gt Western & L[ondon] & South Western. do
12.   do   Gt Western & Llynvi & Ogmore.   do
13.   do   Gt Western & Rhymney.   do
14.   do   Gt Western & Metropolitan.   do
15.   do   Gt Western & Monmouthshire.   do
16.   do   Gt Western & Vale of Towey [ie Towy] do
17. Director of Llanelly Railway.
18.   do   Anglo[-American] Tel[e]g[rap]h Co.
19.   do   Globe Tel[e]g[rap]h Co.
20.   do   Telegraph Trust.
(Inserted in pencil Cape Cable Co.)
21.   do   Gt Western Hotel.
22. Magistrate, County of Berks.
23. Dep[u]ty Lieutenant for   do.
24. Grand Master, Berks & Bucks 1868.
25. Grand Supt,   do   1875.
26. Dep[u]ty chairman, Railway Association.
    Chairman [blank]
    Director of Taunton & North Devon Railway.

[A piece of folio [443] of the ms has been torn away, affecting two lines]

By [*two words illegible*] advice we went to Folkes[tone on] the 7th. We stayed at the West Cliff Hotel. Our situation is good as it is on the high ground and a fair sea view may be had from it, but the hotel is in a sad state of repair, both furniture and rooms; no paint on the wood work nor wool on the carpets. Our feeding was very good and in spite of the state of the house we were very comfortable. We stayed there until yesterday. The weather was bright but with a cold north wind; this we did not feel so much under the cliffs. We had a good deal of walking; one day we went to the camp and back—it was a lovely day—and we, of course, went to see the steamers come in and go out. The place is a fine bracing air, but I should think very hot in summer as there is no kind of shelter. Yesterday morning, when we left, the ground was white with snow.

APL 14. The last few weeks have been a very anxious time in and out of Parliament. Lord Derby, Foreign Secretary, has resigned (we were at his reception at the Foreign Office the night before his resignation) and war with Russia looks very much on the cards. Russia has been playing a very false game, as she always does. Matters are looking a little more like peace today, but all is very uncertain. Yesterday I went to see the Oxford and Cambridge Boat Race, the first time I ever did so. We had an invitation from Lever to go in the saloon steamer, the Victoria, leaving the House of Commons stairs at 8.45. We had on board the Prince of Wales, the Crown Prince of Denmark, Duke of Teck and two of his boys, with some other swells, a party of about 25. The day was all we could wish, but altho' we had the privilege of following the race we really saw very little of it as the boilers of our steamer were priming badly and we got behind some other steamers. The scene was a very wonderful and beautiful one, and we enjoyed it very much, getting home again about 3 oclock. The Oxford boat won by about 10 lengths, so that it was a bad race. It came on wet just as we got home and a good deal of rain fell. It was a very English sight to be sitting with the Prince of Wales smoking cigars very much as tho' he was of equal rank with us, yet there he was, the heir to a vast possession, the finest kingdom in the world, and Emperor of India.

IMPERIAL HOTEL, MALVERN. APL 18TH, 1878. We came down here by 6.30pm train last night, Dunning with Hellen and two of his boys also came with us. Today has been a lovely day; we walked to St Ann's Well in the morning and drove in the afternoon to E[a]stnor Castle. Hellen went with us.

GOOD FRIDAY, APL 19. There has been a good deal of rain during the night but the day has been dry, altho' not bright. We had a drive in the afternoon.

APL 20. There was a steady soft rain today until between 2 & 3, and it then cleared up, so that we got a walk and the evening was very fine.

APL 21. This has been a fine Easter Sunday, with a few light showers. We went to the Abbey Church and had a drive in the afternoon, taking Dunning with me.

APL 22. Had a walk in the morning, went to Blackmore Park to lunch with the Hornyough[s] [*ie* Hornyolds]. They have a nice house, nearly new, and being a Roman Catholic family have a very pretty chapel attached to the house. They gave us a good lunch and were very civil. It was their son who went on his wedding day to Clewer to spend a week a few months ago. We had a long walk before dinner; day was very fine.

TUESDAY APL 23. The Dunnings left this morning. We had a long walk to the North Hill; in the evening it came on wet.

ROYAL HOTEL, ROSS. FRIDAY 26TH. The last few days have been very fine and we have taken long walks each day. We left Malvern at 11 this morning to drive to Ross, sending John with the luggage by rail. We have been very comfortable at the hotel at Malvern. The chief fault in the house is the eating dept, but we did quite as well as I care for, and if you have your own servant you do not feel the want of waiters so much. We have enjoyed our visit very much; the weather has been all we could wish and the country has looked beautiful, the cherry and pear blossom being wonderfully fine. The town of Malvern is certainly the cleanest and nicest place I know, with grand fresh air. The drive from Malvern to Ross by way of the Wych cutting is very pretty. We stayed at Ledbury a couple of hours, had lunch and a walk about the town, and reached Ross at 4 through a lovely country, and at the present time a garden with the blossom on the fruit trees. We took a walk along the river before dinner. We have very comfortable rooms here and a lovely view over the valley of the Wye.

Ross, SATURDAY 27 APL. This has been a glorious day. We went before lunch up to the top of a high hill close to the town, about 700 feet high, covered on the upper part with wood and full of wild flowers. It was a lovely walk and the views very fine. It is said there was once a camp on this hill. After lunch we walked up the side of the river, a pretty walk. The sun set from our window tonight was lovely.

SUNDAY 28 APL. We went to the old church this morning; it is under repair and is a fine old church. Service very nicely done. After lunch we drove as far as Michel Dean and had a walk after our drive. There are some young trees growing in the front of a window inside the church; they are shoots from the fine elms outside, but are near 20 feet high, not very prosperous looking. Day has been lovely. (*On opposite page* Hotel at Ross very comfortable.)

BEAUFORT HOTEL, MONMOUTH. APL 29. We left Ross this morning at 11 and drove here by the valley of the Wye, some very beautiful scenery on the road; distance about 11 miles. We reached here for lunch and afterwards took a walk; the malitia were out, we watched them exercise for some time. This is a poor town, with an old church, but the situation is very pretty. We had some slight showers of rain during the day. Cannot say much for this hotel.

CHEPSTOW, 30. Had a long walk this morning and left Monmouth at 2 and drove down the valley of the Wye to this place. It is a lovely drive and we were very favoured in the weather. Billy met us in his trap near Tintern. We found his wife and baby very well, the latter a very good specimen of infant humanity. Very glad to find Billy happy and comfortable in his home.

MAY 1. I went to the Severn Tunnel[3] and spent the day there, going up to the face of the heading. All going on well, but very slow. The day was fine with some showers. This is a very anxious job for me. Richardson, the engineer, has no go in him and does not move without consulting me, making me almost the engineer.

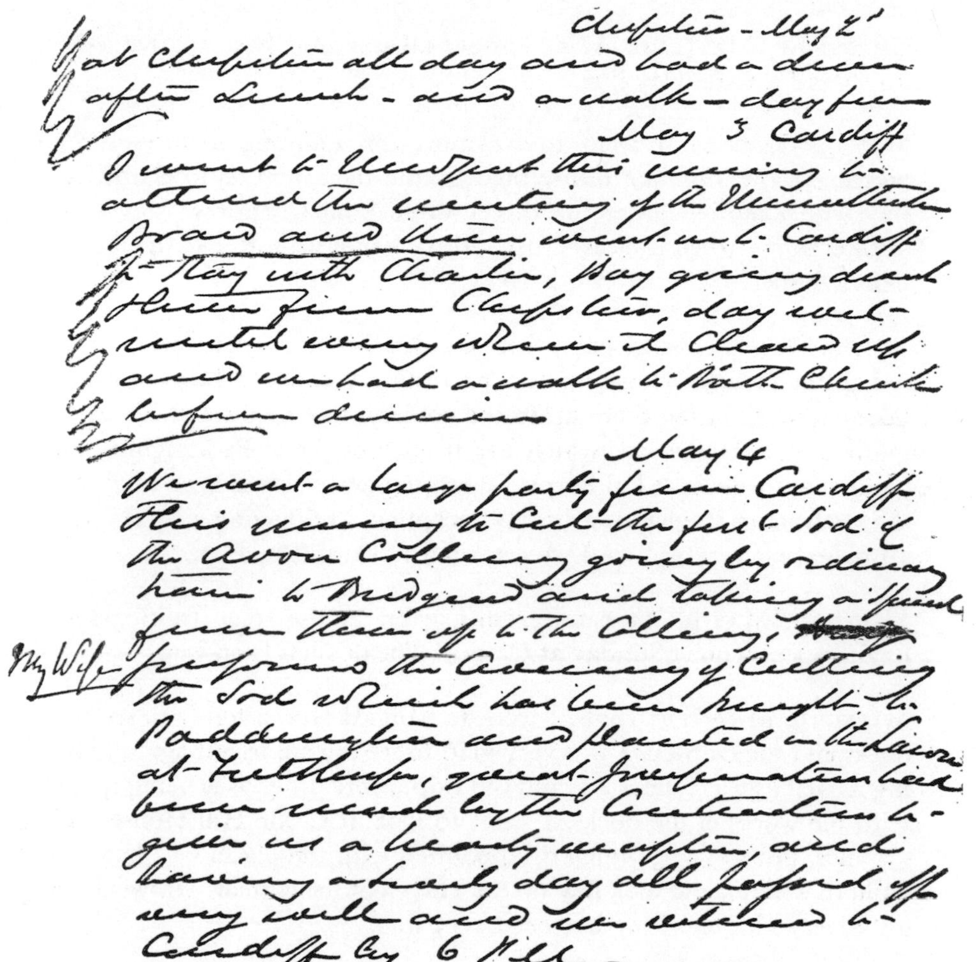

FIG 19   Folio [449] of volume VI, 1–8 May 1878. Note pencil editorial markings by Gooch's widow, indicating passages not for publication in the 1892 edition, and 'Bay' deleted and 'My Wife' substituted

CHEPSTOW, MAY 2ND. At Chepstow all day and had a drive after lunch and a walk. Day fine.

MAY 3, CARDIFF. I went to Newport this morning to attend the meeting of the Monmouthshire board,[4] and then went on to Cardiff to stay with Charlie, Bay going direct there from Chepstow. Day wet, until evening, when it cleared up and we had a walk to Roath church before dinner.

MAY 4. We went a large party from Cardiff this morning to cut the first sod of the Avon Colliery,[5] going by ordinary train to Bridgend and taking a special from there up to the colliery. Bay performed the ceremony of cutting the sod, which has been brought to Paddington and planted in the lawn at Fulthorpe. Great preparations had been made by the contractors to give us a hearty reception, and having a lovely day all passed off very well and we returned to Cardiff by 6pm.

MILFORD, MAY 6. We came from Cardiff by the 10.20 train today, having spent a quiet Sunday at Cardiff. The day has been wet.

MILFORD, MAY 7TH, 1878. I went to Milford Haven today to see the docks and the Gt Ship. I was very glad to see my old friend again looking as well as ever; she is a grand old ship. More progress is being made with the works of the docks. I went to look at Castle Hill House and grounds, but was very much disappointed with the place. Got back to Milford about 5 and took Bay up the Haven in the launch; Haswell has got a very nice one. Day has been very fine.

WEDNESDAY 8. Had a long walk over the works and ships this morning; had the launch after lunch and we went down the Haven as far as Thorn Island & called at Milford on our way back and took Bay over the ship. The day was fine and we enjoyed the sail.

THURSDAY 9. We took two long walks today, weather fine.

PADDINGTON, FRIDAY 10. Left Neyland and went to Chepstow and stayed last night with Billy, and came on here today. Both feeling much better for our holiday and which we have thoroughly enjoyed. Found the dogs very glad to see us. Home is a very comfortable place.

MAY 24TH, 1878. We brought a long debate of 4 nights on the Eastern Question, chiefly as to the movement of Indian troops to Malta, to a close early this morning. The Govt had a complete victory and a majority of 121 in a very full House. The Liberals are playing their cards very badly.

SATURDAY 25 MAY. We went to a reception at the Foreign Office to-night (Lady Salisbury). There was a great collection of big people, Crown Prince & Princess of Prussia. The Russian Ambassador begged my landau, a very proper thing to do. Count Schouvaloff has just re-turned from Russia, and we hope has brought peace with him.

MONDAY 3RD JUNE. Attended Levee held by Prince of Wales.

JULY 3RD. I held my Pro Grand Lodge at Windsor today. We had a large meeting and all went off well. The Lodge was held in Windsor.

JULY 13. The Berlin Treaty was signed today. May we hope it will bring peace, altho' I have no faith in Russia.

FRIDAY JULY 19TH, 1878. We went to Weymouth on Monday and dined there with Henry Edwards. On Tuesday morning we sailed at 6 in one of our steamers for Sherbourg, arriving at one oclock, and dined with the directors of the Western of France Railway in the evening. They gave us a capital dinner. We left Sherbourg at one am for St Malo, arriving there at about 10, leaving again at one pm for Gersey, where we arrived between 9 and 10 at night. We spent Thursday on the island, made a regular drive round it. It is quite a garden and I was quite surprised to see what excellent condition all the houses were in; we saw no dirty cottages. The Channel Islands Steam Boat Co gave us a dinner in the evening, and we left for Weymouth on Friday, returning home to Clewer. This was an experimental trip for a new steamer ser-vice between Weymouth & Sherbourg, in partnership with the Western of France Co, to begin on the 1st August. I fear it will take some time to work up a trade that will pay, yet it must, like everything else, have a beginning. We had lovely weather for our trip and enjoyed ourselves very much.[6]

AUGT 29. We held our Gt Western half-yearly meeting today; it went off very well. We managed with difficulty to pay the same dividend as last year, but the trade of the country is in a dreadful state, and all railways are suffering greatly, but chiefly those dependent on the coal & iron trades. There must be great suffering next winter as matters are growing worse. Whether the prospect of peace will do any good it is difficult to say, but I hardly see how. Annexed is an account of our meeting; I also annex an article in the Masonic Chronicle of a complimentary character as regards my Masonic life.

CLIFTON DOWN HOTEL, CLIFTON. SUNDAY SEP 1, 1878. We left Clewer at one last Friday and came on here. The dogs looked very sad when they saw us start; I believe they knew we were leaving them for some time. We had our dinner at 7 and I took a walk afterwards. On Saturday we had some rain, but it cleared up about 10 and I had a walk. Mr Wall[7] called at 11 to take us for a drive in his carriage. We went over the country between Clifton and the Severn by Weston[8] and to a hill at the village of Almondsbury from which there is a very beautiful view over the Severn into Wales, and the flat, cultivated land between the hill and the Severn. The day was a little dull, but still the view was very fine. We returned to the hotel for lunch and afterwards walked across the chain bridge and for some distance on the road to Portishead; it is a pretty walk. After dinner I had my cigar on the hill. Weather a little cold, but fine and bracing. Today, Sunday, we had a long walk by the dock entrance, and from there up to the Downs and so home. Afternoon we went to the c[at]hedral at Bristol. The interior is very fine [and] has just been restored. The outside is not very striking, tower very dumpy. We drove from the cathedral to make a call upon Mr & Mrs Wall. After dinner I had my cigar on the hill. This is a very pretty place with beautiful air and good walks and drives. A few weeks might be spent here very pleasantly; the hotel is also very comfortable. We leave tomorrow for Dunster.

LUTTEREL ARMS, DUNSTER. SEPT 4TH. We left Clifton on Monday by midday train for here, and arrived here at 3pm. The country round here is very pretty, very undulating and a good deal of wood. The castle stands well upon the top of a hill. We took a long walk after our arrival. The town is very old and quaint, and so is this hotel. It was once a priory and the first sitting room shewn to us was certainly a little old chapel, with open roof &c and no light. It did not look cheerful, so we selected a less important but a more comfortable one. The house dates from the 15th century. Our bed room has a splendid carved chimney piece going up to the ceiling, see rough sketch. The landlady is Miss Cruwys. The town is ¾ of a mile at least from the Channel.

The weather on Monday was very fine and on Tuesday it was a glorious day and we walked to the top of the hill close to the town, called Grabbist Hill; it is a good pull up but the view from the top, and on a bright clear day such as we had is, I think, the finest I ever saw; the whole stretch of the Channel to the north, with the Welsh coast and hills beyond, Dunster Castle on its hill just below with the town and church, and the Quantock Hills in the distance to the east and all around you beautifully wooded hills and dells. We spent some time in the enjoyment of the scene and the beautiful air. On our way up we went into the old church; it has just been restored—it is very well done. There are two distinct churches inside, divided by a solid wall with only very small arches through. There is a very beautiful oak carved rood screen and some fine old monuments, one to the Lutterel family, a very old family at the Castle. After lunch Mrs Lutterel called upon us to ask us to dine with them on Thursday; this we could not do, but arranged to lunch with them today. After lunch yesterday we drove to the ruins of Cleeve Abby, a property of the Lutterels. It is an interesting old place and parts in very good preservation. The roof over the refectory is very perfect. The Lutterels have lately done a great deal to clear out the rubbish and shew the old walls. I got some photographs.

After our return we took a walk before dinner. This morning we had a walk and lunched at the Castle. The Lutterells were very kind, Mrs being a very pleasant woman; they shewed us all over the Castle and grounds. There is some fine specimens of painting on leather; the entrance hall is very fine and the carved stair case the richest in wood carving I ever saw. The rooms are not large but nicely furnished and comfortable. After our visit we walked down to the beach on the Channel. It was low tide and the water goes out a long way, and there is no sand to enjoy so is not a bathing place. We heard today of the awful loss of life on the Thames.[9] We have been very fortunate in the weather and very comfortable at this hotel.

CASTLE HOTEL, LYNTON. SUNDAY SEP 8. We left Dunster at 10am Thursday morning with a carriage for this place, sending our luggage by cart as the hills are something awful. We drove first through very pretty country, passing Wotton Courtney, Luckham [*ie* Luccombe] & Horner to Porlock Wear, arriving there a little after 12; had a sit on the big stones (there is nothing to see) and after getting lunch left at 2 by a zig zag road to reach the high ground which took us 1¾ hours to get to the top. It can only be done at a slow walking pace all the way. The height we climbed was 1,350 feet. The road is very pretty, through woods, up the side of the hill, on the top open moorland, with distant views. A bad hill takes you down into Lynmouth and a worse one up to the hotel at Lynton, which is 450 feet above and accomplished in a short distance.

A large addition has recently been made to this hotel; we are in the new part and the rooms are very good with fine views from the windows overlooking the sea. We took a short walk before dinner & after dinner walked to the Valley of the Rocks. The moon was bright and the effect of the dark shadows of the rocks was very pretty. The whole of the day the weather was lovely. On Friday we had a most perfect day; after breakfast we walked by the carriage road to the Valley of Rocks. They are exceedingly fine, the Castle Rock standing out by itself with a high vertical side to the sea, I should think 300 feet high; it is 150 feet above the carriage road. We, of course, got up to the top and enjoyed the fresh air and beautiful views, both over the sea and land. The Welch coast was not clear, from a haze, but the number of white sails on the sea gave life and animation to it. There is a pretty place called Lea Crest just at the end of the Vally of Rocks. We walked back to the hotel by the path along the face of cliffs, a nice walk.

After lunch we walked down to Lynmouth and followed the vally of the East Lyn by a foot path to Waters Meet, I think the most lovely walk I ever took, and the weather was so perfect for us, bright gleams of sun shine shewing in places amongst the overhanging trees. The water is a succession of rapids and water falls, with beautiful ferns along the banks. The distance is about 1½ miles from Lynmouth; the height at Waters Meet is about 300 feet high, so that the water falls that height in the 1½ miles. We returned by the same path, rather tired, and it was a dreadful pull to get up to the hotel. It was altogether a very enjoyable day. We see the lights of our docks on the other side of the Channel at Porthcawl.

On Saturday we walked to the Valley of Rocks by the cliff path and sat about until lunch time, enjoying the fine air, and after lunch went to see the town and port of Lynmouth; no sands. It rained after dinner. Today we again walked along the cliff path, weather fine with good air; and after lunch we walked up the valley of West Lyn. I have had a long chat with Mr Baker the landlord of the hotel this morning. He came and sat with us in our room; he is an old man of 76 years of age and has lived all his life here. When he was a boy there was no wheel carriage in the district and no road on which wheels could travel. We have been very comfortable at this place and have enjoyed its beauties very much. They are very anxious to get a railway to it, but too many people would spoil it.[10]

ILFRACOMBE HOTEL. MONDAY, ILFRACOMBE, SEP 9. We left Lynton this morning at 12. A good carriage and pair of horses; we sent our luggage by cart. Before starting we went up a pretty high hill to look at some ponies Mr Baker has to sell; he breeds these Exmoor ponies. We saw two, both nice animals, and I bought one for 30£ and am to pay 3 guineas for breaking it in to saddle and harness. We were very comfortable at the Castle Hotel and it certainly is the most beautiful place I have yet seen. The road to this place is not very interesting; we passed over a height of about 1,000 feet and stopped for lunch at the King's Head (a queer old house) at Combe Martyn. We walked down to the beach, or rather harbour of rocks; it is not a place that could be made into a good harbour, but at a very large cost, and the hill out of it is something awful and would always make it a bad place for a harbour. Lord Fortescue has often urged its merits upon me. The road from Combe Martyn here is very pretty and some of the coast scenery is very fine; Watermouth is a beautiful place. We arrived here at 4 oclock, but just as we left Combe Martyn it began a small rain and this has continued. I got a walk, however, after dinner. Charlie and Emma, who are in lodgins here, came to us in the evening. It will be fine weather, I think.

ILFRACOMBE, WEDNESDAY SEPT 11. We had a lovely day on Tuesday and a *very* glorious moon at night. I think rocks and mountain scenery look better by moon light than by day; the dark shadows give such a grand and massive appearance to the rocks. I went in the morning to look at our Gt Western stables, as we run coaches from here to Barnstable. From there we went to the pier and saw the steamer come in and go out. After lunch we walked to the top of Hillsbro' Hill; a very

261

splendid view is obtained from this. After dinner I went out for my moonlight walk and saw a most curious scene. Under a large overhanging cliff on the path up Capstone Hill there was a gentleman surrounded by some lamps hanging to the rocks, and a large number of people were singing hymns. The voices were well tuned and it had a strange effect. The gentleman read some short prayers and read portions of Scripture; the service seemed to be entered into very earnestly by a large number of the people. Many were young women.

Mr Leeman, chairman of the North Eastern Railway is here. I had a chat with him and his wife during the day, and they came into our room for a while in the evening. Charlie & Emily dined with us. Today, Wednesday, has been another very lovely day and tonight beautifully moonlight. We went this morning along the walk on the face of the cliffs under the Torrs, and so got up to the top of the said Torrs. It is a well made path for the use of which a penny is charged. After lunch we had a carriage and drove to Mort and walked down into Wollacombe Bay. The cliffs are very fine round the point, but there is about 2 miles of beautiful sands and sand hills in the bay. There were a good many visitors wandering about. On our return we passed through Lee, a pretty little dell and village. Since dinner took a walk round Capstone Hill and heard some more of the singing &c I saw last night.

The hotel here is a large, good building with good rooms, but not cheap and the cooking is very bad, but the rock scenery of the coast is very fine and I should like to see it in a storm. It has been a rapidly improving place, and now that there is a railway connexion as well as our service of coaches, people can get at it easily.[11]

NEW INN, BIDEFORD. SEP 12. We left Ilfracombe this morning at 10 by rail and reached here at half past 11. This inn stands on the side of the hill in the town, a little way from the bridge leading from the station, and the distance being so short we determined to walk it. Just as we got on the middle of the bridge it came on a very heavy shower of rain and we had to run and make the rest of our way up the steep hill, getting rather damp in the operation. It did Bay no good; the rain did not last long and the day got out very fine. I had a walk about the old town before lunch, but it has not the appearance of age I expected to find.

The view from our sitting room window is very beautiful and when the tide was in nothing could be finer. The old bridge is rather a curiosity; it is very old and the arches differ very much in size. The roadway has been lately widened by carrying the footpaths on iron girders resting on the angle of the piers thus [*sketch*]. After lunch we had a carriage and drove to Westward Ho. It is quite a new bathing place springing into life; the situation is very good, fine sand & splendid open sea. A large college has been built here. There is a curious ridge of large, rounded stones along the beach, forming a strong sea wall. We returned by way of Northam; the drive in both directions was very pretty. There are a great many good residences in all directions, both round the town of Bideford and towards Westward Ho. The River Torridge has not very much water in it, but there is a good tide up to the bridge of 14 or 15 feet of water. The valley above the bridge looks very pretty, but we had not time to go up it. This is a comfortable, old fashioned hotel and we have been well cared for.

FALCON HOTEL, BUDE. FRIDAY SEP 13. We left Bideford at half past 9 this morning and had a lovely drive to Clovelly, where we arrived at ¼ to 11. The country is rich and well wooded all the way. Before reaching Clovelly we turned into the park belonging to Clovelly Court. The woods cover the cliffs and high land along the coast for a couple of miles, and there are 3 little ravines round which the wood winds. The views over Bideford Bay and the country beyond are very beautiful. It is a pity there are not more openings made through the trees. We paid a toll, I think 6d, for the carriage entering the lodge. The carriage stopped at the top of the hill above Clovelly & we had to walk down to the village and of course down to the beach. The hill and street in the village is very steep and donkeys are employed to carry every thing, including luggage. The New Inn is a mere china shop, and very little of an inn. The old lady pretends to sell old china, but the old china looks to me very new and there is no doubt it is so, and made for the express purpose. We did not buy any & were very glad we had not settled to sleep there. It is worth a short visit, and we left at 2 and reached here at 5. Some of the rocks at Clovelly are very beautiful. I have [had] a walk to the beach here and it is a lovely moon light night.

SATURDAY 14. We had a walk over the sands, eastward, and over the sand hills. The rocks are very fine both east and west and at low water there are good sands, but very flat, and they are not long uncovered. After lunch we walked along the west cliffs and sat a little on the Compass Rock. The waves break very finely amongst the rocks. The day was dull in the morning but the sun got out in the afternoon. I am rather disappointed with this place. There is a fine view of the point on which Tintagnal [*ie* Tintagel] Castle stands; Trevose Head is also visable. They say the former place is well worth seeing but the distance to get there is considerable, 21 miles, so that I shall not attempt it. There is a very good canal from the sea here which runs some way into the country. There is a lock down to the sea level and a good-sized basin. The stratification of the rocks here are very curious, thrown in all directions, much of it slate and shale.

SUNDAY 15. We had a walk before lunch. It was very windy and the sand blowing about in a very unpleasant way. About 4pm it began to rain and has been a very wet and stormy evening, the glass falling. The son of Mr Mills[12] called on us; he is one of the gentry here, living in a good house on the hill. He is (*in pencil above* the father) Member for Exeter.

KING's ARMS, LAUNCESTON. MONDAY SEP 16. We left Bude by a carriage this morning at half past 10 and reached here a little before 2. I doubt whether Bude will ever be a large bathing place; the cliffs are too high to build upon them, and there is no space to do so under them, and the district inland is not tempting. The sea was very fine this morning. I walked down to the breakwater before starting; it had been a very rough night but is fine this morning, and we have had a fine but windy day. The deep Devonshire lanes have an advantage in such weather as they give capital shelter. There are the remains of an old castle or circular keep, standing well on a conical hill at this place. It is a pretty object and the grounds about it are very nicely kept as gardens. We got hold of the gardener and went with him to the top of the keep from which very fine views are obtained. The grounds are open to the public.

The old church here is a very curious piece of work. It is built of granite and every stone is deeply carved; it must have been a work of great labour, said to have been built about 1560. There are various subjects and texts represented on the stones. The road was not pretty or interesting as we came along today, hills moderate after those between Dunster and Ilfracombe.

ALVERTON, TRURO. SEP 17. Anniversary of our wedding day, now 8

XV The GWR as Gooch knew it in his later years. Oil painting by B. D. Knox dated 27 March 1876, showing an up mail train passing Reading, with South Eastern Railway in middle distance. The engine is an 8ft single 'renewal' almost identical to Gooch's original series of 1847. It is fitted with an experimental cab of which this is the only known illustration

XIII *(Above)* The only available photograph of Clewer Park, Windsor, app
taken after services' occupation during the second world war and not long befor
demolished

XIV *(Below)* A typical page of pressed flowers mounted by Gooch in the mar
of the diary. These were picked at Mr David MacIver's at Ambleside

Yellow Poppy

Mr Mac Iver
Sept 1st 1880

years ago. How fast years roll on and in what different parts of the world have I spent the 8 days anniversaries. I thank God for the good and loving wife given me on that day.

We left Launceston by train at 10.45 this morning and spent a couple of hours at Plymouth between trains, reaching here about 6pm. The day has been very fine. We were made very comfortable at the hotel at Launceston. I was glad to find Jane looking very well on our arrival and glad to see us.

TRURO, WEDNESDAY 18. The morning was wet until between 10 & 11 when it got out bright and fine and has continued through the rest of the day. I went before lunch to call on Robt Tweedy. In the afternoon Jane [13] took us a very pretty drive down the river. In the evening Mr & Mrs Smith [14] & Mr Tweedy dined with us. This is a very pretty place and Jane keeps it in very nice order. They are all very full of an election that comes off in a few days, in place of Sir F. Williams, who died. Col Tremaine is the Conservative candidate.

QUEEN's HOTEL, PENZANCE. SPT 19. There have been sharp showers of rain today with sun shine between, but it came on very wet about half past 5 and is a very wet night. We left Truro by the 1.30 train. Col Tremaine and Sir James Hogg,[15] with Mr Smith, met us at the platform to shew our men at the station which side they ought to vote. After we reached here we had a nice long walk to Newlyn and back, the weather at the time being beautiful and the view over the bay very lovely. St Michael's Mount is a very pretty object in the bay.

PENZANCE, FRIDAY SEP 20. We had a carriage and drove to Logan Rock and Land's End this morning. The drive to the Logan was very pretty. From the Land's End we returned a shorter way over the higher ground and it was more barren; the road to the Logan lay across and along several pretty valleys. The rocks at the Logan are splendid; the rocking stone is still in its place; I did not try to shake it, but there are men there who, for a consideration, are quite willing to give it a shake. The day has been lovely for our purpose, a clear north wind and bright sunshine. We had a short shower of rain as we drove to the Logan. The water was very clear and green and the sunlight on the broken waves on the little sandy beach just under the rocks was very lovely. You have to walk ¾ of a mile from your carriage to get to the rock.

We drove on to the Land's End; the hotel there looks very comfortable on a small and moderate scale. They gave us a good piece of cold beef for lunch. The first and last house is a little cottage close at hand on a head, which a small and inteligent boy who lives in it with his grandmother told us was the real Land's End, and I suppose it is the extreme point. The rocks are very grand here and the sea looked beautiful. They are indeed mighty stones piled up one upon another. I should like to be here in a heavy storm. We got back to Penzance at 6 oclock, having left the Land's End at 4½ after a very lovely and interesting day. We pass[ed] two churches on the way; one is St Buryan, near Logan. There is a fine old cross just outside the church yard and one inside. The church we passed on our return is at Sennen.

SATURDAY 21 SEP. This has been a lovely day but the wind has been in the south and the night is dark, likely to have wind and rain. We had a long walk in the outskirts of the town; got some good photographs. Went to the harbour and watched the fishing boats come in. After lunch we found out a very pretty path to Madron church. The church is worth seeing, being very old; there is a fine old font in it. The view from the church is very pretty.

SUNDAY 22 SEP. This morning was very wet up to half past 12, after a very rough and stormy night. The Bishop of Peterburgh, Dr Magee, is staying in the hotel and we had service in one of the rooms, with a sermon. After lunch the day got out fine and we walked to Gulval church. It is a quaint and very old building; the churchyard is beautifully kept, well planted with shrubs and flowers. It had been the day for harvest thanksgiving and the interior of the church was very prettily decorated. The walks about Penzance are very pretty in all directions, adding a great charm to the place being able to leave the sea and get into nice shady walks. I have been much struck by the large size of the men in Cornwall, big fine fellows they are. The weather has come on wet again tonight and the sea is making a great noise.

TREGENNA CASTLE, ST IVES. We left Penzance this morning at 12 and came here. The hotel at Penzance is very badly managed and great complaints are made. The situation of this house is very fine; it is a castle within its own grounds of about 70 acres, a great part of which are gardens & woods with pretty shady walks. The Gt Western Co have taken it and opened it as a hotel to encourage the traffic in the west.[16] The house feels more like a private house than a hotel; the views from it are very fine, looking over the town and bay of St Ives and along the coast as far as Trevose Head. With the bright sun shine today the view was lovely. Robinson, one of our directors, came to us at Penzance yesterday and came on here with us.

TUESDAY 24. This has been a very nice day. [In the] morning we walked into the town and on the head. After lunch we went to the monument on a hill above the Castle and in the grounds. It was placed there by a person of the name of Johannes Knill in 1782, as a place for him to be buried. There is a long story about the mayor and 9 virgins dance round the monument every 5 years, some funds being left for the purpose of a dinner &c. The view from the monument is very fine. The sea is seen on both sides of the land.

WEDNESDAY 25TH. The weather was fine this morning, but dull, and there had been a great deal of rain during the night. We went for a walk on the sands near the Hawks Rock, but by the time we got there it came on a fine rain and we had to get back. The day did not clear up.

THURSDAY 26. This has been a very fine day and we had long walks morning & afternoon. We have not been fortunate enough to see a catch of pilchards; the boats lay watching in the bay all day, 5 or 6 of them, with 8 or 10 men in each boat. They rig up a comfortable awning to keep out wet or sun. I was told today that in 1871 there was so large a take that it did great damage to the Cos and almost ruined them, for the business is worked by Cos who employ the men, paying them a fixed wage of 11/- per week and a percentage on the value of the fish taken. The take in question amounted to 1,600 hogshead, each containing from 2,000 to 2,400 fish, so that if the average is taken at 2,200 the total amounted to 3,520,000 fish. When the quantity is large the price falls, and on the occasion in question were only worth about 20/- per hogshead; they sometimes reach 80/- and they say when the quantity is small and prices high the best result is obtained. What they like is a take for the season of about 25,000 hogsheads and a price of about 50/-. Each of the Cos take their turn in watching and claim all the fish that are taken during their time of watching.

FRIDAY SEPT 27. We heard the sad news this morning of the death on the 25th at Boulogne, on her way home from a Continental trip, of my poor godchild Maud Pavy; it will be a dreadful blow to her poor parents as they are very devoted to their two girls. Poor Maud was a sweet young girl, yet full of life. So are the young taken and the old left.

We had a carriage and drove to Gurnard's Head this morning, taking our lunch with us. The day was fine, altho' not bright when we started at 11.30, but it came on a very thick wet fog from the west, and we had this, with gleams of sunshine, all day until, on our return, the fog cleared away for a few hours and we could see the country. The rocks at Gurnard's Head are very fine; both the Head itself and the coast on each side is very fine. The weather was so bad it was not very enjoyable. Bay could not walk to the Head, which is a mile from the hotel, it was so wet. There are some very fine rocks, called Eagles Nest, on the road to Gurnard's Head, near Zennor, and a house built or owned by a London gentleman—a curious place to fix upon.

SUNDAY 29. Yesterday was very fine and we had some good walks. This morning we went to church at St Ives. The service is very high church and the sermon was a very bad one. The building is very old and low like most of these old Cornish churches. The isles [ie aisles] have an arched roof of wood or plaster; the ribs are oak with carved fig[ure]s at the springing of each. There are 3 isles. The congregation was not large. Day has been very fine.

TUESDAY OCT 1. Yesterday was a fine day and we walked to Hawks Point. Poor Maud Pavy was buried (today *deleted*) at Highgate Cemetery. Today there was a high wind and rain early and it had rained hard all night, but the walks dry up very quickly here. The morning turned out lovely, the view from this house is certainly very fine both over the bay and inland, Carn Brea standing up well in the distance. Mr Denbigh[17] came over to see us and we walked over the grounds and to the monument before lunch. Afternoon we walked along the Penzance road as far as Lenant [ie Lelant]. Our hotel is very empty today, only one gentleman besides ourselves.

WEDNESDAY OCT 2. This has been a very fine day and we had a walk on the sands in the morning and to the monument in the afternoon. Mr T. Bolitho[18] and his daughter lunched with us.

DUKE OF CORNWALL HOTEL, PLYMOUTH. OCT 3. We were very sorry to leave pretty Tregenna this morning at 11. It was a nice bright morning and all looked so pretty. We reached here at 3.40 and took a walk; met Mr Brown,[19] who walked with us a little.

FRIDAY 4. Spent the morning at the docks with Margary. After lunch Mr Brown took us for a drive to Saltram, Lord Morley's place, and saw the pictures as well as we could the short time we had at our disposal. There are a number by Sir Joshua [Reynolds], some very beautiful ones. One, a little girl dressed up in her grandmother's cap, and a full-length of a lady. There are also many good Italian paintings by old masters. The house is a fine house as far as we saw it by the reception rooms. The housekeeper knew me, being from Clewer. There is a fine park but matters are not in good order, the house being let. We drove to the forts on the east of Plymouth. There is a splendid view from this high ground.

CLEWER, SATURDAY OCT 5. We left Plymouth by 10.15 train this morning and came direct here. It has been a lovely day and we found all well at Clewer and happy in getting back to our own dear home after a very pleasant trip of 5 weeks, and I thank God for all the many blessings I enjoy.

Nov 9. We left Clewer for London yesterday. Today I have been to Swindon to attend the Wilts Pro Grand Lodge; a testimonial was given to Lord Methuen, it being the 25 anniversary of his being Grand Master. The meeting went off very well and I returned home at night.

DECR 31ST. I had an attack of congestion of the lungs which came on on the 22nd Nov, and kept me in the house until the 11th Decr, when I got down to the station to attend our G.W.R. board. Parliament was called together on the 5th and sat until the 13th on the question of Afghanistan. The govt had two divisions with very large majorities, one of 110 and another 101 votes. I was not able to attend the House. Princess Alice died on the 14th, greatly mourned by every one.

We went to Torquay on Friday the 20 and stayed at Atkinson's Hotel until yesterday, when we returned home. T. Ponsford was with us; the weather was very bad during our stay, frost and snow, & very cold, but I think the rest and change did me good. The hotel is a very comfortable one.

JANY, 1879. We again enter upon another year. I thank God for the many blessings of the past. I have had much reason to be thankful that I have been spared the sorrows and distress I have seen around me. The year has been a most disastrous one to trade, and indeed every one has suffered. The failures of large banks also has brought thousands to ruin. This depressed state of things has now lasted several years and there seems no hope of any immediate improvement. It is not therefore a bright prospect for the New Year. We must hope a change for the better may take place in the spring, things can hardly be worse.

FEBY 1. My friends the Tweedys' bank at Truro stopped payment at the beginning of last month. It is a sad misfortune to the family. A meeting of creditors was held a few days ago and they are able to pay 16s/– in the pound, with the chance of another shilling from Mrs Williams.[20] The meeting was of a most satisfactory character for the Tweedys. Much sympathy for them was generally expressed and a very complimentary resolution passed. The distress in the country seems to grow greater, and we have had a continuance of a cold east wind with frost. This has now lasted about 11 weeks and it is very trying to all us old people; I feel it very much & don't get out in an evening.

MARCH 10. The Gt Western meeting was held on the 28th [of] last month. We were only able to pay 4% as against 4¼ the previous year. There is dreadful stagnation in the trade of the country and railway receipts for the current year shew a large falling-off. The Telegraph Construction meeting was held a week ago and we paid 20%. My health does not get much better; I hope if we get some fine weather like the last few days it will do me good.

GOOD FRIDAY, APL 11, 1879. I went to Highworth on the 6th March to assist in cutting the first sod of the Highworth Light Railway. The day was fortunately very fine and all went off very well. The sod was cut by Mrs Hussey-Freke.[21]

Mr Grant, our chief officer in the Goods Dept, died on Sunday the

16 March after only a few days illness. His death is a great loss to us on the railway; he was a very able and good officer and a truly worthy man.

We went to the Imperial Hotel, Malvern, on Thursday the 20th March. The Friday was a lovely day and we had a long and enjoyable walk on the side of the hills, and to St Anne's Well. From that day we had a week of dreadfully cold weather, ther[momete]r down to freezing, and had hard work to keep our room warm enough to live in, or to get it above 50°. On Wednesday the 26 it snowed hard all day. We had a close carriage on the Tuesday and Thursday and had a drive each day, as we could not go in our open one. This, however, we did on the Friday, the weather having become mild and bearable. We went to the Abbey Church on the Sunday and returned home on Monday the 31 March, feeling better for the change. I attended at the House that night on a confidence division on Zulu affairs; majority 60 at 2am. The weather today is cold and not like Easter weather. The enclosed portrait[22] &c was published a couple of weeks ago. We have just taken a contract to lay a cable from Aden to the Cape.

I went to the Oxford & Cambridge Boat Race on the 5th Apl. Cambridge won very easily. We went in Lever's steamer & were handsomely entertained. Prince Teck & Princess Mary with their children and a lot of other swells were on board. The day was fine but rather cold.

AUG 1. We had a good deal of snow in the middle of Apl and very cold weather. On the 16 went to stay with Alfred at Chepstow and visited the Tunnel on the 27th. On Monday the 19th Apl we went to Milford and spent the morning of 20 on the ship and at Milford docks. In the afternoon we went to Pembroke to see a launch of the Nautilus, a small training ship. Col Phillpot[ts] dined with us & Haswell. On the 20th went to Cardiff to Charlie's; attended a meeting of the Monmouthshire Railway on the 21 at Newport, returning to Cardiff on the 22. Went to the Avon Colliery on the 23, returned home to London. Alfred gave me the dog fox terrier Peter, 7 months old.

On the 6th June I went to stay all night at Mr Lucy's near Gloucester, and the following day went over the works of the Severn Bridge.[23] On the 13th June went with the members of the Telegraph Conference to our cable works at Greenwich. They lunched on board our new steamer Scotia,[24] & dined afterwards at the ship. I did not stay for dinner.

On the 26th June I held my Pro Grand Lodge at Abingdon. We had a very good meeting; about 100 dined. On Saturday the 28th I gave the members of the Telegraph Conference a lunch at Windsor; they had a special train & about 65 attended. The Queen allowed us to see all the private & state app[artment]s of the Castle. Sir John Cowell and Sir [*blank* Henry] Ponsonby went over the rooms with us and shewed us every attention. They also saw the Memorial Chapel, a very beautiful work (I had not seen it before) and also the Chapel. Sir [*blank* George] Elvey played the organ for them while they were in the Chapel. After lunch I provided the party with carriages and they went to Virginia Water. The day was very lovely and they all enjoyed themselves very much. I had my Methuen Lodge at Maidenhead and did not dine with them, but left them in charge of Bay.

JUNE 30. The Agricultural Show was opened at Kilburn; the day was very fine but the only fine day they had. It was in a dreadful state of mud but a splendid show.

AUGT 29TH,[25] CLEWER. On Thursday the 3rd July we went to Clewer for the summer. Weather very cold; on the night of the 5 the temp was only 45°, and we had fires in an evening most days. House of Commons up on [*blank*] Augt.[26] On the 28 Aust we held our Gt Western half-yearly meeting. Altho' our receipts had fallen off we were able to pay the same dividend, or 3 per cent,[27] as this time last year. Railways have all suffered dreadfully from the bad times and I see no opening in the sky. Our shareholders were very content and the meeting passed off very well.

FRIDAY, CHESTER. AUGT 29. We left Clewer this morning and came on here, and on Saturday the 20th we went to Ambleside to stay a few days with Mr MacIver. We spent a very pleasant time with them; one day on the lake, yachting, and another we drove to Grassmere and visited Wordsworth's house and tomb. We had tea with a Mr Fry,[28] a son of my old Bristol friend. He[29] has a steam launch and 3 sailing yachts. On the Sunday we went to the church, day fine; Saturday was also a lovely day. When we left Clewer the floods were out over the park and had been so for a week.

MONDAY 1ST SEPT. We spent the morning in the sailing yachts & in the afternoon went in the steamer to the bottom of the lake and had tea at Lake Side, returning by moonlight to Ambleside. It has been a lovely day.

TUESDAY 2. We walked to the waterfall in the morning & afternoon down to Grassmere.

WED 3RD. We drove this morning to Coniston, and then MacIver & I took the train to Barrow; we walked about the place for a few hours. It is very much larger than the trade, or the trade is, I think, likely to be for many years. We returned by rail to Lake Side station and the steam launch met us and took us home. Day was fine but it came on wet in the evening.

THURSDAY 4. We left MacIver's this morning at 11 & went by rail to Stranraer, through Carlisle. It is a very weary journey after leaving Carlisle. We went to the George Hotel, where we were made very comfortable, reaching there about 9pm; the day has been a lovely one. We were very sorry to leave our happy quarters with MacIver. All were very kind to us; she is a very nice homely woman.

ANTRIM ARMS, PORTRUSH. FRIDAY SEPT 5. Here we are in our old rooms again we had a couple of years ago. They have done nothing towards painting or papering [the rooms] but they are comfortable. We left Stranraer this morning at 10 and had a nice quiet passage in a very good boat, but weather dull. We went on to Belfast where we had lunch and a walk in the town; it came on to rain. We left Belfast about 3pm; they gave us a saloon carriage and we reached here about 6pm.

SATURDAY 6. This has been a very uncertain kind of day, cold with a good deal of rain, but we got a walk before and after lunch.

SUNDAY 7TH. A cold and wet day. I got a short walk on the sands in the west bay in the afternoon. The Lively, with Prince Leopold, came into the bay in the evening.

MONDAY 8. Cold and more or less wet. The Prince went for a drive in a car. Sir Al[e] x[ander] Wood's son was with the party; he is one of the officers on board the yacht.

TUESDAY 9. This day has been bright, but a low temperature. I sat some time on the rocks in the morning, watching some pretty heavy seas. In the afternoon we had a walk on the east sands. Rain came on between 5 & 6.

WEDNESDAY 10. The day has been dull with slight showers. We walked a couple of miles along the Coleraine road before lunch and to the end of the east sands in the afternoon.

THURSDAY 11. It has been wet all day, but we got half an hour's walk before lunch. The rest of the day in the house; I have got a bad cold. Lizzy Seguin was married today.[30]

FRIDAY 12. Wet up to 10.30, when it got out fine but cold. Had a short walk before lunch and a long one after, as far as the quarry on the road to the Causeway.

SATURDAY 13. This has been a fine, bright day and we got long walks morning and afternoon.

SUNDAY 14. Went to church this morning and after lunch took a long walk. Weather dull with a little rain.

MONDAY 15. Day dry, but dull. Walked on the sands in the morning and after lunch walked to Ballawilliam church in the afternoon. It is mostly in ruins but part is yet used as a burial ground, the church being now held in Portrush.

WEDNESDAY 17. Yesterday and today we got good long walks on the sands; weather dry but dull.

THURSDAY 18. We drove to the Causeway this morning; day very fine. This is a very wonderful place. We dispenced with the services of a guide and enjoyed a stroll over the Causeway very much. After lunch we walked to Plaiskin Head, from which the views are very beautiful and the atmosphere was so bright & clear we saw them to great advantage; the Mull of Cantire [ie Kintyre] was so clear we could see the houses on it, so was Rathlin Island and Malin Head, as well as Islay. We enjoyed our day very much, returning home to dinner.

FRIDAY 19TH. We had some walks on the sands today. They have made us very comfortable at this hotel, but the weather has been sadly against our enjoyment of it, and my cold has not helped me.

JURY'S HOTEL, DERRY. SATURDAY 20. We left Portrush this morning at 10.30 for this place. We had a couple of hours to wait at Coleraine for the train, and took a walk to see the town. It is a better place than I expected to find it, some good shops and streets not bad. We reached here about 2 and after getting lunch walked about the town for a couple of hours. The weather was cold, and the night is rough & wet.

SUNDAY. Went to church at the cathedral this morning, very wet. It is a fine church but not large. Did not get out after church, too wet.

MONDAY. Went this morning by the Derry and Lough Swilly Railway to the little town or watering-place on Lough Swilly called Buncrana. The views on the lough are very beautiful. There is a fine old castle here, not in bad condition; it is inhabited. We walked through the grounds and had lunch at a pretty good hotel, and then, as we had time on our hands, walked back along the road to the first station. Unfortunately it came on very wet. Londonderry is a very good town and the wall round it is in good repair and forms a nice walk, with a pretty view of the country round. The river is a fine wide piece of water and some large steamers trade here. It is on the whole a place where two or three days may be pleasantly spent. The situation of our hotel was very bad, in a dirty street in the low part of the town. The Imperial is a much better situation, but of course I do not know what it is inside. I should at any rate try it next time. The inside of ours is nothing to boast of.

SHELBOURNE HOTEL, DUBLIN. MONDAY [recte TUESDAY] 23 SEPT. We left Derry by the 12.30 train today, the Railway Co giving us a retained carriage, and travelled to Dublin where we arrived about 6pm, and have got the same rooms we have had before at this comfortable hotel. The day has been fine and we had a pleasant journey, much of it was new country to me.

WEDNESDAY 24. Have spent the day in Dublin; weather fine but not bright. We went to the Gaiety Theatre at night to see Mr & Mrs Knight.

THURSDAY 25. This has been a cold day, but dry. We went to the picture gallery; it is a nice building and there are some good pictures.

FRIDAY 26. I walked to North Wall this morning to see the L. & N. Western new station there. A large expenditure has been made, but it is a good convenience for passengers over going to Kingstown to embark.[31] After lunch we went by rail to Bray. Here we got a car and drove to the Dargle, a beautiful valley with pretty water cascades. We walked through this and met our car at the other end from which we entered, and drove on through Powerscourt Park to the water fall, a very fine one, and just now in good condition, with plenty of water. We returned past Lord Monck's house and the Valley of the Rocks, and so home by rail to Dublin. The drive was a very lovely one and we had a nice bright afternoon for it, and a civil driver; he charged 10s/–.

SATURDAY 27. Had a drive this afternoon in the Phoenix Park. The day was cold and dull and no enjoyment in driving.

SUNDAY 28. Very wet until middle day; after lunch walked to Donnybrook and back.

MONDAY 29. We went this morning to the railway station to call upon Mr Ward. He was not there but Sir Ralph Cusac[k][32] was; had a chat with him. After lunch we went by tram to Glasnevin Cemetery and the Botanic Gardens. Part of the former is kept in nice order but the bulk very badly. The Botanic Gardens are very nice indeed, well kept and a nice collection of plants. We were very pleased with the Gardens, the day was fine, and we returned by the tram. My first voyage in a street tram.

TUESDAY 30. Went to the Museum. A very good collection. The day was dull and cold.

WEDNESDAY, HOLYHEAD. OCT 1. We left Dublin by the L. & N.W. 9.30am boat this morning and had a beautiful passage here. After dinner, it being a lovely moon light night, we had a walk upon the pier; it certainly was as lovely a night as I was ever out in.

THURSDAY 2. Had a walk with Capt Dent this morning, over the works of the L. & N.W.[33] They will be very fine when completed, and very convenient, but have cost a lot of money. After lunch Capt & Mrs Dent drove us in their pony carriage on to the headland, a pretty mountain drive, and we had tea with them at their house afterwards. They are very kind nice people. The day was cold and rough.

QUEEN'S HOTEL, CHESTER. FRIDAY 3. We left Holyhead at 11.30 this morning and came on here. Day cold and a good deal of rain.

SATURDAY 4. Reached Clewer and found all well.

OCT 17TH. I went today to the opening of the Severn railway bridge.[34] There was a large gathering and, of course, a feast. The day was cold and very uncomfortable. Yesterday we struck a strong feeder of water in the heading under the land on the Welch side, which is more than our pumps can manage, and we are drowned out until we get more power. This is very unfortunate as in a few weeks our heading across the Severn would be complete and I have been looking forward to walking across next month.

NOV 7, 1879. We left Clewer today for the winter.

BURDON HOTEL, WEYMOUTH. DECR 24TH, 1879. I have been laid up in the house with an attack of congestion of the left lung since the 15th Novr, and came down here today in hopes of getting some strength and also for a change both for myself and my wife, who has also been far from well the last few weeks. In addition to nursing me her mother has been ill and died on the morning of the 17th, very suddenly at last. She was a truly worthy woman and my dear wife feels her loss very deeply. We had an invitation to dine with the Prince & Princess Christian on the 5th, but of course were unable to go.

XMAS DAY, THURSDAY. We spent a very quiet day. The weather was sufficiently good to enable us to get a walk before lunch, but did not go out afterwards. Cape cable spliced.

26 FRIDAY. Today has been fine but cold, 40°. Had a walk before and after lunch.

27. A very fine day, 45°. Had a good walk both before and after lunch.

28 SUNDAY. Too wet to go out today, a small rain.

MONDAY 29. The morning was fair & bright, also mild. We got a good walk before lunch. Afternoon was stormy but the evening was beautiful and the moon on the water very lovely. Cape cable opened to the public.

TUESDAY 30. There has been a heavy westerly gale all day with steady, constant rain. We tried to get a walk twice but did not get far until we were driven in again.

WEDNESDAY 31 DECR, 1879. The last day of a very sad old year has been a very rough one; a heavy gale and rain. Few will regret the passing away of 1879. It has been a most disastrous year to all classes, rich and poor, commercial and political, and the weather has been dreadful, brin[g]ing ruin upon the farmers, nay, few have not suffered loss.

The chairmen of two of our leading railways died in the same week: Mr Ellis, chairman of the Midland, and Col Duncombe, chairman of the Gt Northern. It is a singular coincidence that two large Cos should lose their chairmen at the same time, and I was certainly also in a very bad state of health.

BURDON HOTEL, WEYMOUTH. JANY 1, 1880. I think I have only once, since I commenced housekeeping, dined out of my own house on New Year's Day, and this occasion was when I was at York engaged with the gauge exp[erimen]ts. The new year has opened with a great improvement in the weather, today having been fine with a few slight showers, but we got our walk morning and afternoon. There is also a general improvement in the trade of the country the last few months, and a hope is felt that the tide has turned and the new year may be the beginning of a brighter time for all. God grant it may be so.

FRIDAY 2ND. This has been a fine day and I had two good walks as well as spending an hour in the morning in going to look at our steamers.

SATURDAY 3. This has been a lovely day. We took a walk before lunch to Wyke Regis church. It is a very pretty walk and the views from the hill above the church are very beautiful. The church and church yard are kept in very nice order. After lunch we took a walk to the coast guard station and back. This, with my walk to the steamers early, gave me about 5 hours walking, a great improvement.

SUNDAY 4TH JANY, 1880. Went to St John's church today, a very nice service and a good sermon. In the afternoon we walked to Preston. The day has been very fine.

MONDAY 5TH. We left Weymouth by the 12 oclock train and returned home to Paddington. It has been a lovely day, and I am very thankful to feel the change has done both myself and wife a great deal of good, and we were much pleased with Weymouth and very comfortable at the hotel, not a cheap one. However, we were the only visitors.

MARCH 25. Yesterday Parliament was dissolved, and I am not now a Member of Parliament. It is nearly 15 years since I was first elected; I have agreed to stand again, much against my inclination as I do not feel equal to the worry of an election or the night work of the House. I get back my health very slowly. I had a meeting on 15th at Swindon with the principal Conservatives of the borough, and as it appeared clear that if I did not stand we would lose both seats, little choice was left to me, and they promised to take the work off my hands and relieve me from any canvass or attendance at public meetings. Mr Neeld, son of Sir John Neeld, is standing as the other Conservative and the Liberals have brought forward only one candidate, Mr Story Maskelyne, who, I think, has a good chance. Nomination day is on Tuesday next, the 30th, and the polling on Friday the 2nd Apl, so another week will decide the matter. I should not be grieved if Neeld took my place; all I hope for is to save our seat. The election came on very suddenly; I was in hopes it might have been put off until the autumn. I am going to Clewer today until Tuesday for a little quiet, and go to Swindon on Monday or Tuesday.

Our Gt Western half-yearly meeting was held on the 27th Feby. It went off very well; we were able to pay a better dividend than in the corresponding half year by $\frac{1}{2}$ per cent, or $4\frac{3}{4}$ per cent. There has, for the past few months, been a great improvement in the traffic, and I hope the trade of the country has taken a turn for the better; it is much needed.

Our Tel[e]gr[aph] Construction meeting also went off very well; our difficulty here has been to keep the dividend down. We laid a cable to the Cape from Aden and a duplicate Australian cable, with other minor ones, and have just made a contract with the Anglo Co to lay another Atlantic cable this year. In connexion with the Construction Co we have sustained a great loss in the death of Mr Beer. He acted in all our large financial matters for us, and very usefully.

We are having a fine spring; altho' the east wind is cold it is very suitable for farmers drying the land, and I trust we may have a better year. Last year I lost £550 on my little farm at Windsor, perhaps in a great degree from bad management of my bailiff.

MAY 29TH. We went to Clewer this year to spend Easter. We had lovely weather and enjoyed the quiet before going to Swindon on the 30 March for election purposes; we went to the Queen's Hotel. The nomination took place on the 30th at Cricklade, but I did not attend. The parties who were nominated were: Sir D. Gooch; Mr Neeld; Mr S. Maskylene. I did not attend any public meeting, nor make any canvass. I met a few of my old friends on the evening of the 1st Apl and the polling took place on the 2nd, with the result shewn on the other page.[35]

The result of the election throughout the country has been a great surprise to both parties, giving as it has so large a majority to the Liberal party. The cause, no doubt, was the great distress amongst all classes, and a feeling that any change might do good, the Liberal party having also taken great pains to lead the people to believe that they were able to restore prosperity. Altho' the change in number of Liberal members was great, yet the real majority of votes in their favour was only about 5% of the whole. One bad feature in the last election was the breach of good faith on the part of the voters, so large a number making promises which they did not perform. I had over 3,000 promises, yet a little over 2,400 were true; such a thing is much to be regretted. The new House is certainly no improvement on former Parliaments, and I cannot help thinking the Liberal parties will next year tumble to pieces. For myself, I do not care how soon a dissolution takes place.

We went to Chepstow on the 28th Apl and stayed with Alfred all night, going to Milford next day, staying there until the 7th May and returning home, spending a night at Alfred's on the way. We had beautiful weather and enjoyed ourselves on the water a good deal. I visited the Gt Ship on the 30th Apl & 5th May. I wish she was employed, it is a pity to see her idle. We went to Clewer on the 14th May for Whitsuntide and stayed there until the 19th, having lovely weather. Parliament met for business on the 20th. Annexed is copy of my address to my constituents. Lord Beaconsfield called a meeting of the Conservative party on the 19th of Apl at Bridgewater House; it was a large meeting.

Mr Carter has retired from Clewer; a good thing for the parish, but his letters on doing so do him great credit. I annex a copy of them. We spent Whitsuntide at Clewer this year.

MAY 27TH, 1880. We went to a ball at Buckingham Palace tonight. As usual, a very pretty affair.

31ST MAY. Went to Levée held by Prince of Wales.

JUNE 8. We went down to Greenwich today with a large party to see the cable works and the ships just ready to sail with the Cape cable. We had a lunch and dinner. I did not stay for the dinner.

JUNE 14TH. I held my Pro Grand Lodge at Maidenhead today; it was a large meeting and all went off very well, the day also being fine. The Lodge was held in the school rooms, and the dinner also.

JUNE 16TH. We went to Chester today, my wife and several Gt Western directors, to attend the opening of the Holyhead docks tomorrow. There was a special train for us from Chester on Thursday the 17th June, to Holyhead. The Prince of Wales was there, and the programme was we were to have been in time to go with him in a steamer to meet one of the London and North Western Irish boats and so return to the docks in procession. Our train, however, was late, and the boat with the Prince had started before our arrival. We went in another boat and returned to the dinner, a very splendid affair held in the goods shed. The new works are very fine and it gives the L. & N.W. a splendid station for their Irish traffic. We returned to Chester in time for a late dinner and returned home on Friday the 18th. All went off very well, and was very well arranged.

JUNE 22ND. The Lord Mayor of London gave a dinner today to the railway interest. We were a very large party, and many speeches were made, one by me, but short. I was not well. All went off very well. Alderman Truscott was Mayor. It is the first of such dinners and may be continued. He has the stationery for the Clearing House.[36]

Jane Tweedy came to stay a few days with us.

9TH JULY. We went to Clewer today for the summer. The Tel[e]g[raph] Construction Co laid our Atlantic cable this month. It was done in very fine weather and without a hitch, by Halpin. The Scotia sailed from Greenwich on the 21 and arrived at Heart's Content on the 4th Augt, laying the cable as she came back.

TUESDAY, AUGUST 10TH. I went today to Taunton with Grierson and Owen, stayed at Taunton all night and on Wednesday went to Tiverton and took the chair at the half-yearly meeting of the Tiverton & North Devon Railway Co. After the meeting we went to Dartmouth where we stayed all night, and on Thursday had a carriage and drove along the coast to Kingsbridge. It was a beautiful drive, crossing Slapton Sands, through Tor[cross]. Kingsbridge is a very nice little town. Our object was to see how it would suit us to take up the railway from there to Kingsbridge Road station, on the South Devon line.[37] From Kingsbridge we drove to Saltcombe, a beautiful place where Lord Devon has a nice house, but small. The streets are so narrow a carriage cannot turn in them; we had to go into a yard to turn round. It was a lovely day for our drive. We drove back to the railway and had a special train on to Plymouth, where we arrived for dinner.

On Friday morning we went to our docks and had a steamer and went up into the bay and to the brakewater.[38] The fleet were there; it was a pretty sight and the day lovely. After lunch we went to Bridgwater and had a meeting with the townspeople and afterwards on to the Clifton Downs Hotel at Clifton, and on Saturday spent the morning in Bristol and returned home to Clewer in the afternoon. This has been a lovely week for the harvest and great progress has been made with it. We had the Foresters' Fete in the park at Clewer on the 2nd Augt; they had a fine day and all went off very well.

FRIDAY, AUGT 27TH, 1880. We held the Great Western half-yearly

meeting today. The accounts for the half year came out very satisfactorily; there was a large increase in receipts and a consequent increase of [*blank*] per cent in dividend, making it [*blank*].[39] We therefore
had a very pleasant meeting. The report is annexed.

AUGT 28TH. We left Clewer this morning at 9.30 for our holiday, going
direct to Newton[-le-Willows] to stay with Will[40], reaching there at 7 in
time for dinner after a pleasant journey. The day was lovely.

SUNDAY 29TH. Spent the day with Will, went over the Vulcan works.
How much it brought back to my mind the old days when I worked
there and worked hard. The day was very fine.

MONDAY AUGT 30TH. We left Newton at 12 today and joined the
North Western train at Warrington and went to Ambleside to stay with
Mr McIver, reaching his house about half past 2. We went for a sail on
the lake; the day has been gloriously fine and the view of the Langdale
Pikes & the mountains from the lake was very beautiful.

TUESDAY 31ST AUGT. We went out on the lake in the morning, McIver
& his boys to bathe, also a clergyman, a pleasant fellow of the name of
[*blank*]. After lunch we went to have tea with the parson of Wray
church, across the lake. He has a pretty cottage, and the day was hot
and lovely; we were content to sit about in the garden.

WEDNESDAY 1ST SEPT. This has been a wet day and I only got out in
the garden for a little. Mary Redmain[41] and her two boys called upon
us; they are staying in Ambleside.

THURSDAY 2. I walked into Ambleside this morning & then went on
the lake with the bathers. After lunch we drove to Hawkshead and
looked at the church. The man gave me a very old document out of a
large oak chest, a marriage certificate dated [*blank*]. From there we
drove to Mr Fry's[42] and had tea. The morning was very fine but it came
on wet in the evening.

FRIDAY 3RD SEPT. Went in the steamer to Bowness before lunch and
after lunch drove to the Troutbeck valley and looked at the church; it is
a beautiful drive. In the evening Mr & Mrs (? Greening) dined at the
McIvers. The day has been a lovely one.

SATURDAY 4. This has been the hotest day of the summer, and only fit to sit about under the trees and enjoy it, but after lunch we called upon Mary Redmain and went in the launch down the lake and round the islands. A very heavy thunder storm came on about 9pm.

SUNDAY 5. There has been a great deal of rain today and I did not go outside the gardens.

KESWICK HOTEL, KESWICK. SEPT 6. We had a carriage and left Mr McIver's this morning at 11am, after a very kind and pleasant visit. They are very nice, homely people and we have very much enjoyed our visit. We drove through Rydal & Grassmere and past Thirlmere Lake, about to become the water supply for Manchester. It was a lovely drive of about 3 hours. We have got capital rooms at this hotel; we had lunch on our arrival and then walked down to the lake. The views from Friar's Craig is very lovely. The day has also been all we could wish.

TUESDAY 7TH. Walked to Crosthwaite church and Portinscale before lunch, and afternoon had a boat and rowed round the lake. We visited Lodore Falls, but as there was very little water in them it was not a very grand sight. When full they must be pretty. The floating island is a very curious thing; it was up when we were there. It looks as tho' some pressure of water got under the bottom of the lake, probably consisting of weeds and roots, and forced it up, causing a crack through which the water escapes [*sketch*]. It is not constantly in this state. I wonder some one has not taken the trouble to carefully investigate the matter and determine the cause &c. It would not be difficult. The boatman told me they could find no bottom where the crack is, but this is absurd.

WEDNESDAY 8 SEPT. We had a lovely drive today from Keswick by the lake side to Lodore and the Bowder Stone, a large mass of rock, and over the Honister Pass (*in margin* 1,950 feet above lake) to Lake Buttermere, where we lunched and spent some time at the end of the lake, and saw a lot of fish caught with a net. It is very pretty. We returned by another road, the Newlands Valley. All the roads are very hilly and a good deal of walking has to be done, but it was a very enjoyable day.

THURSDAY SEPT 9TH. Walked to Castle Hill this morning. There is a beautiful view of the lake and surrounding hills from it. After lunch we went by rail to Bassenwhaite station. The lake is a small one; there is a pretty view from a hill just above the station. In the evening we went to a concert by Messrs Till & Sons on the rock harmonicon.[43] The music produced from these stones is very sweet and the notes clear and well defined. It was a very interesting evening. The day has been very fine.

SEP 10TH. This has been a very wet day. After lunch we got as far as the pencil works of Messrs Banks and saw the process of black lead pencil making. Bought some exceedingly good ones, but not cheap; we also bought some photographs. Had a good deal of walking in the rain.

SATURDAY 11TH SEP. We walked to the lake before lunch and went to see the museum; there is very little there to see. After lunch we walked for some distance up the path leading to Skiddaw. The day has been very fine and the views were beautiful.

SUNDAY 12. Writing most of the morning. After lunch we took a very long and pretty walk up the Greta Valley. We have enjoyed our visit here very much; the hotel has been very comfortable. Plenty of pretty excursions can be made from this place.

ROYAL HOTEL, EDINBURGH. SEPT 13. We left Keswick by train this morning at 12 and arrived here at 5 after a pleasant journey. We had a walk on Carlton Hill after dinner; it was a lovely night.

14TH. We had a walk in the town this morning. Rain came on middle day and we did not get out again.

WEDNESDAY 15TH SEPT. It has been very cold and wet all day. We were glad to stay in doors and have a fire. In the evening we went to the Theatre Royal and saw Ellen Terry in the play of Shylock, as Portia. Play not well acted.

THURSDAY 16. We walked in the old town and up to the castle in the morning. After lunch we took the train to Portobello where we spent a couple of hours enjoying the fine sea breeze. There is a pier some distance into the sea. After dinner took a walk; the day has been very fine.

SEPT 17TH, FRIDAY. This is the anniversary of my wedding day. We had a good walk in the town and went to the picture gallery and museum on the Mound before lunch; afternoon had a carriage and drove round Arthur's Seat. The day was very fine. This is not a very good hotel, the rooms were good but expensive; try another next time.

ROYAL BRITISH HOTEL, PERTH. SEPT 18TH. We left Edinburgh at half past 12 and came on here by rail. We had time for a walk before dinner. After dinner I went out for a walk; the moon was lovely and I enjoyed a stroll on the South Inch. We have had some showers during the day.

SUNDAY 19TH SEPT. We took a long walk across the river in the morning and after lunch a long walk on the North Inch. After dinner I had a moon light walk. The day has been very fine.

MONDAY 20TH. We went to Dundee by rail this morning and went to look at the remains of the Tay Bridge.[44] It is a very poor structure. We lunched at a shop and had a walk about the town and docks; I see Dundee very much altered. We returned to Perth for dinner; a lovely moon light walk after. The day has been very fine. Hotel bad.

GREAT WESTERN HOTEL, OBAN. SEPT 22 [*recte* 21], TUESDAY. We left Perth at 12 today and came here by rail through Stirling & Bridge of Allan. The scenery was not much until we passed Dalmally, after which it was very fine. We reached here about 6pm after a fine day's travel.

WEDNESDAY SEP 23 [*recte* 22]. It was wet this morning until 10.30 when it cleared up, and had a walk in the little town. After lunch we had a long walk to near Dunstaffnage Castle, or 3 miles off. The view was very beautiful looking over the water and the background of mountains, with the castle standing on a spit of land in the foreground. Altho' a long walk we enjoyed it very much, the weather being all we could desire.

THURSDAY SEPT 23. I took the excursion steamer at 8am this morning (my wife did not go) and made the excursion round the Isle of Mull. It is a beautiful sail and we visited the island of Staffa. We had to land at the end opposite to the caves, and so had a walk along the whole length. The caves were very wonderful, the Giant's Causeway being, of course, similar, but there is not so fine a cave in Ireland. I thought the columns were also larger at Staffa; it is a very interesting spot. We next landed at Iona; this is curious from its antiquity. The ruins of the cathedral are in very good preservation and a good deal has been done of late to preserve them. Just as we left Staffa what had, up to that time, been a fine day became very wet, and it rained very hard while we were at Iona, but cleared up shortly after we got back to the steamer; but it was cold. The coast along the inside or east of the Isle of Mull is very fine. We got back to Oban about 6pm after a very interesting day.

FRIDAY 24 SEPT. We had a long walk this morning along the bank of the lake and returned by a road over the high ground; day very fine, and we enjoyed the walk. After lunch we went over the upper part of the town of Oban and had some fine views. This is a rising little place and I have no doubt, now they have a railway here, it will increase more rapidly.[45] This is a very good and comfortable hotel and well situated. The Alexander [ie Alexandra] is also a new hotel and I am told very comfortable. Sir Wm Harcourt is staying there; I had a talk with him this morning.

SATURDAY 25. We have had showers of rain today, so were confined to short walks about the place.

SUNDAY 26. We had a short walk before lunch; after, a long one on the road to Dunstaffnage, but it came on wet before we returned.

ST ENOCH'S HOTEL, GLASGOW. MONDAY, SEPT 27TH, 1880. We left Oban at 12.45 today and reached here at 6.15pm. The day was fine. We enjoyed our stay at Oban very much; the hotel good and comfortable and not very extravagant for a place with so short a season.

TUESDAY 28. We paid the cathedral a visit this morning; it is a very fine and interesting building. We also went to the Necropolis. After lunch we went to the West Park and the museum in it. Day fine.

WEDNESDAY 29. Walked about the town; day dry but cold. This is a very good hotel but Glasgow is a very dirty, smelly town.

287

THURSDAY 30. QUEEN'S HOTEL, CHESTER. We left Glasgow at 10am today and travelled here; day fine and had a pleasant journey.

FRIDAY OCT 1. We went to Birkenhead today to see the new steam ship Pembroke being built by Messrs Lairds for the Gt Western.[46] Had lunch in the works and returned to Chester for dinner. Day very fine.

CLEWER PARK. SATURDAY OCT 2/80. We left Chester this morning and returned home to Clewer. Had a fine day and was glad to find all well at home. It is always pleasant to be at home again. I unfortunately took cold the day I went to Staffa and have now got a very bad one, which is doing away with the good I got by my excursion. I will hope a little care will remove it. I thank God for my happy return.

The Lord Mayor gave a grand banquet to the Masons at the Mansion House. The Grand Master, the Prince of Wales, and all the great Masonic swells were there. I did not go as I did not feel well enough to run the risk of being out at night.

WEDNESDAY, OCT 27TH, 1880. We left Clewer today for the season, and returned to our Paddington house. We have had very wet weather and the floods have been out over the park.

THURSDAY 28. My wife and I, with the dep[ut]y chairman[47] and Sir James Anderson went to Swindon today. My wife laid the foundation stone of the new church being built. The day was too wet and rough for me to attend the ceremony, but it went off very well and my wife came back armed with a silver trowel and mallet.[48] In the evening we went to distribute the prizes at the Mechanics' Institution. There was a large meeting; it is two years since I was there and was not fit for such a job now, my cough & health being so bad. We returned to London by the last train.

TREGENNA CASTLE HOTEL, ST IVES. SATURDAY, 30 OCT. We came down here from Paddington today, starting by the 11.45am express and reached here at a ¼ past 9 after a very pleasant and not very fatiguing journey. The day was a very fine one.

SUNDAY. This has been a lovely day & we 'had two long walks.

The Order of Service

FOR

Laying the Foundation Stone

OF

ST. PAUL'S CHURCH,

New Swindon,

On THURSDAY, OCTOBER 28, 1880,

(Festival of St. Simon and St. Jude).

At the Temporary Church, Edgware Road,

CELEBRATION OF THE **HOLY COMMUNION** AT 7.45 A.M.

EVENSONG AND **SERMON** AT 2.30 P.M.

Preacher:—

The Rev. J. C. NORMAN,

(VICAR OF HIGHWORTH).

After which the Foundation Stone will be Laid

BY

Lady Gooch.

The Offerings, both at the Service in the Church, and also at the Laying
of the Stone, will be devoted to the Church Building Fund.

"North Wilts Herald" Steam Printing Works, Swindon.

FIG 20 Cover of programme for the stone-laying ceremony at St Paul's church,
New Swindon, after which, as Gooch relates, Lady Gooch 'came back armed
with a silver trowel and mallet

MONDAY Nov 1. There has been a good deal of rain today, but we got one walk.

TUESDAY 2. Very wet all day and kept in the house.

WED 3. This has been a very bright & clear day, wind a little rough and cold, but we had plenty of walking.

THURSDAY 4. This has been a lovely day. We walked to the west sands before lunch and on the Penzance road after. The G.W. new steamer the Pembroke was launched at Birkenhead today. Miss Wynn, daughter of Sir Watkin W. Wynn, christened her. All went off well; I was sorry not to be there.

FRIDAY 5. This has been a fine day, but dull. We got our regular walks. The boats in the harbour were lighted up at night.

SATURDAY 6. Day fine, but dull, with very little sun. We walked to Carbis Bay after lunch. Mr Bolitho called on us.

SUNDAY 7. Morning very wet but fine after lunch, and we got our walk.

MONDAY 8. Very fine, we walked to Knill monument.

TUESDAY 9. A fine day and had good walks morning and afternoon.

WED 10. Day fine; took our long walks morning & afternoon.

THURSDAY 11. A fine day, but had a slight shower as we returned from our morning walk.

FRIDAY Nov 12. This was a wet and rough day. Kept in the house.

SATURDAY 13. We left St Ives this morning by express train, and after a pleasant journey reached home soon after 6 oclock for dinner. The hotel at St Ives was very comfortable and I hope the quiet has done me good, but I am still feeling far from well—such a want of strength and energy.

Nov 19TH. I had a meeting today of the Great Eastern Ship directors and resigned my position of director and chairman. I did so with great regret and reluctance. I have always taken a deep and warm interest in the noble ship, but I do not feel equal to so many cares as I have lately had upon me, and felt compelled to give up some of them. I have been chairman of the ship since the formation of the present company in 1864, and have spent many happy hours on board of her, and many very anxious ones. She has done good work; I doubt, but for her, if we would as yet have the long line of deep-sea cables, and I trust there is yet good work in store for her. Her engines ought to be altered so as to reduce her great consumption of coal. I wish her every success in the future. Mr Henry Brassey[49] took my place at the board.

BURDON HOTEL, WEYMOUTH. DECR 22, 1880. We left London by 10.15am train this morning to spend our Xmas at Weymouth, and had a wet day for our journey until we reached this part of the country, where the weather cleared up.

THURSDAY 23. The morning has been very fine and I got a good walk. After dinner it came on wet; temp about 55°, wind W.

FRIDAY 24. This has been a bright and fine day. We had, after lunch, some showers, but not to keep us in. Temp 62°, wind W.

XMAS DAY. This has been a bright and glorious day, with a crisp, bracing air; very enjoyable. We had good walks and spent a quiet, happy Xmas Day.

SUNDAY, DEC 26. Today has been a dry but dull day; we had ice upon the pools of water. I walked to the coast guard station. In the afternoon it began to rain with a heavy S.W. wind, and has been very rough.

MONDAY. A bright, sunny morning, but wet afternoon. Temp 50°.

TUESDAY 28. Morning very fine, with some rain after lunch. Temp 54°. Capt & Mrs White called in the morning on their way from Gersey [ie Jersey] to Chatham, and Mr Howard, the Mayor, also called.

WEDNESDAY 29. A very wet morning, but it cleared up about 2 and was then bright sun shine, and we got our walk, but it was a wet evening. The Mayor called as I was out yesterday. Temp 52°.

THURSDAY 30. This has been a bright, fine day and very warm and enjoyable. Mr Elliot called. My dear sister Jane Tweedy[50] died this morning at Truro at 8 oclock. She was only confined to her bed for a fortnight. We saw her at the station at Truro as we passed on our way from Cornwall. She was a kind, good soul and I am much indebted to her for her great kindness to me on the death of dear Margaret. Her age was 75; she has passed to a better land to join her sister.

DECR 31, 1880. The old year has retired in a splendid day, a bright sun shine and sharp, clear air; temp 45°. I had a long walk beyond the coast guard station and nearly to Preston, and also two other good walks. May the brightness of today be an emblem of the coming year. The past year has been a hard one to very many, and in political matters affairs look very gloomy. Ireland is in a state of revolution, or nearly approaching it in a large portion of it. All law is in abeyance and a reign of terror exists, and a weak, half Radical government are allowing things to drift on in this state. Parliament meets on the 6th Jany. In the East and in Africa matters wear a very uncertain aspect; in the latter there is open war. May all be made peaceful and prosperous in the coming year.

SATURDAY, JANY 1, 1881. The New Year has come in with bright sun shine and very mild weather. Temp 50°, wind N.W. The day has been a glorious one and we have enjoyed a great deal of it out of doors.

JANY 2ND, 1881. This has been a dull but dry day. We called upon the Mayor. He has a very nice house.

JANY 3. We left Weymouth at 12 oclock today for home, the weather very fine. Found all well at home. We have enjoyed our trip very much at Weymouth, and it has done both of us a great deal of good. The climate of Weymouth is certainly, in winter, very good. When here the Xmas before, while the weather was very bad at all other places, we had it fine there, and so this Xmas, generally throughout the country the weather has been bad; we have been able to get out every day as much as we wished, and some of the time the weather was glorious.

NOTES

1 This should be 26 February.
2 These are only his chairmanships and directorships. There is little doubt that Gooch also had many other connections with railway companies and other concerns in an advisory capacity or as consulting engineer. As early as 1853, for instance, he was consulting engineer to the Geelong & Melbourne Rly, Victoria, Australia, and his great experience would, by the late '70s, have brought him much other work, the extent of which may be judged from the considerable fortune he amassed. Most of the railway directorships he held were as nominee of the Great Western, and although he took his duties seriously it seems he saw the comic side of his position as a railway Pooh Bah. In December 1864, F. G. Saunders, then Secretary of the GW, wrote to Gooch 'would you like to be a director of the East Som[erse]t Line or of the Ely & Ogmore Line or both . . . no liability & lots of dignity attending the position'. (BRB archives HRP1/6, p 28.)
3 *See ante*, V, n 3.
4 ie Monmouthshire Railway. Gooch was a chairman of the joint committee which managed the line. *See* Vol V, n 16.
5 *See ante*, V, n 23.
6 *See ante*, p 151 and *post*, p 318.
7 This was probably J. C. Wall, formerly general manager of the Bristol & Exeter Rly.
8 King's Weston and Lawrence Weston.
9 More than 700 persons were drowned in a collision between two steamers.
10 The only railway that ever reached Lynton was the narrow-gauge Lynton & Barnstaple Rly, opened in 1898 and closed in 1935.
11 The London & South Western line from Barnstaple opened on 20 July 1874. In 1887 the GWR put in a loop to allow through running to Ilfracombe, to replace the road coaches referred to by Gooch.
12 Arthur Mills, MP, not E. W. Mills, the former GWR director.
13 Jane Tweedy (*qv*).
14 Mr Smith has not been identified. He could well be the same as the Mr Smith who was nearly drowned with Gooch while fishing in 1847. (*See ante*, p 63.)
15 The other Member for Truro.
16 Tregenna Castle remained a Great Western hotel throughout the company's existence, and is still (1970) owned by British Transport Hotels Ltd.
17 G. S. Denbigh was superintendent of the West Cornwall Rly. This line, from Truro to Penzance, had been administered by a joint committee of the GWR, Bristol & Exeter and South Devon since 1865. The B & E was amalgamated with the GWR in 1876, and with the absorption of the South Devon on 1 August 1878 the West Cornwall became GWR property.
   See MacDermot, *GWR*, II, chap VIII.
18 Probably Thomas Robins Bolitho, a member of a prominent local banking family. He became a director of the GWR in 1903.
19 Henry Brown *qv*.
20 Mrs Williams was possibly the widow of J. M. Williams, a former partner in the bank.
21 The Swindon & Highworth Rly. Projected by an independent company, but amalgamated with the GWR on 1 July 1882, and opened on 9 May 1883. Ambrose Hussey-Freke, of Hannington Hall, Highworth, was the chairman.
22 A lithographed portrait of the diarist from *Touchstone* for 29 March 1879.
23 The Severn bridge at Sharpness was opened on 17 October 1879. It was severely

damaged when two barges struck it in fog on 25 October 1960, and was never repaired. It was dismantled 1967–8.

    See Paar, H. W. *The Severn & Wye Railway,* 1963.

24 The *Scotia* was the new cable-laying ship for the Telegraph Construction & Maintenance Co. She was originally a Cunard paddle steamer, built in 1862. She was wrecked at Guam in 1904. Gooch sailed in her to Madeira in March 1884 (*qv*).

25 Possibly a mistake for 28th, as the next entry is also dated 29th.

26 ie prorogued, on 25 August.

27 This should be 3½ per cent.

28 Gooch's 'old Bristol friend' may have been Francis Fry of Bristol, a director of the Bristol & Exeter Rly.

29 ie Mr MacIver.

30 This entry refers to the marriage of Lisbeth Gooch Seguin of Curzon St, Mayfair, to Alexander Strahan of Westbourne Terrace Road. The bride's relationship to the diarist has not been ascertained.

31 London & North Western steamers to and from Holyhead had previously run to Kingstown, necessitating a cab ride into Dublin for the Irish railway stations. The LNWR built a connecting line and a new station at North Wall and extended the steamer route so that the boats came alongside the station as at Holyhead.

32 Sir Ralph Smith Cusack was chairman of the Midland Great Western Rly of Ireland. (*See ante*, p 236.)

33 *See ante*, p 235 and *post*, p 281.

34 It was at the luncheon there that Gooch invited the assembled guests to visit the Severn Tunnel, warning them that they might get their feet wet. He had not heard that on the previous day the great spring had burst into the tunnel and flooded the workings.

    See ante, V, n 3.

35 Gooch polled 2,441 and Maskelyne 4,350, and were elected. Neeld polled 1,748 votes.

36 Alderman Sir Francis Truscott's firm, James Truscott & Son, had the contract to supply stationery to the Railway Clearing House. As RCH forms were to be found in every railway station and office in the country, this would be a large and valuable contract.

37 The branch to Kingsbridge was built, being opened in December 1893, when Kingsbridge Road station was renamed Wrangaton.

38 Millbay docks at Plymouth were originally projected and built by the Plymouth Great Western Dock Company, which was purchased by the GWR and its associated railways in 1874.

    See MacDermot, *GWR,* II, 123, 130.

39 The dividend was at the rate of 5¼%, an increase of 1¾% over the corresponding dividend in 1879.

40 His brother William F. Gooch (*qv*).

41 Mary Redmayne was the married daughter of T. L. Gooch (*qv*).

42 *See ante*, VI, n 28.

43 The rock harminicon was a dulcimer made from bars of a very hard rock found near Skiddaw. For an account of this instrument and the Till family *see Oxford Companion to Music.*

44 The first Tay Bridge had been partly destroyed in a gale on the night of 28 December 1879, when a train carrying about eighty persons fell with part of the bridge into the river.

    See Prebble, J. *The High Girders,* 1956.

45 The Caledonian line to Oban had been opened on 1 July of that year.

46 Launched on 4 November 1880 and put on the New Milford–Waterford service. *See post*, p 290.

47 ie of the GWR, Sir Alexander Wood (*qv*).

48 This was St Paul's, New Swindon.

49 Brother of Thomas Brassey (*qv*).

50 Actually his sister-in-law, his first wife's sister.

VOLUME VII

The Diary 1881-5

FULTHORPE HOUSE. JANY 27TH 1881. We spent our Xmas and New Year Day at the Burdon Hotel, Weymouth. The new year came in with a glorious day, bright sunshine and warm. May God bless us all during this year, and restore my dear wife to health; her health is a great anxiety to me. We stayed at Weymouth until the 3rd when we returned to London both, I think, better for our stay at the sea side, where we were favoured by very fine weather.

Parliament met on the 6th to pass some measures to secure law and order in Ireland, but from that day to this no progress has really been made, the Irish Members having debated the address until last Friday. On Monday the Irish Secretary Mr Fo[r]ster brought in his coercion bill & the night before last Gladstone moved a resolution to suspend all bills until the govt have carried the two bills for the protection of life and property in Ireland. This led to another Irish row, and for the first time in my experience in the House, Biggar, an Irish Member, was suspended from taking any part in the business of the House. The Govt would not give way to the several motions for adjournment and the consequence was the House sat on until two oclock yesterday, Wednesday, and then carried the resolution. What a disgraceful bear garden the House of Commons has become! I shall be glad when my time is over in it.

We have had a dreadful snowstorm and frost. The frost began early in the month and has often been down to zero, but on Tuesday the 18th the snow began, and I think I do not remember so severe a day, wind with constant snow & intense frost. The consequence has been that our railway has been closed in the greater portion of it most of last week; indeed, the last block was only cleared on Monday the 24. In many places it was drifted to a depth of 12 feet. The result on our traffic has been a loss of £40,000 or about ⅓rd of our usual receipts, a sad loss, to say nothing of the great cost in clearing the snow. All the lines on the south of Birmingham have been similarly affected, but none have suffered so much as we have. The L. & South Western are down between 11 & £12,000, the L. & N. Western £28,500. The weather this week has so far continued very bad. Today we have a thaw and I hope we are done with the frost for this year.

I was appointed chairman of the Railway Association on the 13th. Mr Moon, chairman of the London & North Western, was appointed dep[u]t[y] chairman, which office I had held for the last 3 years.

We lighted Paddington Station with the Brush electric light at Xmas. It is a good light, but we have not yet got it into *certain* working. I have no doubt all the difficulties will be overcome.[1]

FEBY 14TH, 1881. We have had to excavate 111 miles of snow on the line, varying from 3 or 4 feet to 10 feet deep, at 142 places. The weather has continued very bad.

In the House of Commons matters have improved very little, another long sitting of 42 hours, and 36 of the Irishmen suspended. It is a disgraceful thing the present Govt have, by their wicked folly, brought this disgrace upon the country. New rules have been now passed, but as yet no real business has been done, the 2nd reading of the Coercion Bill only passed last Wednesday and is now in committee with about 100 amendments. When it will get through it is impossible to say. I have cut out of the newspaper the particulars of the struggle with the Irishmen. It is the end of the House of Commons as the standard of such an institution. What a wonderful change do I see since I entered it 16 years ago; then a body of gentlemen, now a body of roughs, or little better. It is a sad thing for the country; Gladstone has much to answer for.

MARCH 15, 1881. Our Gt Western shareholders' meeting was held on the 3rd March and went off very well in spite of a loss of nearly £60,000 by the snow storm. We managed to pay a 5% dividend, or a ¼ better than the previous year. Our Telegraph Construction meeting was also very short and satisfactory, with a 20% divd for the year.

On Friday last the Govt got their last Irish Bill through the Commons. Ever since meeting on the 6th Jany these two Coershon Bills have stopped the way in spite of new rules made to expedite them.

Sad news came yesterday of the assassination of the Emperor of Russia; poor man, they have succeeded at last after many trials. Who would be Emperor of Russia? Not I.

IMPERIAL HOTEL, MALVERN. MARCH 30, WEDNESDAY. We came down here by the 2.15pm train today for a few weeks, to see if a change of air &c would do both my wife and myself good. She is far from well and I have had a bad cough and feel out of order. We have got our old rooms, and with fine weather I hope it will do us good. The day has been fine.

APL 1ST. Yesterday was a bright, lovely day, but with a N.E. wind. We had pleasant walks under the hills where the wind is not felt. The carriage & horses came down. Today has also been very fine; we walked in the morning and after lunch drove by Wind Point round the west side of the hills, & back by the Wyche pass.

SATURDAY APL 2. The day has been dry but cloudy and cold. We had a walk in the morning & after lunch drove as far as the Wells, but the wind was cold, from N.E., and we were glad to get back.

SUNDAY 3. I had a walk before lunch. After, we drove by the Link and Madresfield, but altho' very bright and sunny the wind was cold.

MONDAY, APL 4. This has been a very bright sunny day; had walk in the morning, and afternoon drove to E[a]stnor Castle along the ridge. This is a beautiful drive and the spring flowers were beginning to look very pretty.

WEDNESDAY 6. Walked yesterday morning and afternoon. Day fine but cold. Today we had a walk in the morning, and afternoon drove round by the Rhydd. Weather bright and calm, making it very pleasant.

THURSDAY 7. We walked up to St Anne's Well this morning; a sharp pull for an old fellow like me. I find I cannot get up these hills as I used to do. Afternoon we drove by the Wells and round by Welland. Day very fine but cold.

FRIDAY 8. Walked morning, and afternoon drove round North Hill by West Malvern & back by Wyche Cutting. The day was very lovely and the views were very beautiful.

SATURDAY 9. This has been a lovely day. I had a long walk in the morning. Bay not very well so did not go with me. After lunch we drove by Madresfield and the nunnery,[2] home by the Rhydd.

SUNDAY, 10TH APL. The day has been fine with light clouds and the wind has gone to the south. We did not drive.

MONDAY 11TH. It rained until about 12 oclock today, after which it got out very fine and we drove by Cowleigh and back by the Link.

TUESDAY 12. We went by rail to Langley Green to lunch with my sister Fanny Laing, getting back to dinner. The day was very fine.

WEDNESDAY 13TH. We drove to Ledbury this morning by the ridge-way and lunched with Mr Biddulph; he has a very pretty place there. The day was very fine and we enjoyed the drive.

APL 14. This has been a very fine day. There was a shower of rain in the middle day.

GOOD FRIDAY, APL 15. This has been a lovely day. I had a long walk before lunch and in the afternoon we drove by the Rhydd and by Powick, home by the Link. We ought to have a good railway traffic with this weather.

SATURDAY APL 16TH. Walked into the town before lunch, afternoon drove to the Wyche and got out there to walk to the Wells by a capital path along side of the hills, with beautiful views all the way. We tasted the water at the holy well and after a good walk the carriage picked us up in the main road at the Wells. The day has been very fine.

EASTER SUNDAY, APL 17. This has been a lovely day. I had a long walk before lunch and drove by the Rhydd in the afternoon.

MONDAY 18. A fine day. Bay not very well. I had a walk in the morning. Afternoon we drove by the holy well and round the Camp hill, back by the Wiche Cutting. A good many holiday people about.

TUESDAY 19. One of England's greatest men died at 4.30 this morning, Lord Beaconsfield. He had been ill for some weeks and the greatest feeling has been exhibited by all classes and parties in his condition. Few men have had a more remarkable career and will be more mourned on their death. The day has been cold here; we did not drive, but had a walk before and after lunch.

WEDNESDAY, APL 20. The day has been cold; we had a walk in the morning and drove to the Rhydd after lunch, but it was too cold to be pleasant.

THURSDAY, 21 APL. Went by rail to Tukesbury [*ie* Tewkesbury] and back today. We had a couple of hours there, which we spent in looking over the beautiful old Abbey church; it has recently been cleaned, and in part restored. There are some very beautiful and interesting monuments there. The town is a decaying place and does not look so old as I expected. The day was fine.

FRIDAY 22ND. We sent our horses back to London yesterday, so have had all our exercise by walking today. It has been a very fine warm day.

LONDON, SATURDAY 23. We returned home to Fulthorpe by the 1.30pm train today; very sorry to leave the beautiful air of Malvern. It certainly is a very healthy place and has done us both good.

JUNE 13TH 1881. We went to Clewer on the 3rd to spend the Whitsun week and returned to Paddington today. The weather has been very fine and we much enjoyed the quiet week. We were quite alone.

JUNE 20TH 1881. I held my Pro Grand Lodge today at Aylesbury. We had a large and successful meeting.

JULY 8, 1881. We went to Clewer today for the summer.

JULY 9TH. There was a large review of the Volunteers in Windsor Park today by the Queen. About 56,000 men were present, and the day being fine it was a beautiful sight. The railways had a heavy day; we carried to Slough and Windsor about 27,000 men and all was done with punctuality and safety, to the great credit of our staff.

AUGT 13. We have had some very hot weather, particularly the latter part of July. I changed my farm bailiff today; got rid of Parker and appointed Beasley.[3]

MONDAY, AUGT 22, 1881. We dined today at Cumberland Lodge with Prince & Princess Christian, dinner hour 8pm. We drove from Clewer & started at 7.20; this gave us rather too much time, 7.30 would do. We did not dine until 8.30 and left at 10.30. These parties are very pleasant; I sat next the Princess and she was very chatty & kind.

MONDAY AUGT 29TH, 1881. We left Clewer this morning to go to Harewood, about 6 miles from Ross, to stay with the Dunnings. It is a pretty place, with beautiful trees in a large park. The house is a large one but much out of condition. The property belongs to a Miss Stubbs; the Dunnings[4] have got it very cheap for 6 or 8 weeks. We arrived there about half past 3. A good deal of rain had fallen and the roads &c were very wet.

30TH AUGT. This has been a very fine day and I had some amusement in nutting in a wood near the house. It is long since I scrambled through a wood in pursuit of nuts, but we all enjoyed the fun and got plenty of nuts.

31ST. We have had a fine day today and taken long walks; the country is very pretty. We walked to the bank river [*ie* river bank].

THURSDAY, SEPT 1. At Harewood. Took good walks; day fine.

MILFORD, FRIDAY 2ND. We left Harewood this morning and came here by way of Monmouth, Pontypool Road and Newport, reaching here at 7.15pm, and find ourselves in our old quarters.[5] The day has been very fine.

SATURDAY 3. This has been a lovely day. During the morning I went over our ships and after lunch we went in the steam launch down the Haven to Dale Bay. This is a glorious haven.

SUNDAY 4. This has been a beautiful day; we had a walk. Capt & Mrs Parkins called upon us.

MONDAY 5. The day has been dull and there was a little rain in the afternoon. After lunch we went to call upon Capt Parkings, and went over the dockyard and the ironclad Majestic, which is now building. She is a wonderful ship of iron, not very like any thing that has to float on the water. Except for the loss of life I should like to see the result of a fight between ships of this class.

TUESDAY, SEP 6. This has been a dull day, but no rain. We went up the Haven in the steam launch; had Col Phillpots & Haswell to dine with us. The Col is leaving the command here to go to Edinburgh; he has charge of the forts & engineering works.

WEDNESDAY 7TH. This has been a very fine day. We went in the afternoon over the Gt Eastern; she is advertised for sale, but I doubt if any sufficient bid will be made for her. £75,000 has been fixed as the min[imu]m price at which she is to go. Poor old ship, I wonder if I will ever go over her again. I have had my old cabinet that stood in my cabin during my cable voyages, and the table, sent to me.

SEPT 8, THURSDAY. We left Milford this morning by the 10.30am train and went to Carmarthen. We have had a special to go over the Carmarthen and Cardigan line (which we have just purchased) to the Llandyssal station in the valley of the Teify, where we had a carriage and drove down that beautiful valley to this place, Castle Malgwyn, to stay with my old friend Mr Gower. He was an original director of the Great Western and remained so for many years after I joined the Co. He is now an old man of 86, but hale and hearty. I was very glad to see him again and he was pleased to see me. He has a very pretty place here, a very good house and beautiful grounds. The river Teify is also very pretty; it passes close to his house. We had a dinner party in the evening. Newcastle Emlyn is a very pretty village in the valley, about 7 or 8 miles from Llandyssall. We are about to continue our line on to this place.[6] There were very heavy showers of rain this morning, but after leaving Carmarthen it got out very fine and we much enjoyed our drive.

FRIDAY, SEP 9TH. I walked to Mr Gower's slate quarries on the river, about half a mile from his house, this morning, and we afterwards drove to Cardigan and called upon Canon Miles, a brother of our old director John Miles, and came back by way of Castle Cilgaran [ie Cilgerran], an old ruin. The valley is here very beautiful. After lunch we drove to Tynone [? Ffynone], a beautiful place belonging to a Mrs Colby, a lady who dined with us last night. Her gardens are very good and grounds and timber very fine. We had a dinner party in the evening; I met Mr Lloyd, the late Member for Cardigan. The day, on the whole, has been very fine; we had a few showers.

SATURDAY, SEP 10. We walked about the grounds this morning and went to see the gardens which are a good ¾ of a mile from the house. They are very old, with a great deal of wall, but not in very good order. After lunch we left Mr Gower's and he sent his carriage with us to the Crimich [ie Crymmych] Arms station, where we took the 3pm train to our Whitland station. Mr Owen,[7] the chairman of this branch, accompanied me over his line. It is not in a very good state; I suppose we will one day take it over. At Whitland I had a special which ran us down to Neyland in time for dinner. The day has been fine. A large ship[8] loaded with timber was burning in the bay. She took fire last night. We have had a very pleasant visit to Mr Gower's; both his two daughters & his son, Capt Gower, shewed us every attention.

SUNDAY 11. This has been a very fine day. I had a good walk and went to church in the evening.

MONDAY 12. Had a good walk in the morning. After lunch went down the Haven in the steam launch to see the remains of the burnt ship, which were still smoking. A very fine day.

TUESDAY 13. Had a walk in the morning and went up the Haven in the launch after lunch. It was a lovely day and we enjoyed our sail very much. Got aground once or twice, but this gave us a reason for chaffing the Admiral.

WEDNESDAY, SEP 14. We went today to Haverfordwest to lunch with Admiral Stokes; Haswell went with us. We were received very kindly and shewn all the sights of the place. The town is a much better one than I expected to find it. The Admiral has a pack of hounds which he shewed us. He gave me a walking stick he had brought from some distant country which I forget. Both he & Mrs Stokes were very kind and we had a pleasant day which was beautifully fine. We returned to Neyland for dinner.

THURSDAY, 15TH SEP. I went to sea for a few hours today in our new steamer the Pembroke. We went nearly to Tenby. The day was a lovely one and the trip most enjoyable. We had in our party the Parkins [and] Col Phillpots. Mrs Parkins did not go but some lady friends did, also the Major of the regt at Pembroke. We had a good lunch on board. After our return we called on Mrs Parkins to say goodbye to them.

FRIDAY THE 16. Had a walk in the morning and after lunch went down the Haven in the launch. We picked up Canon Miles and his brother Col Miles & Mrs Miles; they have been here for a couple of days. We went to Dale Bay; had tea on board. It was a lovely day.

SATURDAY, SEPT 17. We left Milford this morning and went to Cardiff to stay with Charlie. The day was dull, with showers.

SUNDAY 18. At Charlie's in the morning; afternoon we walked to Llandaff Cathedral and attended the service. Day fine, with little rain.

MONDAY 19. We went to lunch with the Bishop of Llandaff. He is a very pleasant man, very hale for his age. The day has been fine.

TUESDAY 20. I had a special train this morning and visited both our collieries, and went on to Porthcawl to look at our dock works there. Lunched with [blank]. The day was very fine and we made a long day of it.

WEDNESDAY 21. We went to the Cardiff Exhibition this afternoon; it is a very good one. There are some good pictures on loan. I also went after dinner to see the electric lights, several of which were there. I was disappointed with the effect of the Swan light. The day has been fine with some showers.

THURSDAY 22. We left Cardiff today and went to Chepstow to stay with Alfred. Day fine.

FRIDAY, SEPT 23, 1881. I spent today at the Severn Tunnel. The works are progressing favourably. I went into a finished part of the tunnel; it looks well. We have had a fine day.

SATURDAY 24. Got out first thing this morning but rain came on at 11 and continued the rest of the day.

SUNDAY 25. This has been a fine day. We drove to Crick to call upon Mr Lawrence after lunch, and afterwards had a walk.

MONDAY 26. The heading of the tunnel was got through tonight, so you may now pass through under the Severn. We had some walks today, it having been very fine. (*On opposite page:* This was the heading between Sudbrook shaft & the English side or Sea Wall shaft, on that part under the river.)

TUESDAY 27. Left Chepstow and returned home to Clewer. Day fine. Found all right at home. We spent a very pleasant few days with Billy; the country at Chepstow is certainly very beautiful & the view from Billy's gate very fine.

FRIDAY, OCT 14TH, 1881. We had a fearful gale of wind all last night and today. When I left Clewer to go to London this morning many good-sized branches were scattered about the park, but when I returned in the afternoon the place looked a perfect wreck. One splendid elm at the [*illegible*] was torn up by its roots, and a vast number of very large branches broken. Some trees nearly stripped. The gale was at its height between 11 & 2 oclock. I was glad to find the cedar was not damaged, altho' the large elm on the lawn had lost a big branch.

SATURDAY 15. We came to Margham [Margam] to stay a few days with Mr Talbot over the time the Prince of Wales is to let the water into the new docks at Swansea. We found a very nice party here: Lord & Lady Jersey, Lord Mountedgcumbe and his daughter, Lord & Lady Wimborne, and Mr & Mrs Fletcher (Talbot's daughter & son-in-law).

SUNDAY 16. This is a very beautiful place, the ruins of the Abbey being very fine. The old church has been lately restored by Mr Talbot; there are some fine old monuments of the family in it, and one beautiful one of his son who died a few years ago—the figure is very fine. We went to church in the morning; *very high*. After lunch Talbot and I drove to the

Pyle station to see if all the arrang[emen]ts for the Prince were ready. The day has been very fine.

MONDAY, 17TH OCT. Walked about enjoying the beautiful grounds this morning. After lunch Mr Talbot and I went to meet the Prince & Princess of Wales at Pyle. They came to Margham and had what they called tea, but chiefly champagne, and walked about the grounds and the ruins of the Abbey. They each planted a tree. We then went back to the station with them; they went on to Swansea to stay at the Vivians. Day fine, *very* in the afternoon.

TUESDAY 18. This was the day for letting the water into the docks, but so far as this was concerned it was a farce, as the docks are not nearly ready, and a little tap was turned to let in a few gallons of water. We had a special train from Port Talbot to Swansea, and went direct on board Mr Talbot's yacht the Lynx. The town was beautifully decorated and the day all that could be wished, altho' at sea it was too windy for the ladies. The Prince & party came on board the yacht and we went a little way outside the harbour, when we returned and landed them near the new dock. Here lunch was provided, but I did not attend it as Bay was not very well; we lunched on the yacht, also dined on board, where we also dressed after dinner for the ball. This we attended, and got back to our special train at the station soon after 12 oclk, and returned to Margham. It has been a hard but a successful day, all went off so well.

WEDNESDAY, 19 OCT. We left Margham this morning after a very pleasant rest, and returned home to Clewer.

WEDNESDAY, NOV 2ND. We left Clewer today to take up our winter quarters at Fulthorpe House. There was a thin coating of ice on the morning of the 31st Octr.

DECR 12TH, MONDAY. The annual meeting of the Swindon Institution was held this evening. I and Bay went down to distribute the prizes as usual. Sir Theodore & Lady Martin and Capt Douglas Galton went with us. All passed off well. We were fortunate in a fine day.

WEYMOUTH, FRIDAY, DECR 23, 1881. We left Paddington by the 12 oclock train today. There was a very sharp frost, the country being quite white with it. After sunset the ice formed on the inside of our carriage windows, but as we got near Weymouth it was milder.

SATURDAY, 24TH. A very fine day, but no frost, temp 40°. We had 3 good walks. Poor Mr Powell's[9] brother & sister are staying at the hotel. New search is being made for him by dredging, but I fear there is little hope of finding him. It is now a fortnight since the baloon, in which he was, left the cliff at Bridport and was seen by some one to fall into the sea. Nothing is certain but the fact that the baloon is lost.

XMAS DAY, 25. We went to St John's church this morning; had a very nice service. I had a couple of good walks. Day fine but dull, temp 40°.

MONDAY 26. Had 3 good walks; day fine but dull, temp 50°.

TUESDAY 27. We walked to Wyke Regis this morning and back by way of Rodwell. This latter place is growing very fast. The views are beautiful, looking over Portland and the bay. Day fine.

WEDNESDAY 28TH. This has been a lovely day. Before lunch we went to the pier and sat there in bright sun shine, the water in the bay being as smooth as glass, more like a summer day. After lunch we walked to Radipole.

THURSDAY 29. Had my 3 walks today. Wind a little cold, but temp 50°.

FRIDAY 30. We had a carriage today to go and look at the Abbotsbury Railway, which is in progress of being made. Mr Manfield, a large landowner on the line, who acts as the secretary, met us at Broadway and accompanied us.[10] We drove to Abbotsbury and went over the gardens of Lord Illchester; they are badly kept and are only curious on account of the mildness of the climate, permitting a large number of plants to be grown in the open that only live in hothouses in other parts of the country. Camellias like good-sized trees flower out of doors, and some flowers were out when we were there. The house, on the cliff some little distance from the gardens, is very poor. We returned to lunch with Mr Manfield at Portisham. He is the representative of Capt Hardy, Nelson's friend. Capt Hardy was born and lived in the house now occupied by Mr Manfield. It is rather an old house. He has many relics of Capt Hardy, Nelson's capt. They gave us a splendid lunch with a bottle of '20 port. We returned to Weymouth by dusk. Day has been fine, but cold.

SATURDAY 31. Had my 3 good walks today; weather fine. We did not sit up for the New Year.

WEYMOUTH. JANY 1, 1882. A bright sun has ushered in another year. May God grant it may be a happy one to all dear to me. I have much to be thankful for in the many blessings of the past year; my own health has been very much better, and I only wish that the health of my dear wife was better also. May God grant this in the present year.

The early part of today has been fine, and I got my morning walk, but it rained from one oclock to 4, so we did not get out again.

MONDAY, 2 JANY. We left Weymouth by the 12 oclock train and returned home to Paddington. A very fine day.

TUESDAY, 7TH FEBY. Parliament opened today, and the first business was whether Bradlaugh should be allowed to take the oath. After a long discussion a vote was taken and the govt, who supported Brad[l]augh, were beaten by a majority of 58; ayes 286, noes 228. This is the first decision of the session and a heavy defeat for the government, and it will not be the last, and I doubt whether Parliament will last over the session.

FEBY 10, 1882. We had our Great Western half-yearly meeting today, and paid a divd at the rate of $7\frac{1}{4}\%$, carrying over a large balance. As a matter of course all went off very well. This is a large jump in our divd, but 1% at least is due to our changing the date of ending the half year from 31st July to 30th June, and 31st Jany to 31st Decr, getting into the account for the half year the month of July against the month of January, and $\frac{3}{4}\%$ was due to the loss by snow in Jany of last year.

MARCH 2ND. An attempt was made on the Queen's life today as she was leaving our Windsor station, happily without any effect. The man was immediately taken and will I fancy prove to be a madman. Thank God for the Queen's escape.

MARCH 18. We went today to the Crystal Palace, where there is a very interesting exhibition of electric lighting and matters connected with telegraphs &c. The day was very fine and we enjoyed it very much, driving down.

APL 28TH. We went to Clewer the day before Good Friday and have stayed there until today. Generally the weather was very fine and we much enjoyed the quiet. Our Telegraph Construction meeting was held on the 28 March; we paid our usual divd of 20%, but trade is not as brisk as it was. All went off very well.

SATURDAY, MAY 6TH, 1882. I have just heard of the death of my old and dear friend Capt Bulkeley. He is the oldest of our Gt Western directors, and his death will be much regretted by us all. He has only been seriously ill since Tuesday morning when he was attacked with a fit of paralisis & has not since been conscious.

SUNDAY, MAY 7. A dark deed was done last evening in Phoenix Park, Dublin. Poor Lord Frederick Cavendish, who had only that day begun his duties as Chief Secretary to the Lord Lieutenant, Earl Spencer, was with the Permanent Secretary, Mr Burke, brutally murdered in day light, or about 7 oclock. The govt have brought Ireland to a sad state, and how it will end no one can foretel. They have also let out of gaol Parnell and other suspects who have been shut up for some months. The papers of the day will shew the reckless manner in which Gladstone is dealing with this country.

WEDNESDAY, MAY 10. Dined with the Speaker this evening.

REGENT HOTEL, LEAMINGTON. ROOMS NOS 9, 10 & 11. FRIDAY MAY 26, 1882. We came down to Leamington today by 12 oclock train and took up our quarters in our old comfortable rooms in this hotel. Had a walk before dinner, day very fine. Brought carriage & horses.

SATURDAY 27TH MAY. We drove this afternoon to Kenilworth Castle, but it came on a heavy shower of rain and we did not get out, but returned by way of Warwick.

SUNDAY 28 MAY. We drove round by Stoneleigh Abbey this afternoon; a lovely drive and day very fine.

MAY 29. This was Bank Holiday and Whit Monday; the town was very full of people and the day lovely. A procession of upwards of 300 bicycles went to Warwick and back afternoon. We had a drive and about 5pm a baloon went up from the gardens and there were fire works, but we did not turn out after dinner.

30 MAY. We drove to Stratford-on-Avon, starting at 12, and put up at the Red Horse, where we had lunch, and went to see the new theatre &c,[11] returning to Leamington in time for dinner. A lovely day.

WEDNESDAY MAY 31. Had a walk in the morning, and after lunch walked to Warwick and looked at the town, returning in a tram car.[12] These are very good, and run between Leamington and Warwick about every $\frac{1}{4}$ of an hour. The day has been very fine.

JUNE 1ST, 1882. We had a walk in the morning and after lunch drove round by Stoneleigh. The day was bright but a cold east wind.

JUNE 2. This has been a cold and disagreeable day. We had a couple of walks but did not drive.

SATURDAY 3 JUNE. We drove to Coventry, starting at 12. We went by way of Whitley and saw the house I spent a few months in with my mother in the autumn of 1834. I hardly remembered the place and had forgotten the appearance of Coventry, altho' the town is not much altered, I suppose, excepting on the road to Kenilworth where a public garden and good houses now exist. We went to the King's Head Hotel for lunch &c; a dear place and new. Peeping Tom is placed at the corner.[13] We went into St Mary's Hall, a curious old place with some very good portraits of old kings &c, and also into St Michael's church, a fine church. The day has been very dull and we had rain before we got back.

SUNDAY 4TH JUNE. This has not been a nice day, but we had a couple of walks; there have been showers of rain. My horse Emperor got badly kicked by Captain in the stable this afternoon.

MONDAY 5. We left Leamington after a very pleasant visit by the 3pm train, and returned to Paddington.

WEDNESDAY 21ST. We went tonight to the Queen's ball at Buckingham Palace, after dining with Robertson.[14] Scott Russell, the builder of the Great Eastern steam ship, died this month. We also lost by death our old director Capt Bulkely; he has been long a director of the Gt Western and was much esteemed and his loss deeply regretted by us all. He was buried at Clewer and we went down to attend the funeral.

MONDAY 19TH JUNE. I held my Pro Grand Lodge at Reading today; we had a very good meeting.

JULY 5TH, WEDNESDAY. We moved to Clewer today for the summer. My hay making was finished on the 8th, got in very well.

JULY 8TH. Frank and his family came to stay with us at Clewer.

13TH JULY. We went this afternoon to a garden party given by the Prince of Wales at Marlburgh House.

FRIDAY, 4TH AUGT. Went to Bristol today to look over the lines there. Had the Mayor and several of the Bristol people to dine with us. Returned to Clewer on the Saturday.

AUGUST 10TH. Our Great Western half-yearly meeting was held today. We paid a dividend of 5 per cent[15] and the meeting went off very well.

FRIDAY 18 AUGT. Parliament was adjourned today until the 24th October. I have been sitting 2 days a week during the session on the Railway Rates Committee. We finished our report on 27th July. On the whole the report is a satisfactory one for the railway comp[anie]s. It has been a long and weary job, having lasted two sessions.

AUGT 24, 1882. I kept my 66 birthday at Clewer. Had my children (all but Anna) and Charlie & Harry dined with us. Years roll on very fast, but I have much to be thankful to God for.

SEPT 1ST. We went to stay at Neyland, travelled all the way; day wet.

SUNDAY, SEPT 3. Neyland. Yesterday and today have been very wet days; a little sun shine this afternoon.

MONDAY 4TH. This has been a very fine day. We went in the launch to the Gt Eastern. It was pleasant to see the old ship again, but she wants painting outside very badly.

WEDNESDAY 6. Yesterday was a very wet day. Today has been fine and we went in the launch to the Enchantress Admiralty yacht. T. Brassey & Lord John Hay had been down on a visit of inspection. After lunch walked to the hill fort.

THURSDAY 7. This has been a very fine day. Went in the launch to St Ann's Head; did not land. It was a lovely day. My wife did not go. Afternoon we went to a garden party at Capt Parkins' in the afternoon [*sic*].

SEPT 8TH. This has been a lovely day; we went up the Haven after lunch. The Parkins went with us.

SUNDAY 9 [*recte* 10]. Yesterday was very fine and we took 2 good walks. This morning we went to church, and after lunch walked up the road to hill fort, but rain came on about 4 and we had to turn back.

NEYLAND, MONDAY 11TH SEPT. I went over the dock yard this morn- and the new iron clad Edinburgh, now building. After lunch we went up the Haven close to Haverfordwest. Day very fine.

12, TUESDAY. We went to lunch with Admiral Stokes at Haverford-west; a fine day. Found the old people very well and very hospitable.

13 SEP, WED. Went over to Tenby today and took rooms at the Gate House Hotel. Called on the Parkins on our way back; it has been a lovely day. The battle of Tel el Kebir was fought today.

FRIDAY 15TH. Yesterday we got a walk before lunch, but it rained after lunch. Today I went in the launch to St Ann's Head; we landed there. The day lovely. After lunch we went to a garden party at Lady Catherine Allen's.

GATE HOUSE HOTEL, TENBY. SATURDAY 16. We left Neyland this morning and came here by way of Whitland in time for lunch. Afternoon went for a long walk on the south sands; day fine until evening. Could not get into our old rooms as the people had not left; had pretty good rooms just above them.

SUNDAY 17. Walked to Gumesford [? Gumfreston] church in the afternoon; day fine.

TENBY. TUESDAY 19TH SEP. Yesterday was a fine day and we walked on the hill and sands. Today Admiral Haswell came to lunch with us, and we had a walk. He left at 4, when rain came on. My poney Neddy died on the 20th.

FRIDAY 22. Weather since Tuesday has been fine and we have had our regular daily walks.

CARDIFF, SATURDAY THE 23. We left Tenby this morning at 10.30 and came to Cardiff to stay with Charlie. Day fine.

SUNDAY 24. Charlie and I took a long walk today after lunch. Day fine.

MONDAY 25. I had a special train this morning at 9 and visited both our collieries. We had a good deal of rain.

CHEPSTOW, WEDNESDAY 27. We spent yesterday at Cardiff, day wet and bad. Today we came here to stay with Alfred, the day was fine.

THURSDAY 28. Spent the day at the Severn Tunnel, walked through from the English to the Welch side; works are getting on very well.

FRIDAY, CHEPSTOW, SEPT 29. We had a walk in the morning and after lunch Billy drove us to Tintern Abbey. Day was very fine.

SATURDAY, 30 SPT. Went to see a ship launch early this morning at 9;

weather wet. We left Chepstow by 1.30 train and got back to Clewer where we found all right.

OCT 24TH. The House of Commons met today for a autumn session to settle Cloture and other rules of the House.

THURSDAY 26, 1882. We left Clewer today for the winter. A heavy flood just beginning in the river.

FRIDAY NOV 10. The division on the Cloture took place in the House tonight. The govt had a majority of 44 in a House of 564 Members— ayes 304, noes 260. This vote seals the liberty of free debate in the House of Commons; how we are degenerating. What will the House be in a few years? Very different from what it has been and under which the liberties of England have been preserved. Gladstone has been a curse to the country in many ways.

WEDNESDAY NOVR 15, 1882. My old poney Billy died today. He was 25 years of age and has been a good servant.

SATURDAY 18TH. The Queen held a review of the troops who have re-turned from Egypt today, at the Horse Guards. There was a dense fog up to the time she took up her position on the ground, when the sun broke out and all cleared off. I did not venture to go through the fog but it must have been a very interesting sight.

MONDAY 20TH. Went to Swindon today to attend the meeting of the Institution and give away the prizes. Sir Geo Elliot, Mr Bouverie and Grierson went with us. The day was fine and all went off very well.

NOV 23. My dear brother Tom died this morning after a few days ill-ness, peacefully and without pain. He has been a good son and a good and loving brother, and few men are more fitted to meet the Great Change. He died at his house at Saltwell, Gateshead.

WEDNESDAY, NOV 29. My dear brother was buried today at Kensal Green cemetery. He had a vault there in which his only son was buried some years ago. I have had a bad cold and my doctor would not let me go to the funeral. After it was over I drove to the Great Western Hotel to see Ruthanna,[16] who had come up the night before.

BURDON HOTEL, WEYMOUTH. We came down here today and have taken up our quarters in the old rooms.

XMAS DAY. This has been a dreadfully wet day and we could only get out in a kind of rain for a short time in the morning. Yesterday was a lovely day, and Friday and Saturday were also fine days, and we got 3 good walks each day, or rather I did, and my wife 2.

THURSDAY 28. This has been the first fine day since Sunday. Admiral Haswell came to Weymouth and dined with us.

SUNDAY 31ST. The old year has gone out in wet; since Thursday it has been continued rain and we have [had] to get our walks as best we could.

WEYMOUTH, JANY 1, 1883, MONDAY. The New Year has come in with a very wet day. How fast the years go on. I have much to be thankful for in the past year; my health has been better than it has been for 3 years. My dear wife is also, I think, somewhat better than she has been. May God in His mercy bless this year to us and all my dear ones.

JANY 2. We left Weymouth this morning and returned home to Paddington. The day was bright with showers.

FEBY 8TH, 1883. We had a meeting of the Tel[e]g[rap]h Construction Co on the 6th, to approve a bill we have in Parliament to enable us to extend our operations to electric lighting.

Today we held our Gt Western half-yearly meeting, paying 7¼ per cent divd. The meeting went off very well, and was held for the first time in our new room which seemed to answer very well for sound. The shareholders were good enough, on the motion of Mr Adams,[17] to pass a resolution asking the directors to have a bust of myself executed at the cost of the company to be placed in the new room. It is pleasant to feel that all my anxiety and work for the company is appreciated by the shareholders.

THURSDAY, FEBY 15. Parliament was opened today. The Queen did not attend and Gladstone has been at Cannes for some weeks for his health, and has not returned. The floods in the Thames are very high, this being the 5th this winter, the present ones being the highest since 1852.

I went to Clewer on the 17th and had to drive there as the water was over the roads. It is a dreadful state of things for the country, as the floods are universal—and not only in England but over the whole world. What the farmers are to do I don't know, but many must be ruined.

FEBY 19TH. My dear sister Jane died on Thursday. She had been ill only a few days & went to bed on Wednesday night, by herself, very unwell, and passed away during the night. No better spirit ever passed from life; she was indeed a good woman. She was buried today in the vault at Claines church near Worcester. The following appeared in the Birmingham Daily Gazette Feby 20th 1883 [cutting].

TREGENNA CASTLE HOTEL, ST IVES. WEDNESDAY, MARCH 21, 1883. We came here from London yesterday by the 11.45am train, arriving a little after 9pm. The day was wet. Today it has been very cold and wet; we got out for half an hour in the afternoon.

THURSDAY. It has been dry today but a cold east wind, temp 40°. Had a couple of short walks in the grounds.

GOOD FRIDAY. Bright cold day, temp 40, N.E. wind. Mr & Mrs Fowler came to the hotel last night.

MARCH 24TH. Bright cold day, temp 41°, sun hot. Walked in the grounds and into the town; dined at the table d'hôte.[18]

EASTER SUNDAY. A very fine day, but cold, temp 40.

TUESDAY, MARCH 27. Yesterday and today have been very fine but cold, & some heavy showers of hail today.

MARCH 28. This has been a lovely day and much warmer. We walked through the town to the Head.

MARCH 29. This has been a cold and wet day.

FRIDAY. Day very fine, temp 52°.

SATURDAY. This has been a lovely day. We walked to the monument before lunch and had a long walk in the afternoon.

APL 1, SUNDAY. A beautiful day.

MONDAY, APL 2. We left Tregenna today for home, and had a fine day for our journey.

APL 25, WEDNESDAY. My poor brother-in-law Dunning[19] died at 2am today; he has been long ill. I saw him on Sunday afternoon and had little hope of his lasting long. He has left a large family; I hope they are provided for.

SATURDAY, APL 28TH. We went this morning to attend the church service of the funeral of poor Dunning. It was held in [blank] near Warwick Square; it took place a little after 9am. His body was taken to [blank] in Devonshire to be buried. Mrs Dunning and the family went with it by the 11.15 train on the London & South Western Railway.

PADDINGTON, MAY 27TH. We went to Clewer on the 10th and remained there until the 21st. The first two days were cold and wet, Whit Sunday very fine, the Monday wet during the morning, but we had a drive in the afternoon. All the rest of the time was very fine and warm.

Held my Pro Grand Lodge at Windsor June 18th, a large meeting.

JULY 30TH. We went to Clewer on the 5th for the summer. I have been sitting the last month to Mr Boehm for a bust ordered by the Gt Western shareholders for their new meeting room.

FRIDAY, AUG 10TH. Held our Gt Western half-yearly meeting today. All went off very well.

THURSDAY, AUGT 30TH. Went this afternoon to Birmingham. Stayed at the Gt Western Station Hotel; it is very comfortable.

AUGT 31ST. Went to Oldbury to cut the first sod of the branch to that place.[20] We had a large meeting and dined at the Gt Western Hotel afterwards, returning to Windsor at night.

CLIFTON DOWN HOTEL, SEPT 5. We came down here today to stay; found our rooms & very comfortable.

8TH, CLIFTON. Had an interesting day in seeing a large steamer get aground in the river. They were trying all day to unload her and she was got off on the night tide. She had a very narrow escape of breaking her back. I wonder the river has been left in the state it is [in] so long; they are clearing away the rock at this point, but very slowly, and it ought to have been done years ago.

SEPT 11TH. Went through the Severn Tunnel today. Mr Mott and Mr Castle, two of our directors, went with us. We had a fine day.

CLIFTON, SEPT 12TH. I went today into Wales to visit the Avon colliery with Charlie. Mott went with me. Fortunately it was a fine day.

15TH SEP. My wife was very unwell all last night and I had to send for a doctor this morning. Mr Castle recommended Dr Swayne.

17TH. This was a very fine day; we had a drive to Kings Weston in the afternoon. The doctor is doing Bay good.

20TH. We went today to Weston-Super-Mare. Great changes have been made here since I last saw the place. Our new station is a fine building.[21] Day fine, with one shower; Castle went with us.

21ST. I went this afternoon to Avon Mouth docks.

CLEWER, FRIDAY 28. We left Clifton today and returned home. We were very comfortable at the hotel; it is a very dear one. We were fortunate in having very fine weather on the whole. Clifton is a beautiful place, fine fresh air. Dr Swayne has certainly done my wife a great deal of good.

OCT 10TH, 1883. The large spring that broke out in the Severn Tunnel a couple of years ago broke out in a fresh place today, and much greater in quantity, flooding the tunnel, and a couple of days afterwards the tide rose in the Severn, covering the land and getting down one of our shafts. Fortunately, in the first case no life was lost, but in the latter one man was drowned. So high a tide has not been known for 100 years.

PADDINGTON, NOVR 1. We returned from Clewer to Pad today.

NVR 3RD. We heard today of the death of my old cockatoo; it was given me when I first came to live in Fulthorpe House, Sept 1847. What age it was when given to me I do not know, but even the time I had it was a long life for a bird, 38 years.

NOV 8, THURSDAY. We went to Swindon today by 11.45 train to distribute prizes to the members of the Mechanics' Institution. The day was fine. Lord & Lady Lyttelton and Mr Webster, Queen's Counsel, went with us. All went off very well.

REGENT HOTEL, LEAMINGTON. DECR 21ST, 1883. We came down to Leamington by the 1pm train today; found our old comfortable rooms ready for us. Day fine.

MONDAY 24. Saturday and Sunday were fine dry days, so has it been today. The South Warwickshire hounds met this morning in the Parade and went up and down the street; a good lot of them and a mob of people.

XMAS DAY. This has been a day of fog, but we got our walks before and after lunch. Had our Xmas dinner quietly by ourselves. Our South of Ireland steam ship wrecked this morning.[22]

SATURDAY, 29TH DECR. The last few days have been foggy and damp, but not to prevent our getting our walks. Yesterday we walked into Warwick and came back in the tram. Called upon Mr Muntz. Today we left Leamington by the 12.44 train and returned home; found all right. [*Lower part of page torn away.*]

JANY 1ST, 1884. We have entered upon another year and have much reason to thank God for the many blessings of the past year. My health has continued much better and I hope my dear wife is also better; my chief anxiety is on her account. May God bless us both in the year before us and grant us health and happiness.

THURSDAY, FEBY 14TH. We held our half-yearly meeting today of Gt Western shareholders, and paid 7½ per cent, the best dividend we have paid for some 40 years. All, of course, went off very well. My bust by Boehm was placed in the meeting room and was very much liked.

FEBY 26TH. We held our annual meeting of the Telegraph Construction Co today, and paid our usual 20%.

MARCH 8TH. I have had a very bad cold the last few weeks and have had to call in the doctor and stay several days in doors. We have arranged to go to Madeira on Tuesday next in the SS Scotia. She is going to lay a cable from there to St Vincent. I hope the change will do both my wife and me good.

STEAM SHIP SCOTIA. TUESDAY, MARCH 11TH, 1884. Length of ship 379 feet. Beam 48 feet. Tonage 4,660 tons. Draft at starting 25 feet 9", 2 feet [down] by stern. 1,200 miles of cable. 110 hands and the following passengers: myself and wife, Sir George Elliot and a Mr Bellingfield (a friend of his), Mr Wells (Secretary to Eastern Tel[e]gr[aph] Co), who is making the trip for his health.

We left London by the 10.20am train and got on board ship at about a ¼ before 4, one of the Weymouth tugs taking us off to the Scotia. Capt Halpin met us at the station, he having come by the ship from London, and leaves us here. Frank came down with us to see us off. The weather was very fine all day but a few hours after starting we began to feel the motion of the sea and Bay went to her berth. The weather has also changed and we are likely to have a rough night as the wind is now blowing hard from the west. We dined at 6pm; after dinner had our drinks and coffee in a new deck house which is very comfortable. Capt Halpin has made our cabin accommodation very comfortable and airy. I am to sleep in a hammock hung in the cabin. I liked the hammock in the Gt Eastern better than the berth. This is a very fine ship and I hope we may have fine weather to enable us to enjoy the voyage.

WEDNESDAY, MARCH 12TH. We have had a very rough night last night, the ship rolling very heavily. It is hard on Bay who is feeling it very much, confined to her berth. We breakfasted at 8.30. At noon we were in lat 48–9–45 N, long 5–58–20 W. Distance run 211 miles. The sea has been very heavy and a strong gale of wind making the ship very uncomfortable, having to hold on to something to prevent your falling, and at meals the dishes were sent in all directions. What a lot of crockery there must be broken. There is no pleasure in being at sea in this kind of weather, altho' it has been fine overhead, with occasional showers. The moon was very bright last night; it was full moon. I could not manage to sleep in my hammock very well, it swung about too much for comfort.

THURSDAY, MARCH 13TH. I could not stay in my hammock last night, it bumped against the side of the cabin with the heavy rolls every few minutes, nearly throwing me out; so I got up and moved my bedding to the berth, but what wretched work it is trying to sleep! I did not get an hour's sleep all night—roll, roll, and the noise of things being pitched about and the noise of the screws under my cabin and thumping of the seas. How I wished to be in my comfortable bed at home. But everything has an end, so morning came at last and I got up in time for 8.30 breakfast.

It has blown a heavy gale from the south all day. At 12 we had to go at half speed until 7 at night, heavy seas breaking over our bows and endangering our cable tackle. At noon we were in lat 45–1–0, long 8–36–30, and had made 218 miles, making us 842 miles from Madeira. The weather overhead has been fine all day, but cloudy. We passed 2 steamers today making very bad weather of it. Bay has been very unwell. I should not care so much for all this kicking about for myself, were I not so anxious on her account. I fear the voyage will do her more harm than the visit to Madeira will do her good.

FRIDAY, MARCH 14TH. The weather today has been beautiful overhead and the wind much less, yet the sea is very rough and walking the decks has been impossible. Bay was very poorly in the morning but better later in the day. We passed Cape Finistere at about 6 in the morning but at a distance of about 25 miles. We also got our dinner in a little more comfort. How beautifully bright the stars are at night, Venus magnificent. Position at noon: lat 42–21–0 N, long 10–54–0 W, distance run 189 miles, distance from Madeira 654 miles, so we were about half way at noon.

SATURDAY 15TH. All the early part of the day was very fine and bright, wind moderate but still against us. I got Bay into the deck house for an hour before lunch, which she seemed to enjoy, also for a little time after lunch; this was rather too much for her. At noon we were in lat 38-48-53 N, long 13-2-10 W, distance run 233 miles, leaving us 421 miles from Madeira. Passed a large bark trying in vain to get south. In the afternoon the wind got up and we have had a very heavy sea and unconfortable dinner.

SUNDAY, MARCH 16TH, 1884. We had it very rough last night; I did not get a bit of sleep and wished myself anywhere but rolling about in this ship. The wind has gone to the west and is not so high, but the sea is dreadfully rough. Bay had a better night, getting a good deal of sleep. At noon we were in lat 35-16-6, long 14-51-0. Distance run 230 miles, and now 191 miles from Madeira. We had no service on board. We hope to make our port early tomorrow morning. Met one of D. Currie's ships at 11am.

ST CLARA HOTEL, FUNCHAL, MARCH 17TH, 1884. I looked out of my port at day light this morning and saw land, so dressed and went on deck just as the sun was rising. It was a lovely morning and the view of the island as we passed along and so to this place was very lovely. We dropped our anchor at 7. The first view of the town of Funchal is very beautiful, and there was snow on the mountains at the back, which fell yesterday. It is quite an open roadstead, no kind of shelter; fortunately the change of the wind to the west made the water quite smooth. We were soon surrounded with boats and all kinds of things for sale brought on deck—fruit, basket work and jewelry. I bought Bay a splendid ring for a £. I was able to dress comfortably and eat my breakfast without having it pitched into my lap or my neighbour's, but the ship rolled very heavily all night up to as late as 5am. How pleasant it is to feel on land and find you can walk without holding on to something!

After breakfast Mr Cardwell, the manager of this hotel, came on board and undertook to make all the arrangements for our landing, which we did at about ¼ past 10. This is rather an amusing operation; the beach is very steep, certainly equal to an angle of 45°, and consists of large rolling stones 4 or 5 inches in dia[meter]. When the boat gets near the shore she is turned with her stern to it, and a large wave is waited for, upon the crest of which she is cast up in the shingle. A lot of men being ready to lay hold of her, a couple of oxen are quickly hooked on and rollers placed under her as she moves, and is so run up onto the flat. Mr Cardwell attended to our luggage going through the custom house. They opened everything, it was said because the gentleman was in a bad humour. We, however, at once got into one of the carriages of the place—it is a sledge drawn by 2 oxen, and so travelled up to this hotel, where we found very comfortable rooms. The sitting room is a large one with beautiful views from the windows of both sea and hills. We lunched at the table d'hote and also dined there, but will in future use our own room.

I received a long telegram from Sir Jas Anderson, as annexed [*now missing*]. This has put Elliot[23] into a fix as if there is an immediate dissolution of Parl't he is in the wrong place and may have to get back by the mail boat as quickly as he can. The fight with Osman Digna in the Soudan has been a rather serious affair. I am anxious to see the papers & get full information as to the battle, and also Parliament matters. I am glad to find Col Wood[24] is all safe.

I walked into the town for a couple of hours after lunch. We have had bright sun shine with frequent tropical showers of rain, straight up and down. I called at the tel[e]gr[aph] office; Mr C. H. Reynell, the sup[erintenden]t, has also been very attentive to us and done all he can to put us in the right way. Mr & Miss Hinton called upon us and invited us to lunch with them on Wednesday at 1.30. I am looking forward to a good night's rest.

FUNCHAL, TUESDAY 18TH. This has been a lovely day, the heat not very great, about 65 in our room, but afternoon hotter in the sun. We sit with our windows open until nearly sun set, when it gets colder. I am told it has been as low at 50° the last night; on our voyage we had about 60°, not higher than 65 at any time. I spent my morning on the large balcony at the hotel watching our shipping operations. The sea was beautiful for laying the shore end of the cable, and about 12 the ship took up her position off the cable house and commenced the work, and started at 3 on her voyage. God grant it may be a successful one. The ship is in charge of very good hands: Cato, capt. 1st officer Macvittie. 2nd officer Ladd. Chief engineer Slater. Lucas chief engineer in charge of cable. I have been very much pleased with Lucas, having found him a well-informed and very intelligent man. We are fortunate in having so good an officer. Doctor: Wrackham & Dr Wildey, my Dr, who is staying here with us. Brown is the chief electrician, a man of great experience. Donavan is the electrician to be left in charge here. Ford is on board, representing the cable company.[25]

After seeing the ship fairly off, Bay & I went for a walk in the town for 1½ hours, a good result from her after her voyage. This is Sir George Elliot's birth day, so we had him to dine with us. He is 69 years of age. We did not find walking at all difficult; I was told we could not walk at all and must either go in a bullock cart, on horseback, or in a hammock, a most uncomfortable-looking thing. I must try one.

They gave us at dinner yesterday some custard apple; it is grown here, the flavour is very pleasant. How abundant and beautiful the flowers are, roses in particular. Mrs Cardwell sent to our room not a bouquet but a basket 2 feet long × a foot, full of beautiful flowers.

WEDNESDAY, MARCH 19TH. This has been a beautiful day, heat much as yesterday. I was rather inclined to be lazy & did not go out in the morning: the climate does not produce a feeling of great activity. Had telegram saying cable going on all right, position at noon lat 30–44–0, long 18–3. Cable paid out 142·5 k[no]ts, so this is good news.[26] At one oclock we started in a bullock carriage for Mr Hinton's house, called The Til, after the name of a large tree in the garden. It took us about 20 minutes to get there up hill. We were very kindly received by the family, Mr & Mrs Hinton and 3 daughters—Mary a very nice girl. There are also some sons but they were not at home. We had a very nice lunch and some very good light Madeira. After lunch we went into the garden; the flowers are simply a wilderness. I do not admire it as it has a look of untidiness. There is the remains of a very fine old chestnut, about 33 feet in circumfer[ence], but without any life left in it. All their gardens are made ground on the side of a steep hill, and terraced; it must have been costly work moving the soil. A fruit tree called Loquat is now in full bearing, the fruit being in different stages of ripeness; it is yellow, about the size of an ordinary plum. I had some in a tart; it has a pleasant flavour. There are not many orange trees about. Mrs Cardwell sent us a very beautiful bouquet of flowers. We walked back to the hotel from Mr Hinton's and did not go out afterwards as Bay had a bad pain in her head. Mr Blandy lunched with us at the Hintons.

THURSDAY, MARCH 20TH. I walked down to the beach this morning & looked at the market places. There were no fish, I suppose we were too late in the day, and I did not see much in the fruit & flower market. There is a very interesting old gateway leading from the beach into the town, said to have been built by Collumbus; it has a small chapel in the top. Afternoon we went to hear the band which plays Thursdays and Sundays in the public promenade, beginning at half past 4. It is a military band, and they played very well. Report from the Scotia today is at noon lat 28–37–5, long 19–5–0, total cable paid out 297 + 35 knots, or 155 k in the last 24 hours = 6½ k per hour. All going well.

I wonder how they do in cold weather here to keep warm. This large sitting room of ours, with 4 windows, has no fireplace, nor have any of the bedrooms. The public rooms, I see, have one, but even now it is not too warm in an evening, not more than 64° or 65°. Bay saw her doctor this morning, but she is better this evening. The day has been very fine.

FRIDAY, MARCH 21ST. The day has been fine, with a rather cool east wind. I was glad to have my light overcoat on, particularly in the morning. We went down to the beach before lunch. Some steamers came in, one of the British and African Line came from Liverpool. The Cape mail has been expected all day; some people in the hotel are going home in her, Sir John & Lady Johnson.[27] She may arrive during the night. Pleasant to get out of bed and go on board ships. After luncheon today we walked to Jones' Hotel to call upon Mr & Mrs Benett Stanford. He was out but we spent a pleasant half hour with her. I counted 5 steamers in the bay this afternoon. Ship at noon lat 26–27, long 20–14. Cable laid 459·4 k.

SATURDAY, MARCH 22. There was a cold east wind for a few hours this morning, but the wind changed to S.W. and it became warmer. We went to the beach before lunch, called upon Mr Blandy at his office and visited the English club of which I am a member—paid 12/6 for the month. It is a very comfortable club overlooking the sea. After lunch we went to call upon Mrs Blandy at her home, Quinta de S Luzia; it is up a very long & steep hill on the way to the mount. We had a bullock cart, or a carro as they are called. The gardens at Mr Blandy's are like all the others, wild with vegetation. However, there are some beautiful ferns and the view from the garden is very fine. There is no grass anywhere, so I greatly miss our pretty English lawns; they are much prettier than the wilderness of flowers. The Cape steamer has not come in yet. Position of Scotia, noon: lat 24–13, long 21–23. Cable laid 625·7 ks.

SUNDAY, MARCH 23, 1884. This has been a very fine day and some-what warmer than we have had it. I took half an hour's walk before lunch and went into the English cemetery; it is full of flowers, but not particularly well kept. There is a very large pepper tree and they had just cut one down. Afternoon we went down to the promenade to see a great religious procession called, I believe, Mid Lent. It was a very long one, consisting of priests & others. There were also, I should say, 50 children, 3 or 4 years of age, dressed in blue and silver with little wings on their back, each led, poor little thing, by a grown-up person. They carried various things in their hands: one a scourge or whip, another a cross, another a nail and another a hammer. Poor little monkeys, what folley. There was a military band and 60 or 70 soldiers. Great crowds of people were assembled to see it. We afterwards went to see the Duke of Edinburgh Hotel. Mr & Miss Reed were very polite and took us over it. The situation is not a good one. They gave us some flowers from the garden. Mr Reynell was with us during the afternoon and took us into the garden of the new premises they have purchased for tel[e]g[rap]h offices.

Position of the ship today: lat 21–55, long 22–39, cable laid 798 ks, so they are getting on very well; they have had very fine weather. Their last day's work is over 7 kts per hour; they have each day made some little advance in speed.

The Cape mail steamer Spartan came in this morning at half past 8, and left again for England at half past 11. Some of our visitors here went with her.

MONDAY, MARCH 24. A week today since we arrived. The weather has been beautiful and today most lovely. We took a good walk before lunch into the town, and explored that part of it near the fort &c. After lunch we had a long and beautiful walk; a Mr Brown, who when at home lives at Teignmouth, went with us and shewed us the road. We walked up the hill to the east end of the Levada; this Levada is a level road a couple of miles long, 500 feet above the sea and following the contours of the hills. There is a water channel made along it from which the houses below can get water. The views from it are very beautiful and the weather was very perfect. It was a stiff walk for Bay but she managed it and does not seem any worse.

There was a religious procession tonight, similar to that of yesterday;

they came up the hill to the church in the St Clara Convent close to the hotel. Here the effect was pretty as you looked down the street filled with torches wending their way up the hill. After being in the church for 10 minutes they started off again.

Tel[e]gr[am] from Scotia: lat 19–37, long 23–48, cable laid 968·16 kts. They hope to bouy end at noon tomorrow; if so, and they have no special difficulty with the repairs, they ought to be back here very early next week.[28]

The water here is beautifully soft, almost like oil. It quite makes one's skin shine. The drinking water is also very good; it is obtained best from a spring near the shore in the grounds of the Governor, and people send here for it, the ordinary water from the hills not being good for drinking.

MARCH 25TH, TUESDAY. This has been another beautiful day. They had a very bad winter here, no fine weather, until we came, since when the weather has been real Madeira weather, particularly the last 4 or 5 days. We went down to the beach before lunch and sat there an hour. The mail steamer Trojan for the Cape came in just as we got down, or a little before 12, & we were amused in seeing the boats go and come from her. Some of the passengers landed and went a drive in the bullock carts; 7 landed to stay in the islands. She sailed about 4 oclock for the Cape. We got some letters and I was able to borrow some newspapers, as none were sent to me. In the afternoon we went to the cable house beyond the fort; we were fortunate to get there just at the time they were going [to] bouy the end of the cable at St Vincent, and saw the last few test signals, when I was able to send a message of congratulations to them in the ship. They have had splendid weather for the work; if it keeps so a few days I hope they will easily repair the fault.

After leaving the cable house we went to the house of one of our tel[e]gr[aph] staff to see another religious procession composed chiefly of young girls dressed in white. There were a great many of them, but there were also a lot of men and boys, and they sang as they went along; a band also accompanied them. It was rather a pretty sight. Today is a Festa Neve and all the shops are supposed to be closed and no work done. The town was full of people from the country in their Sunday dresses. I am told they walk from all parts of the island to attend & see this particular procession.

Position of Scotia, noon: lat 17–12, long 24–57. Cable laid 1,145 kts.

WEDNESDAY, MARCH 26TH. We have had two new sensations today: a ride in a hammock and down the mountain on a sledge. We had an invitation from Mr Reid, the landlord of this and all the other large hotels, to go to his Quinta Bom Successa on the hill, and lunch. Several of our party were also invited. Bay and I started at half past 12 in hammocks, a most unpleasant mode of travelling—a swinging kind of motion and a very constrained position. I also could not help feeling a kind of sense of shame at seeing the men sweating and blowing as they carried me up the hills. I do not think it will tempt me again. It took us ¾ of an hour to get up. This Quinta was bought by Mr Reid a couple of years ago for 350£; the grounds are large but the house is a cottage. It can be made a beautiful place and the views from it are very fine. The air was also cooler than in the town—we were up about 1,100 feet above the sea. We had a capital lunch with good Madeira, and sat and walked about until 5 oclock, when we started down the hill in a sledge. This is better than the hammock and, of course, we went pretty quick, but I would rather walk if it were possible. When we got down we called in at Miles' Hotel, also belonging to Mr Reed, and looked over the gardens; there are some fine trees and plants. The silver banana grows very large; there is also a fine camphor tree and two large custard apples. He (Mr Reid) gathered a couple of apples for us and we will try to ripen them, which is done by wraping them up in flannel. We gathered strawberries in the garden on the mountain, and were very tired when we got back to our hotel at 6.30.

The cable was bouyed last night in 540 fathoms, lat 17–7–20, long 24–58, and this morning the ship proceeded to grapple for the broken end of the Pernambuco section, but up to this evening had failed to get it. I will hope for better accounts tomorrow. The new caple [cable] is very perfect. The day has been very fine, not too hot; sun temp 80°, shade about 68°. I looked into the St Clara church this morning. One end has half of its area occupied with Clara gratings, beyond which the nuns have their portion of the church. Very few nuns are left in this convent now, no new ones are admitted.

THURSDAY, MARCH 27TH. We went this morning with Miss Mary Hinton to do some shopping. She is a nice sensible girl, and has her head well set on her shoulders. After lunch we called upon Mrs Faber at Quinta S Ivas; we had some difficulty in finding the entrance to the

house. It is a good house when you get into it. We returned to the hotel
and attended a musical reception given by a lady of the name of Beving-
ton and her daughter, who are in the hotel. Found half an hour of this
quite enough and left very early. We had a dinner party in our room;
Mr Reynell, the cable supt here, and his daughter, and Mr Wildey my
doctor. The weather today has been very uncertain, frequent heavy
showers. The news from the ship is they have not yet managed to put
the repairs through. I hope we will hear of its being done tomorrow.
Had a telegram from Richards and Renton this morning, congratulations on success of cable.

FRIDAY, MARCH 28. The cable was repaired this morning and messages have been very plentiful. We will now be able to settle about the
day we leave here. I had a long telegram from Anderson this morning,
but not any striking news. I had a short one between 4 & 5 this afternoon telling me of the sad death of the Duke of Albany; poor Queen, it
will be a great blow to her. May God comfort and support her is my
earnest prayer and will be that of millions of her subjects.

The weather today has been colder; there is a coating of snow on the
mountains and pretty low down. We had frequent showers of rain up to
one oclock, with sun shine between. Had a walk up the hill beyond our
hotel in the morning; stood under a pepper tree for one shower and got
into a carpenter's shop for another. Afternoon we went to see Mr
Hinton's sugar manufactory. I was much astonished at the quantity of
juice there was in the cane; it ran from the rollers in a stream certainly
6 or 7 inches wide and an inch deep. The smell of the place is not very
agreeable. We went from there to the tel[e]gr[aph] office and along to
Mr Reid's, where we had a cup of tea.

SATURDAY, MARCH 29TH. A Liverpool boat came in this morning and
brought letters from Anna & T. A boat also arrived from the Cape and
took home letters, also a boat from Lisbon, so that the bay looked quite
gay. The weather at St Vincent is rough and prevents them completing
the cable. I hope this will not last long. I am quite ready to go home;
this is not a place that will do for a long stay. We had a walk before
lunch and in the afternoon had a carro and went to call upon the
Hintons, then to Dr Grabham's. His gardens are well worth seeing; he
has so fine of [sic] collection of both trees and shrubs. There is a large
tree planted by Capt Cook; he is said to have lived in the Quinta. Mrs

Grabham was very kind and took us over the grounds. They do not cover a large area but are full of beautiful plants too numerous to mention. We went from there to Mr Blandy's, and so back to the hotel at 6 oclock. It was a wet afternoon, frequent heavy showers; fortunately it cleared up for a short time when we were at Dr Grabham's, enabling us to get out into the gardens.

A sad event has occurred in the hotel today. Mrs Cobbold, the wife of a banker at Southampton, came here in the autumn for her health, but has lately gradually got worse and died this afternoon at 5 oclock. I saw the first fire today I have seen in the island; Mrs Hinton had one in her drawing room made of fir cones.

SUNDAY, 30TH MARCH. This has been a cold day and wet most of the afternoon. Before lunch we walked as far as the English cemetery and saw the grave prepared for poor Mrs Cobbold, who was buried this afternoon at 5 oclock. A few of the gentlemen from the hotel accompanied the funeral; I would have gone but was afraid of standing in the cold and wet. We did not go out in the afternoon. Ship says hopes to be here on Sunday next. They broke their grapnell rope when about to make the last splice yesterday afternoon. This will delay them a day I fear. I shall be very glad to find myself back at Fulthorpe; it was a mistake coming so far from home.

MONDAY, MARCH 31ST. Bay was very unwell this morning, a severe attack of sickness came on between 4 & 5 oclock. For the first time in our life she was unable to be with me at breakfast. Dr Wildey gave her some medicine and she is much better this evening and I hope will be all right tomorrow. There must have been something the matter with the fish or other dish at dinner the day before, as I felt some reaching when dressing this morning.

The day has been fine and warmer than yesterday. They have finished the cable, making the last splice this evening between 4 & 6 oclock. I hope the ship will be here by Monday in next week at the latest, and we may get away on Tuesday. I had a walk before and after lunch.

TUESDAY, APRIL 1ST. Bay was better this morning. Several people in the hotel were not well yesterday; they blame a tongue. We did not go out before going to Mr Blandy's to lunch; this is in fact *their* dinner, and they have a strong tea at 7. We had a beautiful lunch and some splendid Madeira wine. Mrs Blandy is a very pleasant woman, young. They have some curious trees, the names of which I do not remember. We kept our cow cart to bring us back as I thought the walk would be too much for Bay. The Scotia leaves St Vincent tonight at 9pm and they expect to be here on Sunday morning. I shall be glad to find myself at home again. Today has been fine but cool, particularly after lunch, and rain came on between 4 & 5 and continues. Snow continues to fall upon the mountains; they are quite white.

WEDNESDAY, APL 2. There have been some showers this morning but I took a short walk. We went to lunch with Dr Grabham at the Quinta de Val. He shewed me his electric clocks & many other curiosities. In his bed room he has a large clock 18″ dia[meter] and the hands are painted with luminous paint so that he can always see the time. He also paints the edges of the doors with it so as to see them in the dark. They were very kind and seem nice people. We had a carriage and pair to take us up and down. On our return we walked down to the beach and back; the evening has been wet with some very heavy rain. The people complain sadly of the weather, which they say is very unusual.

THURSDAY APL 3. Walked down into the town to see the progress made with the trench for the land line between the cable house and the office. In the afternoon we walked to call upon Mr & Mrs Addison, the English chaplain and his wife. They live in a nice little Quinta near Jones' Hotel. On our return we stopped to hear the band play in the promenade. We have had showers of rain all day and tonight it is very wet. The homeward mail has not yet come in; there are several people in the hotel who are going with her. It is very disagreeable to have to be all packed up ready to go on board at a short notice either day or night, as the steamer only stops 4 hours. Elliot talks of going by her, but I hardly think he will turn out in the middle of the night.

FRIDAY, APL 4TH. The mail steam ship Moor came in this morning about 10 oclock, much to the comfort of those who were going with her. We went down to the beach to see the passengers embark. A Lisbon steamer was also sailing at 12 oclock and 22 English people left the island by the two boats. There was a heavy surf on, breakers 6 or 7 feet high, and it was rather good fun seeing the boats getting through them, seldom without a wetting for those on board, and sometimes a good deal of wetting. 2 boats were swamped, but as a rule the men manage the boats exceedingly well. I will hope for fine weather when we have to start.

Elliot went by the Moor; he had not made up his mind 5 minutes before getting into the boat to go on board. He asked Bay should he go, who of course gave no advice, and without saying anything more went and got into a boat without his luggage or any overcoat, sending his servant to the hotel to fetch them, which there was hardly time to do before the boat sailed. I did not see him on the beach, but saw him get into a boat by himself and get a good wetting into the bargain. He had no ticket. The Moor left at 2pm.

After lunch we walked for an hour in the town. There was a rough wind at [sic] it felt cold, and about 5 oclock it came on to rain and has been a very wet evening. The early part of the day was bright. We have had a good deal of rain here; snow continues on the hills.

SATURDAY, APL 5TH. There was a heavy shower of rain between 8 & 9 this morning; the rest of the day has been very fine. In the morning we went down to the beach and along the cable trench, and in the afternoon had a walk. We were very glad during our afternoon walk to see the Scotia in the distance. She reached her anchorage at 5pm, having made a very good run from St Vincent. Captain Cato & Lucas came to the hotel to see me and as they will be able to complete the land line & their coaling by tomorrow midday we have settled to start at 3pm. If we have a good voyage we ought to be at Weymouth on Friday, & so be able [to] get home on Saturday. This will be very nice if we can carry it out. Miss Hinton came and sat with us for half an hour between 5 & 6. She is quite a blessing to her friends. The moon is beautifully bright tonight, the first time we have had it so. I hope we are to have some fine weather as the glass is going up and the snow & clouds have cleared away from the mountains.

SUNDAY, APL 6TH. This has been a very fine day. I went down to the shore to see how they were getting on with the laying of the land lines. There are 4 of them; they hope to finish either tonight or early tomorrow. This being Palm Sunday is a great day amongst the Catholics. I went into the cathedral a little before 11 and went up into the gallery at the west end, where I could look down upon the people and see all that was going on at the high altar. The middle part of the building was filled chiefly with women, the men being in the side isles. The effect of the different col[oure]d handkerchiefs worn by the women as a head dress had a very pretty effect, very like a flower bed. All those who took part in the programme went up to the altar and received from the bishop a palm, very prettily plaited and decorated with flowers, after which a procession was formed and they passed down the side isle out at a side door and, I understand, walked round the church outside and in again at the chief west entrance, so up the middle of the building to the altar. I cannot see what religion there is in all this ceremony.

We went down to the cable again after lunch and called at the Duke of Edinburgh to say good bye to the Reids who have been very civil. Bay attended the English church in the morning. The weather tonight is beautiful, with a bright moon; looking from our sitting room windows the views are very pretty, the mountains one one side studded with white houses, and the sea with 9 or 10 vessels with their lights on the water. Two steamers have come in today but they bring no letters. The City of Paris steamer came in here on Friday to take emigrants to the Sandwich Islands. They expect to take 500 from here; it will be good for the people as there are many more workers than work and much poverty and distress exists. I hope the day will be fine for our start tomorrow.

SS Scotia. Monday Apl 7. We came on board this afternoon at 3 and started at 3.15, so we were very punctual. Fortunately the sea was very calm and we had no difficulty in leaving the shore. It has been a very fine day. I walked down to the Tel[egra]p[h] office in the morning and went into the club for $\frac{1}{4}$ of an hour, all I have had for my 13/4 subscription.[29] Later called upon Mr Blandy. We left our hotel with regret for we had been made very comfortable there. Both Mr & Mrs Cardwell have done all in their power to make us comfortable. I was surprised at the small amount of our bill, as we had good rooms and plenty to eat— tea at 7, breakfast at 9, lunch at 1.30, tea at 4, dinner at 7.30, and coffee or tea afterwards if desired. All these meals and the rooms were charged at only about 2£ per day for my wife & I and 2 servants. Miss Mary Hinton came and sat with us for an hour and had her lunch with us.

Madeira is not a place I should like to make a long stay at; the last few days I have felt better than I did before—I suppose I have got more used to the climate. Dr Grabham says it takes 2 or 3 weeks to do so and then the climate begins to do good, but people had better not come for only a couple of weeks. It has been very enjoyable sitting on the deck and watching the island as we coasted along it, looking back upon the east end. The mountains are very beautiful, very rugged, and [*word missing*] today, with light fleecy clouds hanging about them. We passed the islands of Porto Santa and the Desertas before dark. There is a sharp needle rock standing up by itself at the end of the Desertas you may easily take for a ship. We have had it very smooth so far. Bay dined with us in the saloon. Our ship is making good speed, a little over 12 kts. I hope we will carry good weather with us home. The night is rather cloudy and there has been a shower of rain since dinner.

SS Scotia. Tuesday, 8 Apl. We have had a very fine day, bright sun shine after early morning when it threatened rain. The sea has also been very calm so that it was possible to walk the decks in comfort. Bay has also been very well, with the exception of a head ache. She spent the day from 12.30 to 5.30 in the chart house on deck. Our position at noon was lat 36–12–15 N, long 14–26–30 W. Distance run since start 254 k, or a speed of 12·2 k per hour. If we can keep this up we ought to be in Weymouth on Friday night; it will be very pleasant if we can. The night is slightly cloudy but we can see the moon.

Wednesday, Apl 9th. This has been a very fine day, warm and calm; we were able to walk with comfort. Bay was on deck all day, had her lunch and dinner in the chart house. We will be in the Bay of Biscay about 3 in the morning; I hope the smooth sea will continue. At noon we were in lat 40–35–11 N, long 55–5–0 [W], having made 288 kts. We had to take in the sail during last night as the wind fell off. We are at noon 724 miles from Weymouth. I fear it means early Saturday morning for us to get in. The moon is shining brightly tonight through light clouds.

Thursday, Apl 10th. The day has been cold & cloudy, no sun and occasionally slight rain. We have seen a large number of steamers. The sea has been perfectly calm and we had sail on the forward part of the ship. Position at noon lat 44–46–2 N, lon 8–40–0 W. Distance run 290 miles, leaving 434 miles to Weymouth. We will not be able to land tomorrow night.

GOOD FRIDAY, APL 11TH. We passed Ushant this morning at 10 oclock, close enough to see the land well. It is a wild looking place. The sea was very calm but a cold east wind blowing, day fine with cloud & sun shine. We saw a great number of steamers & ships, all the steamers we passed we left them a long way astern. Off the Start light at 7 this evening, a beautiful clear moonlight night, and we will drop our anchor in Weymouth between 12 & 1. Our speed has been very good, having made quite 12 ks per hour on the whole voyage. It has been a great contrast with our outward passage. Bay has also been very well, dined in the saloon today and has been able to spend her days in the chart house on the deck and get a short walk at times. Lat 48–47–0, long 4–58–30; distance from Weymouth 150 ks.

FULTHORPE HOUSE, APL 12TH. Just a month today since we started. The ship cast anchor at 12.30 this morning and we had our breakfast on board at 8, and the tug took us off at 8.30; a lovely morning. We stayed at the Burdon until the 12 oclock train, arriving at home a little after 6pm and found all well, the dogs very delighted to see us. We are both better for our trip and have much reason to be thankful to God for His many mercies to us.

MAY 4TH, 1884. Since my return home I have been appointed by the Government on a committee to enquire into the conditions under which contracts are invited for the building or repairing of ships, including their engines, for Her Majesty's Navy, and into the mode in which repairs and refits of ships are effected in the dockyards. The committee consists of:

> Lord Ravensworth, chairman
> Sir Daniel Gooch
> Mr Samuda
> Mr C. Palmer
> Mr Ismay
> Mr Burns
> Capt Codrington

We met on Friday last to arrange the mode of our proceedings.

I have been suffering the last week from pain in my head and tooth ache, and yesterday had one extracted, which has given me relief I hope will last.

[*Two leaves removed from the MS*]

JUNE 10TH, 1884. We have spent Whitsun holidays at Clewer. We went down on the 30th May and returned on the 9th June. The first few days up to the Tuesday were very fine, after that wet and cold. The rain was, however, very badly wanted for the grass and crops. Flo & Loo Newton[30] were with us. My poor dog Judy died in our absence from Paddington after only 8 or 10 hours illness. She was quite well when I left but as she was 13½ years old it was not surprising; she died simply of old age. She had been a nice creature & I miss her very much.

I held my Pro Grand Lodge on the 16 inst at Wycombe; we had a very good meeting. After dinner I went to pay a visit to the grave of Lord Beaconsfield at Hug[h]enden and placed some flowers on his grave. The church is a nice old building. I also went over the house and was disappointed not to find it a better building. I was glad to have this opportunity of visiting the place of the great man's home and grave, and gathered a few flowers as on the other side.

We went to Clewer on the 30th May for the Whitsun week. My poor old and faithful dog Judy died on the 4 June while we were away. She died of old age, being 14 years old. I will miss her, poor thing, as she had been a very true and faithful companion.

JUNE 19TH, 1884. Went to Chatham dock yard with the Admiralty committee today to look over the ships and works. I was much disappointed with the extravagant system on which they conduct such large works. The tools are old and out of date and are very costly to work. A private establishment would soon be ruined if they carried on their works in such a manner. We had a good lunch at the home of the chief supt, and returned home in the evening.

We had a bazar on the 13th [&] 14th in our garden and the adjoining one on behalf of the funds of St Saviour church;[31] it answered very well, leaving a balance of about £800.

JULY 3RD. Went with the Admiralty committee today to the docks, to see an iron clad built by Samuda for the Brazilian govt. She is a fine ship and well finished.

FRIDAY, JULY 4TH. We went to Clewer today for the summer. Finished my park hay on the 5th.

JULY 24TH, 1884. Went with some of our Gt Western directors to Bristol.

25TH. We went today through the Severn Tunnel as far as we could; works all going on well. The big spring not so heavy as it has been; hope we are now fully master of it. We returned home at night. We have finished our Admiralty committee and made our report.

AUGT 14TH. We held our Gt Western half-yearly meeting today. The dividend was less than last year by ¼ per cent. All went off very well. The trade of the country is very bad and I see no prospect of improvement.

SEPT 4TH. Left Clewer for the Imperial Hotel at Malvern, where we had our old and comfortable rooms. Day very fine and night lovely, with moon.

SEPT 12TH. The weather on the whole has been fine, and we have had our daily walks. The 6th was cold and we had a fire in our room, but since it has been very hot.

My old friend Mr F. Gower died today at the great age of 90. He was a Great Western director when I first joined the company, and told me that when Mr Brunel proposed to the board to appoint me he had objected to it because I was so young; Mr Brunel said I would mend of this. Upon how little does the course of one's life depend; suppose he had had his way, what might have been my life?

SEPT 25, THURSDAY. We left Malvern for Clewer today. The weather has been very hot, the temp in the shade one day as high as 85°. It has been, on the whole, dry and fine, and I have enjoyed my daily walks. One day we drove round by West Malvern. Bay, I am sorry to say, has not been well, suffering from a swelling in the leg with a great deal of pain, and she has in consequence not been able to accompany me as much as usual. We have been very comfortable at the hotel and it has been very full. Malvern is certainly a very nice place to spend a few weeks, and the air is fresh and scenery very beautiful. We had not been here before when the trees were in leaf. They have now established capital baths at the hotel and bring the salt brine from Droitwich for rhumatic people.

OCT 2ND. There was a very beautiful full e[c]lipse of the moon tonight. The sky was very clear and it was seen to great advantage.

OCT 25TH. Mr Robinson, one of our Gt Western directors, and I went to Cardiff this afternoon. I stayed with Charlie.

OCT 26. We spent today in visiting the collieries. Robinson returned home.

OCT 27TH. I went this morning to the Severn Tunnel. Lord Bessborough[32] met me there. Before lunch we inspected the surface work, and after lunch went below. It fortunately happened that the headings were just meeting & by the time we had finished lunch the men had got a small hole through, making the tunnel open throughout. I was the first to creep through and Lord Bessborough followed me. It was a very difficult piece of navigation, but by a little pulling in front and pushing behind we managed it, and the men gave us some hearty cheers. I am glad I was the first to go through as I have taken great interest in this great work, which is now getting fast towards completion. The spring is now about 7,000 gallons per minute, but is fully under the control of the pumps, and a fresh pump is just ready to start which will give us very ample power, more than double of our present wants. A heading is being driven parallel with the tunnel so as to turn this water from the line of tunnel and so enable us to complete this short length of about 200 yards. The side heading will then be built out. I hope by June or July next the tunnel will be finished.[33] Lord Bessborough went to Ireland and I went to stay with Alfred at Chepstow.

SATURDAY 18. I left Chepstow and returned to Clewer.

OCTR 30TH, THURSDAY. We left Clewer today for London. The past summer has been a wonderfully fine one; I do not recollect so continued fine, dry weather. The water in the country is very scarce. Parliament met yesterday for an autumn session, to try and pass the Franchise Bill.

It has created a great sensation in the country. Throughout the recess Gladstone has been stamping Scotland and all the politicians on both sides have been holding monster meetings, the Lords having thrown out the Bill last session because it was not accompanied by a distribution of seats bill. What will now happen I cannot tell; it rests with the Lords. I think the Lords were wrong in throwing out the Bill. They ought to have passed it, but providing it should not come into operation until a distribution bill was passed.

Oct 29th, 1884. I heard today of the loss of a very dear & old friend in the death of Mrs. F. Pavy. She has been long ill. Some years ago she lost a very favourite daughter, and has since never recovered the shock, but her death was caused by cancer in the breast & throat. She was a good and kind creature and very kind to me some years ago in my great sorrow. I had a note from the doctor informing me of her death.

Nov 18th, 1884. There was a large meeting today at the Carlton Club, of Lords & Commons, to discuss the position of the party with reference to the Franchise & Redistribution Bills; Lord Salisbury in the chair. The offer of the Govt to a joint meeting of the leaders of the two parties to hold a meeting with the hope of agreeing on a distribution bill was adopted, so I hope this useless contest will now come to an end.

Nov 25. The enclosed slip cut from the Windsor paper is a very truthful account of our Members' private smoking room in the House of Commons. We have had this room now about 3 years. Before, the smoking room was open to the friends of members and it was an uncomfortable place. I have very often gone to the new room for an hour before the meeting of the House, and have enjoyed the fun more than the House.

Burdon Hotel, Weymouth. Decr 22. We came down to Weymouth today. The day was very fine with a sharp frost, and are in possession of our old rooms.

Decr 23rd. Very cold and dull, N.E. wind; the coldest we have [had] at Weymouth. The house is also very cold from not being occupied, we being the only customers. Hard work to get our sitting room above 50°. Got my usual walks.

DECR 24. There was a slight covering of snow on the hills this morning. Temp 40°, wind as yesterday. Had 3 good walks; cloudy.

THURSDAY, DEC 25TH. This has been a bright, sunny day, temp 40°. Just before dinner I got a copy of the Telegraph paper and saw what the Gt Western receipts were for last week, and [this] did not add to the enjoyment of my Xmas dinner. I find they were down by £25,159; the largest drop I ever knew in railway receipts. This is partly due to the Xmas traffic not falling in the same week as last year, so that the next return will to some extent recover the loss.

DECR 26. This has been a dull, cold day, N.E. wind, temp 40°. Had a good walk in the morning. Bay did not go out as she had a tumble in her room and shook herself a little.

DECR 27. A very cold N.E. wind, temp 35°. Had a walk about the station and new engine house. Had a very short walk after lunch.

WEYMOUTH, SUNDAY, DECR 28. A wretched cold N.E. wind and dull. Had a walk in the morning but did not go out after lunch. Temp 38°.

MONDAY, 29TH. Still very cold and dull. Temp 39°, wind N.E. I dined with Mr Howard[34] to meet Henry Edwards, M.P. for Weymouth, and a Mr Lundy. We had a good dinner.

TUESDAY 30. The day has been very pleasant as compared with what we have had. I had a good walk in the morning and went over our steam ship the Great Western. Temp 38°, wind N.E.

WEDNESDAY 31. It has been a good deal warmer today. Temp 44°. Capt Lecky came and I went over the s[team] ship Gael with him. Had a long walk after lunch. Wind S.E.

WEYMOUTH. JANY 1ST, 1885. Another year has passed and I have much cause to thank God for His great mercy to me. I have had much better health and have much cause for thankfullness. I regret I am unable to say as much for my dear wife; she has been very unwell during the autumn, but I trust she is now better and will soon be restored to good health. Our stay here has been of service to her. God grant that this year may bring that great blessing to her.

The state of trade in the country is in a desperately depressed condition, and our look out in political matters could not be worse. The extension of the franchise has been carried, giving votes to 2,000,000 extra voters, but that can do no good; it will not create trade nor confidence, and may bring about a change even for the worse. It is difficult to foresee what this large increase of power in the hands of the working classes may produce. The whole power is now in their hands; we can only hope it will be wisely used, and I trust a change in the govt will before long take place and our dear old England be preserved from decline and ruin.

The weather today has been cold, with a S.E. wind.

FRIDAY, JANY 2, 1885. This has been a cold and windy day from S.E., chan[g]ing in the afternoon to N.E. I got my walks under difficulty.

SATURDAY 3RD. We left Weymouth by 12 oclock train today and returned home to London. Day much warmer. We found all well at home and glad to find our own home comforts. The Burdon Hotel has many defects; it is cold and badly furnished and very dear. Our bill was nearly £4 per day, instead of about £3, my usual cost at an hotel. My wife, however, is I think much better for the change and that is worth any cost.

MONDAY, FEBY 2, 1885. My dear grand child Mary Newton[35] died today at her uncle Newton's house, where she had been for some weeks. Poor child, she suffered sadly, and her death was perhaps a happy relief. She is now happy and at peace with her God. Who would call back so pure a spirit to the cares and troubles of this world?

THURSDAY, FEBY 5TH. Bad news reached us today from Khartoum, the town has fallen to the Maida [Mahdi] and General Gordon is either killed or a prisoner. Our Govt of old women have wickedly brought upon the country the disgrace and sorrow of this event upon us [sic]. It is very sad to be ruled by such a lot of wretched Radicals, who have no regard for the honour of the country. I hope when Parliament meet they will hear the truth from the country and be kicked out of office with the contempt they deserve. On the other side is a short account of the proceedings in the matter of Egypt.

FEBY 6TH, 1885. My dear grand child was buried today in Kensall Green Cemetery. I was not able to be present. Poor child, she had a sweet disposition. God takes those whoom He loves.

FEBY 11TH, 1885. There is sad news today from the Soudan of the slaughter of General Gordon, only a couple of days before a part of the relieving force under General Wilson reached the place, only to find it in the possession of the enemy. What an account of blood guiltyness the Govt have upon their hands, a miserable lot of old women, reckless as to the honour of England [and] the lives of her soldiers, only seeking place and party interests. I hope in the coming Parliament they will be called to a rigid account and cleared out of office, for they have got the country into a sad mess both at home and abroad, the contempt of Europe. But what can be expected from such men as Chamberlain, Dilke & Co? How Ld Hartington and a few of the others sit at the same table with them & incur the responsibility of their acts I cannot understand. Poor Gordon has been sacrificed to their willful mismanagement.

THURSDAY, FEBY 12. We held our Gt Western half-yearly meeting today. It was a full meeting and all went off very well, our divd being 7% as against 7½ in 1883, but this was better than I expected from the decrease in our traffic. The trade of the country and agriculture is in a dreadful state of depression, and I see no immediate prospect of any amendment.

FEBY 28TH. We had a great division in the House of Commons last night on a motion of want of confidence in the Govt, particularly on the Egyptian question. The Govt had only a majority of 14, or 302 against 288. This is practically a defeat but I have no doubt they will stick to office. In the Lords a division on the same subject was taken and Govt were defeated by a majority of 121, or 189 against only 68.

MARCH 3RD, 1885. Our Telegraph Construction meeting was held today. We paid our usual 20% divd, and the meeting as a matter of course passed off very well. I hope we may be able to continue it.

MAY 18TH. The country has been for some months on the point of war with Russia, and great naval and military arrang[emen]ts have been made. We are now said to be in a position to obtain peace, but I fear with a great loss of honour and prestige. Affairs in the Soudan & Egypt cannot be worse. We are now recalling the troops from Suakin; they have done nothing beyond killing a lot of Arabs and have laid a few miles of railway in the direction of Berber. It is sad to feel the country in the hands of such imbeciles as our present Govt.

Death has been busy amongst my friends the last few weeks. Mr Samuda died suddenly, Sir Watkin Williams Wynn died a week ago, May 9th, and was buried yesterday. He is an old Gt Western director holding his seat by Act of Parliament. His nephew succeeds him and I suppose he will exercise his right either to come on the board or appoint a representative. Sir Watkin was a kind and worthy man, very much liked by us all. When I joined the board in 1865 he resigned and appointed me in his place, as a vacancy could not be made until the meeting in Feby 1867 [*sic, ie* March 1866], when I was elected by the shareholders and Sir Watkin resumed his position.

My old friend and brother officer on the Great Western since I joined the Co, Mr Owen, died on the 14th of this month. He has for some years past been the chief engineer of the company. His serious illness began in Augt last and he has gradually got worse since that time. He resigned his position on the railway a couple of months ago. He was a good and trustworthy officer and much esteemed by all connected with the company. Year after year fewer of my old friends are left.

MAY 22ND. We went to Clewer today to spend our Whitsuntide and stayed until the 3rd June. We had very fine weather and enjoyed our 10 days.

JUNE 9TH. The Ministers were defeated tonight in the House of Commons. I suppose we will have a new govt. Some election meetings at Cricklade have been held. Michell[36] has retired and Story-Maskaline is to be the Liberal candidate. I had an application from the Conservative party urging me to stand again, but I declined. See copy of letter on other side. I doubt much whether the Conservatives can carry the seat again.

JULY 4TH, 1885. Cyrus Field, who has been in England a few weeks, gave one of his usual large dinners today at Richmond. I went; it was dreadfully slow and I left early without stopping to make a speech it was intended to get out of me. The speeches were awfully long-winded as long as I stayed.

JULY 8. We went to Clewer today for the summer.

24TH. I held my half-yearly meeting of the Telegraph Construction Co today.

AUGUST 14TH. Parliament was prorogued today. I paid my last visit on Tuesday the 11th. Not sorry to feel my work as a Member of Parliament is at an end.

MONDAY, AUGUST 24TH. This was my 69th birth day; I spent it at Clewer. Frank and his family and Flo & Loo Newton were with us.

WEDNESDAY, SEPT 2ND. We left home for a few weeks going to Cardiff today to stay with Charlie.

SEPT 3RD. At Cardiff and went to Penarth in the afternoon. I had not seen the place before.

4 SEPT. I visited our collieries today. We were fortunate in the weather; the hills are not nice when it is wet. Found all very satisfactory.

SATURDAY SEPT 5TH. I took a special train today through the Severn Tunnel. We had a large party and all went off well. Mr Walker the contractor gave us a very liberal lunch at the works. This tunnel is a big work and has been a source of great anxiety to me. The large spring of water we cut on the Welch side a short distance from the Severn has been a great cost and trouble. I hope now the arch is finished it will keep out any serious quantity of water. It will be some months yet before we can open to the public as the permanent pumping and ventilating machinery has to be arranged and fixed. Saunders and Bassett were the only two of our people who turned up. My wife and Mrs Saunders were with us, and several other ladies.

After leaving the tunnel I went to Newport to go over the proposed line called the East Usk;[37] it is down the east side of the river. We returned to Cardiff for dinner. The day was very fine, in which we were fortunate. The newspapers gave some long accounts of our trip, see other side.

The Great Western held their 100th half-yearly meeting on 13th Augt, and I have attended 94, or I think 95, of them; a long service. A full account is given on other side, and all passed off well.

MONDAY, 7TH SEPT. We went from Cardiff today to see Caerleon Castle. It is between 50 & 60 years since I went there from Tredegar with a pic-nic party. It is a very fine old ruin. We had a carriage for the pretty drive, and the day being fine we enjoyed it.

MILFORD, SEPT 8. We left Charlie's at Cardiff today and came to Milford to our old quarters at the South Wales Hotel. Found our rooms comfortable as usual. On the 16th we went over the line from Milford to go over the new piece of line between the present terminus and the town of Cardigan.[38] We had a grand reception and address by the Mayor at the station, and a very good lunch afterwards. The day was very fine. I was sorry my old friend Mr Gower did not live to see this day as he had taken so deep an interest in the extension of the line to Cardigan. We had a nice walk and returned to Milford in the evening, the day being very fine. (See newspaper accounts over).

MILFORD, SUNDAY, 20 SEPT. The Channel Fleet came into the Haven yesterday. After lunch today we went in the launch to visit it, but the day was very wet and cold. We went on board the Leander and Moorhen. They gave us tea on the former; very civil on both.

GLOUCESTER, TUESDAY, SEPT 22. We left Milford today for Gloucester. The weather has been of a very mixed kind while we have been at Milford, and my wife not very well, but the hotel makes us as comfortable as they can. We missed our old friend Admiral Haswell. I see by the papers the old ship the Gt Eastern is to be sold by auction. On the opposite side are some notices of her. We are staying at the Bell here; the hotel is not so good as it used to be.

SEPT 23. I went over the Gloucester & Ledbury Railway today.[39] It has recently been opened. The line is well finished and I hope will bring us some traffic. Went to the cathedral in the afternoon; disappointed at there being no music.

SEPT 24. Left Gloucester and returned home to Clewer. Found all well.

OCT 3RD, 1885. The Conservatives at Swindon had a large meeting to-day in support of their proposed Member Mr Stone; he is a young man and a barrister, but not connected with the district. The meeting passed a complimentary resolution with regard to myself (see printed report and copy of my answer which I consider closes my parliamentary life).

WEDNESDAY, NOVR 18, 1885. The Queen disolved Parliament today, so I am no longer a Member of Parliament after over 20 years service. It is a great relief to me to feel I am not to be mixed up in the coming contest. The House of Commons has been a pleasant club. I have taken no part in any of the debates, and have been a silent Member. It would be a great advantage to business if there were a greater number who followed my example. I have no doubt I will sometimes miss the attendance at the House. The coming election is a very uncertain matter. The large addition made to the voters makes it very uncertain what the results will be, altho' I believe the country is so dissatisfied with the late Govt that a Conservative reaction will take place. We cannot be worse off, and the short time the present Govt have been in office they have done much to improve our foreign affairs. If they are secured in office by a fair majority I think it will give confidence to the country and trade will improve. Chamberlain, by his wild and revolutionary speeches has done much to damage his party and old Gladstone trims to any gale that blows, so long as he can secure office. I trust and believe he will be disappointed; he is a dangerous man and it would be a blessing to the country if he retired into private life. I fear the Irish party will be a difficulty in the new House, as, if the Govt are not very strong, they will be an awkward element to deal with. Ireland is in a wretched state, as in fact it ever has been. They ought to be governed by martial law—they are not fit for constitutional govt.

NOV 29TH. Capt Gosset, the old Serjeant at Arms of the House, died a few days ago. He retired from the office at the end of last Session. He was buried at Richmond. He was a great favourite with every body and I have spent many pleasant evenings in his room in the House of Commons; it was the best part of the House, as the Members having access to it were limited.

I nominated Cohen as Member for the North Paddington district, and voted for him last week. He got in by a large majority. So far the elections have resulted in large gains for the Conservatives. Several of the late Govt have lost their seats, thank goodness.

SATURDAY, DECR 12TH, 1885. My wife and I went yesterday to Swindon to distribute the prizes at the Mechanics' Institution. Sir Robert N. Fowler, Bart (late Lord Mayor) and his two daughters, joined us there and assisted in the operations. The day was fine, with hard frost, and all went off well. Maud Gooch[40] went down with us. We did not get back until the last train at night. We had the Prince of Wales' carriage, so did the journey very comfortably.

DECR 20TH, 1885. The whole of the Members of the new Parliament are now elected, the last completed on Friday. What a change, more than $\frac{1}{2}$ are new men. Gladstone, it is stated, has determined to give the Irish a Parliament of their own. He is mad enough to do any thing, but I can hardly think he will carry his party with him in this. I give on the other side The Times return of the new House. I am very glad I am not one of them.

NOTES

1   There was much activity in the development of electric light at this time, and in 1880 it was installed on the Thames Embankment and in the British Museum. The Brush system was, as Gooch suggests, not entirely satisfactory, and in 1884 the Telegraph Construction & Maintenance Co contracted to light the offices, hotel, platforms and yard at Paddington, and the stations at Royal Oak and Westbourne Park. A hundred arc lights and 4,100 incandescent lamps were used. A generating station was built near Westbourne bridge. This was taken over by the GWR in 1887.

Gooch, as chairman of the TC & M CO, made it clear at their annual meeting in March 1884 that the installation was an experiment, to gain experience.

See The Telcon Story (1950), 77–8. *Great Western Rly Magazine*, 1906, 242–5.

2   Stanbrook Abbey, now renowned for its fine book printing.

3   As long ago as May 1880 the diarist had suspected that his bailiff was responsible for his farming losses. *See ante*, p 280.

4   The Dunnings were related to Gooch by marriage. 'My poor brother-in-law' to whom he refers, *post*, p 316, was Simon Dunning of 2 Warwick Square.

5   At the South Wales Hotel, Neyland.

6   The line from Carmarthen to Llandyssul was built by the Carmarthen & Cardigan Rly and opened in 1864. It had a precarious existence until 1881 when it was sold to the GWR. The extension to Newcastle Emlyn was opened on 1 July 1895.

See MacDermot, *GWR*, II, 178–9.

7   John Owen was chairman of the Whitland & Cardigan Rly. It was, as Gooch prophesied, worked by the GWR from the date of opening of its final section from Crymmych Arms to Cardigan on 1 September 1886, and purchased in 1890.

See MacDermot, *GWR*, II, 192.

8   The *Clarovine*, from Lulea, Sweden. She was towed to Pwllcrochan mudbank and scuttled.

9   Walter Powell, MP for Malmesbury, left Bath on 10 December 1881 in a War Office balloon, the *Saladin*, on loan to the Meteorological Society. After attempting to descend near Bridport, throwing out two of the occupants, Powell was carried out to sea and never seen again.

10   From Upwey Junction to Abbotsbury, opened on 9 November 1885. Worked by the GWR and vested in that company in 1896. The secretary was William Manfield of Portesham House, Dorchester.

11   The Shakespeare Memorial Theatre was opened on 23 April 1879. It was burnt down in 1926 and the present theatre opened in 1932.

12   This was a line of standard railway gauge (4ft 8½in), at that time using horse traction. It was later electrified and the gauge reduced to 3ft 6in.

13   The figure of Peeping Tom, associated with the Lady Godiva legend, was built into a corner of the King's Head in Hertford Street.

14   Probably Sir Henry Robertson (*qv*).

15   Should be 5¼ per cent. The diarist left a space for the fraction, but never filled it in.

16   Thomas Gooch's widow.

17   If this was Thomas Adams, a GW shareholder, as seems likely, it was about the only useful resolution he ever proposed. He was a continual thorn in the flesh at shareholders' meetings, raising objections to anything and everything. He had aspirations as a director, even though his holding at one time was only a few hundred pounds. His antics were reported in the railway press over a long period. *See, eg, Railway News*, 12 March 1864.

18   Gooch mentions this as he usually dined in his own rooms.

19 *See ante*, VII, n 4.
20 Langley Green Junction to Oldbury, Worcestershire. Opened in 1884 for goods and 1885 for passengers. Worked by the GWR and purchased in 1894.
21 Weston-super-Mare was originally the terminus of a branch from the main line to the west, but in 1884 this was superceded by a loop line and a new station was erected at the same time.
22 The GWR steamer *South of Ireland*, bound from Cherbourg to Weymouth, ran ashore in Kimmeridge Bay, Dorset, in dense fog and was a total wreck. No lives were lost.
23 Sir George Elliot (*qv*) was standing again at the election, whereas Gooch was not, and was thus not concerned at being out of the country.
24 Colonel Wood commanded the cavalry at the battle of Tamanieb on 13 March.
25 Ford was probably H. C. Forde, a cable engineer of long experience, and Brown may have been James Wallace Brown, inventor of the Brown-Allan relay used in telegraph cables.
26 Gooch was evidently getting daily reports through the cable from the *Scotia*.
27 Possibly Sir John Henry Johnson, Sheriff of London and Middlesex.
28 In addition to laying the new cable the *Scotia* was to pick up the broken end of a line from St Vincent to Pernambuco, Brazil. *See post*, p 327.
29 According to his previous entry on 22 March he paid 12/6!
30 Probably children or brother- and sister-in-law of his daughter Anna.
31 St Saviour's church, in what is now Warwick Avenue, was close to Fulthorpe House.
32 Formerly the Hon F. G. B. Ponsonby (*qv*).
33 A side heading, parallel to the main tunnel, was driven to intercept the Great Spring and leave the actual tunnel dry. Water was, and still is, pumped from this side heading by machinery at Sudbrook.
34 The Mayor of Weymouth.
35 His daughter Anna's child.
36 Robert Michell, a director of the GWR. For some years up to the time of the 1885 election he had wished to stand as a Liberal for Cricklade, but declined to do so while Gooch was standing as a Conservative. He finally retired from the contest just before the 1885 election.
37 A short branch line from Newport, opened in April 1898.
38 *See ante*, VII, n 7.
39 This was built by two companies, the Newent Rly and the Ross & Ledbury Rly. It was amalgamated with the GWR from 1 July 1892.
40 Probably Agitha Maud Gooch, daughter of Henry Daniel (Harry).

VOLUME VIII

The Diary 1886-9

As we have seen in Volume VII, the entries become less frequent in the last years of the diarist's life. The surviving fragments of the last volume, printed in 1892, show him mourning more and more of his old colleagues, suffering increasing ill-health, but ever watchful of the fortunes of his beloved Great Western, whose progress had been his life's work upon which, surely, he must have looked back with much satisfaction in his declining years.

Sir Daniel presided at a half-yearly meeting for the last time on 14 February 1889, when he was already a sick man. His last months brought him much suffering and he died at Clewer on 15 October, aged 73. The cause of death was said to be gout at the heart. At the request of his widow (no doubt echoing Sir Daniel's own wishes) the funeral was a simple one, attended by the family, the directors and chief officers of the Great Western, some of his surviving friends, and Masonic deputations. He was buried in Clewer churchyard beside his first wife, at the spot he had himself chosen more than twenty years before.

The death of Sir Daniel Gooch marked the end of an epoch on the Great Western Railway. Within three years the last of the broad gauge had gone. The man who shared with Gooch the responsibility for the revival of the company's fortunes, James Grierson the general manager, had died suddenly in 1887, and G. N. Tyrrell the superintendent of the line retired in the following year. Soon, as the century neared its end, new men emerged to lead the company into a new and memorable era. The solid foundations upon which they built the modern Great Western were the outcome of nearly a quarter of a century of patient striving by the writer of this diary and as devoted a body of directors and officers as ever ran a railway.

SATURDAY, JANUARY 9TH, 1886. A coal-train was worked through the Severn Tunnel today from Newport and Cardiff to Bristol and on to Southampton. All went well, and I hope to open for goods and coal on the 1st March. This has been a very anxious work for me, we have had so many serious difficulties. One has felt a doubt whether we ought to persevere with so large an expenditure, but I never lost hope of succeeding in the end. Curiously enough, our trouble has not been under the Severn but on the Welsh side under land, where the water has been our difficulty, and now we must pump a great deal more than I had hoped. We had a pressure of 60 lbs on the inch on the brickwork, and this found its way through. We are now putting pumping-power to the same, with a daily discharge of 30,000,000 gallons. The autumn and winter have been very wet, so I hope in dry weather this will be greatly reduced.

January 20th. The Mersey Tunnel was opened today by the Prince of Wales. It is a big work, and may in time be of use to the Great Western if there is a good central station built in Liverpool.

September. We opened our Severn Tunnel on the 1st for goods traffic.[1] The first train that passed through was a goods leaving Bristol at 6.35pm. Fourteen trains were worked through during the night, and all was most satisfactory. This has been a long and very anxious and costly job. Our estimate for it was about £900,000. We have now spent over £1,600,000. The water is still a large expense to us, but it is under perfect control. I spent yesterday with Sir John Hawkshaw at Sudbrook, where our chief pumping machinery is.

December 1st, 1886. We opened the tunnel today for passenger traffic. It has been a long and very anxious work for me. But I trust it will prove a very beneficial work for the Company.

January 23rd, 1887. The *Times* this morning contains the sad news of the death of my oldest friend, Sir Joseph Whitworth. We have lost the first mechanic of the age. I first knew Whitworth in 1836, when I was about to join the Hawkes in the proposed engine-works at Gateshead, and I went to Manchester to order tools; since then we have been fast friends.

August 14th. This is my Great Western Railway jubilee-day, it being fifty years today since I entered the service of that Company, a few days before I was twenty-one years of age. I was very young to be entrusted with the management of the locomotive department of so large a railway; but I felt no fear, and the result has been a success. I have seen

350

great changes during the fifty years. How few of those who entered life with me, or were connected with the railway world at that time, are left to us! Yet we have a very few. God has greatly blessed me in every way.

SUNDAY, OCTOBER 16TH. I have sustained a great and grievous loss in the death of my friend Mr Grierson. He went to Milan to attend a railway conference held there, and returned home on the 29th September, not feeling very well; but he went to Paddington from Marlow (where his family have been spending the summer) on Friday, returning to Marlow that night. On Saturday he was very ill, and continued so until his death on Friday evening, the 7th October, at 7.30pm. He was buried at Barnes Cemetery on Wednesday the 12th October. His loss to me and the railway interest cannot be replaced.

MAY 19TH, 1888. Our Great Western superintendent of the line, Mr G. N. Tyrrell, retired on Saturday last. He has been forty-six years in the service, and was a most excellent officer and a kind and worthy man. I will miss him very much.

CLEWER, JULY 16TH. We had a jubilee dinner, on Wednesday the 11th, of the opening of the first portion of the Great Western Railway from London to Maidenhead on the 4th June 1838. It was attended by most of the directors and the chief officers. We also had the pleasure of having Mr Walpole, an old Chairman of the Company, with us. The dinner was at the Great Western Hotel, and all went off very well—a party of thirty-one.

Dean gave me a very fine photograph of the old locomotive, the *North Star*. She was one of those that opened the line, and we have kept her in a building built for the purpose at Swindon, as a specimen of the engine of the period. I feel a great interest in this old engine, and am glad to have so good a photograph of her. There is also a good photo of the *Lord of the Isles*, an eight-wheel engine which was in the 1851 Exhibition. This was one of a new and powerful class of engine I built about that period. Several of them are still doing our express broad-gauge work, and are equal in every respect to any we have since built. The *Lord of the Isles* is also put away at Swindon to be preserved as a specimen of this class of engine.[2]

AUGUST 26TH, 1888. A paragraph in the *Standard* looks like the last of the grand old ship, the *Great Eastern*. I would much rather the old ship was broken up than turned to any base uses. I have spent many pleasant and many anxious hours in her, and she is now the finest ship afloat. Some good use might have been made of her.

NOVEMBER. The *Great Eastern* has been sold in detail. Poor old ship, you deserved a better fate.[3]

DECEMBER 11TH. The oldest officer of the Great Western Railway Company died on Sunday the 9th, Mr T. Merriman Ward. He entered the service in September 1833, before the Act was passed, and held the position of Registrar until February 1st, 1876, when he retired on a pension. He was a good servant and a very worthy man.

FEBRUARY 17TH, 1889. I have been very little out of the house since the 17th of last month, when I went into the city and took fresh cold, getting an attack of bronchitis. On the 5th I got down to the station to settle our Great Western Railway report and accounts, and again on the 14th to hold our half-yearly meeting. I got through it pretty well, and as we paid 7¼ per cent it went off very well.

HASTINGS, APRIL 14TH. We came down here yesterday by the 3.40pm South-Eastern train. On the 4th March I was attacked with gout in my left foot, and a week after in my right foot, and I have been laid up ever since. I can now walk a little—but very little—and am sent down here to effect a cure.

SATURDAY APRIL 27TH. We left Hastings today by the 2.30pm train. The South-Eastern gave us a saloon carriage, so we made our journey very comfortably. I do not find my visit to Hastings has done me much good. I hope I will feel the benefit of the change now I have got back to my home.

NOTES

1   The delay in opening was mainly due to the pumping and ventilating plant not being ready.
2   It is to be regretted that during the regime of G. J. Churchward at Swindon both these historic engines were cut up. A replica of *North Star* was made for the railway centenary in 1925, and the great driving wheels of *Lord of the Isles* are preserved. Both are in the GWR Museum at Swindon.
3   The *Great Eastern* continued to lay submarine cables until 1874. She was refitted as a passenger ship but was not a success. She ended her days as a showboat on the Mersey and was sold for scrap in November 1888.

Appendix

Transcript of letter from Gooch to I. K. Brunel, applying for the post of locomotive superintendent on the GWR, 18 July 1837. (From the original in the Great Western Railway Museum, Swindon, by kind permission.)

Manchester & Leeds Railway Office,
Rochdale. July 18th/37.

I. K. Brunel Esqre.,

Dear Sir,

I have just been informed it is your intention to erect an engine manufactory at or near Bristol and that you wish to engage a person as manager. I take the earliest opportunity of offering my services for the situation.

I have until the last two months been constantly engaged in engine building and have worked at each branch of the business, but principally at locomotive engine work. The first 3 years of my time I was with Mr Homphry at the Tredegar Iron Works, Monmouthshire. I left him to go to Mr R. Stephenson and was at the Vulcan Foundry 12 months when I obtained leave from Mr Stephenson to go down to Mr Stirling of the Dundee Foundry Co, Dundee, to get a knowledge of steam boat work. I remained with him 12 months and returned to Mr Stephenson's works at Newcastle where I remained until last October when I left, having had an offer from a party in Newcastle to take the management of a locomotive manufactory which they intended erecting, but which owing to some unavoidable circumstances they have now given up the idea of proceeding with, and we have countermanded the orders for machinery. This has left me without a situation, and I am anxious to engage myself to some company where I will have the management of the building of engines. At present I am with my brother on the Manchester & Leeds line, where I have employment until I meet with something more suitable.

I will be glad to refer you to any of the forementioned places for testimonials.

Should you approve of my application I shall be glad to hear from you stating the salary and any other information you may think necessary.

I am, Sir, Yours obly., Danl. Gooch

Biographical Index

Note: The following brief notes are only intended to suggest how the persons mentioned in the text came to be associated with Gooch. References to the *Dictionary of National Biography* (*DNB*) and other sources are given where appropriate. Foreign royalty are shown under countries. Business firms will be found in the general index. Page references appear in italic at the end of entries.

ACLAND, Thomas Dyke (later Sir Thomas), (1809–98). Politician, MP for West Somerset at the time of the opening of the Bristol & Exeter Rly. *44*

ADAMS, George. *96*

ADAMS, W. Bridges. *64*

AIRY, Prof George Biddell, FRS (1801–92). Astronomer Royal, member of the Gauge Commission, 1845.
See *DNB*. *48, 49*

ALBANY, Duke of. *See* LEOPOLD, Prince.

ALBERT, Prince. *See* PRINCE CONSORT.

ALLCARD, William. One of George Stephenson's three resident engineers on the Liverpool & Manchester Rly. Like T. L. Gooch (*qv*) he drove an engine, the *Comet* at the opening. He was later to set up a locomotive works in France with W. B. Buddicom, who was locomotive superintendent on the Grand Junction Rly. *18*
See Nock, O. S. *The Railway Engineers* (1955), 78, 156.

ANDERSON, James. A senior Cunard captain, took command of the *Great Eastern* for the 1865 and 1866 cable expeditions, receiving a knighthood after the latter. He was later director-general of the French Atlantic cable concern and was on board when the ship laid the French cable in 1869. *322*; 1865 cable expedition, *97, 102*; 1866 expedition, *111, 115, 119, 122, 126*; 1869 expedition, *155, 162, 166, 173, 177, 180, 182, 183, 184*; at Swindon, *288*

ARMSTRONG, Joseph (1816–77). In charge of the Wolverhampton works of the GWR 1854–64, and the company's locomotive superintendent from June 1864 until his death.

354

For an account of this interesting family of GW engineers *see* Holcroft, H. *The Armstrongs of the Great Western* (1953). *94, 145, 146, 204, 205, 234, 244*

BAKER, Samuel, of Thorngrove, Worcester. Director of the GWR. Resigned in 1856 over disagreement on the dual role of C. A. Saunders as secretary and general superintendent, and also over the directors' refusal to appoint committees to supervise various departments. He returned to the board in 1858.

Baker was also a director of the Eastern Steam Navigation Co, the first owners of the *Great Eastern*, and chairman of Great Ship Co. *73, 84, 85*

See MacDermot, GWR, I, 211–12, 219. Rolt, L. T. C. *Isambard Kingdom Brunel* (1957), 238–9.

BARBER, William. Chairman of the Great Ship Co and director of the Great Eastern Steamship Co of 1864. He succeeded Gooch as chairman in November 1880. *77, 92, 99, 201, 238*

BARLOW, Prof Peter, FRS (1776–1862). Professor of Mathematics at RMA Woolwich, and a member of the Gauge Commission, 1845. His two sons, Peter William (1809–85) and William Henry (1812–1902) were both railway engineers, the former on the South Eastern Rly 1844–51 and the latter on the Midland Rly as principal engineer from 1844. W. H. Barlow was the inventor of the Barlow 'saddleback' rail used on parts of the Great Western and South Wales Rlys, but soon found unsuitable for heavy traffic. *49, 51*

See DNB. Marshall, C. Dendy. *A History of the Southern Railway* (1936), 396.

BARRINGTON, 6th Viscount. MP for Berkshire 1837–57, joined Great Western board in 1839 and was deputy chairman 1843–56 and chairman 1856–7. *47, 73, 94*

BARRY, Dr Alfred (1826–1910), Canon of Worcester and later Primate of Australia. He was the son of Sir Charles Barry, architect of the Houses of Parliament. *223*

See DNB.

BASSETT, Richard, of Bonvilestone, Cardiff, later of Highclere, Newbury. Director of a number of railway companies in South Wales and the west country, and of the GWR itself from 1863 to 1890. *217, 232, 233, 343*

BEACONSFIELD, Lord. *See* DISRAELI.

BECKWITH, George. Engineer in charge of the paddle engines on the *Great Eastern*. *174, 190, 225, 226, 227*

BEER, Julius. City business man and proprietor of *The Observer*. *280*

BELGIUM, King & Queen of. *43*

BERKELEY or BERKLEY, George. One of Robert Stephenson's assistants. His experiments helped to convince Stephenson of the impracticability of the atmospheric system of railway traction which Gooch's chief, I. K. Brunel, supported. *51*

See Rolt, L. T. C. *Isambard Kingdom Brunel* (1957), 166.

BESSBOROUGH, Earl of. *See* PONSONBY, F. G. B.

BIDDER, George Parker (1806–78). Civil engineer, friend and associate of Robert Stephenson, whom he assisted on the London & Birmingham Rly; engineer of Victoria Docks, London. *49, 51*

See *DNB*.

BIDDULPH, Michael, MP for Herefordshire and a director of the Midland Railway. *298*

BIRKINSHAW or BIRKENSHAW, John. Manager of Bedlington Ironworks. Published, with Michael Longridge, a pamphlet *Remarks on the Comparative Merits of Cast Metal and Malleable Iron Railways* in 1827, which included an engraving of the 'Locomotive Engine Manufactory & Bedlington Iron Works'. *See plate* II. *xi, 9, 24*

BLONDIN. *80*

BOEHM, Joseph Edgar (later Sir Joseph), RA (1834–90). Sculptor-in-Ordinary to Queen Victoria. *316, 319*

See *DNB*.

BOUVERIE, Edward Playdell, of Market Lavington, Wilts. A GWR director. He had previously been a director of the Berks & Hants line which was worked by the GWR. *313*

BRADLAUGH, Charles (1833–91). Elected Member for Northampton, 1880, refused to take the oath and was refused permission to affirm. He was repeatedly re-elected and unseated until 1835, after which he remained MP for Northampton until his death. *307*

See *DNB*.

BRAITHWAITE, John (1797–1870). Engineer. Built the first successful steam fire engine and, with John Ericsson (1803–89) the *Novelty* locomotive which was entered unsuccessfully in the Rainhill trials on the Liverpool & Manchester Rly. He was engineer-in-chief of the Eastern Counties Rly 1836–43.

Braithwaite was one of the founders and editors of the *Railway Times*, a weekly journal commenced in 1837 which was distinctly hostile to Brunel and the Great Western Rly. *39*

See *DNB*.

BRASSEY, Thomas (1836–1918), son of Thomas Brassey the great railway contractor. Created a baron in 1886. A Civil Lord of the Admiralty, 1880–4. *92, 93, 244, 311*

See *DNB*.

BROWN, Henry, of North Hill House, Plymouth. Director of the South Devon Rly and member of the joint committee which administered the Cornwall

Telegraph Construction & Maintenance Co on all three of the expeditions of the *Great Eastern* in which Gooch took part. He gained his early engineering experience on the Great Western Railway. Canning designed the grappling apparatus with which broken ends of cables were lifted from the ocean bed. 1865 cable expedition, *99, 100, 101*; 1866 expedition, *111, 120, 122, 126*; 1869 expedition, *156, 161, 162, 169, 173, 177, 182*
    See DNB.

CARNEGIE, Capt S. T., RN. Director of the Great Ship Co and commander of the *Great Eastern* for a short period after her first voyage to America in 1860. *77*

CARTER, the Rev T. T. Rector of Clewer, Windsor for thirty-six years until his resignation in 1880 after complaints and criticism from some of his parishioners. *131, 192, 281*

CATO, Capt W. R. 1st officer under Capt Halpin on the *Great Eastern* on the Atlantic cable expedition of August 1874. Commanded the *Scotia* from 1884 until 1898, when he moved to the new ship *Anglia*. He retired in 1901. *208, 322, 331*
    See The Telcon Story (1950), 82–5.

CHAMBERLAIN, Joseph. *341, 345*

CHRISTIAN, Prince. *230, 277, 300*

CLARK, George Thomas. Served as a divisional engineer under Brunel during construction of the GWR, being responsible for the first station at Paddington and the bridges at Basildon and Moulsford. In addition to being virtually manager of the Dowlais ironworks, as mentioned by Gooch, Clark was a co-trustee of the Dowlais estate from 1852.

According to *DNB* (*qv*) he was the author of the text of what is always known as J. C. Bourne's *History and Description of the Great Western Railway* (1846), and of the earliest guide book to the GWR (see Ottley, G. *A Bibliography of British Railway History* (1965), 6026).

Clark was perhaps better known as an archaeologist and architectural historian. *38*
    See DNB.

CLARK, Josiah Latimer (1822–98). Engineer and electrician. Engineer to Anglo-American Telegraph Co. His elder brother was Edwin Clark, resident engineer under Robert Stephenson on the Conway and Britannia tubular bridges, where Latimer was also employed. *162, 163, 171, 182, 183*
    See DNB.

CLARKE, George. *See* CLARK, George Thomas.

CLARKE, Seymour. Chief clerk to I. K. Brunel at his office in Duke Street, Westminster, before the opening of the GWR, he became the first traffic superintendent at the London end of the line. His younger brother

Frederick was appointed superintendent at Bristol and when the line was completed Swindon became the boundary of their respective divisions. In 1850 he was appointed general manager of the Great Northern Rly. *51, 65*

See MacDermot, *GWR*, I, 359.

COATES, Rev Henry, BA. *5*

COBDEN, Richard. *48*

CODRINGTON, Capt William, CB, RN. ADC to Queen Victoria, superintendent of Sheerness Dockyard from April 1883. *334*

COHEN, Lionel Louis. Conservative MP for North Paddington, elected 1885. It was a new constituency. *346*

COMMERELL, Capt J. E. (later Admiral of the Fleet Sir John), VC (1829–1901). Commanded HMS *Terrible* during the successful cable-laying expedition of the *Great Eastern* in 1866. *113, 117, 124*
    See DNB.

COOKE, W. Fothergill. *45*

COWELL, Maj-Gen Sir J. C., KCB, Master of the Queen's Household. *272*

CRAMPTON, Thomas Russell (1816–88). As Gooch's chief draughtsman at Swindon he might well have succeeded his chief, though his unorthodox ideas probably best suited him to the freelance career which he afterwards adopted. His locomotives, though tried in this country, only found favour on the Continent, and particularly in France.

He practiced as a civil engineer, mainly in SE England, and was largely responsible for the design and laying of the first cross-Channel cable. *37, 67*
    See DNB.

DEAN, William (1840–1905). Locomotive & carriage superintendent of the GWR from 1877 until his retirement in 1902. *234, 351*

DENT, Capt C. B. C. *235, 277*

DERBY (14th Earl). *112, 127, 128, 192*

DERBY (15th Earl). *See* STANLEY, Lord.

D'ERLANGER, Baron Emile, director of the Societé du Cable Transatlantique Français. With Paul Julius Reuter he held a concession from the French Government to lay the cable. *155*

DESPECHER, Jules. French technical writer whose works include *Projet de Télégraphe Transatlantique* (Paris, 1863). He was on board the *Great Eastern* in 1865 and again in 1869. *181, 187*

DICKS, George T. Member of the GW staff at Swindon works. Assisted Gooch in his first election campaign of 1865, and was in charge of the arrangements for the presentations made to Gooch and his wife on 3 June 1865. *96*

the Atlantic sixty-four times, suffering from sea-sickness every time. *100, 110, 342, 343*

See Field, Henry M. *History of the Atlantic Telegraph* (1866). Bright, Charles. *Submarine Telegraphs, their history, construction and working* (1898).

FIFE or FYFE, Sandy. In charge of locomotives at the Manchester end of the Liverpool & Manchester Rly at the time of opening. He was dismissed with John Melling (*qv*) in 1839 and became Locomotive superintendent of the Northern & Eastern Rly. *20*

See Marshall, C. F. Dendy, *Centenary History of the Liverpool & Manchester Railway*, 1930, 74, and *Great Western Railway Magazine*, Nov 1890, 4.

FOOTE, William, solicitor of Swindon. Gooch's election agent at Cricklade. *146, 204*

FORTESCUE, 3rd Earl (1818–1905), former MP for Barnstaple, author of pamphlets on social questions. *261*

See *DNB*.

FOWLER, John (later Sir John), (1817–98). Civil engineer. Engineer of the Metropolitan Rly, consulting engineer to GWR and later co-designer of the Forth Bridge. *85, 86, 112*

See *DNB* and Mackay, T. *The Life of Sir John Fowler, Engineer* (1900).

FOWLER, John. *66*

FOWLER, Sir Robert Nicholas, 1st Bart (1828–91). Banker, Lord Mayor of London 1883–4, MP for Penryn and Falmouth 1868–74, and for City of London 1880–91. *346*

See *DNB*.

FRANCE, King & Queen of. *43, 47*; Emperor of, *71, 178, 180, 181, 185*

FROUDE, William, FRS (1810–79). Engineer and naval architect, brother of the historian J. A. Froude. He did experimental work for the Admiralty. *232, 233*

See *DNB*.

GALTON, Douglas Strutt (later Sir Douglas), (1822–99), formerly secretary to railway department of Board of Trade. *305*

See *DNB*.

GEACH, Charles, of Birmingham. Born at St Austell in 1808, he rose rapidly in the banking world. Liberal MP for Coventry 1852, and Mayor of Birmingham 1848.

He was brought in as a director of the Eastern Steam Navigation Co when money was being raised to finance the building of the *Great Eastern*. *67*

See Rolt, L. T. C. *Isambard Kingdom Brunel* (1957).

GIBSON, John. Carriage and wagon superintendent of the GWR from 1846 to 1864. *91*

at Swindon, *288, 346*; on *Scotia, 319, 320, 321, 333, 334*; in Madeira, *329, 330*

GOOCH, Emily Jane. Daniel's second child, *b* 13 July 1840, *m* 19 October 1858 William Ponsford. She died 17 March 1901. *40, 74, 84, 102, 193, 222*

GOOCH, Frances (Fanny). Daniel's youngest sister, 5th daughter and 9th child of John Gooch, *b* 29 June 1823, *m* 1865 Rev William Laing, rector of Langley, Staffs, *d* 11 April 1889.

GOOCH, Frank, Daniel's youngest child, *b* 20 July 1847, *m* 1871 Teresa Croskey. The Croskeys were neighbours of Gooch in Maida Hill and another daughter married Henry Gooch. Frank was a captain in the 4th Hussars 1869. He died 29 January 1890. *64, 131, 193, 196, 207, 218, 219, 225, 310, 343*

GOOCH, Henry Daniel (Harry). Daniel's 3rd child and eldest son, *b* 30 December 1841, *m* 23 November 1865 Mary Kelsall Croskey. Director of the Whitworth works at Manchester 1863–5, managing director of slate quarry at Bettws-y-Coed from 1865. Succeeded his father as second baronet and died 24 June 1897. *43, 87, 110, 131, 148, 191, 192, 193, 196, 218, 310*; on *Great Eastern, 77, 80*; at Whitworth's, *92, 110*; at Bettws-y-Coed, *110*

GOOCH, Jane Longridge (Daniel's sister), 3rd daughter and 5th child of John Gooch, *b* 19 September 1814, *d* unmarried 15 February 1883. Lived for at least 35 years in Birmingham where she was much engaged in church and charity work. *315*

GOOCH, John, of Bedlington. Father of Daniel, *b* 17 March 1783, *m* 1805 Anna Longridge; 'cashier' at Bedlington Ironworks and later at Tredegar Ironworks. Died 28 August 1833. *xii, 2, 3, 5, 7, 8, 9, 10, 15*

GOOCH, John Viret, 2nd son and 4th child of John Gooch, *b* 29 June 1812, *m* 1840 Hannah Frances Handcock, who died in 1874. He remarried. Locomotive superintendent of South Western Rly 1841–50 and of the Eastern Counties Rly 1850–6. He died 8 June 1900. *10*

GOOCH, Margaret (Peggy). Daniel's first wife. Daughter of Henry Tanner of Bishopwearmouth (*qv*). Born 10 February 1814, married 22 March 1838 and died 22 May 1868. *xiii*; meets DG, *25*; engagement, *26*; marriage, *32, 33*; in France, *52*; France & Italy, *87*; on *Great Eastern, 77, 80*; presentation to, *96, 97*; death, *xx, 130–3*; mourned by DG, *143–51 passim, 170, 177, 190, 193*; DG dreams of, *148, 156, 158, 178, 188, 192, 196*

GOOCH, Mary Ann (Daniel's sister), 4th daughter and 7th child of John Gooch, *b* 10 August 1818, *m* 1853 Rev A. C. Kingdom, vicar of Bunny St Mary, Nottingham, *d* 29 October 1899. *148*

GOOCH, Thomas Longridge. Eldest son and 2nd child of John Gooch of Bedlington, brother of Daniel. Born 1 November 1808, apprenticed to

George Stephenson at Newcastle in 1823. George Stephenson's secretary and draughtsman during construction of Liverpool & Manchester Rly and later resident engineer at Liverpool. Responsible for arrangements for opening the line and drove the *Dart* engine at the opening. Appointed engineer, under George Stephenson, of the Manchester & Leeds Rly. In October 1831 he joined Robert Stephenson on the London & Birmingham Rly, for which he prepared many of the plans and sections. When work commenced he took charge of a 36-mile section north of Kilsby Tunnel.

Gooch returned to the Manchester & Leeds after its authorisation and became joint principal engineer with George Stephenson. During the Railway Mania he was much in demand as a surveyor of new lines and overwork caused a breakdown in his health which forced him to retire in 1851 at the age of 42. T. L. Gooch died on 23 November 1882. *See Mins of Proc of Inst of Civil Engrs*, Vol lxxii, session 1882–3, part ii, for a good account of his life. *9, 18, 20, 26, 313*

GOOCH, William Frederick. 5th son, 10th and youngest child of John Gooch of Bedlington, brother of Daniel. Born 19 April 1825, became manager of Swindon Locomotive Works of the Great Western Rly in 1857. Daniel Gooch hoped that his brother would succeed him as Locomotive Superintendent, but Joseph Armstrong was appointed by the board and W. F. Gooch went to Newton-le-Willows as Managing Director of the Vulcan Foundry in 1864. *13, 14, 97, 147*; at Swindon works, *73, 85, 91, 93, 94, 95*; at Vulcan Foundry, *95, 283*

GORDON, General. *341*

GOWER, Robert Frederick. A member of the original London committee of the GWR in 1833. *301, 302, 336, 344*

GRANT, Sir Francis, RA (1803–78). Fashionable portrait painter whose subjects included Queen Victoria. *71*
   See DNB.

GRANT, John. Chief goods manager of the GWR from October 1863. *270, 271*

GRIERSON, James (1827–87), was one of the great railway managers. He was secretary of a joint committee of the Shrewsbury lines and the Great Western in 1851, traffic manager of the Shrewsbury lines in 1854, goods manager of the GWR at Wolverhampton in 1855, and in 1857, when he was still only 29, he became chief goods manager at Paddington. In October 1863, after the amalgamation with the West Midland, Grierson was made the first general manager of the GWR.

James Grierson was an able administrator and a very skilful negotiator both with other railway companies and in Parliamentary committees. With Gooch he was largely responsible for the improvement in Great Western fortunes in the twenty-four years before his tragically early death at the age of 59 in 1887. His son, W. W. Grierson, became Chief Engineer of the GWR. *151, 282, 313, 349, 351* time of Gooch's apprenticeship there. His father, also Samuel, was one of the original partners in the Sirhowy Tramroad which ran through Tredegar. *10, 14, 15*

HORSLEY, Mrs. I. K. Brunel married Mary, daughter of William and Elizabeth Horsley. This talented family lived in what was still rural Kensington. *32*

    See Noble, C. B. *The Brunels, Father and Son* (1938), 124 *et seq.*

HUGESSEN. *See* KNATCHBULL-HUGESSEN.

ISMAY, Thomas Henry (1837–99). Ship owner and co-founder of the Oceanic Steamship Co in 1868. *334*

    See DNB.

JEFFERIES, Richard. *xvii*

JENKIN, Henry Charles Fleeming, FRS (1833–85), an authority on cables and collaborator with Prof Thomson (Lord Kelvin). *162, 164, 175, 181, 182, 183, 184*

    See DNB.

JENKINSON, Sir George. MP for the neighbouring constituency of North Wiltshire. *205*

KIRTLEY, Matthew. Three years older than Gooch, he came from Tanfield, Co Durham and was connected with railways from his youth. His very varied experience included a period as fireman on the Warrington & Newton Rly which became part of the Grand Junction, and he is said to have been driver of the first train into Euston Station.

    Kirtley became locomotive foreman of the Birmingham & Derby Junction Rly in 1839 and locomotive superintendent of the Midland Rly in 1844. He died in 1873. *19*

    See Barnes, E. G. *The Rise of the Midland Railway 1844–74* (1966), 89–90.

KNATCHBULL-HUGESSEN, Edward Hugessen, later 1st Baron Brabourne (1829–93), politician. *231*

    See DNB.

LAING. *See* GOOCH, Frances.

LAMPSON, Curtis Miranda (later Sir Curtis), (1806–85), director and vice-chairman of the Atlantic Telegraph Co. Born in the USA, he came to Britain in 1830 and was naturalised in 1849. *127*

    See DNB.

LANE, Michael. Appointed principal engineer of the GWR in April 1860. He was one of Brunel's assistants and had earlier worked on the Thames Tunnel. *132*

LARDNER, Dr Dionysius (1793–1859). Scientist and author, whose theories were widely publicised and believed at the time. Among his pronouncements was one to the effect that a train whose brakes failed would reach a speed of 120mph in running down the 1:100 incline in Box Tunnel. *33, 37, 38*

    See DNB and MacDermot, *GWR*.

LAWRENCE, John, of Crick House, near Chepstow. Deputy chairman of Monmouthshire Railway Co. *304*

LECKY, Capt Squire Thornton Stratford (1838–1902), navigation expert. He had been appointed marine superintendent of the GWR in 1884. *339*

    See DNB.

LEEMAN, George, MP for York, deputy chairman, North Eastern Rly, 1855–74, chairman 1874–80. *262*

LEOPOLD, Prince. *148, 230, 273, 328*

L'ESTRANGE, Lt-Col Paget W., of the 15th Brigade Artillery, Woolwich. *208*

LLANDAFF, Bishop of, Alfred Ollivant. Born in 1798, he was 83 when Gooch met him, and he died on 16 December 1882. He completed the restoration of the cathedral begun by his predecessor. *303*

    See DNB.

LOCKE, Joseph (1805–60). Assisted George Stephenson on the Liverpool & Manchester Rly, was engineer to the Grand Junction line, the South Western and the Caledonian, and built several lines on the Continent. Like his contemporary T. L. Gooch (*qv*) he wore himself out and died in 1860 at the age of 55. *9, 49, 61, 65*

    See DNB, Devey, J. *Life of Joseph Locke, Civil Engineer* (1862) and Webster, N. W. *Joseph Locke* (1970).

LONGRIDGE, Michael. *xi, 3, 55 n 4*

LONGRIDGE, Thomas (1751–1803). Ironmaster of Gateshead, Daniel Gooch's maternal grandfather. *3*

LOPES, Sir Lopes Massey, 3rd Bart (1818–1908). MP for Westbury 1857–68. Scientific farmer and agricultural improver. Deputy chairman of South Devon Rly. *217*

    See DNB.

LUCAS, Francis R. Chief Engineer of the Telegraph Construction & Maintenance Co during the 1884 cable-laying voyage of the *Scotia*. *322, 331*

LUCY, William Charles, chairman of the Gloucester & Berkeley Canal and of the Severn & Wye and Severn Bridge Rly. He lived at Brookthorpe, south of Gloucester. *271*

LYTTELTON, Charles George, 5th Baron (later 8th Viscount Cobham), (1842–1922) of Hagley Hall, Worcestershire. A director of the GWR and a keen supporter of the temperance movement, being president of the GWR Temperance Union. *318*

An Eliza Minet was godmother to Gooch's son Frank. *65, 72*

MONCK, 4th Viscount (1819–94). First Governor-General of Canada, 1866. *276*
See *DNB*.

MORIARTY. Capt Henry Augustus, RN (1815–1906). Navigator on the *Great Eastern* during the cable-laying expeditions of 1865–6. Charles Bright in *Submarine Telegraphs* . . . called him 'one of the ablest navigators in the world'. *98, 120, 122, 126*
See *DNB*.

MOZIER, Joseph (1812–70). American sculptor working in Rome. *88, 91*
See *Dictionary of American Biography*.

MUNTZ, Philip Henry (1811–89). Mayor of Birmingham 1839–41, MP for Birmingham 1868–85. Gooch paid him a call at Somerset House, Warwick Street, Leamington. *318*

MURPHY, Patrick (1782–1847). Writer on natural science. He correctly predicted that 20 January 1838 would be the coldest day of the year. *31*
See *DNB*.

MUSGRAVE, Sir Anthony (1828–88), Governor of Newfoundland. *126*
See *DNB*.

NEELD, Sir John, 1st Bart (1885–91). MP for Cricklade 1835–59. *279, 280*

NEWTON. See GOOCH, Anna L.

NORVAL. Gooch's Newfoundland dog, presented to him, as a puppy, by Capt Anderson, to whom he was given when the *Great Eastern* was at Heart's Content after laying the 1866 cable.
Norval returned to England with Gooch, and in 1869 did the round trip to his birthplace during the laying of the French cable. He died at Clewer on 5 or 6 March 1876. Given to DG, *119*; at Clewer, *126, 146*; on *Great Eastern, xiii, 166, 167, 170, 172, 178, 190, 196*; death, *223, 225*

O'NEIL, Henry Nelson, ARA (1817–80). Historical painter and writer. *99, 100*
See *DNB*.

OSBORN, Capt (later Rear-Admiral) Sherard (1822–75). Succeeded Richard Glass as managing director of the Telegraph Construction & Maintenance Co in March 1867. Resigned 1874. *155, 156, 164, 168, 169, 192, 200, 201, 218*
See *DNB*.

OWEN, William George. Assistant engineer in charge of Box Tunnel during the building of the GWR main line, and succeeded Brunel as chief engineer

POYNDER, William Henry, DL, JP, of Hartham Park, Chippenham. A prominent local landowner. *204*

PRINCE CONSORT, *43, 44, 45, 74, 245*

PRINCE OF WALES (later Edward VII). *43, 119, 202, 217, 224, 288*; at Boat Race, *252*; DG meets, *224*; DG at levée, *224, 257, 281*; at Holyhead, *281*; at Swansea, *304, 305*; garden party, *310*; carriage, *346*; at Mersey tunnel, *350*

PRINCESS ROYAL. *74*

PRUSSIA, King of. *43*; Crown Prince of, *74, 257*

RAE, Stewart Keith, first medical officer of the GWR Medical Fund Society at Swindon.

For an account of this important body, and Gooch's letter to the GWR board which led to its foundation, *see* Darwin, Bernard, *A Century of Medical Service* (Swindon, 1947). *64*

RAVENSWORTH, Earl of (1821–1903), president of Institute of Naval Architects, 1880, and of the North of England Steamship Owners Association. *334*

See G. E. C. *The Complete Peerage*, X (1945), 747.

RAWSON, Philip, Director of the Telegraph Construction & Maintenance Co. *162*

REA or RAE, Minard C. Works Manager at Swindon 1850–7 in succession to Sturrock. He had previously been locomotive superintendent of the Bristol & Exeter Rly.

His name was spelt Rea in the original edition of MacDermot's *History*, and elsewhere, but among that author's corrections published by Michael Robbins in *Jnl Transport History*, Vol I, No 3 (May 1954), 187, and since incorporated in the revised edition of the book, the spelling was amended to Rae. There is, however, an indenture in the GWR Museum at Swindon bearing the signature Minard C. Rea, thus spelt. *73*

REA, Stewart K. *See* RAE, Stewart K.

REYNELL, C. H. *322, 325, 328*

RICHARDS, Rear-Admiral George H., CB, FRS. Succeeded Rear-Admiral Sherard Osborn (*qv*) as managing director of the Telegraph Construction & Maintenance Co in 1874. *208, 328*

RICHARDSON, Charles. *247 n 3, 254*

ROBERTSON, Sir Henry (1816–88), of Palé, Merioneth. Liberal MP, engineer, railway promoter and mineral owner. His best-known civil engineering works are the Dee and Ceiriog viaducts on the Shrewsbury & Chester line, of which he was engineer. *71*

See Lerry, G. G. *Henry Robertson, Pioneer of Railways into Wales* (Oswestry, 1949).

Sims, William Unwin. Chairman of the Great Western Rly from October 1837 until his death by suicide in November 1839. *39*

Smith, Lt-Col (later General) Sir John Mark Frederic, RE (1790–1874), Inspector-General of Railways, 1840, member of the Gauge Commission, 1845. *48, 49*

 See DNB.

Smith, Willoughby (1828–91). Electrician and manager of the Gutta Percha Co and later of the Telegraph Construction & Maintenance Co. He was one of the pioneers of cable manufacture and made the cross-channel cable of 1849–51 and the first Mediterranean cable of 1854. *161, 162, 163, 169, 181, 182*

 See DNB.

Stanley, Lord (later 15th Earl Derby). *117, 125, 252*

Stephenson, George (1781–1848). It would be impertinent to attempt a summary of the life and achievements of George Stephenson in a short note. As L. T. C. Rolt has said (see below) 'it is not too much to say that the railway engineers, and in particular the two Stephensons, created the Victorian Age'.

 George Stephenson was already on the road to fame when the little Daniel sat upon his knee at the Gooch home in Bedlington. At that time he was engineer of the Stockton & Darlington Railway, and his greatest triumph, the Liverpool & Manchester line, was soon to come. He was nearing the end of his life when the confrontation occurred between Gooch, as champion of the broad gauge, and 'old George' as protagonist of the narrow, at the Gauge Commission hearings in 1845. *xi, xii, 9, 18,19 ,48*

 See Smiles, S. *The Life of George Stephenson* (1857 and later editions). Rolt, L. T. C. *George and Robert Stephenson* (1960).

Stephenson, Robert (1803–59). George Stephenson's son was much more than a junior partner of his father. The success of the *Rocket* at the Rainhill trials was very largely due to the multi-tubular boiler designed by Robert. But the younger Stephenson's fame rests largely on his work as a civil, rather than a mechanical engineer. The London & Birmingham Railway, the high-level bridge at Newcastle, and the great Britannia tubular bridge over the Menai Straits (tragically destroyed by fire in 1970) are his lasting monuments, though he achieved much else at home and abroad before his early death at the age of 56.

 Daniel Gooch would have known him well. He was at the Vulcan Foundry of which Stephenson was a partner, in 1834, and at the Forth Street works at Newcastle in 1836, while his brother Tom was one of Stephenson's assistants on the London & Birmingham line. The gauge trials of 1845–6 brought Robert, as well as his father into a sharp clash with Gooch and Brunel; it says much for the characters of Stephenson and

Brunel that in spite of their wide differences of opinion on the gauge question and other matters they remained firm friends. *xi, 47, 81*; Vulcan Foundry, *18*; Newcastle works, *24, 25, 26*; gauge controversy, *49, 50, 61, 62*

See Smiles, S. *Lives of the Engineers—George and Robert Stephenson* (1861-2 and later editions). Jeaffreson, J. C. and William Pole. *The Life of Robert Stephenson, FRS* (1864). Rolt, L. T. C. *George and Robert Stephenson* (1960).

STOKES, Admiral John Lort (1812–85), commander of HMS *Beagle* during surveys in the Pacific, 1841–3, and surveyed New Zealand, 1847–51. He lived at Haverfordwest and was a director of the Milford Rly (Johnston to Milford) opened in 1863 and worked by the GWR. *302, 311*

See DNB.

STORY-MASKELYNE, Mervyn Herbert Nevil, FRS (1823–1911), mineralogist. He was Member for Cricklade as a Liberal until 1886, and as a Liberal-Unionist from 1886 to 1892. *279, 280, 342*

See DNB.

STUART-WORTLEY, the Rt Hon James, QC (1805–81), chairman of the Atlantic Telegraph Co. He was the youngest son of the first Lord Wharncliffe, who was chairman of the committee on the Great Western Rly bill in the Lords in 1835, after whom the Wharncliffe Viaduct at Hanwell was named. *127*

See DNB.

STUBS, Peter, founder of the engineering firm of Peter Stubs & Co, Warrington. *40, 64*

See Ashton, T. S. *An Eighteenth Century Industrialist* (1939).

STURROCK, Archibald. Born in 1816, he was apprenticed to James Stirling at the East Foundry, Dundee at the time Gooch was there. He became Gooch's assistant on the Great Western in 1840, and three years later was made manager of the locomotive works then being built at Swindon. He left the GWR in 1850 to become locomotive superintendent of the Great Northern Rly.

Sturrock retired in 1866 and was succeeded by Patrick Stirling. He died in 1909 at the age of 92, perhaps the last survivor of a great generation of locomotive engineers.

See Ellis, C. Hamilton. *Twenty Locomotive Men* (1958), chap VII, and Brown, F. A. S. *Great Northern Locomotive Engineers*, I (1966), 38–9, in which the former belief that Sturrock was related to the Stirlings is discounted. *22, 44*

SUTHERLAND, 3rd Duke of (1828–92). Not only carried out agricultural improvements on his Highland estates, but actively encouraged railways, building his own line from Golspie to Helmsdale with a station on his estate at Dunrobin. *129*

General Index

Names of persons will be found in the Biographical Index, but those of business firms are included here.

Sub-headings are arranged in the order in which they appear in the text, with the exception of the principal sub-headings under Great Western Railway, which are alphabetical. References in bold type refer to the Biographical Index.

2G*